Computing in the
Humanities

Lexington Books Series in Computer Science
Kenneth J. Thurber, General Editor

Computing in the Humanities

Edited by
Peter C. Patton
Renee A. Holoien
University of Minnesota

LexingtonBooks
D.C. Heath and Company
Lexington, Massachusetts
Toronto

Library of Congress Cataloging in Publication Data

Main entry under title:

Computing in the humanities.
Includes index.
1. Humanities—Data processing. I. Patton, Peter C. II. Holoien,
Renee A.
AZ105.C59   001.3'028'54   79-3185
ISBN 0-669-03397-9

International Standard Book Number: 0-669-03397-9

Library of Congress Catalog Card Number: 79-3185

To Dr. Frank Verbrugge, director of University Computer Services, University of Minnesota, under whose creative administrative and financial leadership the University Computer Center has grown from a service activity in the natural sciences to become a truly all-university resource for instruction, research, and public service.

Contents

Contents ix

Acknowledgments

The editors wish to acknowledge the cooperation of the University Computer Center (University of Minnesota) staff and the special editorial staff, without whose efforts this book would not exist. The University Computer Center staff activity was managed by Mary Dickel, executive secretary and office manager. A special note of thanks goes to Karen Prince, principal secretary, who took responsibility for typescript production through its many drafts. Paula Goblirsch took responsibility for editing bibliographic references for completeness and consistency as well as the word processing for the final typescript.

The editorial work for the book was initially assisted by Nicki Harper, who helped define goals and formats for the chapters. Later in the project Joe Miller and Kellen Thornton assisted our authors with the editing and organization of their chapters. Vicky A. Walsh and Kevin McMahon took responsibility for their respective sections of the book and provided considerable expertise to the authors of their sections from their own specialized computer-applications experience. We also acknowledge the cooperation of our authors, who were willing to put forth special efforts to describe their research in its current state of development within the common format requirements we established for this book.

In concept, this book began several years ago with a survey carried out by Professor Douglas Anderson of the Educational Psychology Department. On a summer research grant from the University Computer Center, Professor Anderson interviewed faculty members in every department of the College of Liberal Arts that indicated interest in computing. His report on the use of computers in the humanities at the University of Minnesota was not published because he found many beginnings but little progress. Although unpublished, the report was a success because it focused University Computer Center and Computer Services attention on the need for support in this promising application area. This book is in some sense a consequence of Professor Anderson's final project as manager of statistical computing at the University Computer Center.

1

Introduction to Computing in the Humanities

Peter C. Patton and
William C. Roos

The computer is simply a tool, a modern and powerful tool, which traditionally has been applied to the solution of problems first in the natural sciences and the engineering sciences, then to business data processing, industrial process control, and commerce generally, and only more recently to the social sciences. Our interest in this book is applications of an even more recent nature to humanistic research and instruction, primarily in higher education. The application of the digital computer to the humanities is the current step of a progression that began in the late 1940s. During World War II computers were developed for ballistic calculations and the solution of difficult problems in military logistics and later of problems in atomic physics. The first nonmilitary applications of computers were to research applications, such as the computation of mathematical functions, and then to engineering applications, primarily in the aircraft industry. The aircraft industry was the first major commercial user of large-scale digital computers. On the business side or in commercial application, the first users of computers were insurance companies.

The first computer applications in the commercial area were to the further mechanization of accounting operations of tabulating machines. Subsequent applications to new areas of data processing were far less successful, amounting to little more than automating existing paperwork systems. The technical and economic consequences of those early, often ill-conceived, applications were soon overcome, but their adverse effect on personnel and clientele engendered a negative attitude which remains today in the average person's conception of the computer and its role in society. Both of these early application areas called for new tools able to manage large quantities of complex data. The computer quickly proved itself up to the task in both the aircraft industry and the insurance industry and has gone from that secure double footing to its present-day widespread use throughout business and industry worldwide in fewer than twenty-five years.

In the university the computer was first used for research in applied mathematics, the engineering sciences, physics, and astronomy. During the 1950s there was an explosion of new applications of computers to university research in the so-called hard natural sciences. During the 1960s attention turned to the development of computer-supported methodology in the social sciences. At first, computers in the social sciences were used primarily through the vehicle of statistical packages such as the Statistical Package for the Social Sciences (SPSS). The introduction of data-base technology in the 1970s not only expanded the usefulness of the computer as a tool to more disciplines, but also allowed a more systematic, cost-effective application of computing in disciplines that had long enjoyed its use. In the middle to late 1970s, a number of pioneering applications were made in support of humanistic research. This is not to say that there have not been some impressive but isolated results earlier. The work of Mosteller and Wallace[1] on the authorship of the Federalist Papers and the brilliant analysis of Ellegard[2] for the authorship problems of the Junius letters could be mentioned, among a number of others. But these first applications were the results of lonely pioneers who happened to enjoy some computer expertise along with their specialized training in a humanistic discipline.

The journal *Computers in the Humanities* was founded in the late 1960s, and it reports many of these pioneering efforts in the humanistic application of computers. Although one can read of many interesting applications, it was the rare university that had more than one humanistic scholar doing anything with a computer, even in the mid-1970s. By the late 1970s conferences were beginning to be held on the application of computing to the humanities, historical research, and the study of languages and literature. Readers interested in the development area can find much interesting source material in *Computers in the Humanities* beginning in 1967, in the *Journal for the Application of Computers to Ancient Literature and Languages,* published in Belgium beginning in 1971, and in *The Association for Literary and Linguistic Computing Bulletin* published in Great Britain, beginning in 1975.

In this book we illustrate the current state of computing in the humanities by presenting and reviewing work from a number of projects underway primarily at the University of Minnesota. These presentations follow our general introduction to computing and are of a brief but somewhat tutorial nature, which is necessary in this case because we wish to introduce a diversity of application techniques to as broad a humanistic audience as possible. Our introduction need not develop and motivate the technology itself since two excellent books for this purpose have recently appeared. Susan Hockey's book introduces the reader to our subject with a discussion of the concept of an algorithm as it is defined in terms of programmer-oriented languages.[3] The book by Robert Oakman starts with a more basic machine-oriented section entitled "Fundamentals of Literary Computing."[4] Both books cover a wide variety of literary and linguistic applications with extensive reference for further study. This book represents a sequel to either of these in the sense that we present more fully detailed examples of the applications. We also present a wider variety of applications, including examples of applications to music, history, archaeology, language instruction, and the fine arts. Our scope, however, is limited by the fact that we present the results of both completed and ongoing research projects that began at the University of Minnesota. In part I the area of interest is applications to languages and literature, including linguistics, lexicography, and literary data processing generally. A similar but somewhat more specialized area of interest also included is the use of the computer for biblical and religious studies. In part I applications to New Testament research problems are presented, as well as an application to rabbinic literature. There are numerous ongoing applications of the computer to other religious studies at Minnesota, particularly to the Old Testament, to classical mythology, and to the Vedas, which are not represented in this book. A second major area of interest treated in part II, is the application of computers, particularly using data-management techniques, to archaeology and history. A number of archaeological applications have been investigated at the University of Minnesota, including site-oriented data bases, problem-oriented data bases, collection and museum data bases, pottery classification, and, to a lesser degree, remote sensing and graphics. In history, applications have been made to cuneiform archives, to prosopographical studies, and to economic history studies, particularly of the economic history of ancient Babylonia. Applications to the fine arts at the University of Minnesota are relatively few and are not as fully developed at Minnesota as are other areas, such as language, literature, history, and archaeology; but we do include a few significant projects conducted at Minnesota and some references which interested readers may pursue. This book includes in part III applications on the educational side of humanistic research and instruction at the University of Minnesota. Computer-aided instruction (CAI) applications involve the computer in the teaching of ancient languages such as Greek, Latin, Sumerian cuneiform, and Egyptian hieroglyphics. Also (in part II) chapter 14 discusses the use of simulation approaches to an instructional application in Greek prehistoric archaeology.

The computer is a tool like any other, but it is—in the sense of any tool people use that is an extension of some human capability or trait—a prosthesis. Marshall McLuhan has referred to the computer as a prosthesis in assistance of human intelligence.[5] The computer may thus be considered as an intellectual prosthesis or an amplifier of human intelligence. As such, it is almost unique among tools since most tools are extensions of physical rather than intellectual human qualities, for example, tools that augment capabilities such as locomotion, speech, grasping power, and so on. Although the computer as an intellectual extension is widely used and, if only indirectly, touches the life of almost every person in every civilized society, the ultimate role of the computer in society is not yet fully understood.

The computer industry today has been likened to the automobile industry in 1918 or 1920. Automobiles today do not differ greatly in fundamental characteristics from automobiles made in 1918. The major differences in the automobile as a vehicle over the last sixty years have been in technological improvements, cost-effectiveness improvements, and standardization. In fact, the diversity of automotive engineering concepts in use today is far less than existed in 1918, and attempts to introduce older concepts, such as steam-powered automobiles, have not been successful because this thread in the development of automotive technology has lain too long unraveled to be woven back into the current pattern of technological development. The major difference between 1918 and now is the social impact of the automobile. In 1918 the automobile was a toy and a novelty and was used productively at first primarily by physicians. Load-carrying versions, or trucks, were used for city delivery and certain hauling functions, although they by no means replaced horse-drawn carriages and did not completely do so for years. The most significant factor about automobiles as a transportation system is that they have allowed, mostly since the late 1920s or early 1930s, a form of personal, mainly family-oriented, transportation not available in any other means of mass transportation before.

The computer may stand on the same sort of threshold today that the automobile occupied after the first twenty-five years of its development. Today's computers probably represent more technological diversity than they will twenty years from now. Aside from being more standardized, in the future they will be smaller, lighter, more reliable, much less expensive, more cost-effective, and faster; but probably they will not differ significantly in form and function from today's computers. They may, like the automobile, be so ubiquitous that we cannot get along without them. One already sees indications of this trend in the tremendous popularity of personal computing, that is, small computers for hobby applications. Although personal computers or hobby computers have been available for several years, by far the majority of programs run on these computers are for game playing or essentially toylike or hobbylike applications. But aside from primitive, useful, computer-controlled home-systems applications such as bookkeeping, tax accounting, and small-business data processing, personalized computers are finding more sophisticated nonhobby applications. For example, a sophisticated application of a very small microcomputer that came to light at the November 1978 conference on computers in Biblical studies at Ann Arbor, Michigan, was that of an Apple II microcomputer to a study of definitions given by the church fathers in their Latin works to Hebrew names in the Old Testament.[6] The scholar using this computer has recorded the text of a number of church fathers who analyzed Hebrew names in the Old Testament in the Latin originals onto Apple II computer minidisks and has written computer programs to scan the Latin text for analyses of Hebrew names. Another application of this sort developed recently is the use of a Terak microcomputer to develop a lexicon of Sumerian Emesal dialect terms from native lexical lists.[7] Although the biblical scholar or the Sumerian lexicographer having a microcomputer at home is a rarity today, a decade from now this may very well be commonplace. The personalized computer will be as common as the electric typewriter and no more expensive than a quality color television by 1985. The sophisticated user will be able to subscribe to a computational "utility" service that will provide data-base and computational backup to the small machine, which will appear to the utility or "network" as an intelligent terminal or "smart appliance."

Like the automobile, the computer is a tool that has multiple levels of utility. Just as one can employ the automobile for personal transportation in several different modes, such as using a taxi, or being driven in one's own car, or being driven in someone else's car, or driving one's own car, so the computer can be dealt with on several different levels of personal involvement. The first level of involvement (and the one requiring the least technical knowledge of computing) is simply that of specifying one's problem in an unambiguous, algorithmic format to a computer professional, who can then carry out the solution and return the results to the user for verification and utilization. The user can then carry out a research plan based on the program prepared by someone else; until recently, most computing research in the humanities was done in just this way.

The second level of involvement is to prepare a system analysis or program description, which again may be programmed by another person, but not necessarily someone as expert or experienced a computer professional as in the first case. A programmer or coder can then implement the program specification or design and carry out the computer runs.

The third level of involvement is to learn the specification language of a program package such as SPSS and then to code one's data, enter them into the computer, and apply the program or some of its features to the data in order to obtain the desired results.

The fourth level of involvement is to learn to program and write one's own programs. Many humanistic scholars have already done so. An early language which was very popular for those doing work in literary studies was SNOBOL, a language designed for dealing with strings of alphabetically encoded or textual data on a computer. A popular current language for such applications is named after the French mathematician Blaise Pascal. This language has extensive capability for string manipulation and provides a powerful tool to a scholar willing to invest the time and effort into learning yet another language, albeit an artificial rather than a natural one.

The fifth and most sophisticated level of interaction with the computer—and one that is often employed by users of small, personalized computers—is interactive involvement with the computer program. In this type of human-machine relationship, the program is written so that it involves the user interactively in dealing with the data. An example of an interactive program to be used in literary analysis would be an editing program, a tagging program, or a program that does grammatical analysis of textual data. Such a program, used on a small computer or an interactive terminal connected to a large computer, allows the user first to scan a text or other data and give instructions to the computer program, by means of the keyboard, and then to inspect intermediate results immediately on the terminal screen and modify the commands or develop a command sequence that carries out precisely the operation specified and produces the desired results for a part of or all the text.

In describing the computer it has become traditional to separate a computing system into subsystems and then into components to better understand the function of the system as a whole. The computer can be readily broken down into two fundamentally different entities called hardware and software. The term *hardware* is associated with the machinery that makes up the computer. The machinery is then further divided into a processing unit, which actually carries out the computer commands on the data it is given, and the memory, which is itself a subsystem and may be divided into a hierarchy of high-speed, internal memory; slower-speed, external, disk memory, and even slower-speed, magnetic tape memory. The memory holds the program instructions or commands and the data on which they operate. The processing hardware must then be complemented with machinery to read in data from punched cards or punched paper tape, terminal keyboards, or some other graphic input device; and machinery to output data, such as line printers, devices for displaying graphic data, magnetic tape devices for exchanging programs and data with other computers, and so on.

In contrast to the hardware is the body of systems and application programs usually referred to as *software*. In the early days of computing, hardware was so called because it was made of machinery components, in contrast to programs, which were not hard, physical objects and were thus referred to as software. Programs are usually manifested by paper listings of computer instructions and data. Software is developed for a computer by a process called programming or coding. It requires that problems be stated in a formalized language or notation and then described to the computer in formal or artificial language. The first artificial languages were designed for solving mathematical formulas. One such language, FORTRAN, an acronym for *for*mula *tran*slator, allowed the mathematician to describe mathematical formulas to the computer in such a way that another computer program, called a compiler, could generate in machine language a computer program which the machine hardware decoded directly and then executed as commands on the given data. Later applications were made to business data processing and many years later to literary data processing. The example of SNOBOL has already been given. The design and development of computer hardware are much better understood today than those of software. The written instructions in the software are not really the software itself, but only a partial manifestation of it. Some computer scientists consider software to be what the programmer thinks and then writes on paper, to be transferred by the program (compiler) to the computer as machine instructions, to be executed by the hardware. The description of a computer program as a statement in a formal language, or really as an effective statement in a formal language, has analogies to music. For example, one can compare the computer, the machine which carries out the function and produces the effective result, to the orchestra which is, like the computer, an ensemble or a system of separate instruments. The control unit of the computer which reads the program and sequences the machinery can be compared to the conductor. The conductor functions to some extent as the basic clock of the orchestra, just as the control unit times or sequences the computer. The written program itself is comparable to the musical score which the conductor reads and directs the musicians to play. The musical notes of the program are comparable to the commands which the computer executes. To extend this analogy, the programmer is, of course, analogous to the composer of the musical score.

From a functional rather than a physical perspective, it is necessary to understand the concept of a procedure to understand what a computer does. Informally defined, a *procedure* is a set of instructions for carrying out some repetitive task. The computer is simply the machine that executes or performs the procedure. Actually, in this simple definition the computer is not limited to be a machine; in fact, in the 1930s and 1940s computation was done by large groups of people sharing the computation. The earliest computing methods were thus designed to be performed by people working cooperatively with individual calculating machines. Older dictionaries, such as the *Oxford English Dictionary,* define a computer as a person who computes. Thus, a procedure may be carried out not only by a machine (computer) but also by a group of human beings. For example, business procedures are carried out in most cases by one or more clerks or bureaucrats. Humans give little thought to procedures per se. Rather, the final goal and the objectives to be accomplished to achieve it are their major concern. In directing someone to carry out a well-defined task, usually no explicit, step-by-step instructions are given. The doer implicitly understands what to do and normally does the task; however, a good supervisor explains what to do in detail the first time. In many ways this varies from person to person and very often differs from the way that the person delegating the task might carry it out. That is, different procedures can achieve equivalent results; moreover, humans can tolerate vagueness and ambiguity in procedural instructions that computers cannot. This notion leads to the problem of how we communicate with machines, which is inextricably connected with how the machine performs its function. For this reason, learning to communicate procedures to computers has evolved with rather esoteric programming languages. The program is simply a communication, a message from the human user to the computer, which defines to the computer in a precise, unambiguous artificial language a method by which the desired results can be obtained.

To understand how programs can direct computers to execute procedures so as to produce the desired results, the basic kinds of operations that a computer can perform must be understood. Further, the data on which they operate must be studied as to how they are transformed and represented. Instead of listing the operations that can be performed, more insight might be gained through a problem chosen from literary data processing. An easily understood example is the authorship problem. The solution of this problem is based on a theory that there exist, in written discourse, unconscious signatures of the author, representing basic individual thinking patterns which are deeper in the structure of the written prose or poetry than the surface structure we call style. If this is true, then it is possible to examine a work attributed to an author and compare it to other works known to be written by that author; if one can identify a sufficient number of unconscious characteristics or mental signatures of the author, then one can attribute the unknown work to an author or conclusively state that a given author did not write the unknown work. To do this, the computer must be able to accept and store texts in the language in which they were written, as well as identify structural aspects of these texts, that is, chapters, paragraphs, sentences, phrases, and so on. In addition, the computer must be able to search for and identify patterns, either known patterns for comparison or unknown patterns, by abstracting similarities or differences from text segments.

Finally, the computer must be able to do arithmetic operations on tallies and numerical quantities derived from recurrences of various characteristics or aspects of the text. Breaking these major functions required for authorship analysis down into primitive tasks which the computer can carry out, we usually find three groups. The first is arithmetic operations, that is, addition, subtraction, multiplication, and division. Second is logical operations, that is, comparison and/or logical functions based on logical AND, OR, and NOT. The third group is control functions, that is, those commands which change the control sequence of the machine by given criteria depending on data and program conditions. Referring to the analogy of the computer program as a musical score, we could compare the arithmetic, logic, and control functions of the program to the melody, harmony, and rhythm of the musical score. The set of instructions in any procedure can also be assigned to one of these three groups. The functions of arithmetic operations are usually simple, but provide the user intellectual advantage or gain on the computer because of the great speed at which they are performed. From the procedure point of view, logical functions involve comparisons, shifting, and modification of data. These functions usually result in setting special data values which can be used by the control instructions later. Control operations allow the instructions to be executed in a nonsequential order. This is important to avoid unnecessary repetition that could result in procedures of enormous length (in terms of the number of instructions).

To understand how a computer can execute a set of instructions comprising a procedure, the idea of data representation, storage, and retrieval must be understood. The human has learned to recognize and manipulate data through five physical senses, but the computer has no such sense or perception. It is essentially told or programmed what to do.

Computers range in size from devices no larger than a typewriter to huge machines occupying rooms 3,000 square feet in size. These machines, from the largest to the smallest, are capable of fundamentally similar operations, but carry them out on vastly different scales. Machines of all sizes seem to find application in most research fields, even in the sophisticated natural sciences, such as atomic physics, which usually require the largest, most sophisticated computers for realistic research. Students find application for the smallest microcomputers in student laboratory and other instructional settings. Likewise, the humanist may find applications for very small computers as well as medium- to large-size computers. An example of a problem that generally requires a large computer is building a concordance of a long or complex text. As an example, consider a biblical concordance; the first concordance of the King James Bible was made by Cruden in 1728. Cruden spent seventeen years making this concordance with purely manual means and made only six mistakes. The first computer Bible concordance was made on the Univac I in 1955. A concordance was made of the Nelson Bible in 1,000 hours of Univac time, a significant time saving compared to seventeen years. If one assumes 2,000 effective worker-hours per year, the computer was thirty-four times faster than the human being and made no mistakes. Recently at the University of Minnesota, a concordance was made of a fully analyzed text of the Greek New Testament, comparable in size and complexity to making a concordance for the entire Bible. This concordance required only 19 minutes of computer time on the Cyber 74 computer. This is an improvement factor of more than 3,000 over the Univac I time. As an example of a small-computer application to an equally complex but much smaller data base, consider a Terak microcomputer starting with the native lexical list from materials for a Sumerian lexicon. This small automatic lexicon allows the translator rapid access to the Emesal vocabulary and, initially, only Sumerian and Akkadian cognates. However, as lexicographic decisions are made by the translator and these decisions are entered into the data base, the system rapidly builds up a very useful historical lexicon of this dialect based on the native lexical list, for structure, and the text being translated, for content. The case studies presented in this book illustrate both large- and small-computer applications in humanistic research and instruction.

Notes

1. F. Mosteller and D.L. Wallace, *Inference and Disputed Authorship: The Federalist* (Reading, Mass.: Addison-Wesley, 1964).

2. A. Ellegard, *Who Was Junius?* (Stockholm, Almquist and Wiksell, 1962) and *A Statistical Method for Determining Authorship: The Junius Letters 1769–1772* Gothenburg Studies in English (Göteborg, Sweden: Acta Universitatis Gotheburgensis, 1962).

3. S. Hockey, *A Guide to Computer Applications in the Humanities* (Baltimore, Md.: Johns Hopkins University Press, 1980).

4. K.L. Oakman, *Computer Methods for Literary Research* (Columbia: University of South Carolina Press, 1980).

5. M. McLuhan, *Understanding Media* (New York: McGraw-Hill, 1964).

6. L.V.D. Parunak, ed., ''Computer in Biblical Studies'' (Proceedings of a conference held at the University of Michigan, Ann Arbor, in February 1980, publication forthcoming).

7. S.R. Sparley, D.D. Reisman, and P.C. Patton, ''A Computerized Lexicon of the Sumerian Emesal Dialect,'' *ALLC Bulletin* 7, no. 3 (1979):283–294.

Part I
Computing in the Analysis of Language and Literature

Peter C. Patton

The application of computing technology to linguistic and literary "data" or texts was the first nonnumerical application of the computer. Early research was often inhibited by the general perception of the computer as a large, high-speed calculator; but once it was realized that a computer is really an arbitrary symbol manipulator and that "9" and "a" are simply encoded symbols subject to different operators and rules of combination, many new computer-application opportunities became available. Unfortunately, early attempts at machine translation of natural languages outstripped their theoretical basis, producing some serious setbacks. Meanwhile, the computer has assisted the linguist to obtain a better understanding of natural language, and today interest in computer-aided language translation is experiencing a resurgence in the hope that theory has begun to catch up with technological potential. While language-translation and even language-decipherment interests on the part of our authors instigated many of the research projects reported in chapters 2 to 9, our concerns here are more fundamental, if less spectacular.

Chapter 2 by Timothy Friberg and Barbara Friberg reports the development of a Greek New Testament data base of interest to the linguist, Bible scholar, and Bible translator. Beyond the M.A. and Ph.D. theses, the results of this project will be a series of analytical tools to be published in 1981 and 1982. The analytical text of the New Testament will be followed by a lexical-focus, analytical concordance, a grammatical-focus analytical concordance, and finally an analytical lexicon of the New Testament. While only the specialist will be interested in these works, anyone interested in the use of the computer for either literary or linguistic analysis, in particular discourse analysis, will be interested in that chapter.

Chapter 3 describes a systematic approach to computer-assisted lexicography for the Sumerian language. An earlier project in computerized Sumerian lexicography was undertaken by Professor Miguel Civil of the University of Chicago's Oriental Institute.[1] We were inspired by this pioneering research and by a suggestion from Professor Daniel Reisman of our own Ancient Near Eastern Studies Department of the University of Minnesota.[2] Chapter 3 reports the methodology developed for a system

employing both large (Cyber 172) and small (Terak) computers. Two major
lexical series coming down to us from the ancient native lexical tradition
were entered into the computer. After several stages of data processing,
more than 10,000 items were grammatically analyzed and finally printed out
as page proofs for an index. Again, only the specialist will be interested in
the results, but the techniques described, especially the use of a microcomputer as a page- or screen-oriented editor for a language or translation
scheme employing a non-Latin alphabet, will concern many readers.

While most of the chapters in part I report methodology and technique,
two describe program packages which are available for the general user.
The EYEBALL program developed by Professor Don Ross is available for
both CDC Cyber and IBM 360/370 computers. Instruction manuals and the
program file are available from the University of Minnesota for interested
readers.[3] The TAGEDIT system developed by Eric Inman while he was an
undergraduate at Minnesota is also available as a Pascal program suitable
for any large computer able to compile a Pascal program. User reference
manuals are also available from the University Computer Center, University of Minnesota.[4]

Three chapters in part I illustrate computer applications to a variety of
literary as well as linguistic studies. Professor Larry Mitchell's computer-
aided research on Old English manuscripts (chapter 5) not only has served
the literary scholar by indicating previously unsuspected breaks in scribal
continuity, but also has documented the historical development of linguistic
phenomena during the early stages of the English language. The work of
Roger Brooks and Professor Zahavy (chapter 6) illustrates a computer
approach to form criticism in an ancient text of considerable religious and
historical interest, the Mishnah. Chapter 7 by Nicki Harper and Tom Rindflesch describes a pioneering technique they have developed and applied to
Etruscan and Minoan Linear A. Their initial results are already promising,
and graphemic analysis may offer considerable potential as a computer-
based method for the study of undeciphered languages.

Chapter 9 on troubadour poetry in Old Occitan describes a concor-
dance-oriented study which may soon yield a machine-readable data base
for the entire literature in Old Provençal, as a result of the collaboration of
Professor Akehurst of the French department with a colleague who has
similar interests in Provençal prose. A similar effort currently underway on
the part of Professor Evelyn Firchow of the German department will yield
the complete literature of Old Icelandic as a computer data base.

Notes

1. M. Civil, "Lexicography," *Sumerological Studies in Honor of
Thorkild Jacobsen,* Assyriological Studies 20 (Chicago: University of
Chicago Press, 1975), pp. 123–157.

2. S.R. Sparley, D.D. Reisman, and P.C. Patton, "A Computerized Lexicon of the Sumerian Emesal Dialect," *ALLC Bulletin* 7, no. 3, (1979):283–294.

3. D. Ross, "Description for EYEBALL" (English Department, University of Minnesota, 1973), rev. 1976, 1979.

4. R.A. Holoien, and E.E. Inman, "TAGEDIT User Reference Manual," UCC Technical Report, forthcoming.

2

A Computer-Assisted Analysis of the Greek New Testament Text

Timothy Friberg and
Barbara Friberg

For millenia inquiring minds have been fascinated by the phenomenon called language. What is it and how does it work? One discovery about language, indisputable to linguists, is that language has structure. It is not like so many grains of sand on the seashore. Instead, language is composed of units which together form patterns in certain identifiable, but restricted ways, to form larger units which in turn group into patterns. This process, repeated hierarchically to a depth of several layers, makes language learnable and usable. Such structuring is both linear and hierarchical. It is hierarchical in that units on one level are made up of smaller units on a lower level, illustrated nontechnically by sentences being composed of words and words being composed of sounds (or letters). It is linear in that left-to-right order is significant: *PIT* does not signal the same unit as its backward spelling *TIP*, nor does the two-unit sequence *book reservations* represent the same message as the sequence *reservations book*.

The study of language has been segmented rather naturally into subdisciplines. By one reckoning there are three: phonology, syntax, and semantics. Phonology is the study of the sounds of language and the structuring by which they carry significant communication. Semantics is the study of meaning, the message encoded on the physical signal of speech. Syntax relates sound and meaning, focusing on the placement of the meaningful units of language with respect to one another.

Whether by accident or by design, the focus of syntactic studies has been the sentence. Working within sentence boundaries, linguists have made great advances in their understanding of language, advances of both practical and theoretical value. For all the progress, however, many questions have not been answered by inquiries made solely within the domain of sentential syntax. Recent research has looked beyond the sentence to the larger units of language (paragraphs, and so on) for answers to these questions. Why does the sentence "David was too far away to see," ambiguous as it stands (". . . for anyone to see" or ". . . to see anyone"), register unambiguously when preceded by "Martha scanned the area in vain"? These larger units, the contexts of any smaller unit, are called discourse. Discourse is therefore usually taken to be the larger whole to which the smaller part belongs. Discourse analysis is the study of the structure of language removed from the artificiality of the laboratory and returned to the environments from which it naturally arises. Discourse analysis actually has had a long and important history under other names: rhetoric, literary criticism, and exegesis.

Scholarly treatment of Koine Greek (Common Greek, roughly from 300 B.C. to A.D. 300; hereafter often simply Greek or Koine) is representative of how languages have been analyzed. Our knowledge of its phonology and morphology (word structuring) is at an advanced state compared with what is known about its syntax. And some of what has been observed about Koine syntax is suspiciously complex with respect to its statements of the language's organization and structure. The state of research in Koine Greek parallels that of general linguistics, in that recent research is expanding its focus to include the realm of discourse, for the sake of both what can be learned about the larger organization of the language itself and what light that organization might throw on lingering uncertainties about intrasentential syntax.

The Problem

The Greek New Testament (GNT) is the exemplar of Koine Greek. Written as twenty-seven discrete manuscripts across some fifty years' time by perhaps eight or nine authors, it is probably the single most studied literary text on earth (and that apart from translations). Numerous scholarly lexicons and grammars and countless commentaries are available. However, the general problem in linguistic research across world languages is also the specific problem in GNT studies: Its discourse structure is relatively unknown, both undescribed and unexplained.

That there is an area unexplored by human inquiry is perhaps reason enough to enter into new searches. In the GNT case, however, there are at least three practical reasons why its discourse structures should be probed, that is, justifications for the project here described. First, a proper understanding of the message itself requires such an inquiry. In speaker-hearer exchanges within the same language, all meaning-significant elements of the structure of the language, at any level, are understood by the participants as part of their largely unconsciously acquired competence in that language. Paragraphing, focusing, and backgrounding techniques (to name a few) are language-specific. To understand the total message of a foreign language, one must understand the entire range of meaning-carrying apparatus. Second (and derivative from the first), adequate translation across languages requires an understanding of the meaning-signaling devices of both source and target languages. As by far the world's most translated book, the New Testament must be well understood in its original form if faithful translations are to be produced. The discourse structure of the GNT must be part of that understanding. Finally, insights gained into the discourse structure of Koine Greek are sure to answer riddles within smaller units of the language, particularly at the sentence level and below. To look at sample entries in a GNT lexicon compliments the Greek mind. Only a great mind could handle with any competence the twenty-five shades of meaning typically assigned the Greek function word *kai* (and)! The observations of the senior author are that the distinctions of meaning into which a single Greek word is analyzed may fade at the level of discourse. The big picture is often a whole new picture.

Some work has been done in the area of GNT discourse analysis. Before reviewing specific efforts at this research, however, we discuss some general complications implicit in any approach to discourse analysis. A serious complication to any proposed research in this area is that the organizing principles behind discourse structures are mental; language is but a reflection of the mind. As in any psychological study, many of the proofs are indirect. The principles a researcher has internalized in the course of learning to speak his native language are real, but elusive. How much harder it is to identify those principles in Koine Greek where there are no longer any living native speakers! Another complicating factor is the size of the relevant data. The *Good News by Matthew,* one of the twenty-seven constituent GNT manuscripts, is roughly 18,000 words long, a significant increase over ten-word sentences, which form the domain of traditional grammatical analysis. A final complicating factor cannot be overemphasized; Greek is, to a high degree, a free-word-order language. Although there are some constraints on moving words around, Greek has much more ordering freedom than a language such as English because Greek is a highly inflected language. This means that, where English depends on a largely fixed word order (subject, verb, object) to identify the relation of a noun to a verb, Greek accomplishes the same result by a set of suffixes attached to every noun. A noun thus identified is free to signal other discourse-related information, for example, focus and emphasis, by its position. Any adequate study of Greek discourse structure must determine the significance of the possible orderings of words.

In order to heighten appreciation of the contributions others have made to an understanding of Greek discourse patterns, it is appropriate to elaborate on Greek word order. Prerequisite to evaluating the significance of possible orderings in a Greek sentence is enumerating them. An example will illustrate the difficulties. Three items, a, b, c, can appear in six logically possible orders:

a	b	c
a	c	b
b	a	c
b	c	a
c	a	b
c	b	a

Although these might be the essential items in a sentence order, other elements may also occur. Of these, some might have independent placement, while others will be related dependently to a, b, or c. Rather than the array given above, it is more likely that the following is representative, in which the sentence length is arbitrarily limited to ten items, but chosen from a vocabulary of twenty-six items. The task is simply to find the orderings of a, b, c:

u	c	b	l	d	g	v	a	p	v
f	h	x	b	k	c	h	o	a	r
a	o	l	g	c	m	q	b	z	s
j	w	m	u	a	e	b	x	k	c
b	a	c	y	i	r	k	d	s	a
t	y	n	c	q	p	u	f	a	b

One final observation about the rather mechanical task of enumerating the relevant orders is that the second array represents both some items which are single words and some items which are only suffixes, that is, grammatical markings, to words.

Previous efforts to discover the discourse structure of Koine Greek might be grouped under three approaches. First, many attempts have followed the traditional approach of literary criticism, focusing on a particular book of the New Testament. Valuable information as to theme and focus, setting and participants, introduction and climax has come out of this approach, which is foundational to work in discourse analysis. If there has been any one deficiency worth comment, it is that some statements as to how a particular semantic effect is achieved have not been borne out by exhaustive study. Statements making exactly opposite claims can be cited; for example, one nonexhaustive study has claimed that the verb in Greek is sentence-initial, while another has asserted it to be basically sentence-final. Clearly the neutral position cannot be both, although numerous examples of both placements are found in the data. Moreover, many potentially useful statements derived from literary criticism are too vague and too general. That moving an element forward in a sentence gives it prominence is useful information, but the fact that this is nearly a universal phenomenon detracts from its importance.

A second approach to discourse analysis, statistical analysis of vocabulary, has been developed by Wake,[1] Morton and McLeman,[2] and Michaelson and Morton.[3] With techniques of statistical analysis, the unity of a text (or set of texts) can be shown by identifying recurring elements, on the assumption that an author's use of vocabulary is consistent. Methods of statistical analysis are easily implemented on a computer, so that large texts can be evaluated in relatively little time with a high degree of accuracy. The weakness of this approach is twofold. First, the approach tries to harvest before it sows. For example, much research under this approach has been undertaken to determine authorship of the various manuscripts. But the research base is too small for such a goal. There are more variables involved in questions of authorship than those of vocabulary frequency and use of function words (noncontent words—for example, *the, to, for, of*). Before one can profitably pursue what is variable, one must decide what is constant. In particular, the discourse structures of Koine Greek must first be determined. Without an understanding of what discourse structures reflect which genres, the significance of individual items cannot be evaluated. Second (and much more serious), work under this approach has focused on lexical items (whether they are content words or function words) and their frequency and distribution. It has not given the requisite attention to grammatical items, for example, categories of case, tense, mood, voice, gender, number, and person.

A third general approach to discourse analysis, a theory that relates syntax and semantics, is represented by work being done under the guidance of John Beekman of Wycliffe Bible Translators.[4] The strength of his approach is that, while doing discourse analysis of individual New Testament books, he is developing a theory of discourse. Combining the insights of Greek scholarship with those of modern linguistics, he is not only contributor to, but recipient of, recent developments in the investigation of the universals of discourse, as they are being discovered by Bible translators and linguists. The disadvantage of this approach to date is only quantitative. The size of the corpus has hindered the quick development of this theory. Some statements, such as those in the first approach mentioned above, await exhaustive substantiation. On the other hand, the slower pace has added depths of thoughtfulness to Beekman's theory.

Our work is greatly indebted to that of Beekman. Seeing the difficulty Beekman and his associates have had in giving attention to grammatical information in extended texts was a prime motivation for developing the project this chapter describes. The grammatical analysis described below reflects discourse-level considerations that are consistent with those of Beekman's approach.

The Solution

A solution to the problem of determining the discourse structure of Koine Greek texts will be intrinsically valuable, as will the means to that solution. In the following section these are discussed as they pertain first to discourse analysis of the GNT; second to the larger disciplines of linguistics, translation theory, and Greek studies; and finally, in a very general way, to other disciplines.

As discussed below, the means that has been developed to discover discourse structure is a combined text, incorporating the standard scholarly edition of the Greek New Testament (see Bibliography) with an interleaved grammatical analysis. This format of word-analysis-word-analysis will be valuable in all discourse-related approaches to the text. Whether using one of the printed formats of the project or the equivalent computer data base, this approach will make possible studies of vocabulary in context, the grammatical relations within the text, and the interplay of both vocabulary and grammatical relations. Only the first of these, the Greek text itself, has been available in any useful format previous to this project.

This means is applied to a specific end: determining the relationship between the New Testament Greek word order and discourse-related meaning. This has been done previously only in a limited and an unsystematic way. With computer-assisted speed and accuracy an exhaustive search for word-order patterns is intended to result in a correlation between grammatical patterns and their functions which will be definitive for the literary genres represented in the New Testament. The result will serve as a confirmation of previous work and will undoubtedly raise new questions to which the combined text may be reapplied.

Within the larger area of linguistics and translation theory, the combined text should serve as a model as well as a tool. In linguistics, discovery procedures which, when applied to a text, will automatically identify its structural composition have generally been eschewed as unavailable. At the same time, practical insights into various approaches to the data have always been welcome. This project can serve as a model for serious discourse studies, particularly in highly inflected languages where suffixation plays such a determining role. The projected study of Greek word order in light of discourse considerations is expected to add measurably to an understanding of linguistic universals. Linguistic universals are lawlike statements of either absolute (all languages have verbs) or implicational [if a language has inflectional case markings (as does Koine Greek), it may have free word order] import. Since there are linguistic universals relevant to phonology, syntax, and semantics, there is every reason to believe that there are universals waiting to be discovered at the discourse level of language, of both syntactic and semantic relevance.

The combined text will provide a new tool for translation theory, which seeks to identify the ingredients crucial to the process of saying meaningfully in one language what is meaningful in another. This is especially significant in that so much of translation theory has been developed from insights gained in Bible translation. (To date, the GNT as source text underlies some 2,000 target-language translations either completed or in progress.) One question with far-reaching implications concerns the correspondence between syntax and semantics. There is no doubt that some skewing exists between the two areas, as is obvious in the example of asking a question (syntactic form) in place of issuing a command (semantic meaning): "Would you please open the window?" The combined analytical text can serve translation theory as a grammatical base against which the propositional statements of meaning can be checked for just such correspondences. Such an extension is only one possibility. Additional extensions might profitably include the following: development of a higher level of grammatical analysis, built on the combined text, which would go beyond the individual word analysis to analyze phrases and clauses as to their grammatical constituents; adding a level of analysis which would analyze the roles of nouns with respect to their verbs (for example, as agent, beneficiary, time, location).

The actual discoveries made about discourse will serve to establish further the role of a proper treatment of discourse structure in translation. As universals of discourse structure are enunciated, a typology of discourse will result. Practically speaking, as Greek and every other discourse-analyzed language are assigned a type, significant factors far beyond vocabulary compatibility can be assessed as to their contribution to the overall ease and effectiveness of translation. For example, a knowledge of what is universal and what is particular about the argumentation subtype of the expository genre in Greek will certainly benefit the translation process into the discourse-analyzed languages of preliterate cultures wherever they may be found.

In time, Greek studies will profit from this project in proportion to the linguistic distance, in terms of time, between the particular stage of Greek being studied and the Koine Greek of this project. One of the existing aspects of this project is a central computer file containing each lexical form (the word with its inflectional status, "as is") encountered in the GNT with every matching grammatical analysis (for example, first person, singular pronoun, and so on). The Septuagint (the Greek translation of the Hebrew Old Testament, third century B.C.) is of interest to Greek, Hebrew, and biblical scholars, as well as to translation theorists. By using procedures not unlike those described below for this project in the Greek New Testament, the accumulated grammatical information in the central file could be semiautomatically transferred to the Greek Old Testament. That is, the analysis of any word-analysis pair could be transferred to every matching word in an unanalyzed text. This could also be done for the Greek writings of the church fathers in the centuries immediately following the writing of the GNT.

The GNT texts are almost entirely prose. However, there is a massive body of Greek literature, from the Homeric poems down, which consists of poetry and other genres not found in the GNT. The results of the discourse discoveries of this project and related studies should prove to be very valuable for inquiries into these untried genres.

Of interest to both linguistics and Greek studies are grammars of the Greek language at the various stages of its development. And yet the existing grammars of Greek are not complete. This is due in part to the fact, as noted above, that some sentence-level questions will remain unanswered until the mysteries of the structure of larger units of the language are uncovered. Not only will the project text allow quick access to the large GNT corpus in constructing a grammar of Koine Greek, but also the discourse factors which bear on grammatical choices and which are exposed by applications of this project will contribute to a more complete grammar. Grammars of a language at different points in its ongoing development are very important to diachronic linguistics (a study of language change through time). Diachronic studies will greatly profit from adequate grammars written for the progression of Greek (Mycenean, Homeric, Classical, Koine, Byzantine, Modern) through some 3,000 years of change. This project can make a visible contribution to that goal.

This project should offer a valuable model for historical and literary studies. Any study that works with observable forms or entities and some related, though distinct, information about those forms derivable from them, but not coextensive with them, can conceivably pattern its research on the model schematized here as word-analysis-word-analysis. By way of example, the vessels of the archaeologist's pottery inventory are analogous to the lexical forms of the Greek text. What he can learn from them (use, type, manufacture date, and so on) corresponds to the paired grammatical analysis.

Methodology

The general approach to the problem has been to develop a complete grammatical tag for each successive word in the Greek text. A grammatical tag contains, encoded in a short abbreviation, all the grammatical information contained in a prose statement of a form's analysis. Each Greek word is analyzed for the grammatical information it contains in itself. In addition, contextual information is provided from elsewhere in the sentence to resolve any ambiguities inherent in the form itself. Two examples will illustrate this. *Diōkōn,* a participle meaning "persecuting," contains the following grammatical information (where underlining represents letter abbreviation in subsequent tag): it is a Verb, Participial in form, Present tense, Active voice, Nominative case, Masculine gender, and Singular number. (See a Greek grammar, for example, Smyth,[5] for extended discussion of these categories.) This information is all contained in mnemonic form in the tag: VPPANM-S. (The hyphen marks the place where the identification of the person of a verbal form—first, second, or third—is indicated; it is not relevant to an analysis of this word.) *Heautōn* (themselves) is tagged as NPGMYP to encode the following grammatical analysis: it is of the general class Noun, a Pronoun by subclass, Genitive case, Masculine gender, second person (Y), and Plural number. This form is ambiguous as to gender and person. That it is, say, masculine gender and second person is information supplied from the context, since the form itself could be masculine, feminine, or neuter and first, second, or third person. The grammatical choices employed in the analysis are presented in Appendix 2A.

The analysis of the forms of the New Testament text reflects all the major distinctions provided by traditional Greek grammatical analysis. Contextually supplied information is generally limited to information which cannot be determined unambiguously by looking at the form in isolation, but which is distinctive somewhere within the paradigm (a grouping of related forms, basically the same, but differing, say, by suffixes). In the above example, the Greek for *themselves* is nondistinct as to gender, but only in the genitive case form *heautōn;* the accusative case forms show that the three genders are distinct: *Heautous* (masculine), *heautas* (feminine), *heauta* (neuter). Additionally, although use of this project is meant to yield new but vital information about the discourse structure of Greek, the analysis in tagged form already contains discourse-related information. For example, the Greek conjunction *alla* (but) is potentially tagged as CC, CH, or CS according as it functions to coordinate, superordinate, or subordinate the Greek clause it heads to the preceding material. This grammatical information can only be ascertained from the discourse as the clause following *alla* is observed to relate to its context. Finally, the position of each letter in the tag is significant. The analyses have been divided into seven major areas: adjectives, conjunctions, determiners, nouns, prepositions, particles, and verbs. An A in third position (NPA-YP) represents information about the accusative case when the first position is filled by N (as for all nouns and pronouns), while an A in third position (VPAANM-S) represents the aorist tense when a V is in first position (as for all verbs).

The resulting extended or combined (word and analysis) text becomes the basis from which searches for lexical or grammatical or lexical and grammatical information can be made. The Greek text underlying this grammatical analysis is called simply the *lexical text*. The resultant text which includes word and grammatical analysis we call the *combined text*. The simple combined-text format looks like this (see Appendix 2B for Greek character, English transcription equivalents):

2.18   KAI (CC) JSAN (VIMA--ZP +) HOI (DNMP) MATHJTAI (N-NM-P)   MK   02.18

IWANNOU (N-GM-S) KAI (CC) HOI (DNMP) PHARISAIOI   MK   02.18

(N-NM-P) NJSTEUONTES   MK   02.18

Here 2.18 (leftmost, first line) represents chapter 2, verse 18. Such a reference occurs at the beginning of each new verse. And MK 02.18 represents the full reference (MK = *Good News by Mark*). Such an index follows and fully identifies every line.

Prior to the decision to give grammatical tags of the form already described, the value of a GNT text itself for discourse-related analysis was considered. The following discussion illustrates some shortcomings of such a text. The lexical text does contain a significant number of discourse-relevant words, particularly function words such as *kai* and *alla* (but). But there are numerous grammatical markings, mainly as suffixes, that are relevant to a discourse approach. If there were no overlap in suffix functions, such a text would suffice for extensive discourse research. The real situation, however, is much more complicated. For example, the final Greek letter A marks accusative neuter plural forms, nominative neuter plural forms, and nominative feminine singular forms, among several others, and is thus not unique to one grammatical form.

Language maintains a balance with respect to its distinctive elements. It has enough distinctions to be understandable but as few as possible for the sake of efficiency. The blurring of the distinctions noted above is possible because the speaker-hearer team is monitoring meaning. A hearer can usually tell from the context when, for example, the ending A is meant to distinguish the Greek accusative case from the nominative case. This is a straightforward matter for the speaker-hearer, but to the analyst it presents a problem. The researcher who wants to study all the accusative case forms for some purpose cannot get to them merely by recovering, manually or with computer assistance, all occurrences of words ending in A. This is the case because A marks, in addition to the accusative case, some nominative case forms as well as other functions, some of them verbal. Furthermore, not all accusatives are marked by A. If limited to the simple GNT text, the researcher has no choice but to monitor meaning in order to recover the accusative cases desired in his study. His task is not impossible, but standard methods are inefficient.

An approach to discourse analysis requiring reference to the grammatical information of the GNT cannot be made without monitoring the meaning of the text. Fortunately, however, the monitoring must be made only once. Once marked in the form of grammatical tags, the information is available to successive searches. Such a text is what has already been introduced as the extended or combined (word and analysis) text, in contrast to the simple or lexical text.

This project envisages searches to a degree of complexity which elevate computer assistance from being merely convenient to being all but necessary. The advantage of mechanical processing over manual processing is seen in the aspects of speed and accuracy. Searching for occurrences and orders of a, b, and c among a full alphabet of symbols is anything but speedy; accuracy is also likely to suffer. Indeed, it seems to be the case that manually conducted searches can, at best, have either speed or accuracy, but never both. Later in this chapter an example will show convincingly how computer-assisted analysis of language patterns is fast and accurate for searches made over an extended text.

The strategy, then, is to build an extended text in the word-and-analysis format. Built into that analysis is the grammatical information derivable directly from a form as well as from its context. This contextual information is of two types—information from the immediate context which supplies what is nondistinct for a given form, but distinctive to the paradigm (compare the *heautōn* discussion above), and information from the potentially wider context which supplies clues to discourse structure (compare *alla* above). Further, we have opted for the assistance of the computer because it can deliver both speed and accuracy. Finally, implicit in this discussion is the twofold nature of the solution: the project result is both the means (the combined text) and the end (answers to questions about discourse patterns in the GNT).

In order to explain the specific steps taken to arrive at the combined text, it is necessary to illustrate the several formats of the text to which reference will be constantly made. First, the simple GNT text, termed the *lexical text,* is basically identical to a traditional, printed Greek New Testament. This text is stored in computer memory in transliterated English characters (see Appendix 2B). The following illustration is from the *Second Letter from Peter.*

1.1 ' SUMEWN PETROS DOULOS KAI APOSTOLOS IJSOU CHRISTOU   2P01.01
TOIS ISOTIMON HJMIN LACHOUSIN PISTIN EN DIKAIOSUNJY   2P01.01
TOU THEOU HJMWN KAI SWTJROS IJSOU CHRISTOU: 2P01.01

1.2   CHARIS HUMIN KAI EIRJNJ PLJTHUNTHEIJ EN EPIGNWSEI   2P01.02

TOU THEOU KAI IJSOU TOU KURIOU HJMWN.   2P01.02

A second format used in developing the project solution is the *lexical concordance*. Figure 2-1 is part of a page from the lexical concordance of the *Second Letter from John*. As can be seen in the figure, the concordance format is a listing of all identical forms found in a given lexical text. These identical forms are grouped or concorded together. Each word is focused on in turn as the *key word*. Right and left contexts are included around each key word in order to permit examination of the form in context. The context allows the user to determine how the word is used, whether, for example, *salt* is a noun ("Wars have been waged over salt") or verb ("They salt their speech with witticisms"). An index stands at the right margin to identify the location of the key word in the lexical text. This seven-place index corresponds to the reference system already in use in biblical studies: book, chapter, verse. The concordance index permits easy reference to the source text when it is necessary to consult larger texts than those provided.

The *combined text,* already introduced and illustrated, is a third project format. It is useful both as a tool in developing the combined text, as is explained below, and as an analytic tool itself. Refer to the sample on page 24.

The *combined concordance* format relates to the combined text as the lexical concordance relates to the lexical text. Its features are identical to those of the lexical concordance, with the additional feature of being able to focus on both lexical and grammatical items, a reflection of the nature of the combined text. As the combined text contains the lexical GNT, so the *lexical focus* puts the spotlight on instances of identical lexical forms, that is, words. It differs from the simple lexical concordance in that it contains the grammatical tags as part of the concordance context. See figure 2-2, a page from the *Letter to the Galatians* combined concordance. Since the combined text also contains the grammatical analysis of the GNT, the *grammatical focus* puts the spotlight on instances of identical grammatical tags. The accompanying words which the grammatical tags analyze are included as part of the concordance context. See figure 2-3, also a page from the *Letter to the Galatians* combined concordance.

The following paragraphs offer a description of how each of these formats was developed and how it contributed to the development of the project as a whole. The production of the combined text is also discussed. Those developing projects analogous to that described here might profit from the pitfalls encountered and the lessons learned.

Since no computer-readable tape of the United Bible Societies' third edition of the GNT (hereafter UBS3) was available, we developed our own.

KEY WORD   PAGE 00005 IDENT

      ERGOIS

00001 OCCURRENCE(S) OF ERGOIS

      ERWTW

KATHWS ENTOLJN ELABOMEN PARA TOU PATROS. 1.5 KAI NUN   ERWTW SE, KURIA, OUCH HWS ENTOLJN KAINJN GRAPHWN SOI ALLA   2J01.05

00001 OCCURRENCE(S) OF ERWTW

      ESTAI

DIA TJN ALJTHEIAN TJN MENOUSAN EN HJMIN, KAI METH HJMWN   ESTAI EIS TON AIWNA. 1.3 ESTAI METH HJMWN CHARIS ELEOS   2J01.02

MENOUSAN EN HJMIN, KAI METH HJMWN ESTAI EIS TON AIWNA. 1.3   ESTAI METH HJMWN CHARIS ELEOS EIRJNJ PARA THEOU PATROS, KAI   2J01.03

00002 OCCURRENCE(S) OF ESTAI

Figure 2–1. Lexical Concordance

KEY WORD   PAGE 00001 IDENT

      ADELPHON

(VIAA--XS), EI (CS) MJ (AB) IAKWBON (N-AM-S) TON (DAMS)   ADELPHON (N-AM-S) TOU (DGMS) KURIOU (N-GM-S), 1.20 HA   GA01.10

0001 OCCURRENCE(S) OF ADELPHON

      AGAPJ

(N-NM-S) TOU (DGNS) PNEUMATOS (N-GN-S) ESTIN (VIPA--ZS)   AGAPJ (N-NF-S), CHARA (N-NF-S), EIRJNJ (N-NF-S), MAKROTHUMIA   GA05.22

00001 OCCURRENCE(S) OF AGAPJ

      AGAPJS

TJY (DDFS) SARKI (N-DF-S), ALLA (CC) DIA (PG) TJS (DGFS)   AGAPJS (N-GF-S) DOULEUETE (VMPA--YP) ALLJLOIS (NPDMYP). 5.14   GA05.13

AKROBUSTIA (N-NF-S), ALLA (CC) PISTIS (N-NF-S) DI (PG)   AGAPJS (N-GF-S) ENERGOUMENJ (VPPMNF-S). 5.7 ETRECHETE   GA05.06

00002 OCCURRENCE(S) OF AGAPJS

Figure 2–2. Combined Lexical and Grammatical Category Concordance— Galatians (Lexical Focus)

KEY WORD   PAGE 00113   IDENT

	KEY WORD	IDENT
(VIAP--XP) KAI (AB) AUTOI (NPNMZS) HAMARTWLOI (A--NM-P), ARA	(QT) CHRISTOS (N-NM-S) HAMARTIAS (N-GF-S) DIAKONOS (N-NM-S)	GA02.17
(CC) GNWSTHENTES (VPAPNMYP) HUPO (PG) THEOU (N-GM-S), PWS	(QT) EPISTREPHETE (VIPA--YP) PALIN (AB) EPI (PA) TA (DANP)	GA04.09
EI (CS) PERITOMJN (N-AF-S) ETI (AB) KJRUSSW (VIPA--XS), TI	(QT) ETI (AB) DIWKOMAI (VIPP--XS) $ ARA (CC) KATJRGJTAI	GA05.11
W (QS) ANOJTOI (A--VM-P) GALATAI (N-VM-P), TIS	(QT) HUMAS (NPA-YP) EBASKANEN (VIAA--ZS), HOIS (NRDMYP) KAT	GA03.01
(VPPMNF-S). 5.7 ETRECHETE (VIMA--VP) KALWS (AB): TIS	(QT) HUMAS (NPA-YP) ENEKOPSEN (VIAA--ZS) [TJY (DDFS)	GA05.07
(N-AN-S), HOUTWS (AB) KAI (AB) NUM (AB). 4.30 ALLA (CC) TI	(QT) LEGEI (VIPA--ZS) HJ (DNFS) GRAPHJ (N-NF-S) $ *EKBALE	GA04.30
HWS (AB) CHRISTON (N-AM-S) IJSOUN (N-AM-S). 4.15 POU	(QT) OUN (CH) HO (DNMS) MAKARISMOS (N-NM-S) HUMWN (NPG-YP) $	GA04.15
KECHARISTAI (VIRM--ZS) HO (DNMS) THEOS (N-NM-S). 3.19 TI	(QT) OUN (CH) HO (DNMS) NOMOS (N-NM-S) $ TWN (DGFP)	GA03.19
KAI (CC) OUCHI (AB) IOUDAIKWS (AB) ZJYS (VIPS--YS), PWS	(QT) TA (DANP) ETHNJ (N-AN-P) ANAGKAZEIS (VIPA--YS)	GA02.14
00009 OCCURRENCE(S) OF		
PNEUMATOS (N-GN-S) HUMWN (NPG-YP), ADELPHOI (N-VM-P): AMJN	(QS)	GA06.18
CHRISTOS (N-NM-S) DWREAN (AB) APETHANEN (VIAA--ZS). 3.1 W	(QS) ANOJTOI (A--VM-P) GALATAI (N-VM-P), TIS (QT) HUMAS	GA03.01
HA (NRANZP) DE (CC) GRAPHW (VIPA--XS) HUMIN (NPD-YP), IDOU	(QS) ENWPION (PG) TOU (DGMS) THEOU (N-GM-S) HOTI (CS) OU	GA01.20
(DAMP) AIWNAS (N-AM-P) TWN (DGMP) AIWNWN (N-GM-P): AMJN	(QS) 1.6 THAUMAZW (VIPA--XS) HOTI (CS) HOUTWS (AB) TACHEWS	GA01.05
00004 OCCURRENCE(S) OF ,	(QS)	

Figure 2-3. Combined Lexical and Grammatical Category Concordance—Galatians (Category Focus)

For the great bulk of the GNT this was accomplished by transliterating (eliminating most accent marks) the Greek text at a computer terminal and, for a much smaller part of the text, by taking a different source text[6] already available in computer-readable form and adapting it to the UBS3 standard. The results of both procedures were proofread against the text of UBS3. The result was the GNT lexical text in computer memory, excluding any UBS3 reader aids such as the editorial critical apparatus, section headings, punctuation apparatus, or cross references. It does, however, include verse and chapter numbers, an optional index, editorial bracketting within the text, the equivalent of UBS boldface type to indicate Old Testament quotes, and full punctuation. This text is available in the American Philological Association standardized transliteration (see Appendix 2B, column 3) with or without accents.

The lexical text thus developed was the basis of the next step. The University of Minnesota Computer Center (hereafter UCC) computer program GENCORD (*gen*eral con*cord*ance program) was applied to the lexical text.[7] In order to use GENCORD and to have manageable-size units, the GNT was divided into its twenty-seven constituent book lengths, ranging in length from 152 words (*Second Letter from John*) to 19,628 words (*Good News by Luke*) compared to a total GNT length of somewhat less than 140,000 words. The result of applying GENCORD to these book-length files was twenty-seven lexical concordances.

The lexical concordances were, in turn, the basis for the tagging operation, giving a grammatical analysis to each successive word. The initial choice of how to proceed was obvious enough: Either tag the first word, then the second, and successively each word in the GNT until all words had received a grammatical analysis, or somehow tag all identical words in one operation. The latter approach seemed more efficient.

This approach was optimal for a large number of words, that is, those whose grammatical analysis is identical or unambiguous. These words are of that type—*gar* (for), *hina* (in order that), *hoti* (that)—for, even though there may be some difference of usage within a given example, that difference is below the level of detail treated by this analysis. This approach to tagging like groups of words all at once made extensive use of the lexical-concordance format. Thus where *hina* is encountered on the concordance page, a single tag CS (subordinating conjunction) was given to all instances at once.

The question arises, however, whether it is more efficient to do this procedure on twenty-seven individual book-length lexical concordances or on a single GNT-length lexical concordance. The word *hina* potentially occurs in every New Testament book. If a single tagging can correctly identify five instances of *hina* in the lexical concordance of the *Second Letter from John,* it appeared that a GNT lexical concordance would be even more efficient, for there the more than 600 occurrences of *hina* in the GNT would appear all together and could thus be tagged CS in one fell swoop. Appearances notwithstanding, the approach that gave tags to the individual book-length lexical concordances was chosen. There were several reasons for taking this approach. First, the initial project began with a single book, the *Letter to the Galatians*. It was not initially obvious that interest and funding would permit a GNT-length project. Second, the number of words that would receive identical tags is less than the GNT total, there being a higher percentage of types than tokens. In addition, some words receiving a single identical tag have a restricted distribution, occurring in just one or a small set of GNT constituent texts. Third, the process of taking a given grammatical analysis and automatically attaching it to all words thus analyzed, was found to be more cost-efficient when performed over shorter lengths of texts, since the computer must scan only the books where the words occur, rather than the entire twenty-seven-book corpus.

A large number of words are not represented by single, identical tags. These are words of the "salt" type explained earlier. They are ambiguous in that, depending on their contexts, they have one or another grammatical analysis (noun or verb; nominative or accusative; adverb or particle; and so on). A given ambiguous word is usually either one analysis or a second, but twelve or more analysis tags potentially occur. [*Hepta* (seven) and *dōdeka* (twelve), two frequently occurring GNT numbers, have numerous tags because they belong to a subset of numbers which do not take the variable inflectional endings for gender and case.] These words need individual attention, for each must be examined for its use in context.

Figure 2-4 gives a sample page from the lexical concordance of the *Good News by Matthew*. It illustrates two points. First, some words are ambiguous. Specifically, *dia* is a preposition which demands an accusative or genitive case in the following word, depending on whether *dia* means "because of" or "through," respectively. At the end of the *dia* listing, two grammatical tags are handwritten: PG, representing "preposition governing genitive case," and PA, representing "preposition governing accusative case." These are numbered, respectively, 1 and 2. Instances of *dia* are then identified as matching one or the other of the grammatical analyses. A 2 is marked before PA analyses while the absence of any mark indicates a PG analysis. Second, the script illustrates that the tags are marked manually. The place of hand-marked tags will become evident as the discussion continues.

The lexical-concordance format also served as a check against errors of spelling in the lexical text. While tagging the lexical concordances, a number of errors were observed which had been missed during the proofreading process that followed the preparation of the lexical text. Since each grouping of identical words needs to be given one or more tags, misspelled words come under scrutiny. Assuming that misspelled words are infrequent and that the same word is not consistently misspelled, they are most likely to occur as the only instance of a form.

The goal was to give a grammatical analysis to every word of the lexical text in order to arrive at a combined (word and analysis) text. The means to that end was to hand-tag the lexical concordances. (Figure 2–4 represents one such page of the process.) From the hand-tagged concordance pages each grammatical analysis had to be taken and added, following the matching word(s) in the lexical text (see, for example, *dia* in figure 2–4). For this the computer provided valuable assistance, the specific operations of which are explained below. The approach allowing the most fully automatic computer assistance possible was chosen. The least costly approach would have been to begin with the first word of a given text, locate its tag in the alphabetically listed hand-tagged lexical concordance, enter it at the terminal, and then repeat the process for the second and succeeding words. This word-by-word approach could have employed a Greek scholar at the terminal, thus obviating the prior hand-tagging on the lexical concordance. However, the volunteer Greek experts available to assist the project were scattered near and far. Providing them each with a computer-printed lexical concordance for hand-tagging the words was more reasonable than flying them in to do their grammatical analysis at a UCC terminal or providing them with long-distance terminal connections with UCC computers. In addition, the volunteer experts acknowledge the benefit of having all the occurrences of a given Greek lexical form grouped together. Their grammatical analysis was made more accurate by their being able to examine all instances of a Greek word in a given book at one glance. Thus there was no need to have the tag entered by a Greek expert at the computer terminal. But the method just described (tagging the first word, then the second, and each succeeding word in a text) was also not employed. In terms of human time it was too costly to look up each successive word in a text in the lexical concordance.

Already ruled out is a GNT-length tagging approach by any method as well as a successive-word method on shorter lengths, for reasons stated above. In working with the alternate approach, book-length files, the most costly approach in terms of computer time would have been to tag a given word in its every occurrence in a whole lexical text. In actual fact, the longer book files were divided into two to five smaller files. This shortened the size of the file through which the computer had to search, but increased the number of times the person sitting at the terminal had to go through a given lexical concordance, looking up the tag for a word. When a word was found whose tag was consistently the same, the computer was told to find all the instances of that form of the word and give each the tag. When there were multiple distinct tags for a given form, each location of the form under review was found by the computer, and the one correct tag for that form in

EGERTHJSONTAI KAI PLANJSOUSIN POLLOUS: 24.12 KAI 2 DIA TO PLJTHUNTHJNAI TJN ANOMIAN PSUGJSETAI HJ AGAPJ TWN   MT24.12

ALLA PROSKAIROS ESTIN, GENOMENJS DE THLIPSEWS J DIWGMOU 2 DIA TON LOGON EUTHUS SKANDALIZETAI. 13.22 HO DE EIS TAS   MT13.21

EIPAN AUTW, EN BJTHLEEM TJS IOUDAIAS: HOUTWS GAR GEGRAPTAI DIA TOU PROPHJTOU: 2.6 *KAI *SU, *BJTHLEEM GJ IOUDA   MT02.05

OUDEN ELALEI AUTOIS: 13.35 HOPWS PLJRWTHJ TO RJTHEN DIA TOU PROPHJTOU LEGONTOS, *ANOIXW *EN *PARABOLAIS *TO   MT13.35

AUTOUS. 21.4 TOUTO DE GEGONEN HINA PLJRWTHJ TO RJTHEN DIA TOU PROPHJTOU LEGONTOS, 21.5 *EIPATE *TJ *THUGATRI *SIWN   MT21.04

TJS TELEUTJS HJRWDOU: HINA PLJRWTHJ TO RJTHEN HUPO KURIOU DIA TOU PROPHJTOU LEGONTOS, *EX *AIGUPTOU *EKALESA *TON   MT02.15

TOUTO DE HOLON GEGONEN HINA PLJRWTHJ TO RJTHEN HUPO KURIOU DIA TOU PROPHJTOU LEGONTOS, 1.23 *IDOU *HJ *PARTHENOS *EN   MT01.22

IWANNOU TOU BAPTISTOU, 14.9 KAI LUPJTHEIS HO BASILEUS 2 DIA TOUS HORKOUS KAI TOUS SUNANAKEIMENOUS EKELEUSEN DOTHJNAI   MT14.09

EKBALLW TA DAIMONIA, HOI HUIOI HUMWN EN TINI EKBALLOUSIN S 2 DIA TOUTO AUTOI KRITAI ESONTAI HUMWN. 12.28 EI DE EN   MT12.27

DE OUK ECHEI, KAI HO ECHEI ARTHJSETAI AP AUTOU. 13.13 2 DIA TOUTO EN PARABOLAIS AUTOIS LALW, HOTI BLEPONTES OU   MT13.13

IWANNJS HO BAPTISTJS: AUTOS JGERTHJ APO TWN NEKRWN, KAI 2 DIA TOUTO HAI DUNAMEIS ENEPGOUSIN EN AUTW. 14.3 HO GAR   MT14.02

SOI HEWS HEPTAKIS ALLA HEWS HEBDOMJKONTAKIS HEPTA. 18.23 2 DIA TOUTO HWMOIWTHJ HJ BASILEIA TWN OURANWN ANTHRWPW BASILEI   MT18.23

ECHIDNWN, PWS PHUGJTE APO TJS KRISEWS TJS GEENNJS 23.34 2 DIA TOUTO IDOU EGW APOSTELLW PROS HUMAS PROPHJTAS KAI   MT23.34

AN KAI OUK AN EIASEN DIORUCHTHJNAI TJN OIKIAN AUTOU. 24.44 2 DIA TOUTO KAI HUMEIS GINESTHE HETOIMOI, HOTI HJ OU DOKEITE   MT24.44

KATAPHRONJSEI: OU DUNASTHE THEW DOULEUEIN KAI MAMWNA. 6.25 2 DIA TOUTO LEGW HUMIN, MJ MERIMNATE TJ PSUCHJ HUMWN TI   MT06.25

KAI *ESTIN *THAUMASTJ *EN *OPHTHALMOIS *HJMWN 21.43 2 DIA TOUTO LEGW HUMIN HOTI ARTHJSETAI APH HUMWN HJ BASILEIA   MT21.43

EMOU ESTIN, KAI HO MJ SUNAGWN MET EMOU SKORPIZEI. 12.31 2 DIA TOUTO LEGW HUMIN, PASA HAMARTIA KAI BLASPHJMIA   MT12.31

PANTA LEGOUSIN AUTW, NAI. 13.52 HO DE EIPEN AUTOIS. 2 DIA TOUTO PAS GRAMMATEUS MATHJTEUTHEIS TJ BASILEIA TWN   MT13.52

HOUTOS EPHJ, DUNAMAI KATALUSAI TON NAON TOU THEOU KAI DIA TRIWN HJMERWN OIKODOMJSAI. 26.62 KAI ANASTAS HO   MT26.61

PALIN DE LEGW HUMIN, EUKOPWTERON ESTIN KAMJLON DIA TRUPJMATOS RAPHIDOS DIELTHEIN J PLOUSION EISELTHEIN EIS   MT19.24

AKOUSAS EN TW DESMWTJRIW TA ERGA TOU CHRISTOU PEMPSAS DIA TWN MATHJTWN AUTOU 11.3 EIPEN AUTW, SU EI HO ERCHOMENOS   MT11.02

EIS POLIN LEGOMENJN NAZARET, HOPWS PLJRWTHJ TO RJTHEN DIA TWN PROPHJTWN HOTI NAZWRAIOS KLJTHJSETAI. 3.1 EN DE TAIS   MT02.23

EN EKEINW TW KAIRW EPOREUTHJ HO JJSOUS TOIS SABBASIN DIA TWN SPORIMWN: HOI DE MATHJTAI AUTOU EPEINSASAN, KAI   MT12.01

DIA   1[PGJ 2[PA]

00053 OCCURRENCE(S) of DIABLEPSEIS

EKBALE PRWTON EK TOU OPHTHALMOU SOU TJN DOKON, KAI TOTE DIABLEPSEIS EKBALEIN TO KARPHOS EK TOU OPHTHALMOU TOU   MT07.05

00001 OCCURRENCE(S) of DIABLEPSEIS

VIFA--YS

DIABOLOS

KURION *TON *THEOU *SOU. 4.8 PALIN PARALAMBANEI AUTON HO DIABOLOS EIS OROS HUPSJLON LIAN, KAI DEIKNUSIN AUTW PASAS   MT04.08

DIA *STOMATOS *THEOU. 4.5 TOTE PARALAMBANEI AUTON HO DIABOLOS EIS TJN HAGIAN POLIN, KAI ESTJSEN AUTON EPI TO   MT04.05

TOU PONJROU, 13.39 HO DE ECHTHROS HO SPEIRAS AUTA ESTIN HO DIABOLOS: HO DE THERISMOS SUNTELEIA AIWNOS ESTIN, HOI DE   MT13.39

KAI *AUTW MONW *LATREUSEIS, 4.11 TOTE APHIJSIN AUTON HO DIABOLOS, KAI IDOU AGGELOI PROSJLTHON KAI DIJKONOUN AUTW. 4.   MT04.11

DIABOLOS 00004 OCCURRENCE(S) OF

AP-NM-S

DIABOLOU

EIS TJN ERJMON HUPO TOU PNEUMATOS, PEIRASTHJNAI HUPO TOU DIABOLOU. 4.2 KAI NJSTEUSAS HJMERAS TESSERAKONTA KAI NUKTAS   MT04.01

DIABOLOU 00001 OCCURRENCE(S) OF

AP-GM-S

HOI KATJRAMENOI EIS TO PUR TO AIWNION TO HJTOIMASMENON TW DIABOLWY KAI TOIS AGGELOIS AUTOU: 25.42 EPEINASA GAR KAI OUK   MT25.41

DIABOLWY 00001 OCCURRENCE(S) OF

AP-DM-S

DIAKATHARIEI

HAGIW KAI PURI: 3.12 HOU TO PUTUON EN TJ CHEIRI AUTOU, KAI DIAKATHARIEI TJN HALWNA AUTOU, KAI SUNAXEI TON SITON AUTOU   MT03.12

DIAKATHARIEI 00001 OCCURRENCE(S) OF

VIFA--ZS

DIAKONJSAI

HO HUOIS TOU ANTHRWPOU OUK JLTHEN DIAKONJTHJNAI ALLA DIAKONJSAI KAI DOUNAI TJN PSUCHJN AUTOU LUTRON ANTI POLLWN.   MT20.28

DIAKONJSAI 00001 OCCURRENCE(S) OF

VNAA

DIAKONJTHJNAI

Figure 2-4. Lexical Concordance—Hand-Tagged

that context was added. This costly approach was made more efficient by performing the above procedure for all but the most frequent tag of a given form. Then, for that remaining tag, the untagged occurrences of the word were automatically tagged by one command to the computer. For example, if for *kai* (and, also) in a given book thirty occurrences were analyzed as AB (adverb) and seventy were analyzed as CC (coordinating conjunction), only the former would have to be tagged one at a time. The more frequent CC tags could automatically be added to the remaining untagged *kai* forms.

The task of building combined texts out of lexical texts was made easier by using the computer for automatic tagging wherever possible. Since it was desirable to tag automatically all occurrences of a word previously encountered, a *central file* was developed to keep track of all lexical items and their associated tags. The computer read the input text one word at a time and looked up the word in the central file. The procedure was semiautomatic and was used interactively.

One of three cases obtained.

1. Where the word encountered was identified in the central file as uniquely tagged, the computer supplied the tag for the output text.
2. Where the word encountered was identified in the central file as ambiguous (having two or more tags), the computer put an empty parentheses set following the word for later filling in.
3. Where the word encountered was new to the central file (that is, not found), the computer asked for its tag. The person at the terminal, after consulting the lexical concordance, supplied the appropriate tag. If the word-tag combination was unique, then the tag was supplied. If the new word form took one of several tags, the most frequent tag, as observed in the concordance, was supplied. This word and its tag were then added to the central file for future reference (a scratch file was used at this stage). The central file was permanently updated after the editing process described below.

The process continued until every word in the text was supplied with a unique tag or marked by empty parentheses as being ambiguous. The output text (combined text) consisting of a word-tag-word-tag format then had to be edited. The blank tags were filled in by looking up the word in the lexical concordances from which the appropriate tag could be ascertained. The less frequently occurring tags were first filled in one at a time (or as efficiently as possible for a given book) and the remainder automatically tagged. New ambiguities, overlooked by case 1 above, were caught at this point and corrected.

The complications due to ambiguous words greatly increased the tagging time but could not have been avoided. In a given text up to 20 percent of the forms were ambiguous. The manual tagging of these words consumed a major portion of the man-hours required to tag the texts. The newly acquired combined text of each book was used as input for a GEN-CORD run. The resultant combined concordances were then checked for errors page by page against the hand-tagged lexical concordances. Such errors as new ambiguities and mistyped tags were caught with this vital check. The most cost- and time-efficient means of making corrections was to edit the combined text and then rerun the combined concordances.

With the combined text edited and mostly error-free, the central file was then updated. The computer read each word-tag combination and checked the central file. If the word was not already in the file, the word was added along with its tag. If the word was in the file but the tag was different, the new tag was added and the word was marked as ambiguous for subsequent central-file uses.

The process of making combined concordances of individual GNT combined texts was followed by making a single GNT combined concordance. The purpose was developmental: The combined texts of individual books needed to be checked for accuracy and internal consistency as a set. Since the individual combined texts reflected the grammatical analyses of several Greek experts, it was necessary to unify the analysis over the text of the entire Greek New Testament. The single GNT combined concordance proved valuable both in developing a unified system of grammatical analysis and in applying that analysis to points where the particular analysis of individual Greek experts differed from it. This second value has been realized by checking unit subsections of the whole GNT combined concordance against the system analysis. The grammatical focuses have been especially valuable here. For example, the noun subsection lists all nouns by their tags, subgrouped by the constituent elements of the noun tags. Thus all the genitive case, masculine gender, singular number nouns of the entire GNT can be examined in a single operation for membership in that tagged analysis (N-GM-S). The final residual errors of the GNT tagged text have been eliminated by this approach.

As we have already noted, the project is both an end in itself and a means to other ends, specifically answers to inquiries about discourse. In both respects the technology and resources provided by UCC were indispensable. Apart from hand-tagging the lexical concordances, UCC computers were crucially involved in every aspect of the project. Because the focus of this project has been to develop research materials and because large texts have been involved, a computer with large storage facilities and fast access to them was needed. The UCC Cyber 172 was more than adequate. In addition to the machines themselves, UCC programs were very valuable. GENCORD turned lexical and combined texts into lexical and combined concordances scores of times. The availability of such an efficient concordance program cut months off the time to complete the project. XEDIT,[8] the editing system most available and easily usable, although not the most flexible, was used extensively, both in entering tags for ambiguous words and in correcting the texts. UCC grants for central processor time and for supplies were crucial to the project. The skills of a computer programmer were necessary in developing, correcting, adjusting, and manipulating computer programs and files. All resources, human and mechanical, needed by the project were available, although the timing of their availability might in some cases have made the project development simpler and more efficient.

Various programs had to be developed in the process of completing this project. The central file called LEXCATS (*Lex*emes and grammatical *cat*egories) used 2.6 million characters of disk space. It was structured into storage blocks which could be randomly located by mathematically converting the Greek word in question to a number, used as the index to the block. Since every word in a text had to be looked up in the LEXCATS file, speed was of paramount importance. Random access to this file was the only viable approach. Figure 2–5 shows the structure of the storage blocks, each potentially containing sixty-four entries (but empty entries are not printed).

Several programs were developed which manipulated the central file. The programs are written in Pascal but employ several COMPASS (CDC assembly language) routines specifically to set up, access, and write on the LEXCATS file. One program used the lexical text as input and interactively filled in the text with appropriate tags (as described above), yielding a combined text. A second program used the combined text as input and updated the central file. Another program accesses the file to extract any information desired (say, all tags for a given word).

LEXCATS, in its final form, is itself a valuable tool. It can be used as a lexicon to tag other Greek texts (say, the Septuagint). It is also used as the basis for an analytical Greek lexicon, described on page 44.

Several programs under development can extract information from the combined texts. The possibilities are almost unlimited. Emphasis is given to identifying various patterns in the distribution of grammatical tags and lexical items pertinent to the study of word order. One such program, illustrated below, gives as output all occurrences of circumstantial participles. Another supplies occurrences of a head noun and its corresponding adjective and/or genitive noun. These programs, written in Pascal, handled the text in chunks (with some punctuation marks or specific words serving as delimiters).

Figure 2–5 illustrates three adjacent file blocks from the central file. Each Greek word within a given block has the same numerical value as every other. "False" in the first of the true-false columns indicates that the entry is a word; "true" indicates that it is a grammatical tag. A second column "false" indicates that the entry form appears entirely on its entry line. "True" indicates that the word had to be stored in two locations (adjacent lines). In the last two numeric columns, a nonzero entry in the first column indicates, for words, where the next word begins and, for tags, where the next tag (for the same word) begins (zero when no more tags follow). The second column numbers indicate, for words, where the initial tag is located and, for tags, where its corresponding word is indicated. For example, *CHARJTE* (block 1992, line 4) is identified as a word not needing a second line for full storage as having VSAP--YP as its tag and VMAP--YP as its second and final tag. These tag locations in turn point back to *CHARJTE*.

THIS IS FILE BLOCK #1991

0.	GOMORRA	FALSE	FALSE	2	1
1.	N-NF-S	TRUE	FALSE	0	0
2.	KATARGJSAN	FALSE	TRUE	5	4
3.	TOS	FALSE	FALSE	0	0
4.	VPAAGM-S	TRUE	FALSE	0	2
5.	EXAPATWSIN	FALSE	FALSE	7	6
6.	VIPA--ZP	TRUE	FALSE	0	5
7.	EMNJSTHJSA	FALSE	TRUE	10	9
8.	N	FALSE	FALSE	0	0
9.	VIAP--ZP	TRUE	FALSE	0	7
10.	ENTALMATA	FALSE	FALSE	12	11
11.	N-AN-P	TRUE	FALSE	0	10
12.	APHIETE	FALSE	FALSE	0	13
13.	VIPA--YP	TRUE	FALSE	0	12

THIS IS FILE BLOCK #1992

0.	PISTEWS	FALSE	FALSE	2	1
1.	N-GF-S	TRUE	FALSE	0	0
2.	EPILOIPON	FALSE	FALSE	4	3
3.	A--AMS	TRUE	FALSE	0	2
4.	CHARTJE	FALSE	FALSE	6	5
5.	VSAP--YP	TRUE	FALSE	12	4
6.	GINWSKEIN	FALSE	FALSE	8	7
7.	VNPA	TRUE	FALSE	0	6
8.	EUCHARISTI	FALSE	TRUE	13	10
9.	AS	FALSE	FALSE	0	0
10.	N-AF-P	TRUE	FALSE	11	8
11.	N-GF-S	TRUE	FALSE	0	8
12.	VMAP--YP	TRUE	FALSE	0	4
13.	EISPOREUOM	FALSE	TRUE	16	15
14.	ENOI	FALSE	FALSE	0	0
15.	VPPMNM-P	TRUE	FALSE	0	13
16.	PROSTHEINA	FALSE	TRUE	19	18
17.	I	FALSE	FALSE	0	0
18.	VNAA	TRUE	FALSE	0	16
19.	BOWNTWN	FALSE	FALSE	21	20
20.	VPPAGM-P	TRUE	FALSE	0	19
21.	EKBLJTHJSO	FALSE	TRUE	24	23
22.	NTAI	FALSE	FALSE	0	0
23.	VIFP--ZP	TRUE	FALSE	0	21
24.	HJTOIMAKA	FALSE	FALSE	0	25
25.	VIRA--XS	TRUE	FALSE	0	24

THIS IS FILE BLOCK #1993

0.	ESCHATJ	FALSE	FALSE	2	1
1.	A--NFS	TRUE	FALSE	0	0
2.	APOPHEUGON	FALSE	TRUE	5	4
3.	TAS	FALSE	FALSE	0	0
4.	VPPAAM-P	TRUE	FALSE	0	2
5.	PARAKLJSEW	FALSE	TRUE	8	7
6.	S	FALSE	FALSE	0	0
7.	N-GF-S	TRUE	FALSE	0	5
8.	ANOMIWN	FALSE	FALSE	10	9
9.	N-GF-P	TRUE	FALSE	0	8
10.	BOJTHOS	FALSE	FALSE	12	11
11.	N-NM-S	TRUE	FALSE	0	10
12.	BAPTISMATO	FALSE	TRUE	15	14
13.	S	FALSE	FALSE	0	0
14.	N-GN-S	TRUE	FALSE	0	12

Figure 2–5. Central File

Results

The chief result of the project to date is the completed, combined text of the
GNT. The value of the product can probably not be more forcibly presented
than by way of an example. The example which follows is taken from a list
of possible computer searches for discourse-related information in the
GNT.

Like English, Greek has participles which can modify either a noun (1)
or a verb (2):

1.   The *fleeing* soldiers left everything.
2.   *Coming* unannounced, Mortimer ruffled some feathers.

Greek constructions having participles modifying the main verb, as in item
2, are called circumstantial participles. These constructions are much more
common in Greek than in English, where the participle is usually replaced
(that is, in translation) by a specific subordinating word, a subject, and a
finite verb, as in 3 and 4:

3.   *Because he came* unannounced, Mortimer ruffled some feathers.
4.   *When he came* unannouced, Mortimer ruffled some feathers.

Consider one subset of circumstantial-participle constructions in
Greek, those in which, as in 2 above, the unexpressed agent of the action of
the participle is identical with the expressed subject (agent) of the main
clause. Further information necessary to understand the discussion includes
the following: the subject of the main clause of sentences having these
constructions is in the nominative case; the main verb is finite; and the
participle itself is in the nominative case. There are then three crucial ingredients in a construction of this type: a nominative case noun (N), a finite
verb (V), and a nominative case particle (P).

Now, if Greek really is a language allowing a free ordering of the words
in a sentence, the three elements crucial to the subset of circumstantial
participles and conveniently labeled N, V, and P might be expected to occur
in any of the six logically possible orders given earlier for a, b, and c and
repeated here for convenience as N, V, and P:

N	V	P
N	P	V
V	N	P
V	P	N
P	N	V
P	V	N

Furthermore, assuming that this free word ordering really is free, a frequency distribution for the occurrence of each of these six orders might be expected to be in the vicinity of 1/6, or 16 percent. If, on the other hand, the distribution does not prove to be random, some explanation should be sought for the observed distribution, perhaps in terms of some controlling influence.

The first step in the test is to write a computer program which will recover from the combined text just those sets of three elements, N, V, and P, as defined, that are definitive for the nominative subset of circumstantial-participle constructions. Then the computer is asked to search a combined text (in this example, the *Good News by John*) in response to the dictates of the program. Finally, the results are evaluated.

The results are presented first, with various comments to follow. In the format of a simple array, the interesting frequency distribution of circumstantial-participle constructions in this combined text can be observed:

Orders			Instances	Percentages
N	V	P	8	11
N	P	V	30	42
V	N	P	17	24
V	P	N	1	1
P	N	V	16	22
P	V	N	0	0
			72	100

The above figures hardly represent a random distribution. Two explanations are suggested by these results. The first is that there is some discourse function being served by these various orders. Perhaps an item is moved to the beginning of a sentence in order to achieve some discourse-particular prominence. Possibly an item is inserted in the middle of a sentence to put particular attention on the item that follows it. The second explanation is that there may be "pure" syntactic constraints influencing these orders. For example, a given item must be last in a sentence; if it cannot be last, then it must be first. A subordinate clause is last in a given sentence, displacing the item in question to the head of the sentence. The first explanation explains in terms of voluntary movement. The discourse aims are directly served by using a given order, so the speaker-writer arranges items to achieve that order. The second explanation explains in terms of constrained movement. A given element A gets placed and so displaces a second element B. But by what principle is A placed? By discourse principles of voluntary movement. The authors view these as explanations of discourse. Ultimately, satisfying explanations will be expected to involve the interrelationship of a number of factors. The most that can be said at this point is that word-order patterns have met the expectations of nonrandom distribution.

An indication of how useful the computer was in obtaining these results may be approached anecdotally. It is reported that Alexander Cruden, the compiler of the Bible concordance that bears his name, spent seventeen years at his project and went blind doing so. By way of significant contrast, the computer run that resulted in the combined concordance of the entire GNT (just less than 280,000 words and tags) took less than twenty minutes of central processing time.

In order to evaluate the project further, consider the cost and efficiency of obtaining the statistical information given above for circumstantial participles by three methods. The first method is that described above, programming the computer to uncover the desired patterns from a combined text. The second method evaluated is that of manually searching a combined text for the same patterns. The third method is manually searching a lexical text, that is, a printed Greek New Testament. A fourth possible method, that of computer-assisted analysis of a lexical text, is not even evaluated because of the difficulties inherent in using that approach.

The first method required writing a computer program. It is very hard to evaluate the time investment in developing the program, but at the outside it took twenty hours. The many variables in Koine Greek—not only word order, but also the inflectional co-occurrences of number, gender, and case—make the data structures (how the data is stored in the computer's memory) in the program rather complicated. However, what is not known about Greek is more difficult to account for than what is known. For example, there must be a limit on the span of the text the computer searches across for any one pattern. Shall it be punctuation, specific words, or another construction? The programming time included running the program several times with subsequent tightenings or loosenings of the program to achieve the desired end.

The actual computing time to run the program over the combined text was less than sixty seconds. The length of the combined text of the *Good News by John* is 31,519 words and tags. The time involved to evaluate the results statistically was about one hour.

The second method is evaluated only by guess. There would be no programming time necessary other than to get a computer-printed output of the combined text in question, perhaps two minutes. The project development time may be assumed to be free and not to be computed in these estimates (although method 3 presupposed no project at all). The manual search would make use of both the words and tags of the combined text. We estimate ten hours of search time, give or take 50 percent. There are many variables to consider, including both expertise in Greek and familiarity with the project transcription and tags. By assuming that the search findings were noted directly on the combined text (a replaceable item), the evaluation time may be estimated at two hours.

The third method assumes working through a Greek text without grammatical tags and noting the patterns on a separate sheet of paper. No programming or computing time is involved, but the search presupposes someone totally familiar with Greek. We estimate the manual search to take 20 hours, give or take 50 percent. Statistical evaluation requires 4 hours.

At first glance, the second method seems to be most time-efficient. This is a vote for the combined text with doubtful testimony for the computer. With respect to dollar costs, the variables are immensely complicated. There are also a number of less visible factors such as schedules, supervision, and quality control. The reader may calculate the cost of buying the computer programming or doing it himself. UCC costs for central processing time explained in the first method were less than five dollars.

A harder look at the methods and long-range research goals suggests some changes. Should the grammatical-pattern findings under any method be inconclusive and the decision to extend the search over the length of the New Testament be made, the total investment can be found by multiplying the relevant figures by 10 (the *Good News by John* is 10.7 percent of the GNT). In the first method we have: computer programming, no additional expense; computer processing, 10 minutes; statistical evaluation, 20 hours. The second method yields: manual search, 100 hours; statistical evaluation, 20 hours. By the third method we get: manual search, 200 hours; statistical evaluation, 40 hours. The computer suddenly becomes the only reasonable approach to the suggested research.

Koine Greek, for all its intricacies, is a single language. As research on it continues, the programming involved is expected to drop drastically as a result of the reusability of whole or parts of existing computer programs. In addition, as the research progresses, it is expected that the programming itself can be simplified as a result of the advances in understanding the actual patternings involved.

The work described so far is only the beginning. This data base can be put to good use in evaluating word-order patterns of a wide variety. In the one example already presented, the occurrences of the logically possible orders of three rather independent items (N, P, V) were obtained. More of this work is expected. For example, a basic neutral order for the three elements subject (S), verb (V), object (O) might be determined. However, because the correlation of subject with nominative case and object with accusative case is not complete, these investigations may themselves be less than exhaustive. This state of affairs would hopefully spur others on to build on the project's data base. Extending the data base could profitably include role relations, that is, the relation a noun has to its verb, and thus contribute to the determination of the neutral order of S, V, and O placement.

The ordering investigations suggested above are related in that they are among independent grammatical items. Other investigations might include items dependent on one another. For example, we hope to investigate the order of modifiers (adjectives and genitive nouns: piece *of paper, Bob's* pencil) with respect to their head nouns. A more complicated but very crucial investigation will involve finding out what can go before the verb, as well as the relative orderings of these items.

A number of people are interested in a data base such as this for related but different ends. Such interests include authorship studies, searches for material common to the synoptic gospels (the *Good News* accounts by Matthew, Mark, and Luke), an investigation of evidence for Semitic syntax patterns in the GNT, and questions of Septuagint style (Old Testament quotations in the GNT usually reflect the Septuagint as the source rather than the Hebrew Old Testament). For these investigations to be fruitful, some innovative thinking and challenging computer programming will be necessary.

The computer-assisted searches described thus far have been limited to those for mere listings of instances of this or another pattern. Beyond this, there is more the computer can do to assist in research. The evaluation of three possible approaches to research considered the time necessary to make statistical evaluations. Such time can be reduced considerably. First, the computer could be programmed to concord like patterns rather than merely list them. As in finding the data in the first place, the computer would have to ignore intervening but irrelevant items. But the computer can go one step further to give actual statistical information on the patterns obtained and concorded. Whereas general statistical computation is a big service already provided by computers, it is by no means a trivial matter in regard to the patterns of natural language that interest linguists. Consider an example. In the discussion about finding the orders of circumstantial participles above, some complicating factors were ignored. Although the search was limited to six simple orders, complex patterns were also evident. A typical complex pattern was NPVP, that is, two participles with a single noun and finite verb. Is this one complex pattern or two simpler ones (NPV and NVP)? Such examples are easily handled in listing patterns; they prove much more difficult when computer assistance is sought in statistical summaries.

In the following paragraphs the various formats of the project, not as they figured into the development of the combined text, but as they will be available to scholars, are described and indications as to their possible use are presented.

In conjunction with the computer-tapes format to be described below, UCC plans to issue some of the project in printed form. Baker Book House

(Grand Rapids, Michigan) will publish the printed work in three parts of six total volumes. Part one will be the combined text in altered format, to be called the Analytical Greek New Testament, consisting of one volume. A sample from the *Letter to the Galatians* follows. Its chief difference from the combined text is that the grammatical tags are located interlinearly rather than between the words.

ΠΡΟΣ ΓΑΛΑΤΑΣ

1.1 Παῦλος ἀπόστολος, οὐκ ἀπ᾿ ἀνθρώπων οὐδὲ δι᾿ ἀνθρώπου ἀλλὰ
   N-NM-S   N-NM-S   AB   PG   N-GM-P   CC   PG   N-GM-S   CC

διὰ᾿ Ἰησοῦ Χριστοῦ καὶ Θεοῦ πατρὸς τοῦ ἐγείραντος αὐτὸν ἐκ
PG   N-GM-S   N-GM-S   CC   N-GM-S   N-GM-S   DGMS   VPAAGM-S   NPAMZS   PG

νεκρῶν, 1.2 καὶ οἱ σὺν ἐμοὶ πάντες ἀδελφοί , ταῖς ἐκκλησίαις
AP-GM-P   CC   DNMP   PD   NPD-XS   A--NM-P   N-NM-P   DDFP   N-DF-P

Part two will consist of the printed equivalent of the combined concordance of the whole GNT, and it will be called the Analytical Greek (New Testament) Concordance. It will include a two-volume lexical focus, of which the following is a sample:

    λέγω
    •
    •

ἐν PD τῇ DDFS σκοτίᾳ N-DF-S ἐίπατε VIAA--YP ἐν PD τῷ DDNS φωτὶ   LK 12.03
ἀναγνῶτε VSAA--YP . 4.17 καὶ CC ἐίπατε VMAA--YP Ἀρχίππῳ N-DM-S , Βλέπε   CO 04.17
τὸν DAMS δεῖνα AP-AM-S καὶ CC ἐίπατε VMAA--YP αὐτῷ NPDMZS ,Ὁ DNMS   MT 26.18
ἐν PD τῇ DDFS σκοτίᾳ N-DF-S ἐίπατε VMAA--YP ἐν PD τῷ DDNS φωτί   MT 10.27
    •
    •

It will be complemented by a two-volume grammatical focus, as the following exemplifies:

    ABT
    •
    •

οἱ DNMP γραμματεῖς N-NM-P τὸ DANS πῶς ABT ἀνέλωσιν VSAA--ZP αὐτόν NPAMZS,   LK 22.02
NPG-YP ἔσομαι VIFD--XS; ἕως CS πότε ABT ἀνέξομαι VIFD--XS ὑμῶν NPG-YP ;   MT 17.17
AP-GM-P , βασιλεύ N-VM-S . 26.8 τί APTAN-S@ ABT ἄπιστον A--NM-S κρίνεται VIPP--ZS   AC 26.08
τὰ DANP τοῦ DGMS κόσμου N-GM-S πῶς ABT ἀρέσῃ VSAA--ZS τῇ DDFS γυναικί   1C 07.33
    •
    •

Part three will be a single-volume Analytical Greek (New Testament) Lexicon. It will represent the information contained in the project central file as well as English glosses and sample references. A preliminary page of samplings is included as figure 2-6.

The printed format described above will please several audiences. The analytical text will appeal to a large number of intermediate Greek students simply for reading the GNT. The analytical concordance will appeal to research-oriented Greek students, for in it there is a great amount of information available on which even the speed and efficiency of a computer cannot improve. For example, the editorial additon of question marks will be included as one of the items concorded in the analytical concordance. Or, the use of regular and emphatic pronouns (for example, *moi* versus *emoi*) can be contrasted by consulting the combined concordance where their common grammatical tag is listed (for the example, NPD-XS). The analytical lexicon has obvious grammatical and lexical uses. It spells out in prose the totality of uses a lexical form has.

We also expect to have the above printed forms as well as some additional material produced in microfiche. The additional material would involve combined concordances of individual New Testament books as well as combined concordances of author or genre sets (for example, writings of John, synoptic gospels). The microfiche set could easily be extended to include concordances based on morphemes (smallest meaningful elements) rather than words. This microfiche format should appeal both to scholars who want to carry on research on subsets of the GNT as well as those in the field (for example, Bible translators) who carry whole libraries on microfiche.

Finally, all the above material will be available on magnetic tapes from the University of Minnesota Computer Center. In addition, both lexical and combined GNT texts will be available, in both accented and unaccented versions. The holdings of UCC will also include the project's central file. Magnetic tapes will have two definite advantages to serious scholars. First, any scholars who wish to do their own computer-assisted research would need access to the data base described here. Second, access to the combined texts would allow printed outputs of them to be generated on demand. Scholars can add their notions freely to such printouts, which can be easily replaced.

Acknowledgments

This project has been crucially forwarded by many helpful hands and clear heads. Without willing and eager help, most of the project would not have reached even the dreaming stage. In the following the senior author wishes

ἐν   dative preposition   in, on, at; near, by, before;
                            (John 3.22)   among, within; by, with;

     •
     •
     •

ἐβουλόμην   verb, passive form, active function;   βούλομαι
                            indicative, imperfect, first person singular (Acts 25.22)

     •
     •
     •

ὁ, ἡ, τό   definite article   the, this, that

ὁ   1. article; nominative, masculine, singular (Hebrews 4.10)
           2. article; vocative, masculine, singular (Mark 15.29)
           3. article; nominative, masculine, singular *used as*
              pronoun; nominative, masculine third singular (Luke 14.16)

ὅς, ἥ, ὅ   relative pronoun,   who, which

ὅ   1. relative; pronoun; nominative, neuter, singular (Luke 12.2)
           2. relative; pronoun; accusative, neuter, singular (Romans 1.2)
           3. relative; pronoun; accusative, neuter, singular *used as*
              indefinite pronoun with τι (John 2.5)
           4. relative; pronoun; nominative, neuter, singular *used as*
              pronoun; nominative, neuter, third singular (1 John 2.8)
           5. relative; pronoun; accusative, neuter, singular *used as*
              pronoun; accusative, neuter, third singular (Acts 9.6)
           6. relative; pronoun, accusative, neuter, singular *used as*
              pronoun; indefinite, accusative, neuter, singular (Mark 7.11)

     •
     •
     •

κἀγώ   1. coordinating conjunction *and* pronoun, nominative first singular
                              (John 17.22)   καί, ἐγώ
             2. adverb *and* pronoun, nominative first singular (Ephesians 1.15)

     •
     •
     •

ταῦτα   1. pronoun; demonstrative; nominative, neuter, plural (Luke 1.20) οὗτος
             2. pronoun; demonstrative; accusative, neuter, plural (Romans 8.31)
             3. adjective; demonstrative; nominative, neuter, plural
                              (1 Corinthians 13.13)
             4. adjective; demonstrative; accusative, neuter, plural (John 8.20)

Figure 2–6. Analytical Lexicon

to make detailed acknowledgment of the contributions of many, moving outward beginning with those most centrally involved.

First I want to thank God. An acknowledgment of Him—much more His work—might seem out of place in a chapter whose end is to provide a scientific analysis of a historical document. However, I acknowledge the Greek text to be His word. God's ways and thoughts are beyond finding out, even after exhaustive computer searches. I further gladly acknowledge the development of this project to be nothing short of a minor miracle. Details are available on request.

I would also like to thank my wife and colleague, Barbara, certainly the central figure in the success of the project. Her contributions are innumerable and invaluable. In this project description, *we* often means *she*. She put 71 percent of the Greek text into the computer without understanding Greek. She has been responsible for all aspects of the project that directly relate to the computer, whether programming, sitting at the terminal, or liaison with UCC offices. Enlarging the text to include the grammatical tags was entirely her accomplishment. In immeasurably many and varied ways, her contributing actions and attitudes are humbly and lovingly acknowledged.

Dr. Peter C. Patton, director of UCC, and his staff have been helpful beyond our best imagination. Dr. Patton has consistently looked beyond my limited sights to encourage and guide. UCC grants have carried the day in the project development stage, providing access to the central processor and supplies. I also gratefully acknowledge the director's secretary, Mary Dickel, for her pleasant helpfulness.

I acknowledge the insight and helpfulness of Dr. John Werner, who has exchanged hundreds of pages of correspondence with me over three years' time as he and I have carefully sought an analytical system of the most powerful sort with a minimum of contradictions. His expertise in Greek (Classical, Koine, Modern) has proved invaluable as he has graciously and carefully checked each resulting combined concordance for errors of various sorts. Indeed, John is the closest thing to a living native speaker of Koine Greek that I know. I would also like to thank Dr. John Beekman, for releasing Dr. Werner for his consultative and checking roles.

I acknowledge with thankfulness the help that I received from a number of Greek scholars in hand-tagging the lexical concordances. This work was foundational. They knew the challenge of grammatical choices and the tedium of detailed analysis. They include Winifred Weter; Clarence Hale; and Peter Davids and his students, Robert R. Richard, Kirk A. Troxler, Frank G. Schmunk, William Hall Hunt, and John F. Brandau.

The work of another group of scholars has enabled us to check the entire GNT for accuracy and internal consistency. I gratefully acknowledge their help. They are Philip Clapp, David Clark, Howard Cleveland,

Richard Gould, Harold Greenlee, Clarence Hale, Verlin Hinshaw, Arthur Killian, David Lewycky, Neva Miller, Edward Peters, and Charles Stephenson. Each one has looked at every occurrence of a given Greek word or grammatical tag as part of the accuracy check.

Steven Sparley made 29 percent of a tape of Souter's text compatible with the UBS3 which we gratefully accepted. Eric Inman has attended to a number of details for us, including some traveling. Thanks are also due to Bruce Downing and Thomas Kraabel for commenting on an earlier draft of this chapter. Various other friends in Minneapolis and scattered elsewhere have given valuable suggestions.

Notes

1. W.C. Wake "Sentence Length Distribution of Greek Authors," *The Journal of the Royal Statistical Society* 120A (1951):331–346, pt. 3.

2. A.Q. Morton and James McLeman, *Paul, the Man and the Myth: A Study in Authorship of Greek Prose* (London: Hodder and Stoughton, 1966).

3. S. Michaelson and A.Q. Morton, "Last Words: A Test of Authorship for Greek Writers," *New Testament Studies,* no. 8 (1971):192–208.

4. John Beekman, and John Callow, "The Semantic Structure of Written Communication (Dallas: Summer Institute of Linguistics). A theory of discourse analysis and a manual of how to do it (based largely on the Greek New Testament) are available in prepublication form.

5. Herbert Weir Smyth, *Greek Grammar* (Cambridge, Mass.: Harvard University Press, 1956).

6. A. Souter, ed. *Novum Testamentum Graece* (Oxford: Clarendon Press, 1947).

7. R.L. Hotchkiss and S.K. Graffunder, "GENCORD: A Concordance Program" (University Computer Center, University of Minnesota, 1977).

8. P. Genes, B. Wells, and D. Meers, "XEDIT Users' Manual" (University Computer Center, University of Minnesota, April 1978).

Bibliography

Beekman, John, and Callow, John. *Translating the Word of God.* Grand Rapids, Mich.: Zondervan, 1974.
This is a standard work on Bible translation problems. It includes a discussion in interclausal relationships.

Friberg, Timothy. "The Discourse Structure of the Greek Text of Gala-
    tians." Master's thesis, University of Minnesota, 1978.
    This is a typical discourse analysis of a Greek text.
————. "A System Overview".
    The system behind the grammatical choices made in the GNT text
    analysis project is discussed.
The Greek New Testament. 3d ed. New York: United Bible Societies, 1975.
    This is the standard school text of GNT; the text by itself is identical to
    Nestle-Aland GNT (26th ed., 1979).
I Timothy: Literary Semantic Analysis n.d. Dallas: Summer Institute of
    Linguistics.
    The discourse structure of Paul's First Letter to Timothy is discussed;
    this is the first in a New Testament series. Others prepared include
    Colossians.
Notes on Translation (*NOT*) (quarterly). Dallas: Summer Institute of
    Linguistics.
    This has articles on all aspects of Bible translation.
Pickering, Wilbur. "A Frame-work for Discourse Analysis." Ph.D. disser-
    tation, University of Toronto, 1977.
    An independent theory of discourse analysis is applied to Paul's Letter
    to the Colossians.
Selected Technical Articles Relating to Translation (*START*). Dallas:
    Summer Institute of Linguistics.
    This journal has articles on translation theory and practice dealing
    directly with Greek and Hebrew texts.

Appendix 2A:
Symbol Listing

The capital letter in each word represents the symbol in the tags.

Noun	Pronoun	Vocative	Masculine	X = first person	Singular
	—	Nominative	Feminine	Y = second person	Plural
		Genitive	Neuter	Z = third person	
		Dative	—		
		Accusative			

Verb	Indicative	Present	Active		Vocative	Masculine	X = first	Singular
	Subjunctive	Aorist	Middle		Nominative	Feminine	Y = second	Plural
	Optative	Future	Passive		Genitive	Neuter	Z = third	
	iMperative	peRfect	Either middle or passive		Dative	—	—	
	iNfinitive	iMperfect	middle Deponent		Accusative			
	Participle	pLuperfect	passive depOnent		—			
			middle or passive depoNent					

Adjective	Pronominal	Cardinal	Vocative	Masculine	X = first person	Singular
	adverB	Ordinal	Nominative	Feminine	Y = second person	Plural
	—	Relative	Genitive	Neuter	—	—
		Indefinite	Dative	—		
		inTerrogative	Accusative			
		Demonstrative	—			
		coMparative				
		Superlative				
		—				

Preposition	Genitive
	Dative
	Accusative

Conjunction	Subordinating
	Coordinating
	H(yper) = superordinating

Determiner	Vocative	Masculine	Singular
	Nominative	Feminine	Plural
	Genitive	Neuter	
	Dative		
	Accusative		

Q = particle	Verbal
	Sentential
	inTerrogative

+ periphrastic (VIMA--ZS+) . . . (+VPPPNM-S)
[external brackets in text
/ internal brackets in text
* bold face (Old Testament quotes)
& crasis, and: KAGW (CC)&(NPN-XS)
@ function, 'used as': NUN (AB)@(A--NM-S)
# or: LEGETE (VIPA--YP)#(VMPA--YP)
= dash, -
< left parenthesis, (
> right parenthesis,)

Appendix 2B:
Greek-English
Character Equivalences

1	2	3		1	2	3
α	A	A		ν	N	N
β	B	B		ξ	X	C
γ	G	G		ο	O	O
δ	D	D		π	P	P
ε	E	E		ρ	R	R
ζ	Z	Z		σ, ς	S	S, J
η	J	H		τ	T	T
θ	TH	Q		υ	U	U
ι	I	I		φ	PH	F
κ	K	K		χ	CH	X
λ	L	L		ψ	PS	Y
μ	M	M		ω	W	W
iota	Y	I		.	.	.
subscript				.	:	:
rough	H	(		;	$	;
breathing				'	'	'
smooth		)				
breathing						

Column 1 is Greek characters. Column 2 is the intermediate working English transcription, equivalent to traditional, standard transliteration with the exception of J (= ē), W (= ō), Y (usually ignored). Column 3 is the final, completed project, English transcription to be identical with the standardized American Philological Association system widely used in computer studies.

3 Computer Aids to Sumerian Lexicography

John F. Mulhern,
Steven R. Sparley, and
Peter C. Patton

One area in the humanities in which computers may be of considerable use is the study of ancient languages. The computer can be used, for example, to aid a researcher in gaining a fundamental understanding of an undeciphered ancient language, perhaps by assisting in a statistical analysis of the relative frequency of the symbols used to write it. But even after the writing system of a particular language has been deciphered, additional scholarly work must be done to reveal the finer structure of the language. Investigations concerning the possible meanings of any word or particle of speech must be pursued in order to establish a basis of understanding on which a dictionary of that language can eventually be written. More commonly, however, instead of making a dictionary, scholars of ancient languages undertake the writing of what is called a lexicon.

A lexicon differs from a dictionary in that, in addition to defining the words in a language, it also gives examples of their use by citing instances where they occur in the literature of the language. The more elaborate lexicons are arranged with long entries for each word which give examples of the word's use in different historical periods, in various geopolitical settings, and in several genres of literature. From such a lexicon, a scholar may glean an accurate sense of the range of meanings and probable contextual environments for any word. This is of particular importance to scholars of ancient languages who cannot, of course, gain any firsthand knowledge of the language they are studying from living native speakers. The writing of a lexicon for any language, ancient or modern, is an enormous undertaking which may require that millions of citations from passages of literature be collected, sorted, and compared in order to create the individual entries for all the words in the language. These citations are typically prepared by both those scholars working directly on the lexicon of a language and numerous other scholars working in the field. The scholars must read through many of the available works of literature in the language and collect citations of the use of both common and uncommon words, noting for each word the context in which that word occurs and the literary source of the citation. The labor of collecting the citations can be measurably reduced if the major literary works in a language have already been indexed in a reasonably complete fashion. Such indexes would provide an immediate source of citations for the words occurring within an indexed work, thereby obviating the need to collect and sort citations for that work. This chapter specifically discusses the use of computers in making indexes of Sumerian literature. The Sumerian language, because of its structure and rather complicated writing system, presents several special problems in indexing. Before we discuss these problems, their solution, and the methodology of computer-assisted index production, a brief background on the Sumerian language is in order.

Background

Sumerian was the dominant spoken language of southern Mesopotamia from at least the late fourth millenium until sometime around the end of the third millenium B.C.[1] The extant cuneiform tablets dating from this period establish Sumerian as the world's oldest known written language.[2] The majority of the early tablets are administrative in nature and contain valuable economic and demographic information concerning ancient Sumerian society. By about 2600 B.C., Sumerian literature had become considerably more diverse in its content and had grown to include such literary forms as myth and epic in addition to the more mundane administrative and economic documents. These later written records contain extensive and varied information on numerous facets of the Sumerian culture and the cultures on its periphery. The Sumerian written legacy taken as a whole constitutes the single richest source of information on the earlier history of the ancient Near East. Thousands of cuneiform tablets attest not only to a richly developed religious and literary heritage, but also to an inventive society engaged in architecture, ceramics, metallurgy, agriculture, mathematics, and medicine.

The field of Sumerology (the study of the Sumerian culture and language) had its inception in the last century only after it was realized that the cuneiform tablets discovered by archeological expeditions in Mesopotamia were written in not one, but two languages. One of the languages, Akkadian, was rather quickly recognized as a member of the Semitic language family and, as such, soon was well understood. By analogy with the then known Semitic languages of Hebrew and Arabic, scholars were able to posit a workable grammar of Akkadian and were further able to derive the meanings of a great number of Akkadian words from known Semitic roots. The other language found on the tablets was Sumerian. Although Sumerian was also written in cuneiform script, it lacked the linguistic affinities of Akkadian and hence was not as quickly deciphered. Only toward the end of the nineteenth century had a fairly accurate picture of the linguistic structure of Sumerian been drawn, based on the collective work of many scholars. In the first quarter of this century, attempts were made to write both a grammar[3] of Sumerian and a lexicon.[4] While both these works were monuments of scholarship and remain useful to this day, they were hampered by what was then the paucity of the Sumerian textual corpus, as well as by an incomplete understanding of the nature of the Sumerian language and writing system. To date, there is neither a definitive lexicon of Sumerian nor a generally accepted grammar.

Although both Akkadian and Sumerian are written with the same cuneiform characters, they nevertheless belong to very distinct linguistic groups. Sumerian is agglutinative[5] in grammatical structure whereas Akkadian is an inflected language.[6] And while Akkadian is Semitic and closely related to the other members of that linguistic family, Sumerian has no known cognates.[7] Both languages are commonly said to be syllabically written, that is, written with each cuneiform sign representing an individual syllable and collections of signs in turn constituting words. This description, however, is only partially accurate with regard to Sumerian. Sumerian writing, in fact, is fundamentally logographic in nature; that is, each cuneiform sign has a root conceptual meaning associated with it. For example, the cuneiform sign which is transliterated **ka** has the basic meaning of "mouth" or "forepart of the face."[8] However, this same sign can also have several other phonetic values, each with a meaning that is in some way connected to the original root concept. Thus, the cuneiform character **ka** can also be transliterated as **zu, kir, gu, enim,** or **dug,** meaning, respectively, "tooth," "nose" or "forehead," "voice," "word," and "to say." In addition, if this same sign, **ka,** is combined with the sign **a,** meaning "water" or "drink," it can be transliterated as **nag,** meaning "to drink." Again, if **ka** is combined with the sign **ninda,** meaning "bread" or "food," the composite sign is transliterated as **ku,** meaning "to eat." The specific meaning of a sign is ultimately determined from the context in which it occurs.

A further complication in the Sumerian writing system stems from the fact that, in addition to a cuneiform sign having more than one possible phonetic rendering, as in the case of **ka** above, a single phonetic value can also frequently be represented by more than one sign. Thus, in addition to the **ka** sign with the meaning of "mouth," there is another sign, also transliterated as **ka,** which means "gate" or "city gate." Other cuneiform signs may have as many as a half a dozen such homophones or more. Whether Sumerian simply has a large number of homophones or whether some vocal quality helped to distinguish between the apparent homophones is a question that may never fully be answered. The scholarly convention has been merely to distinguish the various homophones with identifying subscripted numbers. Hence, the cuneiform sign with the meaning "gate" is ka_2, and the sign for "mouth" is **ka**, that is ka_1, but conventionally the subscripted 1 is dropped.[9]

Sumerian writing, however, is not entirely logographic in nature. Some cuneiform signs apparently have more than one root concept associated with them. It has been proposed that these signs assumed other meanings simply because their phonetic values corresponded to the sounds of other Sumerian words for which there were no signs. For example, the cuneiform sign til₃ can mean either "arrow," which is its original meaning, or "life," an abstract concept which lacked a sign of its own. In this instance it could be said that Sumerian is being spelled syllabically, since the word meaning "life" is being spelled with the sound of the til₃ sign. Furthermore, some morphological elements, such as verb tense or mood, are indicated in written Sumerian, and again this could be construed as syllabic writing. This practice was very rare in early tablets, but became increasingly more common until, with the advent of the early Old Babylonian period (c. 1950 B.C.), nearly all morphological elements were being spelled out in the text.

While Sumerian primarily uses cuneiform signs in a logographic manner, the Akkadian language generally uses the signs to spell out words syllabically. The cuneiform signs in the Akkadian syllabary,[10] like the signs used in writing Sumerian, also possessed a wide range of phonetic values, and any given phonetic value could be represented by a number of distinct cuneiform signs. The syllabic values employed in writing Akkadian were usually of the form vowel, vowel-consonant, consonant-vowel, or consonant-vowel-consonant, although a few more complex configurations were also used. Thus, for instance, the Akkadian word *kakkabu* could be written *ka-ak-ka-bu, kak-ka-bu,* or even *ka-ka-bu,* not indicating a double k in the word.[11]

Despite their noted linguistic differences, the Sumerian and Akkadian languages were inextricably linked culturally. Written evidence, even from very early documents, seems to indicate that the two languages coexisted, at least in their spoken forms. The Akkadian tongue is known to have replaced Sumerian as the dominant spoken language of southern Mesopotamia sometime between 2300 and 1900 B.C. Even though spoken Sumerian eventually died out entirely (certainly by c. 1750 B.C.), in its written form Sumerian was used as late as the first century B.C. by Akkadian scribes. These scribes, the literate persons whose task it was to read and write cuneiform script, had a demanding profession which required that they memorize as many as 600 individual cuneiform signs and the several variant phonetic values associated with each sign. Frequently, instead of laboriously spelling out each Akkadian word syllabically, the scribes simply wrote the Sumerian logographic equivalent instead. As an example, the Akkadian word for "star," *kakkabu,* could be represented by the single Sumerian sign **mul**, instead of using the three or four signs necessary to spell it syllabically. This was a common practice in all Akkadian literature. In certain types of literature there were often more Sumerian words used in this fashion than there were Akkadian words spelled out syllabically.

The Akkadian scribal schools taught Sumerian logographic signs as a form of shorthand. The scribes learned the Sumerian logograms from special lexical tablets kept in the schools. Lexical tablets are simply vocabulary lists of Sumerian words and phrases which were in common use in scribal practice.[12] These tablets are organized only in what appears to be a loosely thematic or associative fashion. They have been found in large numbers throughout the entire Near East and date from the Early Dynastic Period (c. 2700 to 2300 B.C.) to the Seleucid era (c. 300 to 70 B.C.). There are several different types of lexical tablets, the earliest of which are unilingual lists of Sumerian words. In the early Old Babylonian period (beginning about 1950 B.C.), bilingual lexical tablets also began to appear. A bilingual lexical tablet is classified either as Sumero-Akkadian or Akkado-Sumerian, depending on the language on which the ordering of the vocabulary list is based. Many bilingual tablets, in addition to giving the Akkadian equivalent of a Sumerian word, also provide a guide to pronunciation of the word by spelling it syllabically. Although the Akkadian perception of the pronunciation of Sumerian words may be questionable, there is growing evidence that this perception may have somewhat more validity, at least in certain instances, than was previously believed.[13] Hence, these lexical tablets may eventually provide further valuable insight into the phonological nature of the Sumerian language.

Ancient lexical tablets may be viewed as precursors to the modern idea of a dictionary, and their value as source material for a comprehensive lexicon of Sumerian is inestimable. They represent a rich native lexical tradition containing valuable information on items of vocabulary; and as has been seen, they may provide some phonological insight as well. The publication in 1937 of the first in a series of volumes entitled *Materialien zum Sumerischen Lexikon* (*MSL*) recognized the potential wealth of information contained in the lexical tablets.[14] The purpose of *MSL* is to provide complete, critical editions of all the Sumerian lexical tablets. In particular, the volumes of *MSL* contain recensions of a number of ancient canonical collections of lexical tablets which are referred to in modern scholarship as lexical series. Two of these lexical series are of particular interest to Sumerologists in general and specifically to the present research project employing *MSL* at the University of Minnesota. The series **ḪAR-ra** = *ḫubullu,* published in volumes 5 through 11 of *MSL*, consists of nearly 10,000 entries listing mostly material objects including woods and wooden articles, reeds and reed articles, pottery, hides and leathers, metals, stones, and textiles, but also including other items such as animals, body parts, plants, birds, fish, geographic terms, and items of food and drink.[15] The other lexical series of particular interest is *ana ittisu*, which was published in volume 1 of *MSL*.[16] *ana ittišu* contains a list of some 1,700 items of legal and economic terminology.

The textual materials contained in these two lexical series alone are of substantial importance both from the linguistic point of view and from the points of view of the archaeologist and anthropologist to whom, for instance, the contents of the lexical series **HAR-ra** = *ḫubullu* are a virtual catalog of the material culture of ancient Sumer. Publication of these lexical series in *MSL,* however, did not include indexes to their contents, for an index to such a large amount of text, spanning eight volumes of *MSL,* is a substantial undertaking in and of itself. The ancient ordering of entries in a lexical series does not provide easy access to its contents, at least not from the viewpoint of a modern scholar accustomed to alphabetical ordering. Thus, effective use of *MSL* in scholarly work has been essentially limited to those with an intimate knowledge of the native ordering of lexical series.

Goals

The *MSL* research project at the University of Minnesota has directed its efforts toward creating indexes for **HAR-ra** = *ḫubullu* and *ana ittišu.* The most distinguishing feature of the work of the *MSL* project is its use of the computer as a central element in its methodology for producing indexes to these two lexical series. In designing a computer-assisted methodology for the indexing of the Sumerian contents of **HAR-ra** = *ḫubullu* and *ana ittišu,* every effort has been made to make the methodology general enough to be useful for the indexing of not only other lexical series in *MSL*, but also any genre of Sumerian literature. In particular, work is currently underway to also produce an index to the literary account of the rebuilding of the temple of the god Ningirsu by Gudea, the prince of the city of Lagash.[17] The principal elements of the computer-assisted methodology designed for producing indexes to lexical series are essentially unchanged in indexing the more varied literary material represented in the story of Gudea. Plans are also being made to apply the same methodology to a somewhat more restricted indexing of the contents of some economic documents from the Ur III period (c. 2000 B.C.).[18]

As will be seen subsequently when the application of the methodology is discussed, the use of the computer can markedly speed the process of index production. The final indexes which the *MSL* project will produce for the two lexical series will be quite elaborate. They will contain extensive cross-reference information and will quote for each indexed word all the lines in the lexical series where that word occurs. Hence, the indexes will facilitate immediate access to the two lexical series by alphabetizing their contents and, in addition, will allow scholars to compare the various contexts in which any word occurs within the series. Extending this computer-assisted methodology to other types of Sumerian literature, and providing similar indexes, will eventually allow for thorough, comparative studies of the phonological, morphological, syntactic, and stylistic features of the Sumerian language. The underlying motive of the *MSL* project, beyond the production of indexes, is to begin to develop computer-assisted methodological tools that will be of use in an eventual attempt to produce a comprehensive lexicon of Sumerian. The making of other lexicons has consistently been hampered by the sheer magnitude of the task of maintaining enormous amount of lexical material in an orderly, easily accessible fashion. The computer is eminently suited to this task. While the computer-assisted methods used in index production may not be immediately applicable to lexicographic work, it is hoped that the indexes produced by the *MSL* project will at least provide useful additional material for a Sumerian lexicon.

General Methodology

Although ultimately it is intended that the computer-assisted methodology of the *MSL* project extend to broader application in the field of Sumerian lexicography, the immediate task of the project is the production of Sumerian indexes to the lexical series **HAR-ra**= *ḫubullu* and *ana ittišu*. Much of the work toward this goal must be performed by trained Sumerian scholars, as a result of the complex nature of the Sumerian language. Primarily, the computer can provide only a rapid, sophisticated sorting capability. But it is precisely the sorting process which consumes such a great deal of time and human effort in the course of any indexing work. While the use of the computer essentially eliminates the hand-sorting of many thousands of index cards, it also introduces several substantial changes in the methodology of creating an index.

Traditionally, indexes on a scale similar to those that will be produced by this project have been generated for a given text by entering each lexically significant item in the text on an index card together with a citation of its source, and possibly of its context as well.[19] These index cards are then manually sorted in a card file, cross-referenced where appropriate, typeset in galley proofs, corrected, and ultimately published. This process in the Sumerological field has been sufficiently Herculean so as to discourage complete indexes of many of the larger works in the language, including the lexical series.[20] The strategy designed by the *MSL* project to provide indexes for the two lexical series, although not entirely archetypal, will nevertheless reveal the principal differences between the computer-assisted and manual approaches to index production. The most obvious and fundamental difference is the absence of index cards and the card file. The initial step in the computer-assisted approach consists of entering the entire text of the work that is to be indexed into a computer text file. This text file subsequently serves as the basis from which the index is constructed.

The process of creating an index from the text file begins with several stages of editing, the exact nature of which will depend on the work being indexed. Once the text is thoroughly edited, tags are added to the text in the computer to mark the lexically significant items. These tags consist simply of special characters by means of which the computer programs are able to locate lexical items. Cross-reference information may also be inserted into the text file at this point. The resulting text file in the computer may be thought of as an electronic card file which has yet to be sorted. In contrast to the manual methodology, however, the computerized card file may be sorted in literally a matter of seconds. The computer locates and sorts the tagged words in the text and formats the sorted results in an index fashion, complete with cross references. The resulting index may be checked for omissions of errors, and the appropriate corrections of text, tags, and cross-reference information can then be made in the source text file. The file will then be reindexed, and the results will reflect the corrections that have been made.

Before we go into the specific application of this methodology as employed by the *MSL* project, some of its underlying constituents are discussed. An attempt has been made at every step in the process of creating the indexes to tailor the methodology to the needs of the scholar and to avoid forcing the scholar to learn a vast panoply of computer techniques and terminology. Particular attention was given to providing an environment in which text entry and editing could occur with the greatest ease. The manner in which this was accomplished is discussed in considerable detail. The computer programs which sort the text and format the results in index fashion have been designed to accept as input a text file whose format is as unrestricted as possible. This design requirement allows for the indexing of several different kinds of texts by using essentially the same techniques. Finally, the format of the results produced by the computer programs has received special care, with provisions made to generate camera-ready, publication-quality results directly from the computer in addition to the more common line-printer results.

The usual method of entering and editing a text file on a computer is to make use of a line-oriented editing program. While this method is a distinct improvement over former punched-paper-card methods, the experiences of the *MSL* project in this area indicate several drawbacks. Briefly, a line-oriented editor is a large computer program which allows the user to enter and edit a text file, using the computer on an interactive basis. Instructions are typed on the computer terminal keyboard which direct the program to move from line to line in the text file. At each line, the user may issue specific instructions to alter the contents of that line in a particular fashion. For example, the user may wish to change the spelling of a word or to insert an additional line or delete part of a line. All these tasks are accomplished by typing instructions into the terminal and waiting for the editor to respond. The editor responds by redisplaying the current line with the appropriate modifications. In order to edit the entire text file, this process must be repeated over and over on every line requiring modifications.

The first drawback to this process is that it is rather slow, primarily as a result of two factors. First, the editing is being done on a large time-sharing computer, and the time required for the editor to respond to an editing instruction is determined in part by the number of other people using the computer at any given time. As more people use the computer, the time interval between responses lengthens. When the computer is in heavy use, this time lag may amount to several seconds. Also, because of the speed at which the typical computer terminal will operate, it takes an additional couple of seconds for each line to print out. Since most operations of a line-oriented editor require that the current line be redisplayed after each instruction in order to verify modifications to that line or to indicate the present position in the file, this second factor leads to additional substantial delay in editing. The next drawback, and in some ways the most important one, is the notion of line-by-line editing itself for persons not used to the computer. For a scholar accustomed to correcting manuscript proofs in a page-by-page manner, the line-oriented editor may well seem to be awkward and contrived and eventually may serve as a disincentive to using the computer at all.

A final drawback in using the line editor is not really a fault of the editor itself, but rather is due to the nature of the standard computer terminal. The characters which are used to transliterate Sumerian cuneiform signs are not exactly identical to the usual Latin characters displayed on computer terminals. In order to represent all the characters in the transliteration alphabet, certain Latin characters not already used in the transliteration alphabet must be employed. This circumstance forces the scholar to learn, for example, that *fu* is really *šu* (=*shu*), where the character *f*, which does not occur in the transliteration alphabet, is used to represent the transliteration character *š* (=*sh*), which is not available on a computer terminal keyboard. Thus, for the purpose of editing a text on the computer, the scholar would need to become acclimated to both a line-oriented editor and a somewhat peculiar character set.

In order to overcome these impediments, the *MSL* project has adopted the use of a microcomputer for all its text entry and editing purposes. A microcomputer, as the name implies, is simply a very small, single-user computer. Despite its size, however, the microcomputer has several distinct advantages for text editing purposes over the terminal connected to the large time-sharing computer. The microcomputer used by the *MSL* project consists physically of four pieces, as shown in figure 3–1.[21] As can be seen, the entire microcomputer fits on a table within a relatively small space and is comprised of a keyboard (nearly identical to a standard typewriter keyboard), a display screen, and two disk drives. A disk drive is a magnetic

Figure 3–1. Terak Microcomputer

recording device which is similar in some ways to a tape recorder and is used to store the large text files that will be edited on the microcomputer, as well as the necessary computer programs. Instead of storing these text files on magnetic tape, the microcomputer uses what are called "floppy disks." One such floppy disk is shown on the table beside the disk drives in figure 3-1. The floppy disk itself is circular, about the size of a 45-rpm phonograph record, and is encased in a square protective cover. The disk is inserted into the slot in the middle of the disk drive, and when the microcomputer is in operation, information stored anywhere on the disk can be accessed within a fraction of a second. The actual central processor and memory of the microcomputer are contained quite compactly in the top portion of the lower disk drive.

The microcomputer, like the large time-sharing computer, also uses a program called an editor to enter and edit text files. The editor on a microcomputer, however, differs fundamentally from those editors usually found on large computers. Unlike the line-oriented editor, the editor on the microcomputer is page- or screen-oriented in nature. A screen-oriented editor allows the user to continuously view an entire page of text at a time and to move about on a given page by manipulating a cursor. The concept of a cursor is crucial to an understanding of the manner in which a screen editor functions. Figure 3-2 is a photograph of the microcomputer display screen when a text file is being edited. The cursor is seen in the middle of the picture as a reverse-contrast rectangle with an "1" in its middle. This indicates that the cursor is currently positioned on the page over that "1." It may be thought of as a pencil point (or eraser) of the editor. The cursor can be repositioned anywhere on the screen by using special arrow keys provided on the keyboard. Some examples would perhaps best illustrate the manner in which a screen-oriented editor operates using this cursor. In order, for example, to insert characters in front of the "1" over which the cursor is positioned, the user of the screen editor simply types "I" on the keyboard (to enter the insert mode of the editor) and then types the characters to be entered, which are displayed on the screen as typed. A final special key is typed in order to end the insertion. Similarly, in order to delete one or more characters from the text beginning at the current position of the cursor, the user types "D" on the keyboard (to enter delete mode) and then moves the cursor with the arrow keys. As the cursor passes over a character, the character disappears from the screen. When all desired characters have been deleted, a special key is typed to instruct the editor to exit the delete mode.

While these are only two short examples from among the many available editing functions, they demonstrate the advantages which a screen-oriented editor has over a line-oriented one. The screen editor is fast; most operations occur before the user's eyes as the operations are being per-

01·05·009·001	ur₅(=ḪAR)-ra ḫubullu
01·05·009·002	eš-še-de₂-a ḫubuttaatum
01·05·009·003	šu-lal qiiptum
01·05·009·004	še-bal šupiii█tum
01·05·009·005	nig₂-ba qiištum
01·05·009·006	in-na-an-ba iqiiš
01·05·009·007	a-мu-un-na-ru išruk
01·05·009·008	ba-du₃ iipuš
01·05·009·009	ba-an-bal iḫri
01·05·009·010	ba-an-zal issuḫ
01·05·009·011	a-мu-un-na-diм₂ ušeepiš
01·05·010·012	šu giмillu

Figure 3–2. Microcomputer Screen with Cursor

formed. Because the microcomputer is a single-user computer, there is not the delay often found on large time-sharing computers which must respond to the requests of many users. Additionally, since the microcomputer terminal is connected directly with its central processor, its user does not experience the delay due to communication speed that the user of a time-sharing computer must learn to accept. An entire page text can be displayed on the microcomputer terminal screen in about a second. Most important, however, the screen-oriented editor is far more appealing than the line-oriented editor to the novice computer user. An entire page of text is displayed at any given time, allowing contextual decisions in editing to be made easily. The simple editing instructions, consisting usually of a single keystroke, and the essentially intuitive concept of a cursor are both quickly grasped with a minimum of instruction. Finally, again as seen in figure 3–2, the microcomputer permits the editing to be accomplished while displaying the text in the transliteration alphabet familiar to the Sumerian scholar.[22]

It should be noted in concluding this short description of the micro-computer and editor used by the *MSL* project that the actual processing of the texts is accomplished on a large computer.[23] Although the microcomputer possesses the noted advantages for text-editing purposes, its ability to rapidly sort and index a large text file is much inferior to that of a large computer. For this reason, once the text files have been edited, tagged, and marked for cross-referencing, they are transferred to the large computer for processing.[24]

The results of computer processing are usually printed on a line printer which produces typed copy similar, but inferior in quality, to that produced by a typewriter. The correct printing of Sumerian requires, in addition to the transliteration character set previously mentioned, both subscript and superscript characters. No line printers, or for that matter typewriters, possess these capabilities. While the computer programs of the *MSL* project do generate line-printer listings, extensive efforts have been made to provide a more suitable medium for the printing of results. One of the peripheral devices connected to the UCC computer is a high-speed plotter.[25] Although plotters usually evoke an image of graphs of experimental data, they can be used to plot alphabetic characters as well. A computer program was written to allow a specially designed transliteration character set to be created for use on the plotter. This character set is used in conjunction with other computer programs written for the *MSL* project to provide a suitable form for the publication of the indexes produced by the project. The results of the plotting may be seen in several of the figures which accompany the following discussion of the specific methodology of the *MSL* project.

Application of Methodology

The first step in creating Sumerian indexes for the two lexical series was the entry of the material from the published sources. The text was entered by typists having no special knowledge of Sumerian. Only minimal instruction was required to teach the typists to transcribe from the text of *MSL*, as published (figure 3–3), to the computer representation, as seen in the screen editor (figure 3–4). As may be seen by comparing figures 3–3 and 3–4, the correspondence between the text file on the computer and the text of the *MSL* source is quite close. Each entry in figure 3–4 consists of a citation of the location (comprised of tablet number, *MSL* volume number, page number, and line number) followed by the text of the Sumerian column, and (after three intervening periods) the given Akkadian equivalent to the Sumerian. One of the secondary tasks of the *MSL* project is to index the Akkadian words in the lexical series as well as the Sumerian. Hence in this example (figure 3–4) the Akkadian has been normalized in its spelling from the syllabic spelling found in the *MSL* source.[26] Once a text has been entered into the computer, it is first checked for any typographical errors which may have occurred in entry and is then processed by using an Akkadian sorting program. This program isolates and alphabetizes all the individual

ḪAR-ra -*ḫubullu* Tablet I

ḪAR-ra	*ḫu-bul-lu*	*loan with fixed interest*
eš-še-dé-a	*ḫu-bu-ut-ta-tum*	*loan without fixed interest*
šu-lal	*qí-ip-tum*	" " " "
še-bal	*šu-pil-tum*	*exchange rate in barley*
		(used in accounts)
5 níg-ba	*qí-iš-tum*	*compensation (e.g. of a craftsman)*
in-na-an-ba	*i-qí-iš*	*he has granted (e. g. a*
		king to a subject)
a-mu-un-na-ru	*iš-ru-uk*	*he has donated (e.g. to a*
		god or to a daughter
ba-dù	*i-pu-uš*	*he has made, built*
ba-an-bal	*iḫ-ri*	*he has dug*
10 ba-an-zal	*is-suḫ*	*(time) has passed*
a-mu-un-na-dím	*ú-še-piš*	*he has had made*

1 (1) *To be read* ur₅.ra : *cf.* [ú-ur] ur₅ -*ḫu-buk-lum*] Izi H 187 *and* Ea V 119,
     A V/2 : 166 ; ur ur₅ - *ḫu-bu-ul-lu* Sᵃ *Voc.* A 6' (= MSL III 51) ; ur₅ ᵘʳ⁻ᵈⁱ⁻ⁱᵐ
     dí[m]. [ḪA]R.[ẋ] = [ḫ]u-*bul-lum* Nabnītu XXIII 29 f.

2 (1) *?* [eš]-dé-a : F [eš-dé]-a : V₄ [ẋ ẋ]-a : Kish 1 eš-dé-àm : S₁ , S₁₇ eš-še-dé-
     àm (S₂ še-eš-dé-a) : V₁ eš-dé-a-*še* (*collated*). *The form* eš-še-dé-
     a, *which is found neither in Old Babylonian nor in Ḫi., is attest-*
     ed also in Antagal A 116.

5 (2) S₂ *qí-il-tum.*

8 (1) *?*, S₂, Kish 1 ba-dù : ζ [ba]-dù : C ba-an-dù.

    (2) *?*, ζ, Kish 1, S₁ *i-pu-uš* : A, B, C *e-pu-uš.*

11 (1) *Text follows* A, C, *?*, F, S₁ *and* S₂ : Kish 1 *and* 2 mu-un-na-dím.

Figure 3–3. *MSL* Source Text

Akkadian words in the text file. Figure 3–5 shows the results of this initial
sorting as seen on the microcomputer terminal. In the left column of the
figure are the Akkadian words which the program located in the source text
file. These are the so-called target or key words. The item to the right of
each key word is the location of the *MSL* line from which the word was

```
04·05·009·001    HAR-ra...hubullu
04·05·009·002    eš-še-de2-a...hubuuttatum
04·05·009·003    šu-lal...qiiptum
04·05·009·004    še-bal...šupiltum
04·05·009·005    nig2-ba...qiištum
04·05·009·006    in-na-an-ba...iqiiš
04·05·009·007    a-mu-un-na-ru...išruuk
04·05·009·008    ba-du3...ipuuš
04·05·009·009    ba-an-bal...ihri
04·05·009·010    ba-an-zal...issuh
04·05·009·011    a-mu-un-na-dim2...ušepiš
04·05·010·012    šu...gimillu
04·05·010·013    šu-gar...gamalu
04·05·010·014    šu-gar gi...gimillu turru
04·05·010·015    šu-gar-ra ga2...gimillu šakanu
04·05·010·016    šu-dir-ra...usaatum
04·05·010·017    šu-u4-sud-da...usaatum
04·05·010·018    šu-nig2-gal2-la...mešruu
04·05·010·019    šu-nam-ti-la...gimil balati
04·05·010·020    ha-la...ziittum
04·05·010·021    giš-šub-ba...isqu
04·05·010·022    še-ba...epru
04·05·010·023    i3-ba...piššatum
04·05·010·024    sig2-ba...lubuuštum
```

Figure 3-4. Initial Computer Representation of the *MSL* Source Text ▶

aa   04·05·038·357
        he2-diri-ga nam-ba-la2
        litirma aa imti

abu   04·05·025·225
        itu NE-NE-gar
        abu

abušu   04·05·047·113
        ad-a-ni
        abušu

addaru   04·05·026·232
        itu še-kin-kud
        addaru

addaru   04·05·026·233
        itu dirig še-kin-kud
        arhu atru ša addaru

ahatsu   04·017·05·112
        nin-a-ni
        [a]hatsu

ahaatum   04·05·046·096
        nin
        ahaatum

ahi   04·05·035·335
        šeš-šeš-gin5
        ahu kiima ahi

◀ **Figure 3-5.** Text File Sorted by Akkadian Words

extracted. The following two lines contain complete citations of the Sumerian and Akkadian entries for that location.

Since the *MSL* project will, in addition to its primary task of indexing the Sumerian words, also produce indexes to the Akkadian words in the two lexical series, each Akkadian key word must be put into lexical form in order to allow the key words to be subsequently resorted into exact lexical order. This process is roughly equivalent to the manner in which lexicographers would order the various forms of the verb *to be* in an index, dictionary, or lexicon of English words. The word *be* is said to be the lexical form of the words *is, are, was,* and *were.* The Akkadian language is much more highly inflected than English, and nearly all verbs and nouns change form depending on grammatical circumstances. In order to properly index these inflected words, they must be changed into their correct lexical forms. The initial sorting puts the key words into alphabetical order, which is only roughly lexical order. This ordering, nevertheless, greatly facilitates the first editing phase,[27] which consists of determining the lexical forms of all the key words and checking each line of the text in the available lexicons of Akkadian.[28] The Akkadian lexicons cite nearly every line of the lexical texts and provide a valuable reference for verifying the correct form of the key words and for double-checking the normalization of the Akkadian entries as well. Although publication errors are also taken into account in this editing, no attempt thas been made to produce new editions of **HAR-ra** = *ḫubullu* or *ana ittišu.*[29] This is not the task of the *MSL* project. All the work of the project is based on the secondary source materials found in *MSL* volumes 1 and 5 to 11. The *MSL* project will index these publications in their present form with few exceptions.[30]

There are many reasons for this initial editing. In addition to those mentioned above, which primarily concern the editing of the Akkadian words in a lexical text, the Sumerian words may also be edited at this stage. In fact, a chief motivating factor behind sorting the Akkadian into alphabetical order was to facilitate the editing of the Sumerian entries as well as the Akkadian. The modern lexicons of Akkadian cite not only the Akkadian entries of lexical tablets, but also their Sumerian equivalents. Thus, the alphabetical sort of the Akkadian serves a dual purpose in allowing the simultaneous editing of both the Akkadian and Sumerian entries of a lexical series. This is especially important in view of the lack of adequate lexical aids in Sumerian. The initial editing of the Sumerian words involves supplying accepted transliterations for those cuneiform signs about which the original editor was uncertain (represented by capital letters in the text) and correcting both errors arising from the text-entry process and publication errors found in the *MSL* source.

The end result of this editing, which actually involves several additional, more refined stages of resorting and cross-checking, is a carefully edited computerized source file of the lexical series. From this text file, an index to the Akkadian words in the two lexical series can easily be generated although this has not yet been done by the *MSL* project. The edited text file also serves as the source from which the Sumerian index will be produced. The process of making the Sumerian index, which is the primary task of the *MSL* project, begins by resorting the edited text file back into numerical order, that is, back into the order in which it appears in the *MSL* source. The Akkadian key words are then deleted from the text file, and the file is reformatted slightly. The text at this stage, shown in figure 3-2, consists of the *MSL* text location, the Sumerian entry, and, on the following line, the Akkadian entry, all in edited form. The Akkadian entry is retained in the text file to provide a bilingual context for the subsequent tagging and sorting of the Sumerian words.

The sorting of the Sumerian words in the two lexical series has been treated by the *MSL* project in a substantially different fashion from the sorting of the Akkadian words as described above. Because of the agglutinative nature of the language, Sumerian words are, at least to a certain extent, already in lexical form. The hyphenation seen within the text reflects the modern scholarly convention of connecting the transliterations of lexically significant Sumerian logograms with the transliterations of the cuneiform signs which directly modify them. For example, on line 6 of figure 3-2, the Sumerian logogram represented by the transliteration **ba** is connected by hyphens to the three preceding Sumerian signs which express a specification of the verbal meaning of **ba**. In this instance, the item of lexical interest for creating an index is the syllable **ba** alone. On other lines of the text, lexical items might consist of several syllables taken together, which also may not necessarily come at the end of a hyphenated complex. One difficulty in sorting Sumerian arises in that the computer cannot be instructed in a unique and unambiguous manner to extract the lexically important syllables, while ignoring those syllables which provide only morphological information. This difficulty can be resolved by explicitly tagging all those syllables which constitute lexically significant Sumerian words.

There are actually two reasons for tagging the Sumerian text. First, lexically significant syllables, or groups of syllables, must be tagged in order to indicate to the computer program the words which are to be sorted and formatted into index fashion. This tagging might have been accomplished simply by prefixing lexically significant syllables with, say, a "%" character followed by a number to indicate to the program how many syllables following the percent sign are to be taken together as a single lexical unit. The *MSL* project, however, is interested in further differentiating various classes of lexical items within a Sumerian text. This gives rise to the second purpose served by tagging. Currently, the program written to sort Sumerian recognizes some seventeen different tag marks which it uses to distinguish between verbal and nonverbal lexical items. These two main classes of tag marks are further subdivided so as to allow for the discrimination of several

01·05·009·001	ᴸ₁ur₅(=HAR)-ra
	ḫubullu
01·05·009·002	ᴸ₁eš-še-ᴸ₁de₂-a
	ḫubuttaatum
01·05·009·003	ᴸ₂šu-ᴸ₁lal
	qiiptum
01·05·009·004	ᴸ₂še-ᴸ₁bal
	šupiiiltum
01·05·009·005	ᴸ₂nig₂-ᴸ₁ba
	qiištum
01·05·009·006	ᵡin-na-an-ᵥ₁ba
	iqiiš
01·05·009·007	ˣa-ᵡmu-un-na-ᵥ₁ru
	išruk
01·05·009·008	ᵡba-ᵥ₁du₃
	iipuš
01·05·009·009	ᵡba-an-ᵥ₁bal
	iḫri
01·05·009·010	ᵡba-an-ᵥ₁zal
	issuḫ
01·05·009·011	ˣa-ᵡmu-un-na-ᵥ₁dim₂
	ušeepiš
01·05·010·012	ᴸ₁šu
	gimillu

◀ **Figure 3-6.** Tagged Sumerian Text File

different categories of verbal construction, as well as, for example, verbal objects, syllabically spelled words, and logographically spelled words.

Figure 3-6 shows an edited and tagged version of the first several lines of the lexical series **HAR-ra** = ḫubullu. The tags are seen in this figure as small capital letters, sometimes followed by a numeral. In reality, these tag marks are simply characters which are not used in the Sumerian transliteration character set and thus may be used as tags, being represented on the microcomputer screen in a user-defined fashion (for example, the character which appears as a subscripted "L" is actually just replacing the usual "$" character). These tags may be easily and rapidly inserted into a Sumerian text file by using the screen editor. An example of tagging is seen on line 6 in figure 3-6 where the subscripted characters *V1* preceding the syllable **ba** indicate to the sorting program that **ba** is to be construed as a verb represented by a single cuneiform sign. Similarly, on line 12 of the same figure, the syllable **šu** is preceded by the characters *L1* which indicate that **šu** is a logographic Sumerian word consisting of one sign. As a final example, the syllables **šu-lal,** on line 3, are preceded by the tag marks *L2,* which indicate to the sorting program that both syllables following the tag are to be taken together as a single lexically significant, logographically spelled Sumerian word. These are examples of just two of the seventeen marks currently being used to tag lexical items for indexing purposes.

Results

After the Sumerian words in a text file have been tagged, they are sorted into lexical order by a specially designed computer program which recognizes the tag marks. The program generates a parsing list and several indexes from the tagged file. The parsing list, which may be seen plotted in figure 3–7, indicates the words which the computer extracted from each line in the text file. The first line of each entry in the parsing list cites an *MSL* location, indicating which line of the lexical series was parsed and the Sumerian contents of that line. On the next several lines of the parsing list are citations of the Sumerian words located in the parsed line, followed by the classification of those words as determined by the tags which marked them. Using this list, the scholar may verify that all the lexically significant words in each line have indeed been tagged and that the appropriate tag has been assigned to each word.

V 9,1	ur$_5$(HAR)-ra	
ur$_5$		Logographic
HAR		Replaced Reading
V 9,2	eš-še-de$_2$-a	
eš-še-de$_2$-a		Logographic
de$_2$		Non-Finite Simple Verb
V 9,3	šu-lal	
šu		Verbal Object
lal, šu		Non-Finite Compound Verb
V 9,4	še-bal	
še		Verbal Object
bal, še		Non-Finite Compound Verb
V 9,5	nig$_2$-ba	
nig$_2$		Verbal Object
ba, nig$_2$		Non-Finite Compound Verb
V 9,6	in-na-an-ba	
in-na-an-ba		Verbal Complex
ba		Simple Verb
V 9,7	a-mu-un-na-ru	
a-mu-un-na-ru		Uncertain Reading
mu-un-na-ru, a		Verbal Complex
ru		Simple Verb

Figure 3–7. Parsing List for Tablet 1 of HAR-ra = *hubullu*

V 9,8	ba-du₃	
ba-du₃		Verbal Complex
du₃		Simple Verb
V 9,9	ba-an-bal	
ba-an-bal		Verbal Complex
bal		Simple Verb
V 9,10	ba-an-zal	
ba-an-zal		Verbal Complex
zal		Simple Verb
V 9,11	a-mu-un-na-dim₂	
a-mu-un-na-dim₂		Uncertain Reading
mu-un-na-dim₂, a		Verbal Complex
dim₂		Simple Verb
V 10,12	šu	
šu		Logographic
V 10,13	šu-gar	
šu		Verbal Object
gar, šu		Non-Finite Compound Verb
V 10,14	šu-gar gi	
šu-gar		Logographic
gar		Non-Finite Simple Verb
gi		Non-Finite Simple Verb
V 10,15	šu-gar-ra ga₂	
šu-gar		Logographic
gar		Non-Finite Simple Verb
ga₂		Non-Finite Simple Verb
V 10,16	šu-dir-ra	
šu-dir		Logographic
dir		Logographic
V 10,17	šu-uₓ-sud-da	

Figure 3–7 continued.

The sorting program also generates several different indexes of the Sumerian words which it locates in a tagged text file. All the words marked by a particular tag are sorted into a subindex for that tag. Thus, for example, a separate index of all the logographically spelled, nonverbal words is created, as are similar indexes for each of the other tag marks. Additionally, all the words marked by the several different kinds of verbal tags are sorted together into a joint subindex, thereby providing a specialized index of all the verbal forms in the text. Most of these subindexes are created to aid in future linguistic analysis of the Sumerian language by the

MSL project, and they will not necessarily be published. The principal result of the sorting, however, is the main index shown in a somewhat preliminary format in figure 3-8.[31] This index contains all the words from most of the tagging classes sorted into a single index, which eventually will become the published result of the *MSL* project. The main index (figure 3-8) is formatted in two-column, lexical (or dictionary) fashion. Each indexed word is given in boldface type, followed by an enumeration of the locations and contents of all the lines in which that indexed word appears. The subindexes are also formatted in this manner. There remain, however, several deficiencies in the index as represented in figure 3-8, which may be remedied by cross-referencing.

Future Plans

Cross-referencing in these indexes, as in any index, will direct the user of the index from one form of a word to an alternate form. Several different types of cross references are currently being planned for the indexes to be produced by the *MSL* project. An example of the usefulness of cross-referencing is the case of syllabically spelled Sumerian words which also have a logographic spelling. The Akkadian scribes who wrote the lexical tablets most often spelled the Sumerian words logographically. Occasionally, however, they spelled out some of the words syllabically, even though logographic spellings of the words also existed. An instance of this is the case of the Sumerian word **gal**, meaning "great" or "large," which is found in the lexical texts spelled both logographically, with a single cuneiform sign, and syllabically with the signs **gu-la**. Cross-referencing would allow the syllabic spelling to appear in the index with a reference to the more lexically appropriate logographic spelling of the word. A second example of referencing involves variant dialect forms of a Sumerian word which may be cross-referenced to the index entry of the main dialect form for that word. Clearly, cross-referencing will greatly increase the usefulness of the indexes by gathering under a single main index entry all the variant forms of a particular Sumerian word.

The referencing plans indicated above have been implemented only partially to date; as yet, there are no plotted results of referencing to be shown. Work is currently underway to enable the computer programs to recognize and properly index words marked by special referencing tag marks. Other future plans include improving the quality of plotting and perhaps ultimately using a computer-controlled phototypesetter for final publication of the results. A third area of interest is the application of the indexing capabilities developed for the lexical series in *MSL* to several other types of Sumerian literature. Figure 3-9 shows some preliminary results from the indexing of the literary work "Gudea," mentioned above.[32]

du_3

a-$ša_3$-ga

a-$ša_3$-ga
V 13, 42a nig_2-al-di a-$ša_3$-ga

a_2
V 24, 207 u_4 a_2-bi
V 40, 369 a_2-bi i_3-ag_2-ga_2
V 40, 371 u_4 ku_3-babbar a_2-bi mu-un-tum_2
V 41, 374 a_2-bi ib_2-si-sa_2

a_2-ki-it
V 24, 202 u_4 a_2-ki-it

^{itu}ab-ba-e_3
V 25, 230 ^{itu}ab-ba-e_3

ad
V 17, 113   ad-a-ni

ag_2
V 27, 247 i_3-ag_2-ga_2
V 27, 248 i_3-ag_2-ga_2-e
V 27, 249 i_3-ag_2-ga_2-e-meš
V 27, 250   še i_3-ag_2-ga_2
V 27, 251   še i_3-ag_2-ga_2-e
V 27, 252   še i_3-ag_2-ga_2-e-meš
V 27, 253   nu še i_3-ag_2-ga_2
V 40, 369 a_2-bi i_3-ag_2-ga_2

ak
V 20, 157 $buru_x$(EBUR) i_3-ak-a
V 20, 158 $buru_x$(EBUR) nu-ak-a

ban_2
V 40, 368 u_4 1-kam ban_2-še-ta-am_3

ban_3-da
V 15, 92   dam-ban_3-da
V 17, 110   šeš-ban_3-da

$^{itu}bar_2$-zag-gar
V 25, 221 $^{itu}bar_2$-zag-gar

$buru_x$
V 19, 152 $buru_x$(EBUR)
V 19, 153 $buru_x$(EBUR)-$še_3$
V 19, 154 u_4-$buru_x$(EBUR)-$še_3$
V 19, 155   egir-$buru_x$(EBUR)-$še_3$
V 19, 156   mu-un-du-$buru_x$(EBUR)-$še_3$
V 20, 157 $buru_x$(EBUR) i_3-ak-a
V 20, 158 $buru_x$(EBUR) nu-ak-a
V 20, 159 $buru_x$(EBUR)-$še_3$ ba-ra-e_{11}-de_3

dag
V 40, 366 gan_2-ba-an-dag
V 40, 367 u_4 gan_2-ba-an-dag

dag-gi_4-a
V 15, 79   dag-gi_4-a
V 15, 80   ugula dag-gi_4-a

dam
V 15, 87   dam
V 15, 88   dam
V 15, 89   dam-dam

al

V 12, 41	nig₂-al-di

nig_2-al-di

ama

V 17, 114   ama-a-ni

itu apin-du₈-a

V 25, 228   itu apin-du₈-a

arad

V 18, 129   sag-arad
V 18, 132   sag-geme₂-arad
V 40, 373   arad-a-ni šu-ba-ab-gur-ra

ba

V 9, 6   in-na-an-ba
V 35, 338   i₃-ba
V 36, 339   i₃-ba
V 36, 340   i₃-ba-e
V 36, 341   i₃-ba-e-meš

bad₄

V 26, 236   bad₄(KIKAL)-bi-še₃

bal

V 9, 9   ba-an-bal
V 14, 66   maš₂ ba-ra-bal
V 29, 283   ba-ra-bal
V 30, 284   ba-ra-bal-e
V 30, 285   ba-ra-bal-e-meš
V 32, 308   gis gan-na ib₂-ta-an-bal

---

dam-ban₃-da

V 15, 92   dam-ban₃-da

dam-dam

V 15, 89   dam-dam

dam-guruš

V 15, 90   dam-guruš

dam-kaskal

V 15, 93   dam-kaskal

dam-lu₂

V 15, 91   dam-lu₂

dam-tab-ba

V 16, 93a   dam-tab-ba
V 16, 94   dam-tab-ba
V 16, 95   dam-tab-ba

digir

V 33, 312   mu-digir-bi in-pa₃

dim₂

V 9, 11   a-mu-un-na-dim₂

dir

V 10, 16   šu-dir-ra

diri-ga

V 38, 356   ib₂-diri-ga-e-meš
V 38, 357   ḫe₂-diri-ga nam-ba-la₂

dirig

V 26, 233   itu dirig še-kin-kud

du₃

Figure 3-8. Index of Tablet 1, ḪAR-ra = ḫubullu

babbar

a

a.

a1,9 šag_4-^{d}en-líl$_2$-la$_2$-ke$_4$ ^{giš}digna-am$_3$ a-dug$_3$-ga nam-tum$_2$

a2,8   ninda giš-bi$_2$-tag $_4$-šed$_7$ i$_3$-de$_2$

a2,25 ninda giš-bi$_2$-tag a-šed$_7$ i$_3$-de$_2$

a3,7   a nu-tuk-me a-mu ^{d}nanše-me

a3,7   a nu-tuk-me a-mu ^{d}nanše-me

a3,8   a-mu šag$_4$-ga šu-ba-ni-dug$_4$ unu$_2$-a i$_3$-tud-e

a3,12 še$_6$-gi-bar a-gal-la du$_3$-a-me

a3,19 kur a-ta il$_2$-la nina^{ki}-še$_3$

a4,6   ninda giš-bi$_2$-tag a-šed$_7$ i$_3$-de$_2$

a8,15 lugal-mu ^{d}nin-ĝir$_2$-su en a-ḫuš gi$_4$-a

a8,16 en-zid a kur-gal-e ri-a

a8,25 a-e$_3$ a-gin$_x$ gu$_4$-nun-di zu

a8,25 a-e$_3$ a-gin$_x$ gu$_4$-nun-di zu

a9,1   lugal-mu šag$_4$-zu a-e$_3$-a u$_2$-nu-lal zu

a9,20 ma$_3$ ^{d}nin-ĝir$_2$-su a-ḫuš gi$_4$-a

a10,1 a-duru$_2$-mu nam-gal-ki-aĝ$_2$-da

a10,11 a-duru$_2$-mu dug$_3$-ga-be$_2$ mu-ku$_2$

a-ba

a4,23 munus diš-am$_3$ a-ba-me a-nu a-ba-me a-ne$_2$

a4,23 munus diš-am$_3$ a-ba-me a-nu a-ba-me a-ne$_2$

a-gi$_6$-en

a1,8   a-gi$_6$-en nam-šuḫub$_2$ ni$_2$ il$_2$-il$_2$

a-ma

a8,26 a-ma-en-gin$_x$ u$_2$-ru$_x$ gul-gul zu

---

a5,24 ad-im-da-gi$_4$-a

a6,25 ^{giš}gru$_3$-di mu tuk niĝ$_2$-ad-gi$_4$-gi$_4$-ni

a7,25 ^{giš}gru$_3$-di mu tuk niĝ$_2$-ad-gi$_4$-gi$_4$-ne$_2$

a.k

a1,11 e$_2$-ninnu me-be$_2$ an-ki-a pa-e$_3$ mu-ak-ke$_4$

a2,23 e$_2$-ba-gara$_x$-ka eš$_3$-eš$_3$ i$_3$-ak

a4,24 sag̃-ĝa$_2$ e$_3$ ki-kinda mu-ak

a5,21 ki-sikil sag̃-ĝa$_2$ e$_3$ ki-kinda mu-ak

ama

a1,29 ama-mu ma-mu-mu ga-na-tum$_2$

a3,3   nin ama-lagašu^{ki} ki-ĝar-ra-me

a3,6   ama nu-tuk-me ama-mu ^{d}nanše-me

a3,6   ama nu-tuk-me ama-mu ^{d}nanše-me

a3,25 ama-mu ma-mu-mu ga-na-tum$_2$

a4,13 nin-kur-kur-ra-me ama inim mu-ḫad$_2$-da-mu-da

a5,11 ensi$_2$-ra ama-ne$_2$ ^{d}nanše mu-na-ni-ib$_2$-gi$_4$-gi$_4$

an

a1,1   ud a^{r}n-k^{i}a nam-tar-^{r}e-d^a

a1,11 e$_2$-ninnu me-be$_2$ an-ki-a pa-e$_3$ mu-ak-ke$_4$

a2,28 nin-mu dumu an-kug-ge tud-da

a4,14 šag$_4$-ma-mu-da-ka lu$_2$ diš-am$_3$ an-gin$_x$ ri-ba-ne$_2$

a5,13 lu$_2$ an-gin$_x$ ri-ba ki-gin$_x$ ri-ba-še$_3$

a7,4   en-na šag$_4$ an-gin$_x$ sud-ra$_2$-ne$_2$

a9,2   ur-sag̃ šag$_4$ an-gin$_x$ sud-ra$_2$ zu

a9,10 garza-ma$_3$ mul-an-kug-ba gu$_3$-ga-mu-ra-a-de$_2$

a-ma-ru
a 4,18 sig-ba-a-ne₂-še₃ a-ma-ru-kam
a 5,15 ᵈim-dugud₂ᵐᵘˢᵉⁿ-še₃ sig-ba-a-ne₂-še₃ a-ma-ru-še₃
a 10,2 lugal a-ma-ru-ᵈen-lil₂-la₂
a-na
a 9,4 ma₃ a-na mu-u₃-da-zu
a-ne
a 4,16 a-ne sag̃-g̃a₂-ne₂-še₃ dig̃ir-ra-am₃
a₂
a 10,24 e₂-babbar-babbar ki-a₂-ag̃₂-g̃a₂-ma₃
a 3,16 su-mah-za sa-ga a₂-zid-da-be₂
a 4,17 a₂-ne₂-še₃ ᵈim-dugud₂ᵐᵘˢᵉⁿ_dam
a 5,3 a₂ mu-gur li-um-za-gin₃ šu-im-mi-du₈
a 5,10 anše-nitah a₂-zid-da-lugal-ma₃-ke₄ ki-ma-hur-hur-e
a 5,14 sag̃-g̃a₂-še₃ dig̃ir a₂-ne₂-še₃
a 6,3 min-kam-ma ur-sag̃-am₃ a₂ mu-gur
a 6,12 anše-dun a₂-zid-da lugal zag-ge₂ ki-ma-ra-hur-hur-a-še₃
a 6,21 an-kara₂ a₂-nam-ur-sag̃-ka mi₂-u₃-ma-ni-dug₄
a 9,26 a₂-be-a-mu lu₂ la ba-ta-e₃
ab
a 8,23 šag̃₄ ab-gin_x zig-zig zu
a 9,23 e₂-mu e₂-ninnu ma₃ en-kur-ra ab si-a
abzu
a 2,11 ᵈnin-g̃ir₂-su abzu-a gal-di
a 10,15 ti-ra-aš₂ abzu-gin_x
ad
a 5,1 ad-im-da₅-gi₄-gi₄

a 9,11 e₂-mu e₂-ninnu an-ne₂ ki-g̃ar-ra
a 9,15 an im-si-dub₂-dub₂
a 9,16 me izi-hus-bi an-ne₂ im-us₂
a 9,18 mu-bi-e an-zag-ta kur-kur-re gu₂-im-ma-si-si
a 10,9 su-si-sa₂-a-mu an-kug-ge u₃-a ba-zig-ge
a 10,12 an lugal-dig̃ir-re-ne-ke₄
a 10,13 ᵈnin-g̃ir₂-sul lugal išib-an-na
a 10,18 me-gal-gal-ezen-an-na-mu šu-gal-ma-du₇-du₇
an-dul₃
a 3,14 an-dul₃-dag̃al-me g̃issu-zu-še₃
an-kara₂
a 6,21 an-kara₂ a₂-nam-ur-sag̃-ka mi₂-u₃-ma-ni-dug₄
an-še₃
a 1,2 lagašᵏⁱ me-gal-la sag̃¹-an-še₃-mi-ni-ib-il₂
a 4,5 ensi₂ e₂-kisal-sirara_x-ka sag̃-an-še₃-mi-ni-il₂
anše-dun
a 6,12 anše-dun a₂-zid-da lugal zag-ge₂ ki-ma-ra-hur-hur-a-še₃
a 6,18 anše-dun ur₃ u₃-si-lal
anše-nitah
a 5,10 anše-nitah a₂-zid-da-lugal-ma₃-ke₄ ki-ma-hur-hur-e
ba-gara_x
a 2,9 lugal-ba-gara_x-ra mu-na-g̃in sud₄ mu-na-tum₂
a 2,23 e₂-ba-gara_x-ka eš₃-eš₃ i₃-ak
a 10,27 e₂-ba-gara_x ki-banšur-ra-mu
babbar
a 7,2 e₂-ninnu ᵈim-dugud₂ᵐᵘˢᵉⁿ-babbar-babbar-babbar-ra u₃-mu-na-da-kur₉-re
a 7,2 e₂-ninnu ᵈim-dugud₂ᵐᵘˢᵉⁿ-babbar-babbar-babbar-ra u₃-mu-na-da-kur₉-re

Figure 3–9. Index of Gudea, Cone A, columns 1 to 10

"Gudea" has been used by the *MSL* project to ensure that the tagging system devised for the lexical texts is general enough to be applied to the more varied grammatical constructions of a literary genre. With the eventual refinement of the methodology and completion of the indexes, the *MSL* project will have added a flexible and powerful tool to the repertoire of the Sumerian lexicographer.

Acknowledgments

We wish to acknowledge the help and suggestions of Professor Miguel Civil of the Oriental Institute, as well as Professor Daniel Reisman, Dr. Richard Ward, and Professor Marvin Powell. Particular thanks are due to Paula Goblirsch who carefully checked and initially edited every line of *MSL* that entered the computer and who also designed the special character set seen in the plotted figures.

Notes

1. Mesopotamia, literally "the land between the two rivers," is contained almost entirely in the modern country of Iraq. It is properly the flat, alluvial plain and grassy steppe between and on either side of the Tigris and Euphrates rivers, from the Persian Gulf to the Turkish border. Ancient Sumer encompassed that area of Mesopotamia which lies southeast of modern Baghdad.

2. The cuneiform writing system was employed by the peoples of the ancient Near East from about 3400 to 100 B.C. The major languages using this form of writing were Sumerian, Akkadian, Elamite, Hittite, and Hurrian, although greatly modified versions were also used for Old Persian and Ugaritic. Most often the characters were impressed on a moist clay tablet with a reed stylus. The stylus had a triangular point which, when pressed into the clay, produced the distinctive wedge-shaped strokes for which this writing system was named.

3. A. Poebel, *Grundzuege der Sumerischen Grammatik* (Rostock: Selbstverlag des Verfassers, 1923).

4. F. Delitzsch, *Sumerisches Glossar* (Leipzig: H. Reuther, 1914).

5. An *agglutinative* language is one in which words consist of compounds of individual constituents or morphs, each of which expresses a single definite meaning or grammatical nuance. Examples include Turkish, Finnish, and Hungarian.

6. An *inflected* language is one in which the grammatical relationship between words in a sentence is indicated by modification of the form of the

individual constituent words, including both internal phonetic modification and the affixation of modifying elements. Many of the Indo-European and all the Semitic languages are inflected in nature.

7. Attempts have been made to link Sumerian to various other languages including Chinese, because of the logographic nature of its script, and Hungarian and Turkish, because of the similar agglutinative structure of those languages. To date, no language, ancient or modern, has been found to bear anything more than a superficial similarity to Sumerian.

8. Sumerian words and cuneiform signs are represented in this chapter by bold-faced letters.

9. The subscripted numbers serve the purpose of uniquely associating a transliterated syllable with the original cuneiform sign which it represents. The acute and grave accents seen in the *MSL* text shown in figure 3-3 are simply an alternate notation for subscripted 2 and 3, respectively.

10. A syllabary is similar to an alphabet in that it constitutes all the symbols used to write a particular language. In an alphabet, each symbol (letter) represents a single phoneme, which in turn has a more or less restricted range of pronunciation. However, in the complex Akkadian cuneiform syllabary, each symbol (that is, cuneiform sign) represents a combination of phonemes which form a syllable. In addition, as discussed above, most cuneiform signs have several syllabic pronunciations which can be completely unrelated in sound. The Akkadian syllabary is understood as all the cuneiform signs used in the writing of Akkadian and all their possible corresponding phonetic values.

11. Akkadian words and syllables are italicized in this chapter.

12. For more complete discussions of the types of lexical material and the actual configurations of the tablets, see H.S. Schuster, "Die nach Zeichen geordneten sumerisch-akkadisch Vokabulare," *Zeitschrift fuer Assyriologie* 44 (1938):217–270; and M. Civil, "Lexicography," *Sumerological Studies in Honor of Thorkild Jacobsen,* Assyriological Studies, no. 20 (Chicago: University of Chicago Press, 1975), pp. 123–157.

13. S. Lieberman, *The Sumerian Loanwords in Old Babylonian Akkadian* (Missoula, Mon.: Scholars Press, 1977), and, more recently, "The Phoneme /o/ in Sumerian," *Studies in Honor of Tom B. Jones* (Neukirchen-Vluyn: Butzon and Bercker Kevelaer, 1979).

14. B. Landsberger; Civil, M.; Reiner, E. *Materialien zum Sumerrischen Lexikon,* vol. 1 to 14 (Rome: Pontificum Institutum Biblicum, 1937–1979). Currently, four more volumes are envisioned to complete the series, and a further nineteenth volume will contain additions and corrections.

15. The title of the lexical series comes from the ancient Near Eastern practice of referring to a composition by its first line or the first few words of that line (for example, the book of Genesis is called *Bereshit* in Hebrew,

meaning "In the beginning. . ."). The words **HAR-ra** and *ḫubullu* both mean a "loan with fixed interest," where **HAR-ra** is the Sumerian word and *ḫubullu* is its Akkadian equivalent.

16. Sumerologists refer to the lexical series beginning with the line **ki-KI.KAL-bi-šě₃** = *ana ittišu* simply as *ana ittišu*. The terms in both languages mean "upon pertinent notice given."

17. F. Thureau-Dangin, *Les Cylindres de Goudea, Textes Cuneiformes du Louvre,* vol. 8 (Paris: P. Geunther, 1925). A brief discussion and partial translation of "Gudea" may be found in S.N. Kramer, *The Sacred Marriage Rite* (Bloomington: Indiana University Press, 1969), pp. 23–34.

18. The period of the Third Dynasty of Ur witnessed a tremendous increase in the wealth and political power of the Sumerians under the kings of Ur. The extant documents from this period, numbering in excess of 100,000, are almost entirely economic and administrative in nature. They provide a potential mine of information for an economic history of Sumer in the Ur III period. The University of Minnesota has access to approximately 200 such documents, as yet unpublished, whose contents will be cataloged and indexed by using slightly modified versions of the *MSL* project's computer programs.

19. A *lexically significant* item is simply one which would appear in a dictionary or lexicon. In Sumerian, this distinction is particularly important since, because of the agglutinative nature of the language, lexically significant syllables are commonly surrounded by other syllables which themselves have no lexical significance.

20. A partial index to *MSL*, volume 2, was published as an addendum to *MSL*, volume 3 (pp. 227–249) by A. Sachs.

21. The *MSL* project uses an 8510a Terak microcomputer.

22. The Terak microcomputer has programmable character-set-generation capabilities which permit Sumerian transliteration characters to be displayed instead of the standard Latin characters.

23. The project uses a Control Data Corporation Cyber 172 computer. All the computer programs are written in the Pascal programming language.

24. The transfer of information between the microcomputer and the large computer is accomplished via telephone lines by using a special communications program.

25. A Varian Statos 42 electrostatic plotter is currently being used.

26. As was seen in the discussion of the spelling of the word *kakkabu,* an Akkadian word could be spelled using a number of different syllabic configurations, some of which seem to omit or add unnecessary letters in the spelling. The spelling *kakkabu* is, however, the so-called normalized spelling for modern scholarly purposes. The typists were instructed to omit the hyphenation of the Akkadian words (seen in the right-hand column of

figure 3-3) when they entered the text. Subsequent editing by persons familiar with Akkadian put the words into their correct normalized form.

27. The alphabetization of the key words, even though they are not yet in lexical form, is quite useful because it roughly approximates lexical order, at least in those words which have not acquired some grammatical prefix. This rough order significantly diminishes the amount of time required to locate and check each key word in the multivolume lexicons of Akkadian.

28. The *Akkadisches Handwoerterbuch* was initiated by B. Meissner over thirty years ago. Upon his death in 1947, the project was continued by W. von Soden, who published the first installment in 1965. The lexicon will be composed of three volumes (A–L, M–S, and S–Z), published in sixteen fascicles, of which fourteen have been completed.

The *Chicago Assyrian Dictionary* project was begun in 1921 and was subsequently delayed by the death of its first editor and an intervening war. Progress resumed in 1947 under the direction of A.L. Oppenheim and I.J. Gelb, and the first of a planned twenty-one volumes was published in 1956. Each volume, of the total of twenty-one, is devoted to one letter of the alphabet (that is, the tranliteration alphabet used to render cuneiform Akkadian into modified Latin courses). Twelve volumes have appeared to date.

29. Publication errors in the *MSL* source text are replaced with their correct rendering in the computer text file. The erroneous material is retained in the text file in a specially marked format which will allow a cumulative list of publication errors to be generated by the sorting programs.

30. In the Sumerian indexes, the primary exception will be that cuneiform signs which the original editor of *MSL* transliterated with capital letters to indicate his uncertainty have been assigned currently accepted values in lowercase letters. In the Akkadian indexes, the principal exception is the replacement of Sumerian logographic signs with their Akkadian equivalents.

31. The preliminary version of the main index shown in figure 3-8 is the first page of an index to tablet 1 of **HAR-ra** = *ḫubullu*.

32. Figure 3-9 is the first page of a preliminary index to columns 1 through 10 of cylinder A of "Gudea."

Bibliography

General Background

Chiera, E. *They Wrote on Clay*. Chicago: University of Chicago Press, 1938.

Jacobsen, T. *Toward the Image of Tammuz.* Edited by W. Moran. Cambridge, Mass.: Harvard University Press, 1970.

Jones, T.B. *Paths to the Ancient Past.* New York: Free Press, 1967.

————. *The Sumerian Problem.* New York: Wiley, 1969.

Kramer, S.N. *The Sumerians: Their History, Culture and Character.* Chicago: University of Chicago Press, 1963.

Oppenheim, A.L. *Ancient Mesopotamia: Portrait of a Dead Civilization.* Chicago: University of Chicago Press, 1964.

Sumerian Writing System

Civil, M. "The Sumerian Writing System: Some Problems." *Orientalia* 42(1973):21–34.

Diakonoff, I.M. "Ancient Writing and Ancient Written Language: Pitfalls and Peculiarities in the Study of Sumerian." *Sumerological Studies in Honor of Thorkild Jacobsen.* Assyriological Studies, no. 20 Chicago: University of Chicago Press, pp. 99–121.

Grammars and Related Studies.

Edzard, D.O. "*Ḫamṭu, marû* und freie Reduplikation beim sumerischen Verbum." *Zeitschrift fuer Assyriologie* 61(1971):208–232 and 62(1972): 1–34.

Falkenstein, A. *Grammatik der Sprache Gudeas von Lagāš.* Analecta Orientalia, nos. 28, 29, 29a. Rome: Pontificum Institutum Biblicum, 1949–1950, 1978.

————. "Das Sumerische." in *Handbuch der Orientalistik*, Vol. 2. Leiden: E.J. Brill, 1959.

Gragg, G.B. *Sumerian Dimensional Infixes.* Alter Orient und Altes Testament, Sonderreihe 5. Neukirchen-Vluyn: Butzon & Bercker Kevelaer, 1973.

Jacobsen, T. "About the Sumerian Verb." In *Toward the Image of Tammuz.* Cambridge, Mass.: Harvard University Press, 1970, pp. 245–270.

Jestin, E. *Le verbe sumerien.* Paris: E. de Boccard, 1943–1945.

Poebel, A. *Grundzuege der sumerischen Grammatik.* Rostock: Selbverlag des Verfassers, 1923.

Sollberger, E. *Le systeme verbal dans les inscriptions "royales" presargoniques de Lagaš.* Geneva: E. Droz, 1952.

Lexicography and Lexical Materials

Civil, M. "Lexicography," *Sumerological Studies in Honor of Thorkild Jacobsen.* Assyriological Studies, no. 20. Chicago: University of Chicago Press, 1975, pp. 123–157.

Deimel, A. *Sumerisches Lexicon.* Rome: Pontificum Institutum Biblicum, 1927–1950; Part I, sumerische, akkadische und hetitische Lautwerte nach Keilschriftzeichen und Alphabet; Part 2, Vollstaendige Ideogramm-Sammlung; Part 3, Vol. 1, sumerisch-akkadisches Glossar; Vol. 2, akkadisch-sumerisches Glossar; Part 4, Vol. 1, Pantheon Babylonicum; Vol. 2, Planetarium Babylonicum.

Delitzsch, F. *Sumerisches Glossar.* Leipzig: H. Reuther, 1914.

Jestin, R., and Lambert, M. *Contribution au thésaurus de la langue sumerienne.* Paris: College de France, Cabinet d'Assyriologie, 1954–1955, fascicle 1 GAR (1954), fascicle 2 AK(1955).

Landsberger, B.; Civil, M.; Reiner, E. *Materialien zum Sumerischen Lexikon.* Rome: Pontificum Institutum Biblicum, 1937– .

Lieberman, S.J. *Sumerian Loanwords in Old-Babylonian Akkadian.* Missoula, Mont.: Scholars Press, 1977.

Schuster, H.S. "Die nach Zeichen geordneten sumerisch-akkadischen Vokabulare." *Zeitschrift fuer Assyriologie* 44(1938):217–270.

EYEBALL and the Analysis of Literary Style

Donald Ross, Jr.

The notion of *style,* whether of literature, other writings, or other artistic or abstract human activities, has had a complex history. The term is used in many senses which often contradict one another; style is the creator's personality as manifested in the work, it is the audience's reaction to the work, or it is some property of the work, separate from the artist or the audience. A survey of book reviews in newspapers, liner notes on record jackets, or museum guidebooks quickly shows that most comments about style are quite general, and they often tend toward the metaphorical: Keats is "florid," Beethoven is "heroic," Cezanne is "rustic." While these impressionistic comments may be moving or inspiring, they actually convey little information, and they cannot stand up to probing questions about either the definition of the adjectives used or the method by which the labels were chosen. For scholarly and objective treatment of style, it is essential to begin with an identified, well-defined methodology for describing the works being studied, so that interpretations or judgments can be traced to identifiable features of those works.

Since interest in this chapter is focused on the style of literary works, a description of language is an appropriate starting point for this discussion. Linguistic descriptions can become quite detailed and elaborate; the sounds which constitute a word can be broken down into several dimensions, which include how they are articulated, how long it takes to say them, and so on. While it is clear that impressionistic labels convey too little information, an excess of linguistic detail can convey too much. The descriptive procedure requires both that labels can be selected with consideration of all possible linguistic dimensions and that they accurately and adequately characterize how the text is written. Obviously, if several texts are described in the same terms, it is possible to compare their styles, at least within the limits of the descriptions. Finally, while it is of relatively minor concern in this chapter, it is possible to associate such descriptions with assertions about the relationship of an author's personality to his or her work, how the work affects the reader, and even how works are related to impressionistic labels.

The Problem

For a short literary work or a sample from a larger one, it is feasible to perform a linguistic description "by hand," that is, by noting linguistic features, from sounds through syntax, to semantics and diction. The results of such annotation can be gathered (that is, counted) and various generalizations about style produced rather easily. While tolerable for a hundred words or so, the process is tedious, and the error rate increases as a function of boredom. Once the analysis of one text or sample has been finished, the researcher has another problem in keeping track of the results.

To take the last problem first, clearly it makes sense to store linguistic descriptions in a computer, so they can be gathered for analysis. If the data are qualitative, as in a list of words in texts, then information retrieval and comparison of lists can lead to appropriate generalizations. Over the years, the EYEBALL project has gathered data bases from various published books and articles for such well-defined features as word lengths and syntactic categories (nouns, verbs, and so on), whether or not the description involved computer assistance. Some uses of these data are described later.

While the computer is obviously appropriate as a storage device, it is more challenging to see it as an aid for the description of language. Here the advantages are in the consistency which comes from using the same algorithms (computer procedures) to describe several texts, as well as the rigor involved in designing the algorithms. Accurate analysis of language is a complicated task that tends to resist automatic methods. Linguistic codes are notoriously ambiguous, and the ambiguities are intentionally played on by poets, playwrights, and novelists. Furthermore, descriptions of language have proved to be more successful for the linguistic "levels" from sound structures to syntax and rather poor for semantics, and hence for "meaning" or significance. So far, computer-aided descriptions of style have not solved all the problems, but they do point toward some solutions.

The Solution

Computer-assisted language description involves two steps. The first is to decide which features of language should be included and what form the descriptions should take. The second is a more ordinary sequence of data reduction and statistical generalization. The EYEBALL program starts with computer-readable English texts as input and, after several automatic and interactive steps, produces an annotated computer file with several linguistic descriptors attached to each word. The advantages of starting with the text alone are that entry of the data into the computer can be done by an untrained keypuncher and that the researcher can use texts prepared for other projects, most notably for concordances. Annotating the entered text for special features, for example, to identify spelled forms whose function is varied (*like* can be a verb or preposition), necessarily requires that experts be involved, even at this preliminary stage.

Picking the appropriate annotations involves compromises between the scholar's time and precision, on one hand, and the rational use of computer resources to get a job done, on the other. For a couple of simple examples, information about person and number of the pronouns *I* and *he* can be found from the spelled form, so that the only computer task is one of retrieval and enumeration. *You*, however, does not indicate singular or plural. Obtaining this information would require placing a tag on the word when it is stored (*you-s* versus *you-pl*), or a list of all instances of *you* in their contexts, to determine visually which ones are plural. One compromise is to not include this level of "delicacy" in the descriptive apparatus. A reasonable criterion for exclusion is that relatively rare features need not be identified. Thus, sampling theories indicate that anything which occurs at a frequency of 4 percent or less can be reliably reported on only if the sample size is 20,000 items. This criterion makes psychological sense since it seems unlikely that a reader notices linguistic patterns occurring only in very rare instances. In a computer-based project, it makes sense to gather all the data which can be produced completely automatically, but to be judicious if the process involves added time for the researcher. Thus the EYEBALL program, which computes word lengths in syllables, tells the difference between words of five and six syllables, even though the relative frequencies of both are quite low.

The elements of a language tend to occur in two ways—small, closed sets of items, each of which is used quite often, and large sets, the elements of which appear infrequently. For example, articles (*the, a,* and *an*) comprise some 9.7 percent of all English words, spaced at fairly regular intervals, while a given adjective, say *yellow,* may never appear in a text thousands of words long. Similarly, noun phrases come in a few high-frequency forms (pronoun alone, noun alone, adjective plus noun, article plus noun) and a longer list of unusual types (article plus two adjectives plus intensifying adverb plus adjective plus noun). EYEBALL uses automatic procedures for the closed-set items at several levels; the open-set decisions are made by the researcher in intermediate stages. Once all the decisions are checked, the statistical analysis is automatic.

A flowchart of EYEBALL is given as figure 4–1. While it is not feasible to discuss every step of the programming in detail here, some examples will serve to give the reader a sense of the operation. The third sentence in Stephen Crane's *Red Badge of Courage* provides a sample of text which can be used to illustrate the various stages of analysis with EYEBALL:

It cast its eyes upon the roads, which were growing from long troughs of liquid mud to proper thoroughfares.

Assuming that this has become machine-readable, the first step involves dividing the input string into separate words (identified by the blanks),

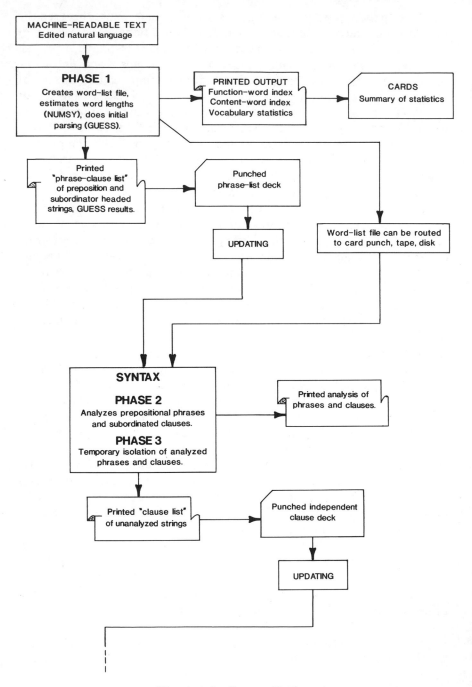

Figure 4-1. System Design

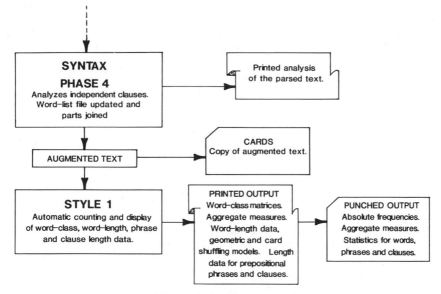

Figure 4-1 continued

separating punctuation marks from the words (the comma after *roads,* the period after *thoroughfares*), and setting up a "file" in the computer with nineteen spaces, one for each word. As the word is isolated, it is first checked against a "function-word dictionary" to see if it is in one of the closed sets that together comprise roughly half of all words in English. The categories in the dictionary are pronouns, determiners (articles and other prenoun words such as *first, most,* and *any*), coordinating conjunctions, intensifying adverbs (*very, only*) that usually appear in noun phrases, auxiliary verbs, interjections, the negative *not,* and, most significant for our purposes, prepositions and subordinating conjunctions. Items in the function-word dictionary are listed in "Description for EYEBALL" (see Bibliography). Words not in this dictionary of some 250 items are assumed to be "content words," for example, members of the open sets of nouns, adjectives, verbs, and regular adverbs. Each word will ultimately be marked in two syntactic dimensions—the "categories," for example, the classes we have just enumerated, and the "function" of the word in its clause. The major functions are subject, predicate, complement (direct and indirect object, predicate adjective), and "adjunct" (essentially adverbial items, a class dominated by prepositional phrases). The category and function are represented by four-character abbreviations, and our sample text will start as follows, with classes as yet unknown indicated by four Xs.

Word	Category	Function
It	PRON	XXXX
cast	XXXX	XXXX
its	DET	XXXX
eyes	XXXX	XXXX
upon	PREP	APRP
the	DET	XXXX
roads	XXXX	XXXX
which	SUBD	XXXX (etc.)

The lengths of function words in syllables are available from the dictionary. The lengths of other words are calculated by a program called NUMSY, the basis of which is that a syllable depends on a vowel or vowel cluster. The program adjusts for such things as silent e's at the ends of words, including plurals, and divides vowel pairs into those which do or do not produce two syllables based on the surrounding consonants. This program is accurate for about 95 percent of all English words, which is probably better than what a human can do, once fatigue sets in.

As each word is taken from the input string, its location is automatically computed in terms of its paragraph and sentence. To set up for the study of vocabulary repetition, particularly for word indexes (lists of the places where each word occurs), each word is checked to see if it has been used before or is new to this text (all words of the example are used once, but several are repeated from the first two sentences in the novel). A final element in the file is a code indicating when a word starts a sentence or ends a clause or prepositional phrase.

A major task of PHASE1 is to prepare for the later steps, when the unknown categories and functions are filled in and any errors which come from the automatic labeling can be fixed. English, like many other languages, is comprised of 25 percent to 33 percent prepositional-phrase words. Prepositional phrases start with a closed-set category word, tend to be relatively short, and are routinely structured. Furthermore, they are independent of the rest of the clause since they are adjuncts whose scope of modification is often the whole clause. They can be removed, yet the clause remains intelligible enough for later analysis. Since most subordinate clauses begin with subordinating conjunctions or adverbs (*if, however*) or relative pronouns (*which, who*), and since each item on the worksheet is accompanied by a punched card which gives its location and category, it is easy to have the computer find their starting points. Work sheets from PHASE1 print out all the prepositions and subordinates in the order in which they occur, along with the next nine words (thus filling about one printout line and generally getting to the end of the phrase or clause). If this is not enough, the number of words printed can be increased later. In the example, the first two items are

PREP   upon the roads which were growing from long troughs of
SUBD   which were growing from long troughs of liquid mud to

The printing stops with a period, question mark, or exclamation point. A more elegant version of the worksheet, developed in 1972, capitalizes on the ability to predict where many phrases end, based on the categories of words which come after the preposition. For instance, if a second prepositional phrase starts, the previous one is probably finished; prepositional phrases do not include auxiliary verbs or subordinating conjunctions. In our example, *which* is assumed to come after the end of the phrase that begins with *upon*, *of* after the *from* phrase, and *to* after the *of* phrase. The programs, called GUESS, which provide this facility are accurate for more than half of the prepositional phrases, and they make a fairly good stab at shorter clauses.

Whether the phrases and subordinated clauses have been analyzed by GUESS or not, all items on the worksheets have to be checked by the researcher. Two tasks are necessary—to determine the last word and to find the main elements of the clause or phrase. Once these are known, the information is translated into a symbolic shorthand which will be keypunched as input to the SYNTAX program.

The SYNTAX program is structured so that the function and category of any word in a text can be marked by entering a number and two four-letter abbreviations. This tedious task is not always necessary, however. As with other aspects of the programming, researchers have been able to capitalize on the consistency of high-frequency items to save time and effort. For example, main verbs always function as predicates, and adverbs are adjuncts, so one-letter codes are used with the location (for example, P7, B15). Noun phrases are "continuous in the sense that verbs or adverbials do not come between the determiner, or adjective, and the noun. Thus, in most cases, all that is necessary is to flag the noun and give its function. The program first marks words outside noun phrases (chiefly verbs and adverbs); then the marking of words in noun phrases goes from right to left or back to front. Since prepositional phrases work as adjuncts, they have to be staked out before their clause is marked. Pronouns whose category is provided from the dictionary are marked as one-word noun phrases. Prepositional phrases are assumed to end with a pronoun or noun, so that designating the final word is enough to specify the rest of the phrase structure. Special coding is available for prepositional phrases containing more than one noun or ending with an adjective. Similar allowances have been made for infinitives and other high-frequency syntactic structures. Ultimately, very few words must be individually marked.

The main elements in the *which* clause are noted below, along with the length of that clause. The input to SYNTAX (Phase 2) looks approximately like this:

Absolute Location in Text	Phrase or Clause Category	Added Input: Length	(First Word) Elements
47	PREP	3	(upon)
53	PREP	3	(from)
56	PREP	3	(of)
59	PREP	3	(to)
50	SUBD	12 Subj at 1, Pred at 3 (which)	

These marks fill in the functions and categories of all words in the phrases and the subordinate clauses, as well as change the phrase-clause location codes. The effect on the file illustrated above is shown in figure 4-2. After prepositional phrases and subordinated clauses are marked, the results are printed out so they can be checked for human error and corrected. Then a second set of worksheets shows the remaining words in the text, with special flags to show what was taken out. These words are the main (unsubordinated) clauses, which have to be marked in a second pass through SYNTAX. For our example, the worksheet will say

It cast its eyes <PREP>, <SUBD>.

The main clauses are marked in the same way as subordinated clauses except that lengths are rarely needed:

43   SENT   Subj at 1, Pred at 2, Comp at 4

After this is keyed on the card and processed through SYNTAX, the "augmented text" is automatically prepared. A total of sixteen keystrokes was needed for the twenty-one words, which is about average for EYEBALL. Again, the results are printed across the page, and corrections can be made (if, for example, one mistakenly said that the third word was a predicate). The vocabulary and location parts of the file are not affected, and, of course, the words and punctuation stay the same. The "horizontal" representation of the text at this stage would be

Vocabulary location of first instance	Location			Syntactic class		Phrase-clause location	Syl. length	Word	Punctu-ation
	Para.	Sent.	Word	Category	Function				
43	1	3	1	PRON	XXXX	1 0 0	1	It	
44	1	3	2	XXXX	XXXX	0	1	cast	
45	1	3	3	DET	XXXX	0	1	its	
46	1	3	4	XXXX	XXXX	0	1	eyes	
47	1	3	5	PREP	APRP	0	2	upon	
1	1	3	6	DET	XXXX	0	1	the	
49	1	3	7	XXXX	XXXX	0	1	roads	,
50	1	3	8	SUBD	XXXX	0	1	which	
51	1	3	9	AUXV	PRED	0	1	were	
52	1	3	10	XXXX	XXXX	0	2	growing	
5	1	3	11	PREP	APRP	0	1	from	
54	1	3	12	XXXX	XXXX	0	1	long	
55	1	3	13	XXXX	XXXX	0	1	troughs	
41	1	3	14	PREP	APRP	0	1	of	
57	1	3	15	XXXX	XXXX	0	2	liquid	
58	1	3	16	XXXX	XXXX	0	1	mud	
27	1	3	17	PREP	APRP	0	1	to	
60	1	3	18	XXXX	XXXX	0	2	proper	
61	1	3	19	XXXX	XXXX	0 0	3	thorough-fares	.

Figure 4-2. Sample Text after PHASE 1

Word	It	cast	its	eyes	upon
Category	PRON	VERB	DET	NOUN	PREP
Function	SUBJ	PRED	COMP	COMP	APRP

Word	the	roads,	which	were	growing
Category	DET	NOUN	SUBD	AUX	VERB
Function	APRP	APRP	SUBJ	PRED	PRED

Word	from	long	troughs	of	liquid
Category	PREP	ADJ	NOUN	PREP	ADJ
Function	APRP	APRP	APRP	APRP	APRP

Word	mud	to	proper	thoroughfares.
Category	NOUN	PREP	ADJ	NOUN
Function	APRP	APRP	APRP	APRP

The augmented text, whether a deck of punched cards or a file stored in the computer on a disk or tape, becomes the input for STYLE1, an automatic program which counts the frequencies of language features. Generally, the information from one column is gathered into either quantitative or qualitative classes. Thus, the sample text has one pronoun, two verbs, five nouns, and so on; two words which function as subject, three as predicates, twelve as prepositional-phrase adjuncts (APRP). It also has fourteen monosyllabic words, four words of two syllables, and one word of three syllables. The program computes relative frequencies, averages and other descriptive statistics, with the most valuable measures automatically punched and ready for more elaborate comparative analysis. The results, in terms both of developing a stylistic methodology and of specific stylistic comparisons, are discussed in the following section. The augmented text for the sample is shown as figure 4–3.

The EYEBALL programs are written in FORTRAN. Versions are available which are directly operational on CDC Cyber computers using the standard FTN FORTRAN compiler and on IBM 360 or 370 machines. PHASE1 uses 131,000 (octal) 60-bit words of storage for a text of 7,500 words and 55,000 for samples or texts of 1,000 words. SYNTAX and STYLE1 require very modest space. The CPU (computer) time to process a 1,000-word text is nine seconds, which translates to a cost of about $1.80. The various operations, including collecting the output, submitting jobs for intermediate processing, doing the analysis for SYNTAX, and punching the input cards, require about one (human) hour for a 500-word sample.

When the project was first organized at the University of Pennsylvania in 1970, the IBM 360 computer had an interactive processor, Conversational Programming System (CPS), which supported the PL/1 programming language. A working version was developed during the following year, with programmer Robert Rasche. When EYEBALL was moved to the University of Minnesota, the programs had to be "translated" to FORTRAN, since CDC had no PL/1 compiler. This inconvenience actually turned out to have two significant advantages. First, nearly every computer has a FORTRAN compiler, and the combined CDC/IBM versions of the programs have been transported to other universities and computer centers—about seventy-five copies have been mailed out so far. Second, FORTRAN uses much less computer time than PL/1. The first FORTRAN version was about three times faster and cheaper. Subsequent improvements in the programs and in CDC compilers have cut even the FORTRAN times, so they are four times faster than the earlier FORTRAN.

Current efforts include designing EYEBALL to fit and run on smaller computers such as the PDP 11. Simultaneously, researchers are developing ways to allow the program to run interactively, especially for SYNTAX steps. With luck, the prototype should be tested during the current year. Of course, the new versions will be adjusted by the suggestions and criticisms expressed by various users.

Application and Examples

Each text analyzed by EYEBALL produces printed and automatically punched results (output) which describe the text's language in various ways.

Vocabulary location of first instance	Location Para.	Sent.	Word	Syntactic class Category	Function	Phrase-clause location	Word	Punctuation
43	1	3	1	PRON	SUBJ	1 0 0	It	
44	1	3	2	VERB	PRED	0	cast	
45	1	3	3	DET	COMP	0	its	
46	1	3	4	NOUN	COMP	0	eyes	
47	1	3	5	PREP	APRP	0	upon	
1	1	3	6	DET	APRP	0	the	
49	1	3	7	NOUN	APRP	1	roads	,
50	1	3	8	SUBD	SUBJ	1 0	which	
51	1	3	9	AUXV	PRED	1 0	were	
52	1	3	10	VERB	PRED	1 0	growing	
5	1	3	11	PREP	APRP	1 0	from	
54	1	3	12	ADJ	APPP	1 0	long	
55	1	3	13	NOUN	APRP	1 1	troughs	
41	1	3	14	PREP	APRP	1 0	of	
57	1	3	15	ADJ	APPP	1 0	liquid	
58	1	3	16	NOUN	APRP	1 1	mud	
27	1	3	17	PREP	APRP	1 0	to	
60	1	3	18	ADJ	APRP	1 0	proper	
61	1	3	19	NOUN	APRP	6 1 6	thorough-fares	.

Figure 4-3. Sample "Augmented" Text

As noted above, these do not constitute a comprehensive description, but they do cover most of the features treated in stylistic studies. The main areas analyzed are vocabulary (in PHASE1), syntax, and word, phrase, and clause lengths (in STYLE1). The structures of vocabulary are described as statistical generalizations about how often words are repeated and as word indexes which show where repeated words appear. The list for content words is alphabetical, so the sample text would start with *cast* (second word in the sentence) and with *troughs* (fifteenth word). Function words are arranged by categories—all the determiners come first, subordinators last. A sample would look like this:

CRANE, RED BADGE

	Loc. no.	PARAG/SENT/WORD			ABS FREQ	REL FREQ
THE	1	1	1	1	8	.131
	2	1	1	6		
	3	1	1	9		
	4	1	1	18		
	5	1	2	2		
	6	1	2	9		
	7	1	2	19		
	8	1	3	6		
AN	1	1	1	13	1	.016

These word indexes are not supposed to be useful for elaborate and detailed tracing of patterns of content and semantic meanings. From the start of the project it was assumed that a concordance which gives the context (surrounding words) of each word was the appropriate computer tool to use for such pattern studies. The GENCORD program at Minnesota or the recently announced Oxford University project would be excellent.

Vocabulary statistics generalize about the degree to which words are repeated. The basic relation is the number of different words (types) to text length (tokens). In the first three sentences from *Red Badge of Courage,* forty-eight types appear; of these, forty-three are used once, *the* appears eight times. EYEBALL produces a table which includes the following information:

CRANE RED BADGE

FREQ.	ABSOLUTE FREQ.	CUMULATED FREQUENCIES	WEIGHTED NO. OF WORDS	CUMULATED SUM OF WTD.
1	43	43	43	43
2	2	45	4	47
3	2	47	6	53
4		47		53
5		47		53
6		47		53
7		47		53
8	1	48	8	61

The relation is expressed as the "type-token ratio" (0.79) or its inverse, the "repeat rate" (1.27). It turns out that these measures depend heavily on the text length—in longer texts, the already-used words start to appear more often, and the proportion of words which appear only once decreases. These difficult relations have been studied often, mostly with an effort to discover general mathematical properties. Since EYEBALL is especially tailored for sampling from long texts or describing related groups of short ones, controlling sample size circumvents the problem. The data gathered from several projects are listed in a technical report. PHASE1 also computes the repeat rates of content words and function words, taken as separate groups. In the example, no content words are repeated (the ratio is 1.0 to 1), and the rate for function words is 1.8 to 1. While both ratios depend on text length, that effect is much less pronounced for content words. These are more open to the free choice of an author, who can use a synonym for *roads* but not for *from*, so the content-word repeat rate is suggested as the best measure of vocabulary "richness."

Syntactic information is presented by STYLE1 in two forms, which depend on the frequency of items in categories and functions. The first set of data form a matrix which tells how many of each cross-classified type were found. For the sample sentence this is:

	SUBJ	COMP	PRED	APRP	...	TOTAL
NOUN		1		4		5
VERB			2			2
ADJ				3		3
PRON	1					1
DET		1		1		2
PREP				4		4
AUXV			1			1
SUBD	1					1
TOTAL	2	2	3	12		(19)

These frequencies are divided by text length to give the relative frequencies of each cross-referenced cell as well as the totals for each category and function. Stylistic studies have developed various ways to generalize about language by combining related categories (nouns and pronouns, auxiliary and main verbs) or computing ratios (adjectives to nouns, auxiliary to main verbs). STYLE1 reports on the "aggregated word-class measures" which had appeared in published studies available before 1970. Since then a rationale has been proposed to describe the word-category classes in a way that both makes linguistic sense and avoids some statistical problems as well.[1]

The printed output from STYLE1 also describes statistically the lengths of subordinated and independent clauses, prepositional phrases, and words (in syllables). Punctuated-sentence lengths are computed in PHASE1. In addition to word lengths, the program computes the extent to which one-syllable words are together in series or spread evenly among uniformly distributed polysyllabic words—the sample has three series of four monosyllables and one of three. S. Keith Lee has shown that one measure, the proportion of monosyllabic words, could predict the other measures of series length quite well.[2] While the statistical procedures are not so well worked out, calculations based on the monosyllable proportion also estimate average word length and the proportions of two-, three-, and four-syllable words. Monosyllable proportion is the best single measure of word length.

The augmented text can also be described in other ways, only a few of which have been explored. As part of a study of Blake, the syntactic categories of words which are first and last in their lines were identified. A more elaborate program, called STYLE2, enumerates the types of noun phrases which function as clause subject, clause complement, and object of prepositional phrase. This program has been developed but not extensively used for style descriptions. Preliminary results suggest that complements are more complex (have more constituents) than subjects, with prepositional-phrase variability between the others. This program also gives schematic descriptions of clauses in terms of their main elements (subject, verb, object).[3]

The most important statistical values for each text are punched on cards. Studies of style should concentrate on samples from long texts or from a corpus (such as the hundreds of sonnets written by Wordsworth). Once samples have been analyzed, they are treated as individual "observations" of a statistical "population"; one group of texts, such as Keats's sonnets, can be compared statistically with another, such as Shakespeare's sonnets. The average value for several style measures can be compared with the *t*-test, a widely used procedure, to reveal similarities between the two groups and identify which features are significantly different. To complete the stylistic analysis, the statistical conclusions can lead to a rereading of the texts to explain them in qualitative and, indeed, literary terms.

Results

The basic methodology was developed for my dissertation on Thoreau's *Walden*, where many of the language features were defined and the counting was done by hand. The programs were subsequently used on poetry samples, initially for a comparison of Blake's "Songs of Innocence" and "Songs of Experience" with Keats' sonnets and odes. At the same time, statistical consultants from the University of Minnesota helped refine the list of features and the appropriate statistical tools. The initial conclusions were that the groups of poems by Blake and Keats had few significant differences, but that the poets differed from each other fairly systematically. The next works analyzed were some medium-length poems by Coleridge, called his "Conversation Poems," as well as the "Rime of the Ancient Mariner" and a sample from "Christabel." Except for the "Rime," Coleridge's poems turned out to be stylistically very close to the two groups by Keats. A look at the poems, say, Keats's "Ode to Psyche" and Coleridge's "Dejection" readily confirms that the styles are similar, especially in the way both poets build up their effects by a series of one-line-long pictures. This conclusion does not explain why critics who do not use computers or statistics have failed to point out the similarities or why the nuances of Keats's style have been discussed with loving care and admiration, while almost nothing has been said about Coleridge's language outside the "Rime of the Ancient Mariner" and "Kubla Khan."

Several basic measures have proved most illuminating so far. The first group is the repeat-rate ratios for vocabulary (all words, function words, and content words), as long as the texts are roughly the same lengths. The largest group has sixteen ratios and proportions carefully selected from the syntactic category and function data. Finally, word lengths (measured by the proportion of monosyllables) and prepositional-phrase lengths reveal similarities and differences quite well. As noted above, word-length data from published and unpublished sources have been gathered and put into a uniform, computer-readable data base against which an author or text can be judged. A similar base has been organized for word-category data, with the largest component outside EYEBALL studies coming from Robert Cluett's studies of prose, known as the York University (Canada) corpus.[4]

The most recent aspect of my study of poetry was to include a sample of Elizabethan sonnets in an effort to see the degree to which poetic genres were written in a common style. When these poems were compared to sonnets by Keats, the differences were striking, even though the five Elizabethans were quite similar. A tentative conclusion has been derived from a preface written by Wordsworth in 1815—that short poems could be divided between the "lyric" and the "idyllic." The former, "containing the Hymn, the Ode, the Elegy, the Song, and the Ballad, in all which for the production of their full effect, accompaniment of music is indispensible," comprises Blake's "Songs" and the Elizabethan sonnets. The idyll includes "the Epitaph, the Inscription, the Sonnet, most of the epistles of poets writing in their own persons, and all loco-descriptive (place-descriptive) poetry," and it describes most of the poems by Keats and Coleridge in our sample.[5] Current plans are to expand the sample to include Keats's long poems, Wordsworth, Shelley and Byron, and some of the sonnets written between the Elizabethans and the Romantics.

EYEBALL has been used to study other texts. Elizabeth Sikes wrote a dissertation at the University of South Carolina based on a fairly large sample of Conrad's *Heart of Darkness*. She was able to demonstrate the consistency of that story and to show many of the nuances in Conrad's heavy reliance on prepositional phrases. Mary Beth Pringle's dissertation on *Ulysses* has given a concrete representation of the wide range of styles that Joyce uses. Furthermore, despite the range, her conclusion that narration and dialogue are systematically different should make it clear that those two elements of a novel must be treated separately.

Richard W. Bailey has studied transcripts of tapes made by Patti Hearst and by members of the Symbionese Liberation Army (SLA) to determine if Hearst or someone else was the author of the tapescripts. He used a multivariate statistical procedure, cluster and discriminant analysis, to reach the tentative conclusion that if Hearst wrote any of the materials, it was most likely the early ones. One methodological problem which Bailey has identified is that a credible effort to isolate an author's personal style can succeed only if the texts are in the same mode and about comparable topics. The absence of political polemics written by Hearst before her SLA experience made an adequate comparison impossible.

Most recently, Joseph Jaynes of the University of Minnesota has studied William Butler Yeats's poems written over many years.[6] Critical tradition has divided Yeats's career into three periods; yet the data from

EYEBALL concerning syntax, vocabulary, and the like show neither significant differences among the periods nor any consistent patterns over time that could be identified by Spearman's rank-order correlation test. The word indexes reveal some patterns of vocabulary, such as Yeats's use of Irish and classical names and technical terms, which differs among the periods. Jaynes and Bailey have shown that the numerical descriptions which STYLE1 produces can be given a variety of statistical treatments. One other instance of this potential is a study by William Baillie of large samples of plays by Shakespeare and Fletcher to see where they contributed to *Henry VIII*. By discriminant analysis, Baillie was able to separate known samples by the two writers and thus to point to a way to sort out the authorship of the collaborative play.

While it should be obvious from the description of the programs, they are fairly complicated. The work to develop a version of EYEBALL which operates in an interactive mode on a small computer may make the programs easier to use. With other projects underway, the body of available data should expand more easily. It is to be hoped that other scholars will have the time and interest to explore their interests and share their results. With the existing bodies of data as starting points, the histories of genres and styles will gradually be filled in.

One other point deserves to be mentioned. The algorithms used in EYEBALL can be adopted to other natural languages, since many other languages have function-word classes analogous to English. One early trial with Old Provençal got to the point of deciding on a dictionary (with spelling variants included) and getting a sample text through the first steps of SYNTAX. An absence of research assistance and time has put this promising start into abeyance for the time being. Nothing has thus far suggested that a significant problem exists with this application.

Language descriptions of the sort developed by EYEBALL can be the basis of objective studies of style. While they do not present a comprehensive view of an author's language, they can make significant contributions toward understanding an author's style. Since studies which use the program produce comparable results, each new study can effectively build on earlier ones. The augmented texts contain cross-classified data which have only begun to be explored. The statistical procedures tested so far are by no means the only appropriate ones. Continued attempts to make the programs more convenient, or expand the data, and to test new approaches to analysis should improve studies of style in the future.

Acknowledgments

EYEBALL has been supported by the computer centers at the University of Pennsylvania (1969–1971), Michigan State University (1972–   ), and, most generously, the University of Minnesota (1971–   ), where support has also come from the graduate school and English department. The chief programmer has been Robert H. Rasche. Additional help has come from student research assistants Jeanine Budnicki and Monica Evans and from users of the programs, William Baillie, Robert Dilligan, Lue Hawk, Elizabeth Sikes, Mary Beth Pringle, Gordon Wood, Joseph Jaynes, Richard Bailey, Richard Brengle, and others.

Notes

1. Donald Ross, Jr., "The Use of Word-Class Distribution Data for Stylistics: Keats's Sonnets and Chicken Soup," *Poetics* 6(1977):169–196.

2. Donald Ross, Jr., and S. Keith Lee., "Statistical Methods of the Distribution of Monosyllabic and Polysyllabic English Words," in *Statistical Methods in Linguistics* (Stockholm, Sweden: Språkförlaget Skriptor, 1975), pp. 51–63.

3. Donald Ross, Jr., "Skimming the Surface: Improvements in the Quality of Syntactic Descriptions for Stylistics," (Leuvin, Netherlands: Institute for Applied Linguistics, in press).

4. Robert Cluett, *Prose Style and Critical Reading* (New York: Teachers College Press, 1976).

5. Donald Ross, Jr., "Stylistics and the Testing of Literary Hypotheses," *Poetics,* 7(1978):389–416.

6. Joseph Jaynes, "A Search for Trends in the Poetic Style of W.B. Yeats," *Journal of the ALLC* 1(1980).

Bibliography

Bailey, Richard W. "Authorship Attribution in a Forensic Setting." In *Advances in Computer-Aided Literary and Linguistic Research,* edited by D.E. Ager, F.E. Knowles, and Joan Smith. Birmingham: Department of Modern Languages, University of Aston in Birmingham, 1979, pp. 1–20.

Baillie, William. "Authorship Attribution in Jacobean Dramatic Texts." In *Computers in the Humanities,* edited by J.L. Mitchell. Edinburgh: University of Edinburgh Press, 1974, pp. 73–81.

Ferguson, A.T., and O'Neil, Stephen, eds. *Karl Marx, Frederich Engels: The Collected Writings.* New York: Precedent Publishers, 1973. (Programs used for attribution of articles.)

Rasche, Robert H. "FORTRAN as a Medium for Language Analysis." In *Computers in the Humanities.* edited by J.L. Mitchell. Edinburgh: University of Edinburgh Press, 1974, pp. 250–257.

Ross, Donald, Jr., "Beyond the Concordance: Algorithms for the Description of English Clauses and Phrases." In *The Computer and Literary Studies,* edited by A.J. Aitken, R.W. Bailey, and Neil Hamilton-Smith. Edinburgh: University of Edinburgh Press, 1973, pp. 85–99.

——— "Computer-Aided Study of Literature." *Computer* 11, no. 8 (August 1978):32–39.

——— "Differences, Genres, and Influences." *Style* 11(1977):262–273.

——— "Structural Elements in Keats's Sonnets and Odes." *Cahiers de Lexicologie* 31, no. 2(1977):95–117.

Ross, Donald, Jr., and Pringle, Mary Beth. "Dialogue and Narration in Joyce's *Ulysses.*" In *Computing in the Humanities,* edited by Serge Lusignan and John S. North. Waterloo, Ont.: University of Waterloo Press, 1977, pp. 73–84.

Ross, Donald, Jr., and Rasche, Robert H. "EYEBALL: A Computer Program for Description of Style." *Computers and the Humanities* 6(1972):213–221.

Dissertations

Pringle, Mary Beth. "A Stylistic Analysis of Dialogue and Narrative Modes in Joyce's *Ulysses.*" University of Minnesota, 1976.

Sikes, Elizabeth. "Conrad's Conscious Artistry: A Computer Assisted Exploration of Style in 'Heart of Darkness.'" University of South Carolina, 1976.

Documentation and Technical Reports

"Description for EYEBALL." Mimeographed. English Department, University of Minnesota, 1973, rev. 1976, 1979.

"OXEYE: A Text Processing Package for the 1906A." Oxford University, 1977.

"Prepositional Phrase Lengths." Mimeographed. English Department, University of Minnesota, 1976.

"Repetition of Vocabulary in Short Poems and Samples." Mimeographed. English Department, University of Minnesota, 1976.

"User's Instructions for EYEBALL." Mimeographed. English Department, University of Minnesota, rev. 1976, 1980.

"Word Length Data and Analysis." Mimeographed. English Department, University of Minnesota, 1975.

Unpublished Conference Papers

Dilligan, Robert. "Measured Language: A Computational Analysis of Tennyson's 'In Memoriam,'" Fourth Symposium on the Use of Computers in Literary Research, Oxford, England, 1976.

Hawk, Lue. "A Comparison, Based on Quantitative Analysis of Conrad's Style in 'Heart of Darkness' and 'The Secret Agent,'" First International Conference on Computers and the Humanities, Minneapolis, Minnesota, 1973.

Pringle, Mary Beth. "Funfersum: Dialogue as Metafictional Technique in the 'Cyclops' Episode of Joyce's *Ulysses.*" Fourth International Conference on Computers in the Humanities, Hanover, N.H., 1979.

Ross, Donald, Jr. "Toward a Definition of 'Sonnet': Computer-Aided Description of Keats's Sonnets." Midwest Modern Language Association, 1973.

5 Computer-Aided Analysis of Old English Manuscripts

J.L. Mitchell and
Kellen C. Thornton

Records written over an extended period can be compared to expose the processes of linguistic change. Applying computer technology to such a problem in philology has produced promising results. An efficient and flexible interactive editing system called TAGEDIT has provided significant new information about texts which have already been the object of much scholarly study. The speed with which the computer handles the data, its infallibility given unambiguous instructions, and its diligence given a monumental and tedious task enhance the possibilities for understanding more of human history as evidenced in the transmission of texts.

Background

In Wessex, at the instigation of King Alfred in the ninth century, works by Paulus Orosius, the Venerable Bede, and others were translated from Latin into the vernacular, and native poetry of Northumbria and Mercia was rendered into West Saxon, the dialect generally recognized as "standard" Old English. It seems to have been in Wessex that the Anglo-Saxon Chronicle began. The significance of the Chronicle is indisputable: it is the only history of England written in the vernacular before A.D. 1200 and for some periods supplies the only available history. The Primary Compilation, which proceeded under King Alfred of Wessex, ends about A.D. 890. It derives from a short chronicle compiled at the end of the reign of Aethelwulf, itself drawn from a century of monastic annals maintained at Canterbury to the mid ninth century, from traditional oral history, and from contemporary events—for the most part affairs of the Church, although the political affairs of Wessex and occasionally Mercia are included. Alfred's scribes added thirty annals involving conflicts with the Danish as well as information drawn from Bede and additional oral tradition regarding events as far back as the beginning of the Christian era.

The Chronicle, particularly the last 180 years (annals 974 through 1154) of its documentation, codifies the creation of a large vocabulary. The style exemplifies literary advances subsequent to the tenth-century monastic revival, considered a great period in English prose writing. At first, entries are short and purely factual; but they get longer, more detailed, and even incline to interpretation in the main body of the work. The final two sections of the Chronicle describe internal distress after the Norman Conquest. An account of the black comedy of Henry of Angely's abbacy at Peterborough (1131) relieves the horror of anarchy and evil during the reign of King Stephen (1137). Although it is historically confusing, the reader obtains nonetheless an excellent grasp of what it was like to live during that time. Ultimately, French replaced English as the prestige language, and by 1154 the language of the Chronicle had evolved into something very close to Early Middle English.

The Anglo-Saxon Chronicle epitomizes the tradition whereby a religious community acquired a historical narrative by copying an available work and continuing it locally. Thus complex hybrids were produced which were, in turn, continued and copied. Local material added in the process of copying, borrowing, and recopying in another location is traditionally referred to as an "interpolation." Of course, sometimes, scribes miscopied material, and sometimes they dated items to suit their own purposes. Furthermore, omissions, erasures, and additions (some made centuries later) create real problems in determining the pedigree of a given manuscript. Seven extant manuscripts and a fragment (traditionally designated by letters of the alphabet, A through H) contain different, but often complementary, versions of the whole work.

Even by 890, several manuscripts were probably circulating. Copies were acquired by various monasteries throughout England and the Continent, but only the Peterborough abbey manuscript was maintained until 1154. The most archaic of the extant manuscripts, the Parker or "A" Chronicle, is at least two copyings removed from the prototype. The Parker is named for its donor Matthew Parker, archbishop of Canterbury (1559–1575). Written in one hand to annal 891, "A" continues in several hands to 920, after which it was removed to Winchester where it was maintained only desultorily until 1001. By 1075, "A" resided at Christ Church, Canterbury, where the scribe of the "F" Chronicle made many interpolations, even erasing passages to accommodate them. Fortunately, before "A" departed Winchester, hence before it was defaced, a copy designated "G" was made. Although virtually destroyed in the 1731 fire which burned much of the Robert Cotton manuscript collection, "G" survives in two eighteenth-century transcriptions.

Manuscripts "B" and "C," also known as the Abingdon Chronicles for their unique references to that locale, are obviously linked. Moreover, only they include annals for 957, 971, and 977, and they incorporated the Mercian Register in a block after a series of blank annals following 915. However, "B" is written in one hand and ends in 977, while "C" continues to 1066 in several hands of the eleventh century. For some reason, the "B" scribe omits annal numbers after 652 but includes the West Saxon genealogy and regnal list which prefaces "A," continuing the regnal list to Edward the Martyr (d. 978). That "C" includes all annal dates and other material and omits the genealogy and regnal list suggests a more complex relationship than simply that "C" used an archetype of "B" as exemplar.

Manuscripts "D" and "E" comprise the Northern Recension as they contain a series of Northumbrian annals (733–806) and passages from Bede which were not incorporated in the earliest versions of the Chronicle. They likely derive at least in part from some ancestor compiled at York, whence "D" or its archetype moved by 1033 to Worcester where it was continued until 1079. Until annal 1031, "D" and "E" parallel each other, although "D" has definitely lost several early folios of northern history which "E" retains, and "E" lacks numerous passages found in all other versions as well as a large amount of material on Margaret of Scotland peculiar to "D." These later discrepancies have been variously explained. Some say an early split of their archetypes from a common Northern Recension ancestor resulted in the fuller account early in "D"; others say that material was simply added to "D" much later; and another group of scholars believes "D" suggests a unification of a "C" and an "E" archetype. Regardless, "E" ceases in 1031 to be a northern version; its ancestor apparently traveled to St. Augustine's monastery in Canterbury where it was maintained at least to the Norman Conquest (1066) and possibly to 1121. There, the "F" scribe based a bilingual chronicle on "E" and copied several passages from it to "A." Then the manuscript or a copy was removed to Peterborough abbey (possibly to replace a chronicle lost in the fire of 1116), and the copy, now called "E" or the Peterborough Chronicle, was made. The initial Peterborough scribe copied through annal 1121, incorporating twenty items of local interest known as the Peterborough Interpolations. He then entered new annals through 1131. Around 1155, a second scribe filled in the next twenty-four years. Finally, through the sixteenth century, various scribes annotated and underlined the manuscript.

The short, bilingual chronicle "F" has already been mentioned. The copy of "A" is known as "G." A fragment called "H" covers events from 1113 to 1114 contained nowhere else. That other versions existed is apparent, considering frequent references in works by Asser (ninth century), Aethelweard (tenth century), Florence of Worcester (twelfth century), William of Malmesbury (twelfth century), Henry of Huntington, Simeon of Durham, Hugh Candidus (twelfth-century chronicler of Peterborough), and others. Considering the devastation wrought by Viking attacks on monasteries and the deliberate destruction of manuscript material during the dissolution of the monasteries in the time of Henry VIII, it is fortunate that so many manuscripts survived.

The Problem

What remains is seven often contradictory, largely anonymous contributions to the history of Anglo-Saxon England. The historical sketch above only suggests the extreme complexity of relationships among the versions of the Anglo-Saxon Chronicle. Scholars have attempted to elucidate the plethora of discrepancies and similarities. Handwriting has been examined in an attempt to obtain information about the textual history. Each scribe's word choices and alterations during copying provide evidence as to time and place of compilation. Even the examination of secondary sources can be enlightening. For instance, the work attributed to Florence of Worcester contains references to the reign of Edward the Elder which can be found only in the "A" text and its copy "G." However, he did not use "G" because he writes *Maneceaster* (Manchester) regarding annal 920 rather than *Manige Ceaster,* which is the appelation in "G." So there are differences, and it could very well be that "G" is copied from an earlier "A" version, rather than the one which produced the existing "A."

Lexical variation, then, has been studied, especially by Cecily Clark [3], although much remains to be done. The circuitous paths by which each version of the Chronicle reached its final form might, for instance, be traced more fully. However, only a detailed analysis of each text will reveal patterns of lexical distribution, and such a comparison has proved too arduous a task to do manually.

The manuscripts have been studied by many scholars, without absolute agreement on such questions as the number of scribes involved, the history of transmission, and so on. For example, Clark, in her discussion of the vocabulary of the Peterborough Chronicle, says that in the so-called Final Continuation written in Peterborough, "the chief, almost the only, Anglian trait of vocabulary to be discerned here is the use of *in* where West Saxon would have had *on*" [3, p. 70]. Yet Plummer [6] reported that the tendency to use *in* for *on* distinguishes "A" from "E" and from other Chronicle manuscripts. Since "A" is almost certainly a Winchester (West Saxon) manuscript, which never went further than Christ Church, Canterbury, the inference is that *in* is a West Saxon trait. From a distributional point of view, it is important to note that Clark's observation referred to the extension of the Anglo-Saxon Chronicle found only in "E," running from 1132 to 1154. Plummer's comments, on the other hand, are couched in very general terms, but are definitely valid for those passages common to both "A" and "E" [5]. Only an exhaustive study of *in* and *on* in both manuscripts can, however, show the distributional complexity of these forms.

Methodology

For the purposes of this chapter, the discussion is restricted to the results obtained from work done on a single problem. The problem involves the distribution of lexical variants of Old English *cyning* (from which comes the Modern English *king*) in the Parker ("A") and Peterborough ("E") versions. But if a computer were to perform the task of searching the texts for the variations on *cyning,* a program had to be developed which could handle Old English and could distinguish between variants. The result was a language-independent interactive editing system called TAGEDIT. For a more thorough explanation of the computer program, see chapter 8.

First, the manuscripts were stored in the computer. Each symbol or letter was encoded to conform to the limitations of the keyboard. The second step established exactly what the variants were. Since *cyning* and a variant *kyning* are Old English relatives of Old Saxon *kuning,* Old High German *kunig,* and Old Norse *konungr,* polysyllabic and monosyllabic bases (for example, *cyning* and *cyng*), *c*-forms and *k*-forms (for example, *cyning* and *cining*), and both rounded and unrounded stem vowels (for example, *cyning* and *cining*) were expected. After consulting Plummer's glossary and doing some experimentation, we instructed the computer to search both manuscripts for the following patterns: *cyn-g-, cin-g-, kyn-g-,* and *kin-g-* where any symbol (letter), or symbols, or no symbol is permitted to replace the hyphens.

A total of 925 occurrences and nine variants was uncovered in the approximately 50,000-word Peterborough Chronicle. In the Parker version of around 30,000 words, eight variants occur among 254 total occurrences. In one form or another, *cyning* is the single noun of greatest frequency in both texts. One pattern *cin-g-* returned ten different variations: *cing, -a, -es, cining, -a, -as, -e, -es,* and the rare *cinigas, -es.* Almost inevitably a few unwanted terms are netted. In this case, they were both proper nouns— *Cynegils* (also *Kynegils*), the first Christian West Saxon king, and *Kyneburg,* one of the endowers of the monastic establishment at Medeshamsted or Peterborough. But these names were easily deleted from the subconcordance.

Computer-generated concordances to large texts are normally produced in one of two formats: some kind of alphabetical order specified by the user or order of occurrence. But the ability to produce an interactive subconcordance allows one to obtain results in both formats. For this Chronicle project, a list of variants in order of occurrence determined by the date of an annal was needed to help locate overlapping and discrete sets. In addition, with close to 1,000 occurrences of nine variants of *cyning,* an alphabetical list proved valuable in bringing together like forms of a word and in highlighting unusual patterns.

Results

In order to reveal underlying distributional patterns in "E," it was necessary to separate the Peterborough Interpolation from the copied annals (entries up to the end of 1121) and from the Peterborough Continuations (annals 1122 through 1154). The two forms of highest frequency, *cyng* occurring 480 times and *cining* occurring 160, were found to be all but mutually exclusive, although the first occurrence of *cyng* (annal 874) overlaps with the last occurrence of *cining* (annal 875). Such a clear-cut division of high-frequency forms can hardly be accidental and strongly suggests the previously unrecognized juncture between two independent sources. Therefore, even the homogeneity of the copied annals to 1121 can no longer be safely assumed.

Rather puzzling in light of these findings is the claim by Clark that in the copied annals Old English y is typically represented in late West Saxon with regular y, except for a few examples, such as *cing, kinehelm, gescrid,* where palatal unrounding is probable [3]. Discounting the *k-* forms, however, which, with one exception (*kining* in 603) are absent from the copied annals, 177 out of 726 forms (roughly 25 percent) are unrounded, hardly an insignificant percentage. Until other linguistic features with a similar pattern of distribution are identified, possible dialect affiliations can only be surmised. Given that "E" represents a version of the Northern Recension, one could make a case for the unrounded variant *cining* being Anglian in origin. Campbell [1, sect. 315] says that *cining* is frequent in one version of the Rushworth glosses (Ru2), and *kining* in the other (Ru1).

The *k-* forms comprise another more or less discrete set. Apart from the exception just mentioned, *k-* forms are found exclusively in the Peterborough Interpolations and in the Peterborough Continuations. Further subdivisions are discernible: polysyllabic variants (*kyning, kining*) are confined to the early interpolated passages (annals 654 through 777), while monosyllabic variants (*kyng, king*) are common to both the Interpolations and to the Continuations. The terms *kyng* and *king* occur side by side throughout the First Continuation (annals 1122 to 1131), but *king* alone is found in the Final Continuation (annals 1131 to 1134). Even where *kyng* and *king* coexist, the pattern of distribution suggests something more than free variation. In some annals we only find *king* (annal 1122, one occurrence; annal 1124, eleven; annal 1125, three) and in others only *kyng* (annal 1129, nine; annal 1131, two).

The suspicion inevitably arises that this is not just the work of one man, as Clark [3, p. xxv] argues mainly on stylistic grounds. Yet the single-scribe hypothesis is resolutely maintained by all contemporary authorities [4, 8] in spite of the changes of ink, handwriting, and even abbreviatory conventions manifest in the First Continuation. The accepted explanation of these admitted differences is that the First Continuation was composed in six blocks over a period of years, more or less as events took place. But the attractive picture of the Chronicle here "being composed before our eyes" [3, p. xxv] may have to yield to a more mundane explanation: the scribe did not compose the entries himself, but merely copied them from existing records. The variation between *kyng* and *king* and the differences in abbreviatory convention could then be attributed to the scribe's use of more than one exemplar. Alternatively, the judgment of Plummer [6, p. xxv] that a number of scribes worked on the First Continuation would account for the peculiar distribution of *kyng* and *king* in terms of differences in scribal practice.

The contrast between "E" and "A" in terms of the distribution of *cyning* variants is quite marked. The standard *cyning* represents, counting even interpolated forms, slightly less than 8 percent (71/926) of the forms in "E"; and its occurrence in only the copied annals strongly suggests that it is a residual form. In "A," on the other hand, *cyning* is overwhelmingly the majority form at 76 percent (192/254). This homogeneity of "A" is quite surprising since between five and eight scribes were involved in its compilation. The first scribe, however, was responsible for most of the entries (his work extends from the beginning through annal 891 to the foot of folio 16a), and he almost always wrote *cyning*. Only 11 times out of 153 did he use a different form: *kyning* (9), *cyng* (2). These variants are widely distributed and may well reflect an earlier stage of textual transmission. Support for such a possibility can be found in the opinion of Sweet [7] who says the use of *k* for *c*, as in *kyning*, was an "archaism" in the Hatton 20 manuscript (Hat) of the Alfredian translation of Gregory's *Cura Pastoralis*. As a matter of fact, *k-* forms are even more prevalent in the fragmentary Cotton Tiberius Bxi manuscript (Cot) of Alfred's prefatory letter than they are in the Hatton version (for example, Cot = *kyning, kytan, Angelkynn;* Hat = *kyning, cytan, Angelcynn*). It is therefore significant that Cot is probably nearest of all to Alfred's first draft [2, p. 179]. Further evidence may be adduced from the "Ohthere and Wulfstan" insertion in the Cotton Tiberius Bi manuscript of the Old English *Orosius:* just as in the "A" manuscript of the Chronicle, *k-* forms are in the minority beside *c-* forms.

The shortest but the most complex section of the Parker manuscript extends from annals 891 to 1070. Sometime early in the eleventh century, the manuscript was removed to Christ Church, Canterbury, and it is therefore to a Canterbury scribe that the discrete set of *king* forms (annals 1017, 1040, 1042, 1043, and 1066) should be credited. However, the annals from 891 to 1001 were the work of at least four scribes, and they show a corresponding diversity of variants. The standard form *cyning* (fifty occurrences) still predominates, but the syncopated variants *cyng* (thirty-five occurrences) and *cing* (seventy occurrences) are much in evidence.

Acknowledgments

The senior author wishes to express his gratitude to the Graduate School, University of Minnesota, for supporting this research with a number of grants; and to Peter C. Patton, director of the University Computer Center, for his interest, encouragement, and generous provision of computer time. All programming for TAGEDIT was done by Eric E. Inman of the University Computer Center.

References

1. Campbell, A. *Old English Grammar.* Oxford: Oxford University Press, 1959.
2. Cassidy, F.A., and Rigler, R.N. *Bright's Old English Grammar and Reader.* New York: Holt, Rinehart and Winston, 1971.
3. Clark, C. ed. *The Peterborough Chronicle, 1070–1154.* 2d ed. Oxford: Oxford University Press, 1970.
4. Ker, N.R. *Catalogue of Manuscripts Containing Anglo-Saxon.* Oxford: Oxford University Press, 1975.
5. Mitchell, J.L., ed. "The Language of the Peterborough Chronicle." In *Computers in the Humanities,* pp. 132–145. Edinburgh: Edinburgh University Press, 1974.
6. Plummer, C.J., ed. *Two of the Saxon Chronicles Parallel.* 2 vols. Oxford: Oxford University Press, 1892–1899.
7. Sweet, H. *King Alfred's West-Saxon Version of Gregory's Pastoral Care.* London: Early English Text Society, 1871.
8. Whitelock, D., ed. *The Peterborough Chronicle.* Copenhagen: Rosenkilde and Bagger, 1954.

Bibliography

Bratley, P.; Lusignan, S.; Ouellette, Francine. "JEUDEMO: A Text-Handling System." In *Computers in the Humanities,* edited by J.L. Mitchell, pp. 234–249. Edinburgh: Edinburgh University Press, 1974.
Dolby, J.L., and Resnikoff, H.L., eds. *The English Word Speculum.* The Hague: Mouton and Co., 1964.
Greene, B.B., and Rubin, G.M. "Automatic Grammatical Tagging of English." Providence, R.I.: Department of Linguistics, Brown University, 1971.
Kucera, H., and Francis, W.M. *Computational Analysis of Present-Day American English.* Providence, R.I.: Brown University Press, 1967.
Whitelock, D., ed. *The Anglo-Saxon Chronicle.* New Brunswick, N.J.: Rutgers University Press, 1961.
Wrenn, C.L. *Beowulf.* Rev. by W.F. Bolton. New York: St. Martin's Press, 1973.

Form Analysis of Mishnaic Sentences

Roger Brooks and
Tzvee Zahavy

This chapter describes a pilot project designed to study sentence forms, employing linguistic tagging as the first stage of rigorous formal analysis of Mishnah. In this chapter we first describe the character and provenance of Mishnah and then outline the current status of the study of Mishnaic sentence forms in the relevant scholarly literature. Later, the focus is on the specific problem within this context which will be addressed and finally on the methodology initiated to solve the problem.

Mishnah is a third-century A.D. Middle Hebrew corpus of rules for religious rituals and of civil and criminal law. It is a collective work containing statements attributed to authorities (called in the work "rabbis") who lived in the first and second centuries. Alongside these assigned statements are anonymous laws presented without specific attribution to any individual master. A single authority or school edited Mishnah at the beginning of the third century A.D. Thereafter, Mishnah became the central normative source of regulation for the ritual and thought of rabbinic Judaism. Later rabbis claimed that Mishnah was divinely inspired. In fact, they said that God taught Mishnah to Moses on Mount Sinai along with the laws of the Pentateuch (the first five books of the Old Testament). Until this century Mishnah was valued by rabbinic Jews as source of divine guidance. The study of Mishnah was, moreover, a religious ritual, and Mishnah's rules and ideas governed proper religious practice and thought. Recent research adds a humanistic dimension to the theological value of Mishnah. In the past generation, scholars in the academic study of religion have used Mishnah as a source for data relevant to the history of Judaic thought and practice.

While Mishnah's topics and ideas naturally provide important information about rabbinic intellectual history, the main focus of this chapter is not on substance, but on a second facet of the Mishnaic evidence, that of its literary form. Research has shown that Mishnah is written in tightly controlled syntactic forms. This project will facilitate the careful identification and differentiation of Mishnah's forms. This analysis is important for several reasons. First, the interpretation or exegesis of Mishnah often depends on the ability of the reader to associate groups of sentences or phrases as coherent units of the text. A text's content is usually enough to rely on for this process; in ambiguous situations, however, sentence form often provides decisive evidence. For instance, if a phrase or sentence uses forms similar to phrases which precede it but markedly different from sentences which follow, that unit "belongs" with the preceding and must be interpreted accordingly. Thus the first use of form analysis is for division of the text into coherent formal units. Second, examination of formal characteristics of the text will reveal defective formal units (for example, incomplete sentences, lists, and so on). This will also assist in the substantive exegesis of the text. Third, and most important for reconstruction of the history of Mishnah's text, detailed form analysis may enable us to propose a "higher-critical" theory of Mishnah. That is as follows. Since Mishnah is the product of editorial processes, rather than the work of a single rabbi or school, it is a collection of different sources. Through form analysis we may be able to identify special characteristics of units of the text. On that basis we may hypothesize several distinct literary "sources" for Mishnah.

The Problem

This project makes use of the results of recent scholarship on Mishnah and carries it forward. Neusner has distinguished several literary forms in Mishnah.[1] Among those forms are disputes (authority X says such and such, authority Y says so and so, contrary to X), lists of items or rulings, and various types of declarative sentences (subject/predicate, duplicated subject, apocopated, and so forth). Neusner,[2] Porton, Zahavy, and others have shown the value of form analysis for exegesis of the text. But in research to date, the categorizing of syntactic forms has not been entirely rigorous. Sometimes all declarative sentences are considered one formal type. Often different scholars use varying categories of form or conflicting labels to identify similar structures. Our first concern, then, is to make more rigorous and subtle the identification and classification of Mishnah's syntactic structures. The meaning of this and the reasons for employing the computer in this process are spelled out below.

The second concern in this chapter, one previously alluded to, is to use the results of sound form analysis to explore the possible formulation of a "documentary hypothesis" for Mishnah. Such analysis would consider whether different literary parts of units of Mishnah point to the existence of distinct pre-editorial documents drawn together by Mishnah's editors in A.D. 200. This inquiry is expected to produce mainly negative results. Most recent research shows that Mishnah's editors significantly revised the forms of earlier material, thus obliterating most distinctive literary characteristics of earlier texts. However, positive results in this inquiry would greatly increase knowledge of the development of Mishnah. It is therefore of significant value to investigate this question by using the new and improved data produced with this research.

Moreover, this inquiry is related to other research into ancient collective literature (for example, the Tanakh or Hebrew Bible, and especially the Pentateuch; the New Testament; the Apocrypha and Pseudepigrapha; other books of rabbinic literature). Scholars dealing with the Hebrew Bible, for instance, have investigated numerous literary critical issues of the text with respect to sentence forms of biblical Hebrew. Inquiry into the history and origin of forms in the text, moreover, itself constitutes a coherent field of investigation often referred to as form criticism. Further attempts to separate the strands of textual material woven together by later redactors fall into the larger field of study known as redaction criticism. Almost identical concerns present themselves in disciplines which study the New Testament literature. New methodology for classifying Hebrew sentence forms and new standards of judging redactional strata would certainly be useful to scholars in these related disciplines.

As the work progressed, the scope of this project narrowed. The factors which constricted initial ambitious goals may be informative to scholars in many disciplines. In particular, the significant disparity between initial goals (above) and ultimate achievements in this pilot project (below) is noted here. Our experience should serve as a caution to others who undertake this kind of methodology in research. The amount of preliminary work needed to make the texts accessible to the computer was found to be a significant obstacle. The complexity of adapting existing programs to fit new analytical goals was a second hurdle. As a result, for the present, this methodology can be used to supplement, but not replace, the slower, somewhat impressionistic and more prosaic manual methods for analyzing texts. Evaluation of the success of this project as limited is perhaps the most instructive aspect of this research. The reasons for these ultimate cautions are spelled out in the following description of the methodology used.

Methodology

The approach to the problem of identifying sentence types or what are loosely called literary forms was as follows. Since sentences are patterns of words, the first task was to develop a mode of identifying a sentence type by classifying the components (words) and their sequential pattern. This pattern is something less than a syntactic description, but it is nonetheless useful. For instance, the pattern of some simple sentences would be described as noun-verb-noun rather than subject-verb-object. This retreat from syntax to morphology was a major movement away from the precise categorization originally sought, but part of the value of the project was judged to be in its ability to utilize software currently available on the Cyber 74 computer at the University of Minnesota Computer Center. This was, in retrospect, a misjudgment. The grammatical characteristics of words were identified; but before the initial goals outlined above could be attained, this work had to be set aside. There was instead some success at designing a method of assigning coded grammatical information (tags) to words of the text, with the assistance of available programs, and the initiation of the first stage of the analysis. This mode of tagging words with grammatical data was tested for a sample of Mishnaic texts taken from the first chapter of Mishnah.

The specific methodology of the actual project was to apply the above approach to samples of Mishnah varying in size from 20 to 100 lines of text. A comparison of these processes with those of the initial research project statement shows significant disparity, which is explained below. First, consider a description of each stage of the actual project, which consisted finally of five stages:

1. Transliteration of Hebrew text into machine-readable code
2. Error identification and data verification
3. Concordance analysis
4. Defining a set of grammatical date "tags" for Mishnaic Hebrew
5. Linguistic analysis

1. The Hebrew alphabet consists of twenty-three graphemes, each of which was represented by a distinctive Latin grapheme. For the present instance, this proved to be the most economical means of representing the alphabet. For a major project using Hebrew texts, acquisition of the necessary hardware and software to allow for use of the Hebrew alphabet without transliteration would be desirable. See Appendix 6A for the transliteration key employed here. (Note that Hebrew reads from right to left, but the transliterated texts read from left to right.) The text was entered with reference codes or pointers to its place in Mishnah (for example, M1:1A = first chapter, first paragraph, first phrase of Mishnah).

2. Once the text was entered into the computer, the UCC program XEDIT facilitated verification and editing of the data. The XEDIT program is interactive so that the text was edited line by line at an output location (either CRT or printer) to correct both typographical and transliterational errors. At this point, all particles normally attached to the beginning of Hebrew words, including the definite article, prepositions, and so on, were separated by XEDIT.

3. A concordance of words in the text was generated by utilizing the UCC GENCORD program. A key word in context (KWIC) concordance was useful for two reasons: It enabled checking for further errors, and the display of all words of the text in concordance form provided data necessary for stages 4 and 5, as explained below. The concording stage of the project was not necessary, but it was undertaken because of the ease of

implementation using GENCORD and because of its potential value in saving time and rechecking results. For larger text samples where the cost of concording may be significant, this stage could be eliminated.

4. The major stage of this project was, in the final analysis, the exercise in tagging the text. Tagging is simply the process of associating a set of code words to a word in the literal text. A tagged word of a Mishnaic text looks like the following:

M1:1I	BYT	[location in text]
PRT	NOUN	[part of speech]
TYPE	COMMON	[see Appendix 6B]
GEND	MASCULINE	[gender]
NUMB	SINGULAR	[number]
PERS		[person]
STATE	CONSTRUCT	[see Appendix 6B]

Figure 6-1. Tagged Word of a Mishnaic Text

The word to be tagged is *byt* (house of). Tags arranged beneath the word identify it as a singular common noun, masculine (Hebrew nouns have gender), in the construct state, thus describing the grammatical data of this word. The aim was to tag each word in the text and then to specify and find patterns of words or sentence forms. While the ultimate goal was to solve the problem of rigorously defining sentence types in Mishnah, for this project only the initial stage of this larger analytical problem was reached, in which a method was devised for assigning grammatical information to words in Mishnaic texts. The information assigned is basic: part of speech, type, gender, number, person, state. Each of these categories is called a *tag field*. Several options for tags are available in each field. A fully tagged word, as shown above, provides the researcher with enough morphological information to do further linguistic analysis. Appendix 6B lists all tags used in this chapter (based on the standard *Grammar of Mishnaic Hebrew*). Appendix 6C shows the sample text fully tagged line by line.

5. The linguistic analysis in this project was modest, but significant. The researchers used a program called TAGEDIT, also reported in chapter 8, to speed the process of tagging the text with grammatical data. For a sample of twenty-two lines of Mishnah, the researchers began by proposing patterns of letters to be tagged. The outline of a simple tagging operation follows. Return to the example shown earlier, the word *byt*. The researchers proposed a set of tags as shown. In the sixth tagging field this word is

identified to be in the construct state (*house of banquet* in the text). But the
same pattern of letters may represent the absolute state (simply *house*). The
researchers, perhaps having forgotten for the moment the latter fact,
entered at the terminal via use of TAGEDIT the tags for *byt*. Figure 6–2
shows the actual process of tagging. First the type of input must be specified, since different texts follow different formats (for example, texts are
accompanied by different types of line designators). Punctuation is defined
next. The number of tags is then specified. For the six tags of this sample,
identifiers are entered. These appear in the margin of each tagged line of
printout. Once the text is printed with line numbers, the researcher then
enters the tagging mode, identifies the pattern, and lists its tags. The
program then prints all occurrences of the pattern. If an erroneous tag is
assigned, it is at this stage that the researcher may change it. For instance,
return to the sample of the tagging process; *byt* may appear in both
construct and absolute forms, and some distinction must be made. If the
tagging pattern of the researcher is accurate, unambiguous, and applicable
to all cases, the program tags each occurrence. For example, all instances of
the definite article are tagged in one operation (see figure 6–3). More clever
tagging patterns may label more words with a single command. *L-W-* (the
hyphen allows for any letter) is a pattern repeated in simple verb infinitives.
Figure 6–4 shows how such a pattern is found and tagged.

Results

The final results of this pilot project were as follows. The object was a
Mishnah text of 126 lexemes (that is, words, including particles). This small
sample constituted less than 1 percent of existing Mishnah texts. The
researchers successfully tagged this text with only fifty patterns (see
Appendix 6B) and from this test case extrapolated that the tagging of all
Mishnah (over 100,000 lexemes) could be accomplished with rapidity by
using the methods described here. As more patterns are defined, repetitive
characteristics in the literature will be automatically tagged. The researchers
estimate they could tag 95 percent or more of Mishnaic texts with but
several hundred different patterns identified and tags established for each
pattern. The research could then proceed to the solution of the initial goals
of this project. TAGEDIT would conceivably assist in defining sentence
patterns based on individual tagged elements of a text, and these patterns
would be studied as hypothetical archetypes of Mishnaic sentences. From
that point the researchers would proceed to solve some more general and
far-ranging scholarly problems based on the entire set of evidence before
them.

```
WHAT TYPE OF INPUT TEXT ARE YOU USING>

  1:   FREE FORMAT TEXT.
  2:   COLUMN FORMATTED TEXT.
  3:   MISHNAIC TEXT.
  4:   GODEAIC TEXT.

3
WHAT CHARACTERS ARE USED FOR PUNCTUATION IN THE TEXT^>^
.,:;-^>^
WHICH PUNCTUATION CHARACTERS CAN ONLY PRECEED A WORD^>^
(NOTE - NONE ENTERED)
WHICH PUNCTUATION CHARACTERS CAN CNLY FOLLOW A WORD^>^
.,:^>^;-
HOW MANY TAGS WILL YOU HAVE FOR EACH WORD IN THE TEXT^>^
6
ENTER THE IDENTIFIER FOR TAG 1.
PRT
ENTER THE IDENTIFIER FOR TAG 2.
TYPE
ENTER THE IDENTIFIER FOR TAG 3.
GEND
ENTER THE IDENTIFIER FOR TAG 4.
NUMB
ENTER THE IDENTIFIER FOR TAG 5.
PERS
ENTER THE IDENTIFIER FOR TAG 6.
STATE
ENTER COMMAND.
PWLN*          (I.E., PRINT WITH LINE NUMBERS)

 1   M.1.1A.   M AYMTY QWRYN AT FMO B ORBYT
 2   M.1.1B.   M FOH F H KHNYM NKNSYM L AKWL B TRWMTN
 3   M.1.1C.   OD SWP H AFMWRH H RAFWNH
 4   M.1.1D.   DBRY RBY ALYOZR
 5   M.1.1E.   W EKMYM AMMRYN
 6   M.1.1F.   OD LCWT
 7   M.1.1G.   RBN GMLYAL AWMR
 8   M.1.1H.   OD F YOLH OMWD H FER
 9   M.1.1I.   MOVH F BAM BNYW M BYT H MFTH
10   M.1.1J.   AMRW LH
11   M.1.1K.   LA QRYNW AT FMO
```

Figure 6-2. The Tagging Process

```
12    M.1.1L.    AMR LHM
13    M.1.1M.    AM LA OLH OMWD H FER
14    M.1.1N.    EYBYN ATH L QRWT
15    M.1.1O.    W LA ZW BLBD
16    M.1.1P.    ALA KL MH F AMRW EKMYM OD ECWT MCWTN OD F YOLH OMWD H FER
17    M.1.1Q.    HQJR ELBYM W ABRYM
18    M.1.1R.    MCWTN OD F YOLH OMWD H FER
19    M.1.1S.    W KL H NAKLYM L YWM AED
20    M.1.1T.    MCWTN OD F YOLH OMWD H FER
21    M.1.1U.    AM KN LWH AMRW EKMYM OD ECWT
22    M.1.1V.    KDY L HREYQ AT H ADM MW H OBRH
ENTER COMMAND
^M    (I.E., MODE)
DO YOU WISH TO CONCORD, TAG OR BOTH^>^
TAG
ENTER PATTERN
(M,K,L,B)  (NOTE: THESE ARE THE PARTICLES IN OUR SAMPLE: THE "PATTERN" THEN IS ONE CHARACTER)
ENTER TAGS.
A.PRT=FUNCTION:TYPE=PREP.2.PRT=FUNCTION:TYPE=PREP.3.PRT=FUNCTION:TYPE=P=FUNCTION:TYPE=PREP.
M.1.1A.                    M AYMTY QWRYN AT FMO B ORBYT M FOH F H KHNYM
M.1.1A.        M AYMTY QWRYN AT F O B ORBYT N FOH F H KHNYM NKNSYM L AKWL B TRWMTN
M.1.1A.        ORBYT M FOH F H KHNYM NKNSYM L AKWL B TRWMTN OD SWP
M.1.1B.    M FOH F H KHNYM NKNSY^ L AKWL B TRWMTN OD SWP H AFMWRH H RAFWNH DRBY RBY ALYOZR
```

Figure 6-2 continued

```
^M
DO YOU WISH TO CONCORD, TAG, OR BOTH>
TAG
ENTER PATTERN
H (I.E., THE "PATTERN" IS AGAIN ONE CHARACTER)
ENTER TAGS.
1.PRT=FUNCTION:TYPE=ARTICLE.
M.1.1A.   QMRYN AT FMO R ORBYT M FOH F H KHNYM NKNSYM L AKHL B TRMMIN OD SWP H AFMMRH
M.1.1B.   NKNSYM L AKWL R TRMMTN OD SWP H AFMMRH H RAFMNH DBRY RBY ALYOZR W EKMYM AMMRYN
M.1.1B.   AKWL R TRMMIN OD SWP H AFMMRH H RAFMNH DBRY RBY ALYOZR W EKMYM AMMRYN OD ECMT
M.1.1G.   GMLYAL AMMR OD F YOLH OMMD H FER MOVH F BAM BNYM M BYT H MFTH AMRM LW LA
M.1.1H.   H FER MOVH F BAM BNYM M BYT H MFTH AMRM LW LA QRYNM AT FMO AMR LHM AM LA
M.1.1K.   AT FMO AMR LHM AM LA OLH OMMD H FER EYBYN ATM L QRMT W LA ZQ BLBD ALA KL MH
M.1.1P.   OD ECMT MCWIN OD F YOLH OMMD H FER HQJR ELBYM W ABRYM MCWIN OD F YOLH OMMD
M.1.1Q.   W ABRYM MCWTN OD F YOLH OMMD H FER W KL H NAKLYM L YMH AED MCWIN OD F YOLH
M.1.1R.   OD F YOLH OMMD H FER W KL H NAKLYM L YMH AED MCWIN OD F YOLH OMMD H FER
M.1.1S.   YMH AED MCWIN OD F YOLH OMMD H FER AM KN LMH AMRM EDMYM OD ECMT KDY L HREYQ
M.1.1U.   EKMYM OD ECMT KDY L HREYQ AT H ADM MN H OBRH
M.1.1U.   FCMT KDY L HREYQ AT H ADM MN H OBRH
ENTER COMMAND.
```

Figure 6-3. Tagging All Occurrences of a Particular Form

```
^M
DO YOU WISH TO CONCORD, TAG OR BOTH>
TAG
ENTER PATTERN
L -W-  (I.E., HERE THE "PATTERN" IS MORE COMPLEX -- FOUR CHARACTERS)
ENTER TAGS.
2.PRT=VERB:TYPE=QAL:STATE=INFINITIVE.
M.1.1A.   ORBYT M FOH F H KHNUM NKNSYM L AKWL B TRMMTN OD SWP H AFMMRH H RAFMNH DBRY
M.1.1M.   LA OLH OMMD H FER EYBYN ATM L QRMT W LA ZM BLBD ALA KL MH F AMRW EKMYM OD
M.1.1R.   YOLH OMMD H FER W KL H NAKLYM L YMH AED MCWTN OD F YOLH OMMD H FER AM KN LMH
```

Figure 6-4. Locating and Tagging a Pattern

For the present, research evolving from this pilot project has been slowed. Real factors of time and cost have entered in to divert our interests. Beyond personal time pressures, though, costs of computer time and research assistants must be considered before proceeding further. The estimated cost of this limited project was modest, but entering, tagging, and concording all Mishnah would cost several thousand dollars. Should the project continue as planned within the next few years, funding will be sought from various sources, including the University of Minnesota, national scholarly funding sources, and government agencies.

It is our conviction that certain issues in humanistic scholarship are amenable to rigorous solution via computer applications. This project suggests one type of issue in linguistic research which may be solved by computer assistance, that is, the study of sentence types in corporate Middle Hebrew Mishnaic texts. During a research leave, one researcher on this project examined other current projects which apply computer assistance to the study of the literature of rabbinic Judaism. Some large projects are currently underway in Israel. At Bar Ilan University in Ramat Gan, a major information-retrieval project for rabbinic texts has been undertaken. At the Academy for the Hebrew Language in Jerusalem, a long-term historical dictionary of the Hebrew language utilizes the most current computer technology for everything from keypunching to concording. Further progress on our project will benefit greatly from the application of techniques used in other computer-assisted projects in rabbinics research to the present issues and methodology.

Acknowledgments

We acknowledge the assistance of Professor Peter C. Patton, director of the University Computer Center and of the Center for Ancient Studies, University of Minnesota, who stimulated our interest in this project; Eric E. Inman and Steven R. Sparley, associates of the University Computer Center, who lent valuable technical assistance: and Joseph Miller, editorial assistant for this book.

Notes

1. J. Neusner *A History of the Mishnaic Law of Purities,* vols. 1 to 22 (Leiden: E.J. Brill, 1974–1977).

2. J. Neusner, *A History of the Mishnaic Law of Holy Things,* vols. 1 to 8 (Leiden: E.J. Brill, 1978–1979).

Bibliography

Rabbinics

Segal, M. *A Grammar of Mishnaic Hebrew.* Oxford, England: Oxford
    University Press, 1927.
Yalon, Hanokh. *Introduction to the Vocalization of the Mishnah*
    (Hebrew). Jerusalem: Magnes Press, 1964.
Zahavy, T. *A History of the Mishnaic Law of Blessings.* 1981 (forthcom-
    ing).
Zaks, N. *The Mishnah with Variants,* vols. 1, 2, ZERA'IM (Hebrew).
    Jerusalem: Yad Harav Herzog, 1972, 1975.

Software Documentation

Genes, P.; Mears, D.; and Wells, B. "XEDIT—An Extended Interactive
    Text Editor." University of Minnesota Computer Center, 1978.
Hotchkiss, R.L. "GENCORD—A Concordance Program." University of
    Minnesota Computer Center, 1976.
Inman, E.E. "TAGEDIT—An Interactive Pattern Matching Program."
    University of Minnesota Computer Center, 1980.

Appendix 6A:
Transliteration Key

Transliteration of Hebrew for computer text input:

ל	כ	י	ט	ח	ז	ו	ה	ד	ג	ב	א
L	X	Y	J	E	Z	W	H	D	G	B	A

ת	שׂ	שׁ	ר	ק	צ	פ	ע	ס	נ	מ
T	F	V	R	Q	C	P	O	S	N	M

(M.1:1)   From what time in the evening may the Shema be recited?)

מאימתי קורין את שמע בערבית?

M.1:1a.   M-AYMTY QWRYN AT FMO B-ORBYT? (input display)

Appendix 6B:
Grammatical Tags

Table of Grammatical Tags

1. PART OF SPEECH: (PRT)

   NOUN, VERB, ADJECTIVE, ADVERB, PRONOUN, FUNCTION

2. TYPE:

   Noun : COMMON, PLACE, PERSONAL
   Verb : QAL, NIPHAL, PIEL, PUAL, HIPHIL, HOPHAL, HITPAEL
   Adjective : COMMON, COUNT, QUANTIFIER
   Adverb : TIME, PLACE, MANNER
   Pronoun : PERSONAL, RELATIVE, INTERROG, DEMONSTR
   Function : ARTICLE, PARTICLE, PREP, CONJUNCT

3. GENDER: (GEND)

   MASCULINE, FEMININE, NEUTER

4. NUMBER: (NUMB)

   SINGULAR, PLURAL

5. PERSON: (PERS)

   FIRST, SECOND, THIRD, ALL

6. STATE:

   Noun : ABSOLUTE, CONSTRUCT
   Verb : PERFECT, IMPERFECT, PARTICIPLE, INFINITIVE, COMMAND

Appendix 6C:
Specimen-
Tagged Text

The following is a copy of the output from TAGEDIT, applied to the sample text of twenty-two lines. The text is tagged as explained in the chapter.

```
ENTER COMMAND.
~PWE*
```

M.1.1A.

	M	AYMTY	QMRYN	AT	FMO	B	ORBYT
PRT	FUNCTION	ADVERB	VERB	FUNCTION	NOUN	FUNCTION	NOUN
TYPE	PREP	TIME	QAL	PARTICLE	COMMON	PREP	COMMON
GEND			MASCULINE		MASCULINE		MASCULINE
NUMB			PLURAL		SINGULAR		SINGULAR
PERS			ALL				
STATE			PARTICIPLE		ABSOLUTE		ABSOLUTE

M.1.1B.

	M	FOH	F	H	KHNYM	NKNSYM	L	AKML	B	TRMMTN
PRT	FUNCTION	NOUN	FUNCTION	FUNCTION	NOUN	VERB	FUNCTION	VERB	FUNCTION	NOUN
TYPE	PREP	COMMON	CONJUNCT	ARTICLE	COMMON	NIPHAL	PREP	QAL	PREP	COMMON
GEND		FEMININE			MASCULINE	MASCULINE				FEMININE
NUMB		SINGULAR			PLURAL	PLURAL				SINGULAR
PERS						ALL				
STATE		ABSOLUTE			ABSOLUTE	PARTICIPLE		INFINITIVE		CONSTRUCT

M.1.1C.

	OD	SMP	H	AFMMRH	H	RAFMNH
PRT	ADVERB	NOUN	FUNCTION	NOUN	FUNCTION	ADJECTIVE
TYPE	TIME	COMMON	ARTICLE	COMMON	ARTICLE	NUMERICAL
GEND		MASCULINE		FEMININE		FEMININE
NUMB		SINGULAR		SINGULAR		SINGULAR
PERS						
STATE		CONSTRUCT		ABSOLUTE		

M.1.1D.

	DBRY	RBY	ALYOZR
PRT	NOUN	NOUN	NOUN
TYPE	COMMON	TITLE	PROPNAME
GEND	MASCULINE		
NUMB	PLURAL		
PERS			
STATE	CONSTRUCT		

M.1.1E.

	M	EKMYM	AMHRYN
PRT	FUNCTION	NOUN	VERB
TYPE	CONJUNCT	COMMON	QAL
GEND		MASCULINE	MASCULINE
NUMB		PLURAL	PLURAL
PERS			ALL
STATE		ABSOLUTE	PARTICIPLE

M.1.1F.

	OD	ECMT
PRT	ADVERB	NOUN
TYPE	TIME	COMMON
GEND		FEMININE
NUMB		SINGULAR
PERS		
STATE		CONSTRUCT

M.1.1G.

	RBN	GMLYAL	AMMR
PRT	NOUN	NOUN	VERB
TYPE	TITLE	PRGPNAME	QAL
GEND			MASCULINE
NUMB			PLURAL
PERS			ALL
STATE			PARTICIPLE

M.1.1H.

	OD	F	YOLH	H	FER	OMMD
PRT	ADVERB	FUNCTION	VERB	FUNCTION	NOUN	NOUN
TYPE	TIME	CONJUNCT	QAL	ARTICLE	COMMON	COMMON
GEND			MASCULINE		MASCULINE	MASCULINE
NUMB			SINGULAR		SINGULAR	SINGULAR
PERS			THIRD			
STATE			FUTURE		ABSOLUTE	CONSTRUCT

M.1.1I.

	MOVH	F	BAM	M	BNYM	BYT	H	MFTH
PRT	FUNCTION	FUNCTION	VERB	FUNCTION	NOUN	NOUN	FUNCTION	NOUN
TYPE	INTRO	INTRO	QAL	PREP	COMMON	COMMON	ARTICLE	COMMON
GEND			NEUTER		MASCULINE	MASCULINE		MASCULINE
NUMB			PLURAL		PLURAL	SINGULAR		SINGULAR
PERS			THIRD					
STATE			PERFECT		CONSTRUCT	CONSTRUCT		ABSOLUTE

M.1.1J.

	AMRM	LM
PRT	VERB	PRONOUN
TYPE	QAL	PERSONAL
GEND	NEUTER	MASCULINE
NUMB	PLURAL	SINGULAR
PERS	THIRD	THIRD
STATE	PERFECT	

M.1.1K.

	LA	QRYNW	AT	FMO
PRT	ADVERB	VERB	FUNCTION	NOUN
TYPE	MANNER	QAL	PARTICIPLE	COMMON
GEND		NEUTER		MASCULINE
NUMB		PLURAL		SINGULAR
PERS		THIRD		
STATE		PERFECT		ABSOLUTE

M.1.1L.

	AMR	LHM
PRT	VERB	PRONOUN
TYPE	QAL	PERSONAL
GEND	MASCULINE	MASCULINE
NUMB	SINGULAR	PLURAL
PERS	THIRD	THIRD
STATE	PERFECT	

M.1.1M.

	AM	LA	OLH	OMWD	H	FER
PRT	ADVERB	ADVERB	VERB	NOUN	FUNCTION	NOUN
TYPE	MANNER	MANNER	QAL	COMMON	ARTICLE	COMMON
GEND			MASCULINE	MASCULINE		MASCULINE
NUMB			SINGULAR	SINGULAR		SINGULAR
PERS			THIRD			
STATE			PERFECT	CONSTRUCT		ABSOLUTE

M.1.1N.

	EYBYN	ATM	L	QRWT
PRT	VERB	PRONOUN	FUNCTION	VERB
TYPE	QAL	PERSONAL	PREP	QAL
GEND	MASCULINE	MASCULINE		
NUMB	PLURAL	PLURAL		
PERS	ALL	SECOND		
STATE	PARTICIPLE			INFINITIVE

M.1.1O.

	W	LA	ZW	BLBD
PRT	FUNCTION	ADVERB	PRONOUN	
TYPE	CONJUNCT	MANNER	DEMON	
GEND				
NUMB				
PERS				
STATE				

M.1.1P.

	ALA	KL	MH	F	AMRW	EKMYM	OD	ECWT
PRT								
TYPE	FUNCTION CONJUNCT	ADJECTIVE NUMERICAL	FUNCTION INTERROG	FUNCTION CONJUNCT	VERB QAL	NOUN COMMON	ADVERB TIME	NOUN COMMON
GEND					MASCULINE	MASCULINE		FEMININE
NUMB					PLURAL	PLURAL		SINGULAR
PERS					THIRD			
STATE					PERFECT	ABSOLUTE		CONSTRUCT

	MCTWN	YOLH	OMWD	H	FER
PRT					
TYPE		VERB QAL	NOUN COMMON	FUNCTION ARTICLE	NOUN COMMON
GEND		MASCULINE	MASCULINE		MASCULINE
NUMB		SINGULAR	SINGULAR		SINGULAR
PERS		THIRD			
STATE		FUTURE	CONSTRUCT		ABSOLUTE

M.1.1Q.

	HQJR	ELBYM	M	ABRYM
PRT				
TYPE	VERB HIPHAL	NOUN COMMON	FUNCTION CONJUNCT	NOUN COMMON
GEND	MASCULINE	MASCULINE		MASCULINE
NUMB	SINGULAR	PLURAL		PLURAL
PERS	THIRD			
STATE	PERFECT	ABSOLUTE		ABSOLUTE

M.1.1R.

	MCWTN	OD	F	YOLH	OMWD	H	FER
PRT							
TYPE	NOUN COMMON	ADVERB TIME	FUNCTION CONJUNCT	VERB QAL	NOUN COMMON	FUNCTION ARTICLE	NOUN COMMON
GEND	FEMININE			MASCULINE	MASCULINE		MASCULINE
NUMB	SINGULAR			SINGULAR	SINGULAR		SINGULAR
PERS				THIRD			
STATE	CONSTRUCT			FUTURE	CONSTRUCT		ABSOLUTE

M.1.1S.

	W	KL	H	NAKLYM	L	YWM	AED
PRT							
TYPE	FUNCTION CONJUNCT	ADJECTIVE NUMERICAL	FUNCTION ARTICLE	VERB NIPHAL	FUNCTION PREP	NOUN COMMON	ADJECTIVE NUMERICAL
GEND				MASCULINE		MASCULINE	
NUMB				PLURAL		SINGULAR	
PERS				ALL			
STATE				PARTICIPLE		ABSOLUTE	

M.1.1T.

	MCMTN	OD	F	YOLH	OMMD	H	FER
PRT	NOUN	ADVERB	FUNCTION	VERB	NOUN	FUNCTION	NOUN
TYPE	COMMON	TIME	CONJUNCT	QAL	COMMON	ARTICLE	COMMON
GEND	FEMININE			MASCULINE	MASCULINE		MASCULINE
NUMB	SINGULAR			SINGULAR	SINGULAR		SINGULAR
PERS				THIRD			
STATE	CONSTRUCT			FUTURE	CONSTRUCT		ABSOLUTE

M.1.1U.

	AM	KN	LMH	AHRW	EKMYM	OD	ECHT
PRT	ADVERB	ADVERB	FUNCTION	VERB	NOUN	ADVERB	NOUN
TYPE	MANNER	MANNER	INTERROG	QAL	COMMON	TIME	COMMON
GEND				NEUTER	MASCULINE		FEMININE
NUMB				PLURAL	PLURAL		SINGULAR
PERS				THIRD			
STATE				PERFECT	ABSOLUTE		CONSTRUCT

M.1.1V.

	KDY	L	HREYQ	AT	H	ADM	MN	H	OBRH
PRT	FUNCTION	FUNCTION	VERB	FUNCTION	FUNCTION	NOUN	FUNCTION	FUNCTION	NOUN
TYPE	CONJUNCT	PREP	HIPHIL	PARTICLE	ARTICLE	COMMON	PREP	ARTICLE	COMMON
GEND						MASCULINE			FEMININE
NUMB						SINGULAR			SINGULAR
PERS									
STATE			INFINITIVE			ABSOLUTE			ABSOLUTE

ENTER COMMAND.
Q

7 A Computer-Assisted Study in Graphemic Analysis

Nicki D.C. Harper and
Tom Rindflesch

The research presented here concerns graphemic analysis, the study of script systems solely in terms of their written symbols. This work forms part of a project in the application of linguistic theory to decipherment. In particular, it presents a new way to determine the language family to which the language underlying an undeciphered or a poorly understood script belongs. Languages are grouped into genetic families in which each filial generation evolves from a common ancestor. Grouping is based on the fact that when sounds change in a language, the change proceeds in a regular manner; hence, linguists can compare the various relatives and reconstruct the ancestor or protolanguage. A decipherer is helped immensely if the language under scrutiny can be identified as a member of a given family of languages.

In the most general terms, a decipherment proceeds as follows: Phonetic values are assigned to the script symbols according to some hypothesis; words and syntactic features now visible in the unknown script are related to some known language or family of languages; comparative information from the related languages is used to hypothesize the meanings of more words in the unknown script; each word is analyzed carefully in every text so that errors can be found and possible meanings for still more words elucidated; and the documents are rigorously translated. Only the translation of the corpus to the satisfaction of other scholars upholds the set of hypotheses made during the course of the decipherment process. As it stands, the decipherment process depends on the assignment of phonetic values to script symbols in order to determine the language family to which the target language belongs. In the strict technical sense, the term *decipherment* means the assignment of correct phonetic values to the script symbols. Here, the term is employed more loosely, indicating the entire process from the assignment of phonetic values to the confirmation of these values through translation of the documents.

The Problem

Phonetic values are not easy to assign. Most poorly understood languages of the ancient world, such as Etruscan, have phonetic values assigned to

135

script symbols on the basis of what may well be an incorrect assumption. The assumption is that when a script is borrowed, phonetic values are necessarily borrowed along with the script symbols. The danger of this assumption is clear from cases of script borrowing in recent times. When some signs from the English alphabet were borrowed for the Cherokee syllabary, for example, not one borrowed script symbol kept the same phonetic value.

For some of the more than seventy undeciphered or poorly understood scripts, such as Etruscan, bilinguals (contemporary translations) provide an independent confirmation of some phonetic-value assignments. But the most desirable goal for decipherers would be a means of determining the linguistic affiliation of the target language on the basis of the script symbols alone. This chapter describes a new application of graphemic analysis which produces that information for alphabetic scripts. A decipherer can now determine the language family to which a target language belongs on the basis of the script symbols, independent of phonetic-value assignment.

Knowledge of the language family can help to verify assigned phonetic values independently and can suggest values of graphemes whose phonetic values cannot be otherwise assigned. The usefulness of the technique can be illustrated by using as an example the problem of deciphering Etruscan. Etruscan texts are abundant, and some notion of their content can be gleaned by analyzing the context and using bilinguals. However, there is no commonly accepted assignment of Etruscan to any language family. On slim evidence, some hold it to be Indo-European, while others relate it to Basque, or Caucasian languages, or other language families even further afield. Because the Etruscans exerted an important influence on the development of Roman civilization, historians would like very much to know just who the Etruscans were and whence they came. Based on archaeological and historical evidence, three hypotheses are nearly equally well supported: The Etruscans lived in Italy before the Indo-European migrations into Italy began (*indigenous hypothesis*); the Etruscans migrated into Italy from Anatolia, bringing with them Near Eastern culture traits which they passed to the Romans (*Anatolian hypothesis*); and the Etruscans migrated from northern Europe, bringing with them culture traits not unlike those of the later Celts and Germans (*northern hypothesis*). If Etruscan could be shown to be related to northern Indo-European languages or to Anatolian languages or to be unrelated to Indo-European languages, that evidence would be strong support for the respective migration hypothesis. Thus by learning the genetic relationship of the language underlying the Etruscan script without relying on the supposed phonetic values of the graphemes, we can answer an important question about the Etruscans before we can read the inscriptions which they left.

The hypothesis was proposed that written versions of genetically related languages exhibit similar patterns of grapheme frequency distribution,

while unrelated languages do not show such similarities. In other words, the
Nth most frequent grapheme in language X will occur with a frequency that
will be close to the frequency of occurrence of the Nth most frequent
grapheme in language Y if X and Y are genetically related languages.
Apparently no work has been done in this area. Kučera and Monroe state
that a close genetic relationship may well be manifest on the phonological
level in similar phonotactics.[1] But both phonology (the study of sound) and
phonotactics (the study of the distribution of sound patterns) concern
spoken languages. What of languages whose pronunciation is unknown?

The hypothesis was first tested on languages whose genetic affiliation is
certain. First studied were those with the simplest writing system: alphabets.
It was postulated that, whatever the form of the alphabet being used,
related languages would have similar patterns of grapheme frequency distribution. But just how complex those patterns might be was not known.
Hence, the study began using the University of Minnesota Cyber 74
computer to count graphemes and calculate their percentage of frequency
of occurrence. The texts were selected from sixteen languages. In the Afro-
Asiatic family were Arabic, Hausa, Hebrew, and Somali. In the Hittito-
Luvian family were Lycian, Lydian, and Mylian. In the Indo-European
family were English, French, German, Greek, Latin, Oscan, Russian,
Spanish, and Umbrian. Each text sample contained about 5,500 graphemes.

Text encoding was devised both to simplify programming and to
increase the efficiency of text entry. For each language, each script symbol
was given a one-character code. For simplicity, and since pronunciation is
irrelevant here, graphemes of each language were encoded in Latin letters.
For example, each letter of the Cyrillic alphabet in which Russian is written
was coded with a Latin letter. Scripts with a character set longer than the
Latin alphabet were assigned the necessary number of arbitrarily chosen
symbols.

The texts were entered on the computer in eighty-unit lines. The lines
began with an abbreviation identifying the language of the text and ended
with a line number. Between the language abbreviation and the line number
appeared the text. Words were divided by slashes; otherwise no punctuation
was recorded. Proofreaders compared the original text to the cards. If the
text had been encoded (for example, Cyrillic), the consultant who had made
the transcription assisted in the proofreading. The XEDIT program allowed
the operator errors to be corrected swiftly and permitted code symbols to be
changed as required.

Eric Inman and Richard Kubat of the University Computer Center
(UCC) wrote all the programs for the graphemic-analysis project. Programs
were designed to count each letter, record its position in the word, and then
perform a frequency analysis. The printout illustrated for the English text
(figure 7-1) names the language and lists in successive columns the

NUMBER OF WORDS—1217
NUMBER OF LETTERS—5599

LETTER	1	2	3	4	5	6	7	8	9	10	11
A	474	104	356	14	8.47	21.94	75.11	2.95	8.55	11.13	1.18
B	93	63	30	0	1.66	67.74	32.26	0.00	5.18	0.94	0.00
C	179	50	125	4	3.20	27.93	69.83	2.23	4.11	3.91	0.34
D	38	58	49	131	4.25	24.37	20.59	55.04	4.77	1.53	11.00
E	680	24	382	274	12.15	3.53	56.18	40.29	1.97	11.94	23.16
F	132	54	35	43	2.36	40.91	26.52	32.58	4.44	1.09	3.63
G	106	26	46	34	1.89	24.53	43.40	32.08	2.14	1.44	2.87
H	319	79	194	46	5.70	24.76	60.82	14.42	6.49	6.06	3.89
I	416	81	335	0	7.43	19.47	80.53	0.00	6.66	10.47	0.00
J	18	10	8	0	0.32	55.56	44.44	0.00	0.82	0.25	0.00
K	23	7	9	7	0.41	30.43	39.13	30.43	0.58	0.28	0.59
L	219	30	149	40	3.91	13.70	68.04	18.26	2.47	4.66	3.38
M	141	47	80	14	2.52	33.33	56.74	9.93	3.86	2.50	1.18
N	412	31	287	94	7.36	7.52	69.66	22.82	2.55	8.97	7.95
O	390	72	281	37	6.97	18.46	72.05	9.49	5.92	8.78	3.13
P	80	29	45	6	1.43	36.25	56.25	7.50	2.38	1.41	0.51
R	325	49	218	58	5.80	15.08	67.08	17.85	4.03	6.81	4.90
S	382	90	140	152	6.82	23.56	36.65	39.79	7.40	4.38	12.85
T	509	190	189	130	9.09	37.33	37.13	25.54	15.61	5.91	10.95
U	176	15	160	1	3.14	8.52	90.91	0.57	1.23	5.00	0.08
V	43	6	37	0	0.77	13.95	86.05	0.00	0.49	1.16	0.00
W	88	57	17	14	1.57	64.77	19.32	15.91	4.68	0.53	1.18
Y	95	6	9	80	1.70	6.32	9.47	84.21	0.49	0.28	6.76
Z	9	1	8	0	0.16	11.11	88.89	0.00	0.08	0.25	0.00
Q	7	4	3	0	0.13	57.14	42.86	0.00	0.33	0.09	0.00
X	11	0	7	4	0.20	0.00	63.64	36.36	0.00	0.22	0.34

1: OCCURRENCE OF LETTER.
2: OCCURRENCE OF LETTER INITIALLY.
3: OCCURRENCE OF LETTER MEDIALLY.
4: OCCURRENCE OF LETTER FINALLY.
5: PERCENT OF OCCURRENCE OF LETTER TO TOTAL OCCURRENCE OF ALL LETTERS.
6: PERCENT OF OCCURRENCE OF LETTER INITIALLY TO TOTAL OCCURRENCE OF LETTER.
7: PERCENT OF OCCURRENCE OF LETTER MEDIALLY TO TOTAL OCCURRENCE OF LETTER.
8: PERCENT OF OCCURRENCE OF LETTER FINALLY TO TOTAL OCCURRENCE OF LETTER.
9: PERCENT OF OCCURRENCE OF LETTER INITIALLY TO TOTAL OCCURRENCE OF INITIAL LETTERS.
10: PERCENT OF OCCURRENCE OF LETTER MEDIALLY TO TOTAL OCCURRENCE OF MEDIAL LETTERS.
11: PERCENT OF OCCURRENCE OF LETTER FINALLY TO TOTAL OCCURRENCE OF FINAL LETTERS.

SINGLE LETTER WORDS
A—32
I—2

Figure 7-1. Frequency of Occurrence of the Graphemes in the English Text

grapheme code, overall frequency of occurrence, frequency of occurrence in each position, and percentage of occurrence for each letter in each position relative to the total occurrences of that particular letter.

Sampling distortion, that is, how much results vary as a result of the particular sample of text selected, was first examined. An assessment resulted from analyzing Latin samples in 1,250-grapheme chunks. With a 5,000-grapheme sample, the cumulative distortion for all twenty-two Latin graphemes was about 1 percent.

In order to test the hypothesis that genetically related languages exhibit similar patterns of grapheme frequency distribution while unrelated languages do not, the following methodology was employed. Composite texts for two language families, Afro-Asiatic and Indo-European, were constructed. The composite Afro-Asiatic text included Arabic, Hausa, Hebrew, and Somali. The composite Indo-European text included English, German, Greek, Latin, and Spanish. An effort to make precise the notion "similar patterns of frequency distribution" was implemented through a program termed the *comparison program* which proceeded as follows. After the occurrences of each grapheme in each individual and composite text had been counted, the comparison program compiled for each text a table in which the grapheme types were listed, with percentage of occurrence, in descending order of frequency of occurrence. Subsequently, each individual language table was compared to both tables for the composite texts in such a way that the percentage of occurrence of the *N*th most frequent grapheme in the text of the target language was matched with the *N*th most frequent grapheme in the composite text, through the comparison program (See figure 7–2, where the target language is English.) The comparison program provided measurements of differences between the individual language and the composite. Of these, the square root of the sum of the squares of the differences was used as an index. As figure 7–2 shows, by comparing graphemes according to their rank-order of frequency, it is not necessary to know any phonetic values for any of the graphemes. The computer performed the following operations: counting graphemes and calculating the percentage of occurrence and the index of difference.

Results

The results support the hypothesis: It is possible to determine the genetic relationship of languages on the basis of grapheme frequency alone. Figure 7–3 displays the results for languages which have not borrowed extensively from sources outside their respective genetic grouping and which are written in script systems that are typologically similar (alphabets which include vowels). Part A shows each language compared with the Afro-Asiatic composite text; part B shows each language compared with the Indo-European;

| Indo-European | | English | | |
Grapheme	Percent	Grapheme	Percent	Difference Squared
E	13.42	E	12.15	1.61
A	8.97	T	9.09	0.01
I	8.89	A	8.47	0.18
N	7.39	I	7.43	0.00
S	7.09	N	7.36	0.07
T	6.97	O	6.97	0.00
O	6.38	S	6.82	0.19
R	6.03	R	5.80	0.05
U	5.38	H	5.70	0.10
L	3.99	D	4.25	0.07
D	3.54	L	3.91	0.14
M	3.28	C	3.20	0.01
H	2.72	U	3.14	0.18
P	2.23	M	2.52	0.08
C	2.20	F	2.36	0.03
G	1.76	C	1.89	0.02
K	1.50	Y	1.70	0.04
B	1.44	B	1.66	0.05
F	1.12	W	1.57	0.20
V	0.75	P	1.43	0.46
Q	0.70	V	0.77	0.00
Ω	0.60	K	0.41	0.04
H	0.53	J	0.32	0.04
W	0.51	X	0.20	0.10
Z	0.45	Z	0.16	0.08
T	0.40	Q	0.13	0.07
Ξ	0.25		0.00	0.07
χ	0.24		0.00	0.06
Θ	0.18		0.00	0.03
J	0.17		0.00	0.03
Φ	0.15		0.00	0.02
Ü	0.10		0.00	0.01
Ä	0.08		0.00	0.01
Ñ	0.03		0.00	0.00
Ö	0.03		0.00	0.00
Ç	0.01		0.00	0.00
				2.01*

*Square root of the sum of the differences squared

Figure 7-2. Frequency of Occurrence of the Graphemes in the English Text
Compared to Frequency of Occurrence of the Graphemes in
the Composite Indo-European Text

part C compares the Hittito-Luvian languages with the two composites.
Hittito-Luvian languages, while admittedly related to Indo-European, are
thought by some to comprise a separate family, so it seemed best to treat
them separately. The smaller the index of difference, the more closely
related are the compared languages. Part B shows that the Indo-European
languages compared with the Indo-European composite have indexes
ranging from 5.1 to 2.0 with a mean of 4.0. The Afro-Asiatic languages are

A. Compared against Afro-Asiatic		B. Compared against Indo-European	
Language	**Index**	**Language**	**Index**
Arabic	6.8	Arabic	14.3
Hebrew	14.4	Hebrew	7.9
Hausa	7.3	Hausa	14.9
Somali	6.5	Somali	13.5
English	12.2	English	2.0
Etruscan	13.4	Etruscan	3.9
French	9.0	French	5.1
German	8.2	German	4.3
Greek	13.6	Greek	4.2
Latin	14.2	Latin	4.1
Oscan	11.7	Oscan	2.7
Russian	12.1	Russian	4.1
Spanish	11.8	Spanish	5.0
Umbrian	13.9	Umbrian	4.9
Mean of the Afro-Asiatic languages: 8.7		Mean of the Afro-Asiatic languages: 12.7	
Mean of the Indo-European languages: 12.0		Mean of the Indo-European languages: 4.0	
C. Hittito-Luvian languages			
Lydian	7.7	Lydian	4.1
Lycian	11.1	Lycian	5.2
Mylian	13.8	Mylian	6.7
Mean of the Hittito-Luvian languages: 10.9		Mean of the Hittito-Luvian languages: 5.3	

Figure 7-3. Indexes of Difference (square root of the sum of the differences squared) for the Languages of the Sample Compared to the Afro-Asiatic Composite Text and the Indo-European Composite Text

all significantly higher. Similarly, in Part A, except Hebrew, the Afro-Asiatic indexes range from 6.5 to 7.3, and the Indo-European indexes are all higher. The mean, including Hebrew, is 8.7 for Afro-Asiatic and 12.0 for Indo-European.

A statistical test (the t-test) determined whether the indexes obtained were significant, indicating that the languages being considered were probably from different populations. This was accomplished by considering the languages compared to the composite as belonging to two samples: Afro-Asiatic and Indo-European. (The Hittito-Luvian languages were not included in the t test.) By computing the t test on the basis of the indexes for the languages compared against the Afro-Asiatic composite, $t = 2.231$. With 12 degrees of freedom, this indicates $p < .025$. This means that the probability of obtaining the difference observed between the two means through sampling error is less than .025. Since .050 is considered to be statistically significant, the actual difference obtained is clearly significant. Therefore, the indexes for the two groups of languages indicate that the Afro-Asiatic languages belong to a different population from that of the Indo-European languages. This methodology is consequently considered capable of yielding results which reliably distinguish the languages of one family from those of another. Similarly, when the t test was computed using the indexes obtained by comparing the individual languages to the Indo-European composite, where the mean of the Indo-European indexes is 4.0 and that of the Afro-Asiatic is 12.7, $t = 7.901$. With 12 degrees of freedom, this indicates that $p < .005$, which means that the differences observed here are highly significant with consequences following as in the Afro-Asiatic case.

In part C, when compared against the Indo-European languages, the Hittito-Luvian languages range from 4.1 to 6.7 with a mean of 5.3. When compared against the Afro-Asiatic languages, the Hittito-Luvian languages range from 7.7 to 13.8 with a mean of 10.9. This seems consistent with a distant relationship to the Indo-European languages: the available text in alphabetic scripts is too small to conclude that Hittito-Luvian should be considered a distinct language family.

Historians want to know whether the Etruscans migrated into Italy and, if they migrated, from where. The assignment of Etruscan to a language family can help answer that question. If Etruscan is Indo-European, then a migration must have occurred. If it is closer to the Hittito-Luvian languages than to the Indo-European languages, then a migration from Anatolia is supported. If it is closer to the Indo-European languages than to the Hittito-Luvian languages, then a migration from the north is supported. A large sample of Etruscan text was subjected to graphemic analysis, comparing it to Indo-European and Hittito-Luvian languages and to Afro-Asiatic languages. Etruscan appears to be an Indo-European language not closely related to the Anatolian Hittito-Luvian languages and not at all related to the Afro-Asiatic languages. This result supports the hypothesis that the Etruscans migrated to Italy from the north.

From a practical point of view, this project could not have been attempted without a computer. The amount of counting and computation necessary would simply have been overwhelming. Had the team even managed to do the counting and arithmetic by hand (perhaps with the aid of a calculator), the inevitable human error involved in counting 104,500 graphemes would have detracted substantially from the reliability of the results.

The application which inspired this project is decipherment of Minoan Linear A, and this procedure was investigated with that specific task in mind. The Minoan culture flourished on Crete from about 2800 B.C. until the takeover of the island by the Greek-speaking Mycenaeans about 1450 B.C. The script of the Minoans is called Linear A and is a syllabary. Once it has been substantiated that languages written with syllabaries can be assigned to language families by using this methodology, just as languages written with alphabets can, graphemic analysis can be applied to Linear A. Graphemic analysis will then be incorporated within the overall scheme for the recovery of the Minoan language.

The plan, then, is to enter nonalphabetic scripts and to apply the technique to them. Cultures which display digraphia (two distinct script systems representing the same language) will aid this effort. Ancient Greek, for example, is written in an alphabet and in the Cypriot and Mycenaean syllabaries. Such phenomena can help pinpoint differences between alphabets and syllabaries. Plans for the data already accumulated include the analysis of positional frequency of occurrence. Positional frequency is the frequency of occurrence of a grapheme in a location as word final, word initial, or elsewhere in the word. Study of these frequencies may allow the assignment of languages to specific subgroups within language families. Other correlations are expected to yield possible universals of script systems.

The large number of unknown and poorly understood languages mentioned indicates the further scope of application of this technique of graphemic analysis. Graphemic analysis will also apply to epigraphy (study of inscriptions) and papyrology (study of documents written on papyrus), since it can predict most probable missing letters without reference to any data beyond the existing graphemes. It also has applications in cryptanalysis, which works with deliberately scrambled texts in modern languages. The methodology developed could be employed in historical linguistics to help determine questions of genetic relationship in contested cases. For example, it is a matter of controversy whether the American Indian languages Yurok and Wiyot are of the Algonquian family. The form of graphemic analysis developed here could contribute to the resolution of this controversy.

This methodology can also contribute to theoretical linguistics. The exact relationship between pronunciation and writing has not been adequately explored. In the work cited earlier, Kučera and Monroe showed that genetically related languages exhibit regularities in their phonotactic structure. This research indicates that genetically related languages exhibit regularities in graphemic distribution, which suggests investigating the relationship between pronunciation and writing. Justeson has done some work along this line in his attempt to recover universals of writing.[2] This work supports his notion that universals of writing are analogous to universals of language and points out the direction for further research in the nature of the relationship between language and writing. Already the specific form of the results reported here indicates that a generalization can be derived regarding the appearances of redundancy and simplicity in written representations of speech.

The study of script systems is barely beginning. The authors believe graphemic analysis can aid in understanding script borrowing, script system design, processes by which scripts are changed to suit changing languages, and the relationship between the script in which a language is written and phonology of the language itself. Although the precise relationship between script systems and phonology is not yet clear, the regularity with which genetic relatedness can be predicted through graphemic analysis should be related to the ways in which languages can change phonetically.

The results of this work were presented at the Linguistic Society of America winter meeting in 1977 and were published in *Minnesota Papers in Linguistics and the Philosophy of Language.*[3] The application of graphemic analysis to Etruscan and the Hittito-Luvian languages was presented at the Minnesota Section Archeological Institute of America Symposium in honor of Tom B. Jones, in April 1978. We hope to incorporate those findings with the results of work now in progress in a paper on the genetic affiliation of Etruscan.

Acknowledgments

The research underlying this chapter was supported by grants from the University of Minnesota Computer Center and the University of Minnesota graduate school. We are grateful to the following people for helpful comments on an earlier version of this chapter: Bruce Downing, Geri Hockfield, Kathleen Houlihan, Eric E. Inman, Tom B. Jones, Richard Kubat, Patrick O'Malley, Peter C. Patton, and Gerald Sanders.

Notes

1. Henry Kučera, and George K. Monroe, *A Comparative Quantitative Phonology of Russian, Czech, and German* (New York: 1980).
2. John S. Justeson, "Universals of Language and Universals of Writing," in *Linguistic Studies Offered to Joseph Greenberg,* vol. 1, edited by Alphonse Juilland (Saratoga, California: Anma Libri, 1976).
3. No. 5, October 1978.

Bibliography

Greenberg, J.H. "Nature and Uses of Linguistic Typologies." *International Journal of American Linguistics* 23, no. 2 (1957):68.
———. "Language Universals: A Research Frontier." *Science* 166(1969): 473.
Packard, D.W. *Minoan Linear A.* Berkeley, Calif.: University of California Press, 1974.

TAGEDIT: A Computer Tool for Literary and Linguistic Research

Eric E. Inman

Textual analysis is a method for solving a variety of problems in literature and linguistics, but textual analysis is a general term that actually includes a broad spectrum of approaches and methods. Examples are graphemic analysis, word-use studies, syntax analysis, semantic analysis, and discourse analysis. These methods can aid in solving such problems as determining the authorship of a text, defining the grammar of a language, or finding the meaning of a word. Textual analysis is a broad field, both in the methods it includes and in the kinds of problems to which it can be applied.

Textual analysis, although valuable, can be extremely arduous because texts must usually be examined word by word. A manual analysis is not practical for most texts because of their size, often numbering in the tens and even hundreds of thousands of words. The speed and efficiency of computer-aided textual analysis, however, allow such a large volume of data to be processed in a short time and naturally draw the user's attention toward global patterns rather than local details. Moreover, the intellectual challenge of textual analysis lies not in the word-by-word investigation, but in determining what type of study is to be performed and interpreting the results of that study. TAGEDIT is a tool designed to free the literary analyst for further investigation by performing some of the laborious tasks of word-by-word text processing. It is intended to assist the user in a general manner by providing some basic functions that can be tailored to suit particular needs of the study.

Computers are currently being used more and more to aid in textual analysis. The usual approach, however, is often different from that conceived for TAGEDIT. Textual analysis programs are usually written for a specific project, text, or corpus. They usually perform one type of analysis on one type of text or for a single genre of literature. If a different analysis is to be performed or a different type of text is to be studied, the computer program must be modified or rewritten. Furthermore, a significant portion of the project or study effort often must be spent developing programs. In contrast, TAGEDIT is a general tool designed both to aid in all types of analysis on all types of texts, and to minimize the need for program development in individual projects.

An earlier approach to the computer-assisted study of literary texts has been to develop programmer-oriented languages such as SNOBOL to

145

include string-processing features. String processing involves the manipulation of strings or sequences of characters from a text, and it is an important aspect of computer programming for textual analysis. SNOBOL and similar languages facilitate programming for textual analysis; but even so, a great deal of effort is still required for program development in support of individual research projects. The main source of this inconvenience results from the fact that the string-processing facility implemented by these languages is character-oriented, whereas the literary analyst usually prefers to work with the word-oriented aspect of the text. The most valuable feature of TAGEDIT is its ability to process a text as a string of words rather than a string of characters. TAGEDIT is written entirely in Pascal, a universal programming language widely used for string data processing on mini- and microcomputers as well as on large machines. The ever-increasing availability of Pascal should allow TAGEDIT to be used at most computer installations. Pascal is especially appropriate for textual analysis applications because of its rich system of data structures.

Concordance programs have proved to be useful tools for textual studies, and often they will do a lot more than produce a simple concordance quickly. They will print the context surrounding each word, compile various data summaries, allow the concording of various portions of a text as well as the entire text, allow alphabetization starting at the end of words instead of the beginning, and so forth. These programs allow the analyst to tailor a concordance to suit the particular requirements of the study. TAGEDIT also includes a concordance-building facility having most of these features.

Requirements

To determine which functions TAGEDIT should be able to perform, the most important needs of textual analysis which could be most effectively met by computer data processing were considered. In programming these functions, the intention was to provide the user with as much flexibility and control as possible so that these functions could be fine-tuned to meet particular needs. TAGEDIT was also made interactive since this feature encourages reactive experimentation by allowing the user to apply a number of different methods conveniently and in a short time.

Textual analysis usually focuses on some type of textual phenomenon, such as occurrences of a certain word or type of word, a phrase, or a type of sentence. Something may be learned about the text by knowing the frequency of that phenomenon, or its distribution, or merely its presence or absence. TAGEDIT therefore includes a system for specifying or describing textual phenomena and a SEARCH function that locates them to determine their frequency and distribution. In designing this system, the primary requirement was that the user be able to specify any desired phenomenon, whether specific or general. Secondarily, but also important, the means of specification were to be kept simple but unambiguous, as required in all computer-oriented research. In addition to meeting these requirements, TAGEDIT was also designed to allow the user to easily focus on inflexion of words and word order. Textual phenomena are specified by patterns. TAGEDIT is given a pattern, and then it searches the text for strings matching that pattern. A pattern consists of a string of letters and punctuation marks which represent words and phrases, and it also includes special symbols for representing various types and combinations of words and phrases. The pattern system has been developed to be highly flexible, and part of the research challenge when using TAGEDIT is to discover patterns that adequately describe the textual phenomena of interest in a particular study.

Many textual phenomena that are of interest to literary scholars would be hard to isolate and identify in conventional computer representations of texts. TAGEDIT, however, allows the production and use of tagged texts, in which each word can have one or more *tags*, or labels, associated with it. The tags supply additional information about given words or about given portions of the text. A common example of tagging is the use of tags to delineate the grammatical parsing of words, but there are many other uses for tags. The scheme for tagging is designed for and tailored to a particular study by the project designer. Fixing the system of tags for optimum research results can be one of the most difficult parts of the research, since the entire project must be thought out carefully in order to develop a system of tags which will yield meaningful results. Tags are also used with patterns in two ways. First, patterns can optionally refer to tags as well as to words. In some instances a pattern may specify merely a sequence of tags, independent of the particular words with which those tags are associated. Second, patterns can be used to supply tags to a text by specifying that all matches to a particular pattern be tagged a certain way. The user soon develops skill in using these general features for a particular text and type of study.

TAGEDIT produces two basic forms of output: the text, or portions of it, and concordances. The text can be printed without tags or with some or all tags. Moreover, there is almost complete flexibility in the format of the output. The output can be formatted as a free-running text or in columns. If tags are also to be printed, they can be placed in interlinear format with free-running text, in separate columns with column-formatted texts, or in a variety of other formats. The concordances produced and printed by TAGEDIT may not be concordances in the traditional sense of the word. The items that they index are not necessarily individual words, but rather matches to a pattern. Thus the key in a concordance entry may be a phrase as well as a word. Concordances produced by TAGEDIT are of the key-word-in-context type and allow the text-output feature.

Before analysis can begin, a text must be converted into a format that TAGEDIT is able to recognize. Texts are normally stored on computer as a series of characters, but TAGEDIT works with texts as a series of words. TAGEDIT performs the conversion from the character-string to word-string format, and the text is then stored in the format suited to TAGEDIT. This special format cannot be printed directly for manual perusal, but is stored in the computer in a code meaningful to only TAGEDIT. The printing facilities mentioned above are provided partially to produce a readable version of the coded text. The conversion process requires that the analyst initially define the format of the text, specifying just how words, punctuation, tags, location markers, and so on are used in the text. The programming for this process is similar to that for formatting printouts of texts.

TAGEDIT orients the text in such a manner that various operations may be limited to certain parts of the text. The text is divided into units, each unit beginning with a location marker. Location markers are simply addresses of units in the text, and they can be specified in many different ways. For example, some texts may use line numbers for location markers, while others may use chapter and pericopae numbers. Unless otherwise specified, each line of the text is considered to be one unit, and the location markers are ignored in processing the text. Location markers may option-ally be printed along with the text. Alternatively, the analyst, rather than TAGEDIT, may determine how the text is divided into units and what the values of the location markers should be. For a biblical text, for example, each verse might be one unit and the location markers could be used to specify the book and chapter and verse numbers. Such a system provides a means of addressing a particular place in the text, by its location marker, and of specifying how much of the text is to be operated on, by specifying a certain number of units to be processed.

The text on which TAGEDIT operations are to be performed is not necessarily the original text, but may be a concordance previously produced from the text by TAGEDIT. The concordance can be manipulated apart from the text, and afterward annotations and tags applied to the concor-dance also may be applied to the respective parts of the original text. Con-cordances are organized in much the same way as texts. Each concordance entry is a unit, and location markers are assigned the relative number of the entry. Most commands have the same application to concordances as to texts, and there are also commands for producing concordances, as well as for turning the operations from concordances back onto the text. Unless noted otherwise, henceforth text will apply to both a derived concordance and the original text.

TAGEDIT is always positioned at a certain unit in the text. For most commands the position determines the point in the text at which further processing is to begin. TAGEDIT is initially positioned at the first unit in the text. After execution of a command, TAGEDIT is positioned either at the last unit processed or back to the first unit, depending on the command given. There are also commands that allow the user to change TAGEDIT's position within the text, so the user has knowledge of and control over what parts of the text are affected by any TAGEDIT command.

As explained above, TAGEDIT focuses on enabling the determination of frequency and distribution of designated textual phenomena. The special text representation, including the tagging system, was developed so that chosen aspects of the text could be emphasized and made retrievable. The patterns are used to describe particular phenomena in the text. The command SEARCH retrieves and lists in concordance form those elements which the user has specified by means of patterns. Tags are added to the text with the TAG command. It is employed exactly as the SEARCH command, except that it also tags the pattern matches it finds. Concordances can be built by either the SEARCH or the TAG command. Once a concordance is built, it may also become the object of TAGEDIT operations. Most commands available for processing or analyzing the text are available with similar results for application to the concordance. In addition, there are two special commands for concordances: SAVE and RETURN. SAVE saves a copy of the concordance that can later be stored or printed. RETURN directs TAGEDIT back to operate on the original text. The concordances that are produced by TAGEDIT are normally in key-word-in-context (KWIC) format. This terminology is used even though the key, being a match to a pattern, is not necessarily a word, but may be a phrase of several words. The analyst has the same control over concordance output as over output of the text. This includes specifying how much context is to be printed, the format of the key and its context, as well as other features provided for text output. The various functions of TAGEDIT are organized in command cycle. Each time the program progresses through the cycle, TAGEDIT prints the message "ENTER COMMAND." The analyst then enters a command, and TAGEDIT interprets and executes it. The commands that can be entered in this cycle permit almost all the functions available to the user. Some commands may cause the printing of additional messages and require further user input.

Examples

The effectiveness of TAGEDIT depends a great deal on how well the pattern system can be used to identify and distinguish the selected phenomena. As stated earlier, an intermediate goal of the analyst will be to develop useful patterns. TAGEDIT cannot be asked to search for a particular phenomenon unless the user can devise a pattern that describes it in an adequate, unambiguous manner. Two concepts that can be useful in developing patterns are content and context. Identifying *content* means specifying what the phenomenon is composed of or includes. A particular phenomenon may be characterized by a certain word or phrase, so that word or phrase would be included in the pattern as part of content. In specifying content, the analyst tries to make sure that all instances of the phenomenon in the text will be matched by the pattern. *Context* comes into play when such a pattern is matched not only by all occurrences of the phenomenon, but also by portions of the text that are not part of the phenomenon. In these cases, context may be brought in as a distinguishing factor. The analyst would then try to include elements in the pattern which do not specify part of the phenomenon, but rather a context of the phenomenon which allows the pattern to be matched only when that phenomenon occurs.

A pattern specifies a set of words and/or phrases that can match the pattern. The simplest pattern is a word pattern, which is matched by a word or a set of words. Phrase patterns are matched by one or more words in the form of a phrase and are composed of word patterns. The simplest word pattern is a word. When a word is entered as a pattern, TAGEDIT searches for every occurrence of that word in the text. There are other types of word patterns, however. For example, the pattern -ION is matched by any word that ends with *ion*, such as *motion, lion,* and *ion.* Patterns of a similar type are IN- -BARK-. The pattern IN- is matched by words that begin with *in*, such as *inactive, inch,* and *in.* The pattern -BARK- is matched by words that contain *bark,* such as *embarks, barking,* and *bark.* Another pattern might be -P-P, which would be matched by words containing two p's, such as *pop* and *purple.* These patterns can be arbitrarily complex. Another possible pattern is -, which is matched by any word. This pattern would be used to produce a complete word concordance of the text, and is often useful in phrase patterns. It is also possible to refer to tags within word patterns. An example of a word pattern that specifies tags is

-ING/POFSP = VERB,MODE = PARTICIPLE

This is matched by any word that ends in *ing* and has at least the two tags POFSP (part of speech) and MODE, where the value of POFSP is VERB and the value of MODE is PARTICIPLE.

Patterns are composed of word patterns. Word patterns consist of any string of one or more letters and dashes, except that two dashes may not occur consecutively. They may also include references to tags. In the following paragraphs, WP is used to denote a word pattern. Phrase patterns are constructed from word patterns. The simplest phrase pattern is a string of word patterns and is matched by a string of words, each word being a match to its corresponding word pattern in the phrase pattern. For example, the pattern THE -ING- could be matched by the phrases *the barking dog* or *the spring day.*

More complex patterns may be developed in two ways. One is by specifying that a segment of the pattern is optional. That is, the match to such a pattern may or may not include a part to match the optional pattern segment. The optional segment of the pattern is denoted by enclosing it in parentheses, and the segment must be a valid word or phrase pattern. Patterns may have more than one optional segment, but the whole pattern may not be optional. For an example, consider the pattern

THE (-) HOUSE

It could be matched by *the red house, the house,* or *the large house.* A segment of a pattern may also consist of a list of patterns, one of which must be matched by the corresponding portion of the match to the entire pattern. Such a segment, in fact, comprises a valid pattern in itself, which is not true for optional segments. The segment is rendered by enclosing the patterns in brackets and separating them with commas, as in

THE [RED, BLUE, GREEN] HOUSE

The example is matched by *the red house, the blue house,* and *the green house.* If the analyst desired that *the house* also be included as a pattern match, the pattern

THE ([RED, BLUE, GREEN] HOUSE)

could be entered. A pattern listed within brackets may be any valid pattern, including those with optional segments. The fundamental patterns are:

WP

WP   WP

WP   (WP)

(WP)   WP

[WP, WP, . . . , WP]

Any pattern that can be constructed by replacing any word pattern with any valid pattern, including the fundamental patterns listed above, is valid.

Since the definition is recursive, patterns may be arbitrarily complex. The actual implementation of TAGEDIT on any given computer system, however, will necessarily impose a restriction on pattern complexity.

A number of additional features are being considered for addition to the pattern-matching system. These include allowing negative operators, count specifications, fences, and references to punctuation. Negative operators would be used to specify letters a word must not contain and words, phrases, and patterns that the match to the pattern must not contain. Count specifications would be used to set the maximum and/or minimum number of letters to be found in a word or portion of a word or the number of words to be found in a pattern or segment of a pattern. Fences would be points in the text that matches could not cross. This happens automatically with concordances, since matches are not allowed to extend into more than one entry. The fences in this case are set at unit boundaries. Finally, references to punctuation would be a part of word patterns. In order for a word to match the pattern, it would also have to have the specified punctuation associated with it.

TAGEDIT is designed not only to allow the analyst to use such patterns, but also to aid in developing and/or discovering those that are effective. Since TAGEDIT is an interactive program, the analyst may experiment with many patterns in a short time. As noted above, the tagging and concordance systems can also be used to make the pattern-matching system more effective. TAGEDIT has been developed to meet some broad and fundamental needs of textual analysis. Time and experience will reveal how useful it is for any particular method or text as well as what additional features will make TAGEDIT more useful. TAGEDIT is not, and may never be, a finished product, but it will develop as the needs of textual analysis and the capabilities of computers for literary analysis become better understood.

Development will continue not only in TAGEDIT, but also in its use and in the collection of data banks which it produces. Use of TAGEDIT can develop primarily by discovering pattern sequences that can effectively tag a text with respect to a certain set of phenomena. A certain pattern sequence may be developed, for example, that will reliably tag texts of Greek prose according to the parts of speech of individual words. One large stage in the analysis of such texts could then proceed automatically. It is not expected that sequences can be found which will completely tag a set of texts, but that such sequences as are detected will enable a high degree of completeness and accuracy, so that most of the manual effort is eliminated. Pattern-tagging sequences may become a major focus in development of TAGEDIT use.

Tagged texts are also useful as data banks for other research, and in a sense they can be considered an end product of TAGEDIT. They are valuable in the same way that texts and concordances are valuable in machine-readable form. In essence, they store a text, plus a certain amount of processed annotation of that text, and can be available simply for data print-outs or for further analysis and processing by other researchers. The production and collection of tagged texts are therefore another aspect in the development of computer-aided textual analysis in which TAGEDIT can play an important part.

Bibliography

Holoien, R.A., and Inman, E.E. "TAGEDIT User Reference Manual." UCC Technical Report, University of Minnesota, forthcoming.

Mitchell, L.; Leavitt, J.; and Inman, E. "KIT and the Investigation of Old English Prose." Computer Science Department Technical Report 78-7. University of Minnesota, May 1978.

9

Concordances of Troubadour Poetry in Old Occitan

F.R.P. Akehurst

In the twelfth and thirteenth centuries in southern France, poets, often members of the nobility, composed verse and music which were performed by professional entertainers, called *jongleurs.* The poets, or *troubadours,* contrary to the modern image, were not itinerant musicians traveling about with guitars slung over their backs. In fact, they never sang their own works, leaving the performance to the jongleurs. Troubadours wrote in a language somewhat different from French, called Old Occitan. Their poetry, always sung in performance, was principally concerned with the joys and despairs of courtly love, although political topics were occasionally treated.

In order to discover the troubadours' notion of *madness,* the author began researching their poems in 1970, manually tabulating in the works of several troubadours the occurrences of words such as *fol, folia, foudatz,* and so on, which mean "mad," "madness," and so forth in Old Occitan (Old Provençal). It became necessary to investigate other words for "madness" when they were associated with those already found. Each time one of these new words was encountered, the process of reading the texts for occurrences of the key words began again. This obviously time-consuming technique led to results reported in a paper read at the 1970 meeting of the Modern Language Association in New York. In the book exhibit at that meeting was Joseph J. Duggan's *Concordance of the Song of Roland,* which indicated exactly how many times the author of the *Song of Roland* had used the word *folie* and in which lines.[1] The research for that information in the concordance took about one minute. It became clear that some concordances of the troubadours' poems would be extremely useful.

There are some 2,500 known poems by these lyric poets, and each poem is about 50 lines long. Thus, there are some 125,000 lines of text to enter into the computer. Grants from the University of Minnesota graduate school enabled the accomplishment of about half of the task in eight years. During that time, the author approached Richard L. Hotchkiss of the University Computer Center (UCC) about writing a concordance program, suggesting certain features in the program which would be useful to literary scholars. The resulting program, GENCORD, has various capabilities and is still actively maintained by the University Computer Center.[2] For the

156   Computing in the Humanities

research reported here, it was used primarily to make key-word-in-context (KWIC) concordances and rhyme concordances.

The concordances of individual poets' works produced along the way during that eight years provided material for several scholarly papers, including "Approaching the Troubadours' Style through Quantification," presented in 1979 at a Troubadour Symposium at UCLA. At the symposium, colleagues were offered machine-readable text of as many poems of whatever troubadour they wished, in return for an equal number by a troubadour not already included in my current data base. In this way, more than 400 poems were acquired at no extra cost, and several people around the country were made very happy.

A second aspect of this work was undertaken in England by Professor Peter Ricketts (formerly of Birmingham University, now professor elect at Liverpool), who applied to the British Academy for funds to enter into the computer the nonlyric corpus of Old Occitan, which amounts to about the same quantity of data as the lyric corpus. As of August 1980, Ricketts has been awarded funds and given access to the new Kurzweil optical scanner at Oxford University. The final third of the lyric corps will soon be completed at the University of Minnesota, making available for computer analysis all the poetry of a very important period of European literature in the Old Occitan language.

Various words are of great importance in the troubadour lyric. It is a somewhat repetitive school, and a small group of words forms a nucleus of sense, where all the words are interconnected and imply one another. It was judged interesting to see just which words were, in fact, the most frequently occurring in such parts of speech as nouns, adjectives, verbs, and pronouns. Old Occitan is an inflected language, so that words appear in various morphological variants, all listed separately in the KWIC concordances. Thus, parts of the verb *esser* (to be) are found under the letters *e, f,* and *s.* To obtain an accurate count, all these variants had to be found and counted. This work was tedious but necessary. A further difficulty was the disambiguation of the listed words; the word *ans*, for example, might mean "years" or "rather" or "go" (subjunctive), according to the context. A side effect of this work was that I learned the Old Occitan language with great thoroughness!

At last, however, it was possible to use a sample of twenty troubadours, who together wrote over 500 poems (therefore one-fifth of the entire corpus), to put together lists of the top twenty most frequently used words in the categories of noun, adjective, verb, and adverb. While experts in the area might have easily guessed which were the most frequently used one or two or three words in each category, there were certain surprises, and the rank of some words was either much lower or much higher than had been expected. A comparison with the lists obtained from a smaller sample of northern French poets of the same period showed that there were also differences between the two groups. These results were reported in papers read at scholarly meetings in Montélimar, France, in 1975 and in Athens, Georgia, in 1977.

The verb listings showed that after the common verbs *esser* (to be), *aver* (to have), and *far* (to make, to do), the next three most common verbs were the so-called coverbs, or modal verbs, *voler* (to want), *poder* (to be able), and *saber* [to know (how)], in almost equal numbers, while another similar verb, *dever* (to have to, must), was well down the list. The ranking of these four verbs was fairly different in the northern group, suggesting that those poets were much more interested in *dever* (which could be translated as "duty") than were their southern counterparts. In addition, the infinitives most often used after these modal verbs in such expressions as *vuelh esser* (I want to be) and *puesc far* (I can do), were discovered. By counting, it was possible to discover which were the most frequently used pronoun subject, modal verb, infinitive after modal, and noun. These turned out to be, in Old Occitan, first person singular, *poder, far, amor.* Arranged into a sentence, these words are as follows: *Ieu non puesc far amor.* The *non* is added because when the verb *poder* (to be able) is used in the first person singular, it is most often negative. This matrix sentence might be translated: "I cannot make love." It is gratifying to note that this sentence, arrived at statistically, as it were, is in fact the major message of troubadour poetry, in which a lover-poet bewails the fact that the high-born lady with whom he is in love will not have anything to do with him.

A further problem concerned the use of certain very frequently occurring words in the privileged poetic position of rhyme word. Since each line of poetry, when keypunched, was ended with an oblique stroke (/), a feature in the GENCORD program allowed the concordance of just those words followed by an oblique stroke, namely, the words at the rhyme in each line. In this way, a list of the words most frequently used at the rhyme was compiled and compared with that of the most frequently used nouns where position in the line was not taken into account. This comparison proved instructive: It became evident that while some "nonpoetic" words appeared fairly frequently at the end of the line because they were needed to make rhymes with "poetic" words, other poetic words were very frequent in the corpus while almost never appearing at the rhyme. Since troubadour poetry often uses a rhyme scheme where the arrangement of rhymes *and the sounds of the rhymes themselves* are repeated in stanza after stanza, it also became clear that there were certain listener expectations: When a rhyme in *-or* was introduced in the first stanza, the listener could be pretty certain that certain words ending in *-or* would be introduced in subsequent stanzas (*amor, valor,* and so on). The fulfillment or nonfulfillment of these expectations might play an important part in the perception of the poem.

The results of these last two pieces of research were reported in papers at scholarly meetings in 1980: on modals at the Medieval Institute, Kalamazoo, Michigan, and on rhymes at the Third Triennial Congress of the International Courtly Literature Society, Liverpool.

The data and the concordance program have supplied information to scholars on the use of certain words: a doctoral candidate in Ghent, Belgium, was interested in the words which had been used for the first time in Old Occitan by a certain troubadour, Raimbaut d'Orange. A list of the unique words used by a group of troubadours who might be considered Raimbaut's predecessors was compared with a list of the unique words used by Raimbaut. The resulting list contained the words that Raimbaut was the first to use. In another stage of inquiry, the last list was used as a special word list to work through the poems of another group of twenty-six poets who could conveniently be termed Raimbaut's successors, to see if any of those words he was the first to use was also used by anyone else later than he. Another scholar who was interested in the words for *play* was furnished with a list of the parts of the verb and noun which occurred in the poems of the thirty-seven troubadours currently available in the data base. Graduate students working on troubadour poetry for their dissertations and scholars preparing critical editions have also received a number of concordances of the works of individual poets. I hope to achieve such notoriety in this respect that in the future a scholar will hardly undertake to prepare a critical edition of a troubadour's poetry without requesting such cooperation. The first of these critical editions, which will include a concordance as part of the critical apparatus, will be published soon by the University of California Press, Berkeley. The poet is Bertran de Born.

Notes

1. Joseph J. Duggan, *Concordance of the Song of Roland* (Berkeley: University of California Press, 1969).

2. "GENCORD User's Manual" is available from University Computer Center, University of Minnesota, Minneapolis, Minnesota 55455.

Part II
Computing
in Archaeology
and History

Vicky A. Walsh

For Part II on computer applications to archaeology and history, we have selected several projects which cover the wide range of current computer applications at the University of Minnesota. These chapters are intended to indicate some of the possible computer application methods that may assist researchers in attempts to reconstruct the culture and society of the past. In addition to the chapters presented here, brief mention is made of several of the many research projects currently underway at the University of Minnesota with the hope of sparking further interest in computer methods for research in archaeology and history.

In the past, computers have been used in archaeological and historical research for mathematical or statistical analyses of artifacts and documents. These statistical studies often have been confined to descriptive statistics, typologies, and seriations.[1] As has been noted in a recent article by D.H. Thomas, statistical procedures can be used profitably, but can also be misused and abused.[2]

Recently, however, there has been renewed interest in computer applications to the study of the past. Problem-oriented research, coupled with rigorous formation and testing of hypotheses, has promoted new applications of statistical procedures. For example, an article by J. Carothers and W.A. McDonald[3] presents a synthesis of some of the data generated in recent work in Greece.[4] Various statistical techniques were employed to generate a prediction of the regional population of Bronze Age Messenia, to investigate the distribution of the population over the landscape, and to attempt to understand the significance of this population distribution.

Perhaps the fastest-growing application area in computer-aided research in ancient studies is that of data bases and data-base management systems. With the increased availability of large-scale computers and adequate storage facilities for the large data bases that archaeological projects usually create, more and more projects are being considered feasible for computerized data storage and retrieval. The project reported here by Dr. Richard Ward and Renee Holoien (chapter 10) and the earlier research report by Debra Katz[5] are good examples of a creative approach to the study of ancient cuneiform documents. These documents serve as the basic source material for a variety of computational and statistical analyses of content, as well as for linguistic and textual procedures. One of the advantages of these applications is the potential for expanding the data base to include a larger corpus of documents. A study with a more specialized focus is represented in chapter 12 by Dr. Linda Ricketts, who presents the development of a data base as a basis for a prosopography of Caesar's associates in Gaul. This prosopography can then serve as the framework for a variety of historical investigations which focus on reconstructing the political, social, and economic structures of the first century B.C. in Rome. Another project now under development is the examination of the Sumerian milling industry. Milling texts from the Sumerian town of Umma will later be accessed and analyzed by the SIR data-base management system. This project is directed by William Brookman.

Archaeological research demands the collection of an enormous amount of data in various categories of information. In many archaeological projects, the first stage is a field survey of a region or area for the purpose of locating sites and collecting various environmental data relating to these sites. A data base for collecting data from a survey of Minnesota sites has been designed by Ruth Tate and is described in chapter 13. Debra Katz has developed a data base for on-site collection and retrieval of data from an archeological excavation.[6] This data base has been in use at Tel Mikhal, Israel, since the 1978 season and will continue to be used on-site for the duration of the excavation. This allows continuous updating of the data-base structure and definitions, immediate responses to the excavators, and modification of excavation procedures as indicated by computer analysis.

Various data bases are being developed for archaeological research at the University of Minnesota. Included are special-purpose data bases for cataloging pottery and glass from the site of Akhmim, Egypt. Thousands of these artifacts are being entered in data-base files for subsequent cataloging and organizing by the System 2000 Data Base Management System for both statistical and traditional analyses. Professor Sheila McNally is the director of the excavations at Akhmim and the data-base project.

A computer technique with great potential as a research tool for archaeology and history is simulation. Simulation is the process of designing a model of a real system and conducting experiments with this model to test specific hypotheses concerning the system and to better understand the system and how it works.[7] This approach allows the researcher to go a step beyond data collection and analysis. Simulation builds on previous analyses to examine the relationships of the entities or processes under consideration and to allow the researcher to test hypotheses based on data already collected and analyzed. Chapter 11, by Holly Morris and Vicky A. Walsh, exemplifies this approach, using a computer simulation of a Roman plantation.

In addition, work is now underway on a computer simulation to aid in activity analysis, specifically, house construction. Based on ethnographic and archaeological data,[8] the simulation attempts to reconstruct the processes and decisions involved in building the houses for a prehistoric settlement such as Nichoria in southwest Greece. This analysis will lead to a better understanding of the interrelationships between human and natural resources, as well as the social and economic decisions made by the ancient inhabitants of Nichoria. The project is under the direction of Vicky A. Walsh.

Locational analysis and sampling are of concern to most archaeologists. Most spatial analyses rely on statistical procedures such as cluster analysis or nearest-neighbor indexes.[9] A project which attempts to test selected sampling techniques on archaeological survey data in a more creative way is that of Jennifer Moody. By simulating the various sampling strategies and comparing these results with the actual survey data, she can assess the validity of these strategies for archaeological field surveys in Crete.

The most recent project to be proposed at the University of Minnesota is an economic analysis of the corpus of Linear B documents. The methodology would involve a combination of textual and archaeological procedures. By implementing an interface between a data-base management system and the TAGEDIT program described in this book, the researcher can access linguistic and contextual information as well as archaeological and word-content data. This project is still in the initial design stages, but could prove to be the prototype for advanced textual and historical studies.

I would also like to draw attention to the project in computer-aided instruction reported in Part II. This teaching module utilizes a simulation of an actual excavation to teach students various archaeological principles and techniques.

Many of these chapters are in the nature of "progress reports," in that the projects are in various stages of completion. Indeed, many will never be completed since, to be useful, these procedures must be continually modified and applied to ever larger sets of data and new areas of research.

Notes

1. J.E. Doran and F.R. Hodson, *Mathematics and Computers in Archaeology* (Cambridge, Mass.: Harvard University Press, 1975).

2. D.H. Thomas, "The Awful Truth about Statistics in Archaeology," *American Antiquity* 43(1978):231–244.

3. Joan Carothers and William A. McDonald, "Size and Distribution of the Population in Late Bronze Age Messenia: Some Statistical Approaches," *Journal of Field Archaeology* 6(1979):433–454.

4. W.A. McDonald and G. Rapp, Jr., *The Minnesota Messenia Expedition* (Minneapolis: University of Minnesota Press, 1972).

5. D.F. Katz, "A Computerized Study of the Aga-uš of the Ur III Period," Report 79001, University Computer Center, University of Minnesota, April 1979.

6. D.F. Katz, J.F. Merkel, P.C. Patton, and R.D. Ward, "System 2000 Applications in Ancient Studies," ASTUTE Conference presentation, Austin, Texas, April 1978.

7. R.E. Shannon, *Systems Simulation: The Art and the Science* (Englewood Cliffs, N.J.: Prentice-Hall, 1975).

8. W.A. McDonald, ed., *Excavations at Nichoria II: Middle and Late Helladic* (Minneapolis, Minnesota: University of Minnesota Press, forthcoming). and *Excavations at Nichoria III: Dark Age and Byzantine* (Minneapolis, Minnesota: University of Minnesota Press, forthcoming).

9. For other simulations in locational analysis, see I. Hodder, ed., *Simulation Studies in Archaeology* (Cambridge: Cambridge University Press, 1978).

10 A Computer Data Base for Babylonian Economic Documents

Richard D. Ward and
Renee A. Holoien

The thousands of Old Babylonian cuneiform texts that have not yet been studied to uncover the historical and philological information they contain beg for analysis by modern data-processing methods. For the project reported in this chapter, a data base was created by using the System 2000 data-base management software package [5]. This data base included all available documents from the Babylonian town of Kutalla. The cuneiform tablet data were entered into the computer in transliterated format, using a special character set developed for Sumerian and Akkadian for a research project in computer-assisted Sumerian lexicography (reported in chapter 3 of this book). This data-base project investigating Babylonian economic documents is seen as a first step toward the computer-assisted analysis of a large corpus of ancient documents.

Ancient Iraq in the second and first millenia B.C. was known as Assyria in the north and Babylonia in the south. In the third millennium B.C., Babylonia was known as Sumer, at least in its southern regions. The languages of this area were Sumerian (mostly third and early second millennium documents), Babylonian (mostly second and first millennium), and Assyrian (mostly first millennium). They were written in cuneiform script on clay tablets. Assyriologists—philologists and historians who study documents in these languages—attempt to reconstruct the political, social, and economic history of these ancient peoples from their actual records.

The Problem

The decipherment and analysis of these documents required complex and unwieldy manual labor during the previous century. Early Assyriological research methodology approached the task of analyzing Babylonian and Sumerian documents as follows:

1. Texts were transliterated into Roman script for ease of reading.
2. Several variables were selected for study and were cataloged on file cards.
3. Selected variables were then manually tabulated, generally chronologically.

4. The tabulated results were then synthesized with previous knowledge
    of the history of the period under examination.

The computer-assisted research project set forth here is an attempt to
support current methods of Assyriological research, as well as to broaden
the scope and efficiency of these methods. The focus is on Old Babylonian
business records, chiefly real estate transactions, of the period around 1800
B.C., known as the Hammurapi period after the most famous king of that
era. Sumerian and Babylonian documents are generally transliterated for
convenience of printing, if not ease of reading; this format has also been
employed in this computerized research.

Most previous efforts to analyze these documents have been manual
tabulations of such data as personal and geographic names. Three computer-assisted projects relate to this effort.[1] G. Buccellati developed
programs for linguistic analysis of a Babylonian epistolary-literature data
base at the University of California at Los Angeles. I.J. Gelb of the Oriental
Institute of the University of Chicago has utilized various sorting programs
for social and economic analyses of Old Akkadian texts, which are
somewhat antecedent to the focus of our project. C. Hamlin encoded
Babylonian documents from a town called Mari and used the Statistical
Package for the Social Sciences (SPSS) for economic analysis at the
University of Pennsylvania [3, 4].

This chapter demonstrates that storage of Babylonian texts in machine-
readable format is both feasible and practical and that printed copy of
transliterated texts is easily obtained. A large computer data base of texts
from many towns would support reliable synchronic as well as diachronic
analyses for historical reconstruction. The dissemination of analytical
studies derived from such a data base would be facilitated with the
computer, since the data base and the studies' results could be available to
other scholars in machine-readable format.

An example of the data utilized in this study is given in figure 10-1. The
document records a real estate sale and is transliterated (figure 10-1b) from
Babylonian cuneiform to Roman script. It is dated in the second year of
king Rim-Sin II, month 11, day 26, or 1740 B.C. (figure 10-1d). Further
reference is made to this document below. An analysis of the contents
(figure 10-1c) and a translation (figure 10-1a) accompany the example.

Typical questions that historians ask regarding this type of real estate
document include:

What indications are there in these documents of economic growth and
decline?

What clues are given to social structure and kinship or association
among residents of a town?

a.   (1) 1 SAR open lot (2) beside the house of Şilli-Ištar, (3) beside the house of the share of the sons of Ubār-Sin; (4) a front at the street (5) and a front at the house of Sin-asû; (8) Şilli-Ištar, son of Ili-sukkal, (9) and Awīl-ilī his brother (10) bought it (6) from Minânum, son of Migrat-Sin, (7) and Ili-turram his son. (12) They paid (11) 3½ shekels silver as its full price. (15) They swore by (var., ᵈRim-Sin) the king (13) forever and ever (14) not to alter [the contract] (var., nor to return to sue). 9 witnesses.

b.   c.

1.   1 SAR E₂. KI. ŠUB. BA   Property Size
2.   DA E₂ ŞI-Ii₂-Ištar   and Type
3.   DA E₂ ḪA. LA DUMU. MEŠ U-bar-ᵈEN. ZU
4.   SAG E. SIR₂   Neighbors
5.   U₃ SAG E₂ ᵈEN. ZU. A. ZU
6.   KI MI-na-ni DUMU MI-ig-ra-at-ᵈEN. ZU   Sellers
7.   U₃ I₃-Ii₂-tu-ra-am DUMU. NI
8.   ᵐŞI-Ii₂-Ištar DUMU I₃-Ii₂-SUKKAL
9.   U₃ A-wi-il-i₃-Ii₂ ŠEŠ. NI   Buyers
10.   IN. ŠI. ŠAM₂
11.   3 1/2 GIN₂ KU₃. BABBAR ŠAM₂. TIL. LA₂. NI. ŠE₃   Price
12.   IN. NA. AN. LA₂
13.   U₄. KUR₂. ŠE₃ U₄. NA. ME. A. KA
14.   NU. MU. UN. DA. BAL. E   Oath
15.   MU LUGAL. BI IN. PA₃
16.   IGI Na-bi-i₃-Ii₂-šu DUB. SAR
17.   IGI I₃-Ii₂-Ip-pa-al-sa₃-am ra-bi-a-nu-um
18.   IGI I₃-Ii₂-I-qi₂-šam DUMU In-ne-run
19.   IGI I₃-Ii₂-I-qi₂-šam DUMU I-nun-E₂-a   Witnesses
20.   IGI I-din-ᵈUTU DUMU U-bar-ᵈEN. ZU
21.   IGI I-ri-ba-am-ᵈEN. ZU ŠEŠ. NI
22.   IGI ᵈUTU-nu-še-zi-ib ŠEŠ. NI
23.   IGI ᵈIŠKUR-i-din-nam DUMU A-na-pa-ni-DINGIR
24.   IGI AN. KA. ᵈNIN. ŠUBUR DUMU A-pil-i₃-Ii₂-šu
25.   KIŠIB. BA. A. NI U₃ KIŠIB LU₂. INIM. MA. BI. MEŠ IB₂. RA   d.
26.   ITI ZIZ₂. A U₄. 26. KAM   Date
27.   MU-ᵈRi-in-ᵈEN. ZU LUGAL
28.   LU₂. KUR₂ LU₂. ḪUL. GAL₂

Na-bi-i₃-Ii₂-šu   AN. KA. ᵈNIN. ŠUBUR
DUMU A-ap-pa-a   DUMU A-pil-i₃-Ii₂-šu
IR₃ ᵈNin-si₄-an-na U₃ ᵈNISABA IR₃ ᵈNIN. ŠUBUR   Seals

ᵈIŠKUR. ILLAT-su₂   MI-Ig-ra-at-ᵈEN. ZU
DUMU A-na-pa-ni-DINGIR   DUMU ᵈEN. ZU-še-ni
IR₃ ᵈIŠKUR   IR₃ ᵈNIN. ŠUBUR

Figure 10-1. Sample Document: Tell Sifr 85

To what extent is private enterprise responsible for real estate activity?

What differences are there in real property transfer in various towns?

What specific factors serve as indicators of property values in Babylonia?

What were the average prices and sizes of various types of property in Babylonia? How do these sizes compare with sizes of excavated houses from the same periods?

What indications do these documents give of bureaucratic functions?

Methodology

A doctoral dissertation written by the senior author [9] in 1973 at the University of Minnesota addressed questions such as these. It consisted of a manual analysis of about 100 published documents from the Babylonian town of Kutalla (modern Tell Sifr, Iraq). This computerized project is an attempt to replicate the analytical methods employed in the dissertation research. Several additional computerized techniques are being developed and tested as well. They include: (1) statistical analysis to determine document provenance (when unknown), by establishing site indexes derived from key variables and then matching the document to these indexes; (2) mapping directional relationships of the sale property with adjacent property types, in order to determine the orientation of a real estate plot; (3) computer analysis of these highly formulaic texts to identify components in the data base by recognizing key words in the text; and (4) computer analysis which uses data such as names of family members to reconstruct genealogical relationships. A further expectation is that this computerized data base will facilitate the compilation and utility of various concordances to the texts.

During the dissertation research, the senior author realized that a simple encoded form of the documents would render much of the data machine-readable. Two 80-column punch cards could handle most of the significant data for computer sorting and analysis. An example is presented in figure 10-2. The major components of the text in figure 10-1 are given numeric equivalents. Thus, columns 1 to 3 on the first card identify the documents (figure 10-2a); other fields on this card represent property type and size (figure 10-2b and c), location information (figure 10-2d to f), price (figure 10-2g), date of the transaction (figure 10-2h); and names of buyers (figure 10-2i). Similarly, card 2 contains the data on names of sellers (figure 10-2j) and witnesses to the transaction (figure 10-2k). (This procedure is similar to that employed by C. Hamlin at the University of Pennsylvania, as noted above.)

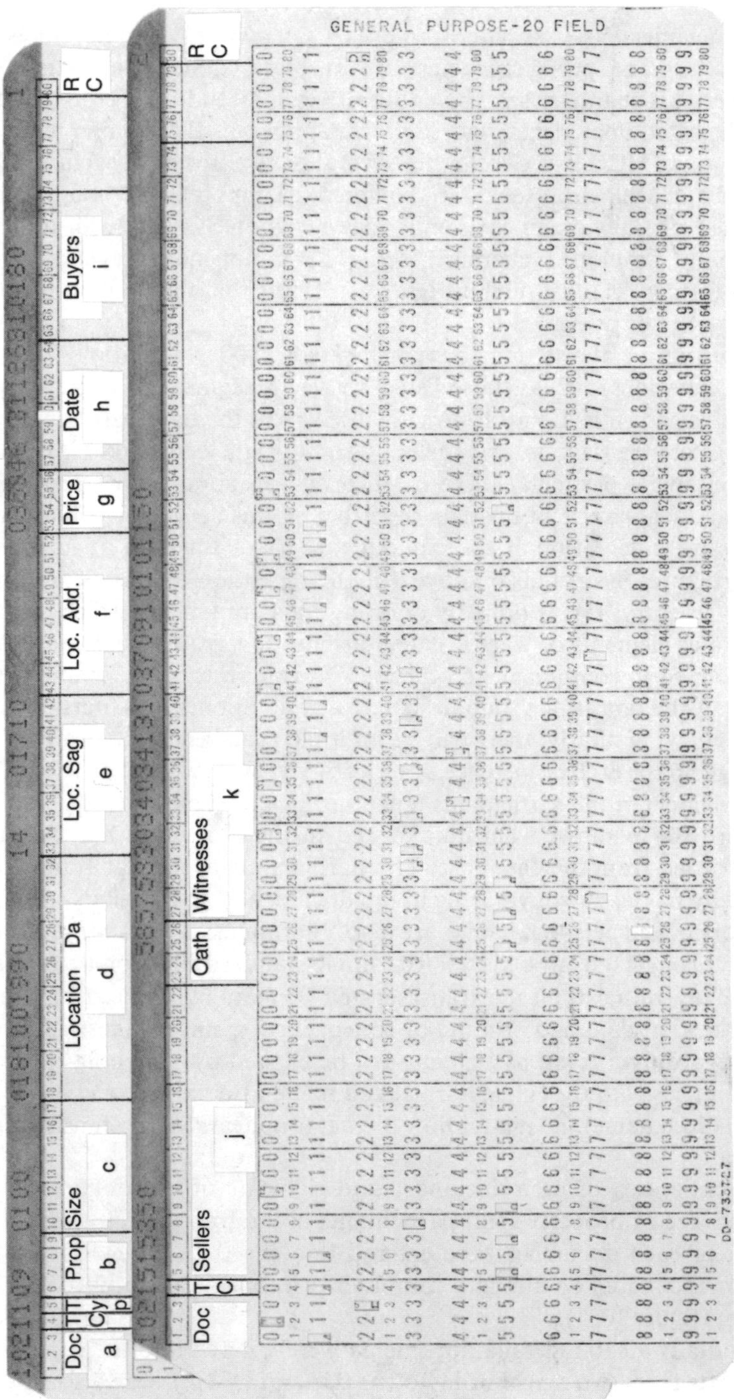

Figure 10–2. Sample Encoded Document: Tell Sifr 85

At the University Computer Center (UCC), a system was developed to represent the set of special characters of transliterated Sumerian texts in the computer. This character set, providing the capability for machine storage of transliterated documents, was similarly applied to Babylonian texts. At the same time, UCC was developing several data bases on System 2000, a data-base management system. UCC offered to support the development of a data base of Babylonian economic documents on System 2000, utilizing the specially developed character set. The major advantage over the encoded format, as illustrated in figure 10-2, was that the original form of the data would be preserved.

Organization of the data base in System 2000 was initially defined based on questions such as those listed above. A segment of the data-base definition is shown in figure 10-3a. Each entry in the data base represents one real estate transaction and includes eighty-eight components, each of which contains a particular piece of information about that transaction. The hierarchical nature of the data described in this definition is illustrated by successive indentation of the components. As a function of its hierarchical structure, System 2000 allows for the repetition of certain information in each entry; this is done by defining the components which contain those data as elements of what is called a repeating group. Thus, information contained in components 65 through 79 can occur more than once as elements of the repeating group designated by component 64 (participants) for each entry. Similarly, there can be multiple occurrences of components 80 through 86 for each occurrence of repeating group 79 (relation), which is itself an element of the participants repeating group.

Figure 10-3b shows what data stored in these components look like when retrieved from the data base. The participants in the sale transaction are listed by name, patronym, role in the document (buyer, seller, witness), and so forth. The personal names are also "normalized": All variant spellings of the same name are reduced to a single standard Babylonian or Sumerian spelling rather than the transliterated format. Normalization facilitates retrieval of data and printing of concordances, since all desired information regarding a given participant can be elicited by searching the data base for entries with the single normalized name as a value for component 66 (normalized name), no matter how the name appears in the transliterated document.

The entire text of each document and elements of information (type, price, and size of property sold, participants in the transaction, and so on) pertinent to each document were entered into the data base. Storing the entire text facilitated obtaining a computer printout of a complete specific document (figure 10-1).

Eventually all 102 Kutalla documents were entered into the computer. Several texts from two neighboring towns (Ur and Dilbat) were also entered

a.

```
64*  PARTICIPANTS (RG)
  65*   NAME (NAME X(60) IN 64)
  66*   NORMALIZED NAME (NAME X(10) IN 64)
  67*   OTHER NAME MU.NI (NAME X(10) IN 64)
  68*   ID NUMBER (INTEGER NUMBER 9(6) IN 64)
  69*   PATRONYM (NAME X(60) IN 64)
  70*   NORMALIZED PATRONYM (NAME X(60) IN 64)
  71*   ROLE (NAME X(20) IN 64)
  72*   TITLE (NAME X(20) IN 64)
  73*   NORMALIZED TITLE (NAME X(20) IN 64)
  74*   ORDER OF OCCURRENCE (INTEGER NUMBER 9999 IN 64)
  75*   SEAL TYPE (NAME X(10) IN 64)
  76*   KISHIB (NAME X(20) IN 64)
  77*   IR3 (NAME X(20) IN 64)
  78*   SEAL NUMBER (INTEGER NUMBER 9999 IN 64)
  79*   RELATION (RG IN 64)
    80*   MOTHER (NAME X(10) IN 79)
    81*   BROTHER (NAME X(40) IN 79)
    82*   SISTER (NAME X(10) IN 79)
    83*   CHILD (NAME X(10) IN 79)
    84*   HUSBAND (NAME X(10) IN 79)
    85*   WIFE (NAME X(10) IN 79)
    86*   RESIDENCE (NAME X(10) IN 79)
```

b.

```
65*  Mi-na-ni
69*  Mi-ig-ra-at-$^d$EN.ZU
71*  SELLER
74*      1

  83*  I$_3$-li$_2$-tu-ra-am


65*  I$_3$-li$_2$-tu-ra-am
69*  Mi-na-ni
71*  SELLER
74*      2


65*  $^m$Şi-li$_2$-Ištar
69*  I$_3$-li$_2$-SUKKAL
71*  BUYER
74*      1

  81*  A-wi-il-i$_3$-li$_2$


65*  A-wi-il-i$_3$-li$_2$
71*  BUYER
74*      2

  81*  $^m$Şi-li$_2$-Ištar
```

▲

◀ **Figure 10–3.** Sample from Data Base: Tell Sifr 85

for comparative purposes. After minimal training, research assistants identified the respective components in these formulaic documents and entered them via interactive terminals. By using XEDIT, a program for the interactive editing of computer-stored text, errors were relatively easy to correct. The special character set, however, hindered error correction, because nonprinting control characters, on which its implementation depended, could not be easily detected or changed.

With the available data, concordances and several special reports were generated with relative ease by means of the TALLY command (figures 10-4 and 10-5) and the REPORT WRITER feature of System 2000. REPORT WRITER enables retrieval of information from the data base in a format predetermined by the user. Figure 10-6 illustrates an example of a report generated by System 2000. Attempts to interface the data base with SPSS for cross tabulations and other statistical analyses were only partially successful—the special character set again caused difficulty.

When the special character set for Sumerian projects was later improved and its methods for input were altered, the same changes were implemented for the Kutalla project. The number of nonprinting control characters was decreased substantially, first by simply eliminating many

```
19"  MU RN DN.E.NE.BI.DA.RA NIG₂.DIM₂.MA.BI
     AL.IN.NA.AN.GU₃.[UŠ.AM₃] ALAM SUB.SUB.BI₂ . . .
     IN.NI.IN.TIL
65"    ᵈIŠKUR.MA.AN.SUM
19"  MU Sa-am-su-i-lu-na LUGAL ALAM SUB.BI₂
     ᵈLAMMA KU₃.GI DILI.DILI.B[I].TA
65"    ᵈIŠKUR.MA.AN.SUM
19"  MU Sa-am-su-i-lu-na LUGAL ALAM.SUB.BI₂
     ᵈLAMMA KU₃.GI DILI.DILI.BI.TA
65"    ᵐBe₂-li-i
19"  MU Sa-am-su-i-lu-na LUGAL URUDU
     KI.LUGAL.GUB ḪUR.SAG ID₂.DILI.DILI.BI
65"    Na-bi-i₃-li₂-su
19"  MU Sa-am-su-i-lu-na LUGAL URUDU
     KI.LUGAL.GUB ḪUR.SAG ID₂.DILI.DILI.BI
     ḪE.NUN ḪE₂.GAL₂.BI TUM₃.TUM₃
65"    Na-bi-i₃-li₂-su
65"    Nu-ur₂-ᵈKab-ta
65"    Nu-ur₂-ᵈKab-ta
19"  MU Sa-am-su-i-lu-na LUGAL ALAM SUB.SUB.BI₂
     ᵈLAMMA KU₃.GI DILI.DILI.BI.TA
65"    ᵐTa-ri-ba-tum
19"  MU Sa-am-su-i-lu-na LUGAL.E ALAM SUB.SUB.BI₂
     ᵈLAMMA KU₃.GI DILI.DILI.BI.TA
65"    ᵐTa-ri-ba-tum
```

Figure 10-4. Tally of Year Names by Scribes

instances where they were previously necessary and second by instead using special signs to indicate certain members of the special character set (for example, ↑ d ↑ instead of superscript ᵈ). With the revised system, the standard transliterated Babylonian or Sumerian text copy appeared only when plotted. (Figure 10–1*b* shows an example of plotted output.)

```
*************************
ELEMENT-        NORMALIZED NAME
*************************
FREQUENCY    VALUE
- - - - - - - - - - - - - - - - - - - - - -
```

1	Aḫi-šagiš
4	Aḫulap-Šamaš
1	Aḫušunn
4	Ali-waqartum
2	An-ka-Ea
1	An-ka-Ninšubur
26	Ana-Sin-emid
1	Anna-...biša
2	Anu-pi-Ninšubur
2	Anum-naṣi
4	Anum-pi-Ea
12	Anum-pi-Ninšubur
35	Apil-Sin
2	Apil-erṣetim
2	Apiša
28	Aplum
1	Ate
2	Awil-Adad
1	Awil-Ningal
53	Awil-ili
2	Awil-Šamaš
2	Beli
14	DUMU.MEŠ
4	Damqi-ilišu
1	Din-iliš
2	E-anna-lu-ti
2	Edublalmaḫ-manšum
2	En-...
3	Enki-bel-ili
2	Etel-pi-Enlil
4	Etel-pi-Sin
4	Etellum
2	Gimillum
1	Hammurapi-lu-dari
2	Hunabatum

Figure 10–5. Tally of Normalized Names

TYPE	SIZE IKU	SAR	GIN_2	SIZE IN SAR	PRICE MA.NA	GIN_2	PRICE IN GIN_2	UNITPRICE GIN_2/SAR
$E_2.GA_2.NUN$	000.00	001.67	000.00	001.67	000.00	004.16	004.16	002.49
$E_2.U_3.GA_2.NUN$	000.00	002.00	000.00	002.00	000.00	005.50	005.50	002.75
$E_2.DU_3.A$	000.00	001.33	000.00	001.33	000.00	007.33	007.33	005.51
$E_2.DU_3.A$	000.00	000.00	000.00	000.00	000.00	014.00	014.00	XXXXXX
$E_2.DU_3.A$	000.00	000.33	000.00	000.33	000.00	004.50	004.50	013.64
$E_2.DU_3.A$	000.00	000.33	000.00	000.33	000.00	004.50	004.50	013.64
$E_2.DU_3.A$	000.00	001.33	000.00	001.33	000.00	007.33	007.33	005.51
$E_2.KI$	001.00	000.00	000.00	100.00	000.00	001.67	001.67	000.02
$E_2.KI$	001.00	000.00	000.00	100.00	000.00	002.00	002.00	000.02
$E_2.KI$	001.00	000.00	000.00	100.00	000.00	001.67	001.67	000.02
$E_2.KI$	001.00	000.00	000.00	100.0C	000.00	002.00	002.00	000.02
$E_2.KI.UD$	000.00	001.33	000.00	001.33	000.00	004.00	004.00	003.01

Figure 10-6. Property Type, by Size and Price

E₂.KI.ŠUB.BA	000.00	002.00	000.00	002.00	000.00	005.33	005.33	002.66
E₂.KI.ŠUB.BA	000.00	002.00	000.00	002.00	000.00	004.00	004.00	004.00
E₂.KI.ŠUB.BA	000.00	002.00	000.00	002.00	000.00	005.00	005.00	002.50
E₂.KI.ŠUB.BA	000.00	001.33	000.00	001.33	000.00	002.50	002.50	001.88
E₂.KI.ŠUB.BA	000.00	000.67	000.00	000.67	000.00	002.00	002.00	002.99
E₂.KI.ŠUB.BA	000.00	001.00	000.00	001.00	000.00	003.50	003.50	003.50
E₂.KI.ŠUB.BA	000.00	002.00	000.00	002.00	000.00	005.25	005.25	002.62
E₂.KI.ŠUB.BA	000.00	001.33	000.00	001.33	000.00	002.33	002.33	001.75
E₂.KI.ŠUB.BA	000.00	001.33	000.00	001.33	000.00	004.33	004.41	003.32
E₂.KI.ŠUB.BA	000.00	001.00	000.00	001.00	000.00	002.50	002.50	002.50
E₂.KI.ŠUB.[BA]	000.00	002.00	000.00	002.00	000.00	003.33	003.33	001.66
KISLAḪ	000.00	000.00	000.00	000.00	000.00	000.00	000.00	XXXXXX
KI.ŠUB.BA	000.00	001.00	000.00	001.00	000.00	002.50	002.50	002.50

Figure 10-6 continued

Because of the programming that would have been required to convert the data to the revised procedures for special characters and the numerous errors in the data base, the decision was made to re-enter the data to conform with the improvements on the character set. All texts were prepared for data entry, and revisions to previous transliterations were made as necessary. The data-base definition was altered slightly to remove some components which had proved unnecessary to the current research and to rearrange others in an order more convenient to the study.

Research assistants again entered data on interactive cathode-ray tube (CRT) terminals. UCC provided ample technical assistance for the data-base management system. Development of procedures for statistical analysis was handled by the senior author. Other needs met by UCC included use of a computer terminal which could be programmed to display the set of special characters required for the project (in this case, the Lektro-media CRT) and use of the Varian Statos electrostatic plotter. The latter machine can be programmed to print any predesigned characters, such as those in the set for transliterated Sumerian, the designs for which are stored in the computer and sent to the plotter as a series of points or dots with horizontal and vertical coordinates. The machine then plots the points and prints the dots, and the result is characters from the special character set. (Again, see figures 10–1 and 10–5 for examples of plotted output).

Results

The Babylonians specified years by names of important events. Lists of such "year names" were compiled to assist scribes by providing a chrono-logical referent against which to record events of their time. These lists have been invaluable to modern historians as a means of establishing the relative sequence of dated documents and, when a known date can be tied into this sequence, of determining absolute dates in years B.C. for events in ancient Babylonia. The data base includes year name, king name, the king's regnal year, month name, number of that month in the year, day number, and absolute year B.C. Figure 10–4 gives the results of a tally of all occurrences in the data base of selected year names (component 19) and names of the scribes who wrote the respective documents (component 65).

In order to study aspects of Babylonian economic history over time, one must arrange all documents in chronological order. For instance, information regarding property values must be arranged by date in order to suggest patterns of economic growth or decline over time. The computer can process a number of variables, such as buyer, date, and price and size of property, simultaneously, and arrange selected information in any order prescribed by the System 2000 user.

Personal names are identified with patronym as well as with other kinships stated in the texts. The spellings are normalized for convenience of reference. A portion of a tally of normalized names in the data base is shown in figure 10-5. Awil-ili, who appears as a joint buyer in the document presented in figure 10-1, line 9, occurs with highest frequency of any of the names listed in this portion of the tally. Most of the names listed, however, occur less than five times. This distribution is primarily a function of the length of time covered by the business archive, on the one hand, and the involvement of a small circle of acquaintances of the principle participant in the archive, on the other. More comparative study on this matter is needed.

Economic history as related to real estate must consider time (date of sale), location (site within the town), property type (houses of various qualities, orchards, fields), property size, price, and parties to the transaction. When changes in price for various types of property are compared over time, and when such information for one town is compared with that for another town, new light may be shed on several aspects of the Babylonian economy. Variables such as time, size, and price indicate economic inflation and recession, reveal significant indexes of value in Babylonian society, and present differences in property values and economic trends among towns. These variables may also be compared with excavated remains of dwellings of the same or other periods, in order to verify or expand on suggested hypotheses.

A report was generated by System 2000 REPORT WRITER to list each sale by property type, size, and price. To compare sales, the sizes and prices were reduced to common units, and then the price per SAR (376 square feet) was calculated. The portion of this chapter that includes the sample text (figure 10-1) is highlighted in figure 10-6. In this instance, the property type E_2.KI.ŠUB.BA with an area of 1 SAR (figure 10-1, line 1) sold for 3½ GIN_2 (shekels) (figure 10-1, line 11). The property size in SAR of this example (indicated by the arrow in figure 10-6) is found in the fifth column; its price in GIN_2, in the tenth column. In the final column is the resulting unit price of the property, in this case 3½ GIN_2 per SAR.

A comparison of similar data from neighboring towns of roughly the same period is given in figure 10-7. Several trends are suggested by this information. One property type [improved house (E_2.DU_3.A)] is highest in both total price and unit price, except at Larsa. Houses at Ur and Larsa were most expensive (at 38 and 32 GIN_2 per SAR, respectively), followed by Dilbat (at 23 GIN_2 per SAR). The market at Kutalla was decidely lower (at 9.5 GIN_2 per SAR). Fields and orchards (E_2.KI, $KIRI_6$, KISLAH, and A.$ŠA_3$) brought much lower prices than houses, regardless of site.

With the results (figure 10-6) compiled for several towns (figure 10-7), certain problems can be viewed from a new perspective. For example,

TOWN	PROPERTY TYPE	AVG. SIZE (SAR)	AVG. PRICE (GIN)	UNIT PRICE (GIN/SAR)	No.
KUTALLA	É.DÙ.A	0.83	5.92	9.58	4
	É.KI.UD	1.33	4.00	3.01	1
	É.GÁ.NUN	1.84	4.83	2.62	2
	É.KI. ŠUB.BA	1.51	3.42	2.44	23
	KI.ŠUB.BA	1.88	4.27	2.29	4
	É.KI	100.00	1.84	0.02	4
LARSA	KI.UD	1.00	36.50	36.26	2
	É.DÙ.A	0.99	31.47	32.32	5
	É.KI.UD	1.17	31.00	26.56	1
UR	É.DÙ + GÁ.NUN	1.33	104.83	78.65	1
	É.DÙ.A	0.61	18.94	38.05	15
	KI.GÁL	0.64	10.67	26.59	3
	É.ŠUB(.BA)	0.58	7.92	24.66	2
	É.KI.GÁL	1.66	11.44	21.70	3
	KIRI$_6$ + dates	135.00	11.25	0.11	2
	KISLAH	100.00	2.50	0.025	1
DILBAT	É.DÙ.A	1.25	33.56	23.10	3
	É.BUR.BALA	0.47	2.48	10.40	4
	A.ŠÀ	501.67	14.75	0.04	6

Figure 10-7. Properties Compared by Town

although Assyriologists had previously assumed that E_2.KI was residential property, when E_2. KI is compared in size and price with various other property types at Kutalla and elsewhere (figure 10-7), its large size and very low unit price suggest that it was a nonresidential property. Furthermore, that neighboring property types were orchard/field types rather than residential types also suggests that E_2.KI was nonresidential property.

The advantages of using the computer in this type of research include convenience and speed of data management. Convenience of text storage, ease of text corrections, rapidity of data analysis (frequency counts, simple cross tabulations, and concordances), and convenience of printed text copy are the major benefits. The use of complex statistical applications available on the computer further enhances the potential in studies such as this. Although the overall cost benefits have not been determined, the initial special character-set problems certainly reduced the cost-effectiveness of the project.

This application could be extended to other research projects. First, the data base can be broadened to include documents of other Babylonian towns for comparative analysis, similar to what is illustrated in figure 10-7. Second, the data base can include other Babylonian text types, such as lawsuits, rentals, and receipts. Third, use of a data-base definition similar in structure and content for Sumerian (third millennium B.C.), Neo-Babylonian, and Seleucid (late first millenium B.C.) economic documents has been investigated and can be implemented. Fourth, the development of concordances of year names, personal names, titles, and professions occurring in texts of the Old Babylonian (Hammurapi) period (c. 1800 B.C.) would be a valuable research tool for Assyriologists. Fifth, documents from other ancient civilizations, such as the Hellenistic economic documents from Egypt, would likewise lend themselves to this data-base structure and analysis.

There are several unresolved problems within this project which other applications could solve:

1. Statistical procedures for identifying contemporaries and kinship groups need development. The entire area of sociometric analysis needs exploration. This new application would be especially suitable for Neo-Babylonian documents (c. 500 B.C.), in which three and four generations are mentioned with many of the personal names of the witnesses to transactions.

2. Computer procedures for identifying and extracting the component parts of a data base from within the full text are being developed at UCC. This system, called TAGEDIT (chapter 8 in this book), will reasonably apply to these economic documents because of the predictable nature of their vocabulary and format. Automatic analysis of the components in the documents for use in the data base will save hours of time formerly spent in manual analysis and preparation of the data. Further, it should substantially decrease the number of errors found in the data base resulting from manual data entry. Similar application of TAGEDIT to Sumerian economic documents of the third and early second millennia should prove especially beneficial because of the enormous quantity of such documents awaiting analysis.

3. Statistical procedures employed routinely in other contexts, such as cluster analysis and multiple regression, should be applied to this data base. It should be possible to develop multiple-regression models to determine missing data (for example, sale price, parcel size, and so on). Such techniques currently assist with real estate value estimation in modern computer-assisted mass appraisal systems.[2] If further analysis of individual document components in relation to known provenance were accomplished and the data base were extended to include documents from a wide variety of known sites, then regression techniques could help determine provenance for the large numbers of documents now available but of unknown provenance. Similar procedures are being used for pottery derivation based on chemical analysis of clays [1].

Reports on this project have been given at various meetings of the American Oriental Society [6], a user conference on System 2000 [7], and property-valuation seminars [8].

Acknowledgments

Financial assistance for the project has come from UCC under the auspices of the director, Dr. Peter C. Patton. UCC research assistants involved in the data entry, editing, and programming were D. Katz, J. Merkel, and R. Holoien, who continues to serve as technical assistant and assisted the senior author with the preparation of this chapter. Other UCC staff, particularly J. Cosgrove, were also consulted.

The source documents for this study are all in the British Museum, having been brought there after "excavation" in 1853. Both published and unpublished documents were made available for study and collation on three occasions by the curator of tablets of the Department of Western Asiatic Antiquities, Dr. E. Sollberger. Thanks are therefore extended to him and to the trustees of the British Museum. The quality of the available data was thereby greatly improved.

Pertinent literature regarding this application is substantially limited to articles and the dissertation of C. Hamlin [3]. Also relevant is a provocative article by J.-C. Gardin, which indicates some important considerations for further computer applications in the humanities [2].

Notes

1. Information regarding these projects is derived primarily from personal communication. Various papers have been presented by the authors at conferences. See G. Buccellati, "The Old Babylonian Linguistic Analysis Project: Goals, Procedures and First Results" (Paper presented at the International Conference of Computational Linguistics, Pisa, August 1973), and subsequent papers.

2. The reader may refer to numerous publications of the Lincoln Institute of Land Policy in Cambridge, Massachusetts. The senior author is a research analyst in the development of computer applications in this area with the Ramsey County Department of Property Taxation in St. Paul, Minnesota.

References

1. Dobel, A.G. "The *Waššukanni* Project: A Progress Report" (Paper presented to the American Oriental Society, Toronto, 1978).
2. Gardin, J.-C. "Logical Effects of Data Bases on the Study of Historical Sources." *International Social Science Journal* 27(1975):4.
3. Hamlin, C.L. "Agricultural Seasonality at Mari and the Problem of

Temporal Variability." In *Bibliotheca Mesopotamica,* vol. 7, edited by G. Buccellati. Los Angeles: UNDENA Publications, 1977).

4. Hamlin, C.L. "Cuneiform Archives as Data: Reliability of the Mari Archive for Agricultural Reconstruction." Ph.D. dissertation, University of Pennsylvania, 1976.

5. MRI, Inc. "System 2000 Reference Manual." MRI Systems Corporation, P.O. Box 9968, Austin, Texas 78766. November 1971, rev. August 1972, August 1974.

6. Ward, R.D. "Computer Assisted Analysis of Babylonian Contracts: The Data Base" (Paper presented to the American Oriental Society, Toronto, April 1978).

7. Ward, R.D. "A Babylonian Real Estate Documents Database," in *System 2000 Applications in Ancient Studies* by D. Katz, J. Merkel, P.C. Patton, and R.D. Ward (Paper presented at System 2000 Users Conference, Austin, April 1978).

8. Ward, R.D. "Computer Assisted Analysis of Babylonian Real Estate Documents" (Paper presented at Lincoln Institute of Land Policy, Cambridge, Massachusetts, June 1978).

9. Ward, R.D. "The Family History of Şilli-Ištar: A Reconstruction Based on the Kutalla Documents." Ph.D. dissertation, University of Minnesota, 1973.

Additional Bibliography

Holoien, R.A., and Inman, E.E. "TAGEDIT User Reference Manual." UCC Technical Report, University of Minnesota, forthcoming.

Katz, D.F. *A Computerized Study of the AGA-UŠ of the Ur III Period.* UCC Technical Report 79001, University of Minnesota, 1979.

Nie, N.H.; Hall C.H.; Jenkins, J.C.; Steinbrenner, K.; and Bent, D.H. *Statistical Package for the Social Sciences.* 2d ed. New York: McGraw-Hill, 1975.

11

CATO: A Computer Simulation of a Roman Wine and Oil Plantation

Holly J. Morris and
Vicky A. Walsh

Around 300 B.C. there emerged in Roman Italy a new, intensive cash-crop system of agriculture often known as the "latifundia" or "plantation agriculture." The plantations represented the evolution of a new kind of farm organization and a shift in some regions from small, one-family subsistence farmers to large landholders. By 50 B.C., some of these extensive cash-crop operations covered 350 acres or more. The main objective of the plantations was to generate profit. Because of land, equipment, and labor costs, owning a plantation entailed a large initial capital investment. Consequently, the owners were often Roman senators and other well-to-do noblemen whose capital had increased as a result of tributes from new provinces. Slaves made up the bulk of the labor base and were an increasingly abundant resource with the expansion of the Roman Empire, although free men were frequently hired at especially busy times (harvest, pruning time, and so on) or on contract basis for special tasks (for example, olive harvest). The owners seldom lived or worked on the farms, but instead hired a manager, often an experienced slave, to oversee the day-to-day operations.

Most plantations had a tendency to specialize in one or two products. In central and southern Italy, wine and oil plantations were common, while in the fertile plains of the northeast, ranching was prominent. Plantation products were sold locally and shipped to markets in the provinces. Despite specialization, plantations worked toward self-sufficiency by producing many of the farm necessities, such as grain for food, and other products needed for the plantation to function, such as reeds for vine props.

Although these plantations were an important new addition to Roman farming, they did not preclude other earlier forms of agriculture. Archaeological evidence has shown the existence of small wine- and oil-producing farms which also produced bread and cheese and often operated in conjunction with small inns [1]. These were usually run by the owner and his immediate family, perhaps with the addition of a few slaves. Small wheat farmers were still operating in the plains and other grain-growing regions, and tenant farming was common.

The plantation is a complex system influenced and changed through interactions with other larger systems. The ultimate purpose of this research is to identify factors and interactions which allowed for the evolution of the plantation and, more importantly, to examine the effect its growth and maturity had on other economic, social, and environmental factors of the ancient Roman world. Our specific approach has been to develop a computer simulation which represents the plantation as a complex system.

Figure 11-1 illustrates how the plantation can be viewed as a part of the larger scheme of Roman life. Each circle represents a system or network in and of itself which is embedded within a larger system.[1] Characteristics of the plantation which were mentioned above are included in the smallest circle. These characteristics set it apart from any other kind of Roman farming and are determined by factors represented in the other three circles. The plantation worked within the framework of an economic system, which included factors of production, distribution, and consumption. Figure 11-1 outlines the major components of each of these economic factors. The economic system is, in turn, embedded in the larger social system. Major social factors which affected the economic system were politics, communications, and religious and other social determinants. The environment is another large system which interacts with the other three systems. Factors such as climate, soil fertility, and access to water and transportation influenced plantation activities as well as economic choices.

The Problem

The sources for studying Roman plantations are of two main types. First, there are the ancient writers themselves, who provided details on farm layout and agricultural production and organization. This collection of writers spans the second century B.C. to the first century A.D. and provides a useful look at how farms changed as the Roman Empire expanded. The first of the important Roman works was Cato's *De Agri Cultura,* probably written in the middle of the second century B.C. Cato's description of a wine and oil plantation is one major source of evidence for this research project. The other important writers were Varro (37 B.C., *De Re Rustica*), Columella (c. 50 A.D., *De Re Rustica, De Arboribus*), and Pliny the Elder (32 A.D.., *Historia Naturale*).

The second major source of information is the archaeological evidence. This source consists of the material remains related to Roman agriculture such as excavated farm and villa sites, farm implements, representations on surviving monuments, and evidence of agricultural settlement and activity revealed by aerial photography. This archaeological record provides details about actual storage capacities, settlement and farm sites, specific crops raised, and the level of technology used to accomplish the daily tasks on a farm or plantation.

Most general histories of Rome have not used these sources effectively;

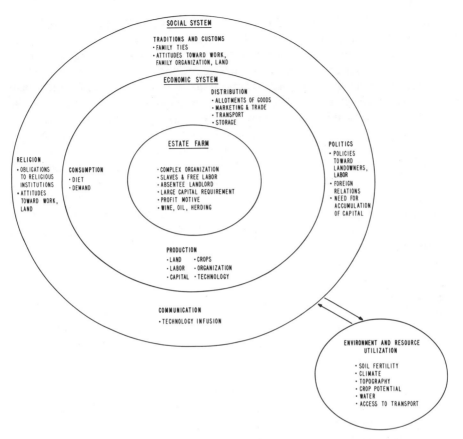

Each circle represents a system in and of itself which is embedded within a larger system. The smallest system is the plantation, which is embedded within the larger economic system. In turn, the economic system is embedded within the larger framework of the social system. Factors from both the economic and the social system influence and interact with the plantation.

Figure 11-1. Relationship between the Systems Associated with Agriculture

nor have they given adequate emphasis to the role of farming in Roman life. "In most standard histories of Rome, and even in works of much narrower scope, the subject is either treated in the most cursory fashion or presented in such a way as to give the impression of a simple primitive structure." [6, p. viii] Many (other) secondary sources have been utilized in gathering and synthesizing the information in the ancient literary and archaeological sources to provide a general picture of Roman farming. Important examples of this kind include works by Carrington [1], Day [2], Tenney Frank [3], and M.I. Rostovtzeff [4]. By far the most sophisticated, up-to-date study of Roman farming is compiled in the works of Kenneth White [5, 6]. He has digested an immense amount of material and has included useful bibliographies and profit estimates of farm productivity. Certainly White, as well as some of the other authors mentioned above, was aware that Roman farming was influenced by and related to other economic and social factors. Although this interaction was not the main thrust, the work of the authors mentioned above, along with other important research, has laid the foundation for the computer simulations described below by providing accessible, accurate information concerning Roman farming. The information provided by ancient and modern sources has been used to understand the general processes of the farming operation and to quantify the important factors related to plantations, as outlined in figure 11-1. For this research, the general approach to the study of the Roman plantation is to view the plantation as a system and investigate the factors and interactions that operate within that system.

Approach

The initial objective is to isolate the plantation from external influences (figure 11-1) and thus concentrate on the internal processes of the system. This approach allows us to construct a mathematical model which represents the plantation system.[2] The model is a working hypothesis dealing with the structure and relationships of various internal factors of the plantation and is, by definition, less complex than the original. These factors or "variables" are divided into four categories: land, manpower, expenses, and revenue (figure 11-2). They are discussed in more detail

I. **LAND**

(% AGE OF LAND IN GRAIN, VINES, OLIVES AND GARDEN CROPS)

II. **MANPOWER**

—SLAVES
—HIRED HANDS

III. **EXPENSES**

—SLAVE RATIONS
—WAGES AND RATIONS FOR HIRED LABOR
—GENERAL FARM EXPENSES

◀ **Figure 11-2.** Categories of Variables

IV. **REVENUE**

—GRAIN YIELD AND MARKET PRICE
—WINE YIELD AND MARKET PRICE
—OLIVE OIL YIELD AND MARKET PRICE

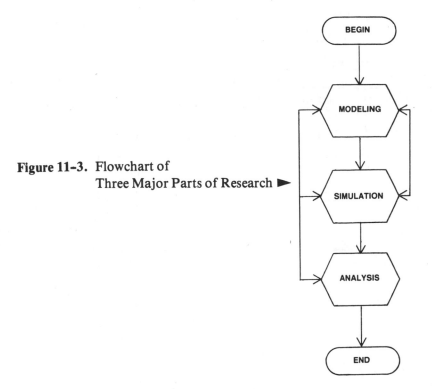

Figure 11-3. Flowchart of
Three Major Parts of Research ▶

below. There are three parts to this research effort: modeling the system, simulating the model, [3] and analyzing the results (see figure 11-3).

It was decided to model the plantation system on a yearly cycle of agricultural activities (figure 11-4), for this would encompass the major objective variables in the four categories mentioned above. The cycle, as represented in figure 11-4, is divided into four seasonal units, and each unit includes variables which define operational costs and revenues. Values and ranges for the individual variables (figure 11-5) were estimated by using a variety of sources, ancient and modern. The major sources were Cato, Varro, Columella, and K.D. White. Archaeological and epigraphical evidence, mainly from Campania, was also useful. The plantation system is evaluated in terms of profit. All variables are selected for their impact on revenue or expenses. Excluding those factors most difficult to assess (the "human" factors, natural catastrophes, supply and demand, and so on), the result is a list of over fifty variables whose interrelationships define an index of profit. The variables are listed in figure 11-5. Each variable name is followed by a value taken from one run of the program, plus a short

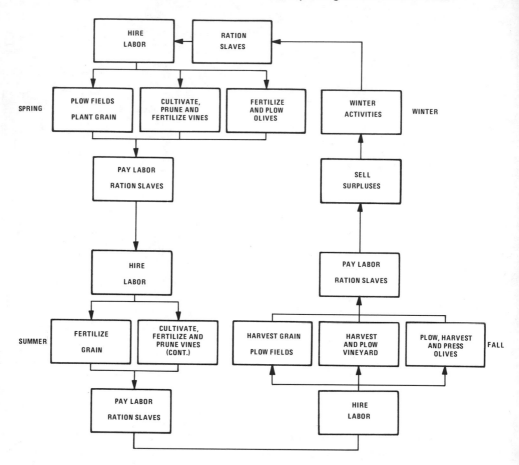

Figure 11-4. Plantation Yearly Cycle

description. The Roman plantation is thus modeled by using a series of mathematical equations employing these variables to produce the profit index.

The second stage is a computer simulation of this model. Since there are over a million possible combinations of variables using three ranges of values (low, medium, high), it was imperative that a computer be used to handle the computations. The computer simulation then computes costs, revenues, and profit for one yearly cycle of the plantation's agricultural activities. This program, named CATO, is written in the high-level language FORTRAN because it is a numerically oriented language which permits quick and easy interactive processing. Interactive processing[4] is important because of the need to "experiment" (see note 3) with different values for any of the variables in order to evaluate the impact of each variable on the

1	TLAND	size of farm in jugera
2	GLAND	percent of total land in grain
3	WLAND	percent of total land in grapes
4	XLAND	percent of total land in non-agricultural
5	RLAND	percent of total land in reeds
6	OLAND	percent of total land in olives
7	VLAND	percent of total land in garden
8	GRFAL	percent of grain land left in fallow
9	SLAVES	total number of males owned
10	SLAVECS	cost of slaves/year (in sestertii)
11	CONLAB	total non-slaves hired/year
12	GRGRCST	grain payment for grain labor
13	GRWNCST	wine payment for grain labor
14	GROLCST	olive payment for grain labor
15	GRMNCST	payment for grain labor
16	WNCRCST	grain payment for vine labor
17	WNWNCST	wine payment for vine labor
18	WNOLCST	olive payment for vine labor
18A	WNMNCST	payment for vine labor
19	OLGRCST	grain payment for olive labor
20	OLWNCST	wine payment for olive labor
21	OLOLCST	olive payment for olive labor
22	OLMNCST	payment for olive labor
24	GRAINCL	men hired for grain labor
25	GRCULT	
26	GRWD	manpower for grain production
27	GRRP	(broken down by seasonal activities)
28	GRFRT	
29	WINECL	men hired for wine labor
30	WNHARV	
31	WNPRN	manpower for wine production
32	WNCULT	(broken down by seasonal activities)
33	WNFRT	
34	OLIVECL	men hired for olive labor
35	OLPRSS	manpower required for olive production
36	OLPICK	(broken down by season)
37	GARDCL	men hired for garden labor
38	VWORK	manpower required for garden
39	WINEPR	price of wine per culleus
40	GRAINPR	price of grain per modius
41	OLIVEPR	price of olives/pound
42	SHTSPR	price of vine shoots
43	WINEYD	yield of wine per jugera
44	GRAINYD	yield of grain per jugera
45	OLIVEYD	olive yield in pounds/jugera
46	SEED	percent of grain yield saved for seed
47	GRAINRT	slave grain ration
48	WINERT	slave wine ration
49	OLIVERT	slave olive ration
50	OWNER	wine stock held for owner
51	YREXP	capital expense

This is a listing of all the variables utilized by CATO to compute the annual profit of the farm. Each variable name is followed by a short description. With CATO, the user can test the relationships among any of these variables. Several Roman units of measure are used: 1 jugera = 0.66 acre, 1 modius = 1 peck, 1 culleus = 120 gallons. SESTERTIUS is a Roman monetary unit.

Figure 11-5. Variables in CATO

system as a whole. Figure 11-6 illustrates the sequence of steps the program must follow to compute the cost and revenue values for one year of the agricultural cycle. After the user enters variable values, the program computes the labor costs, the revenues based on yields and surplus, and the profit. The results of this run are then returned to the user.

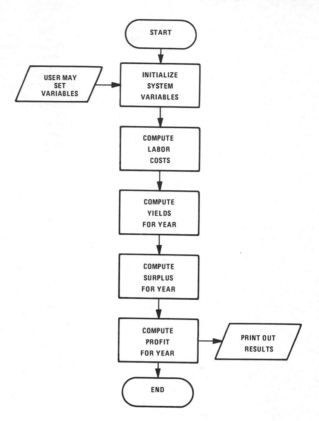

Figure 11-6. Sequence of Steps to Compute Cost and Revenue Values for
One Year

Figure 11-7 shows how one variable, in this case, number of slaves, can
be set to 10, for example, to assess how the number of slaves can affect the
yearly profit. All variables can be set by the user to any value within the
constraints of the system definition or model. In addition, variables not
preset by the user are assigned random values. This allows for a degree of
uncertainty which we feel is inherent in any realistic model of an
agricultural system. The computer simulation allows the user to test hypotheses about which variables should (according to economic principles) or
are said to (according to ancient and modern sources) affect profit. The user
can then preset the relevant variables and run the program to test these
hypotheses. Various decisions about plantation size, configuration (for
example, size of grain fields versus vineyards), number of slaves, and so on
can be evaluated in terms of their net effect on the yearly activities and
ultimate profit for the plantation so described.

```
CATO IS AN ATTEMPT TO MODEL THE ECONOMIC SYSTEM OF A CAMPANIAN
(SOUTHERN ITALY) VINE PLANTATION DURING ROMAN TIMES.  A ROMAN
PLANTATION WAS A SELF SUFFICIENT UNIT, WHICH MEANS BESIDES PRODUCING
ONE OR TWO MAJOR CROPS TO SELL (IN THIS CASE, ONLY WINE) THEY ALSO
GREW SUBSISTENCE CROPS LIKE GRAIN, GARDEN VEGETABLES, AND REEDS
FOR VINE PROPS.  SLAVES WERE THE MAIN SOURCE OF LABOR, ALTHOUGH
HIRED HANDS WERE INVOLVED IN SEASONAL ACTIVITIES SUCH AS THE GRAIN
AND GRAPE HARVESTS.  THE ESTIMATES FOR THE PROFITABILITY OF THE
PLANTATIONS ARE VERY HIGH.  BY ALLOWING US TO VARY THE SIZE, THE
RATIO OF CROPS, THE YIELDS, THE RATIO OF SLAVE VS. HIRED LABOR,
ETC., CATO ALLOWS US TO PREDICT THE PROFITABILITY OF A VARIETY OF
DIFFERENT POSSIBILITIES.  SINCE NOT ALL OF THE VARIABLES MENTIONED
ABOVE ARE KNOWN PRECISELY, ESTIMATED RANGES HAVE BEEN USED IN THOSE
CASES.  ALL OF THE MEASUREMENTS ARE IN ROMAN UNITS.  A JUGERA IS
.66 ACRES, A MODIUS IS ONE PECK, AND A CULLEUS EQUALS 120 GALLONS.
THE MONETARY UNIT IS SESTERSTIUS.

DO YOU WISH TO CHANGE ANY PARAMETERS?
TYPE YES, NO OR LIST
? YES
INPUT PARAMETER TO BE CHANGED (TYPE NO TO STOP)
? SLAVES
INPUT NEW RANGE OR NO
? NO
INPUT NEW VALUE
? 10
INPUT PARAMETER TO BE CHANGED (TYPE NO TO STOP)
? NO
 DO YOU WISH TO LEASE OUT YOUR OLIVE LAND?
? YES
DO YOU WISH AN IMMEDIATE LISTING?
? YES
DO YOU WISH A LONG OR SHORT PRINTOUT?
? LONG

TLAND     MED      100,000    JUGERA
GLAND     MED         .405    PER CENT. OF TOTAL
WLAND     MED         .180    PER CENT. OF TOTAL
XLAND     MED         .045    PER CENT. OF TOTAL
RLAND                 .050    PER CENT. OF WLAND
GRFAL                 .500    PER CENT. OF GLAND
SLAVES    MED       10.000    MEN
```

Figure 11-7. One Variable, Number of Slaves, Can be Set to 10 to Assess How Number of Slaves Can Affect Yearly Profit

The third stage is analysis. The results from these runs are compared with what is known to be true or likely about Roman plantations in order to assess the validity of the model. This analysis, in turn, will produce new or amended hypotheses about the plantation, to be further tested via simulation. Thus the cyclical nature of this research (figure 11-3) allows each stage to aid in the reevaluation of the preceding one.

Ideally, the computer simulation would allow the user to test all possible combinations of variable values in order to ascertain the "best" or most stable Roman-plantation configuration. With the technology presently available at the University Computer Center (UCC), University of Minnesota, this would take an estimated year of computing time, excluding input and output. For this reason, CATO is run interactively (on the CDC Cyber 172), with the user presetting variables according to specific hypotheses, as discussed above. The program can be run as many times as required or desired by the user. The program requires about 60,000 words of central memory and 0.2 seconds to compile and run one data set. Since each run is often dependent on the previous one, a large-batch job with a series of input variables is not feasible at this time.

The Results

The results generated from one run of the program are shown in figure 11–9; all measurements in the program are in Roman units. One "jugera" of land equals 0.6 acre, one "culleus" equals 120 gallons, and one "modius" equals one peck. After all the variables and their values are printed, the program lists the computer yields for each crop, along with the other expenses and the percentage of profit of that specific plantation for one year. Figures 11–8 and 11–9 show the printout for the plantation, with the wine yield per unit of land changed from low to high. In this run the user can see that a plantation with a low wine yield produces a profit of − 11.65 percent, while the same plantation with a high wine yield had a profit of 11.28 percent. Running the program several times and altering one or two items in each run allow the program to test the sensitivity of yields, expenses, and profit to each variable. These results can then be compared to other computer runs, as well as ancient literary data, modern data, and archaeological evidence.

The following discussion illustrates examples of information the user can generate by running CATO several times. These examples are preliminary, but they do point out the effectiveness of computer simulation for testing the effects of certain variables on plantation output. The examples presented relate to the proportion of land dedicated to each crop on the plantation. By using CATO, three variations of the plantation which are relatively stable and profitable have been identified. They are wine plantations, olive plantations, and the "mixed" farm. All three types of farms probably existed in Roman times.

Figure 11–10 shows general conclusions about wine plantations derived from CATO. About half of the land is taken up in grain because of the fallow system of cultivation used in Roman times. Certainly, there were some areas of ancient Italy where fallowing was not necessary [6, pp. 47, 113], which would reduce grain-land requirements. On a fallowing farm, only 30 percent of the land is in vines, but this is enough to give yields as high as 12,000 gallons (95 cullei) on a 66-acre (100-jugera) farm. As a point of reference, a large farm building excavated at Boscoreale in Campania, Italy, had the potential of storing 174 cullei of wine [2, p. 180]. Using CATO, profit outputs were as high as 60 percent in optimum conditions,

```
VARIABLE  RANGE       VALUE     UNIT OF MEASURE

TLAND               100.000     JUGERA
GLAND     MED           .462     PER CENT. OF TOTAL
WLAND     MED           .197     PER CENT. OF TOTAL
XLAND     MED           .037     PER CENT. OF TOTAL
RLAND                   .500     PER CENT. OF WLAND
GRFAL                 1.000      PER CENT. OF GLAND
SLAVES    MED         10.000     MEN
SLAVECS             365.000      SESTERTII
CONLAB               16.000      TOTAL MEN HIRED
GRGRCST   MED           .150     MODII PER MANDAY
GRWNCST   MED           .100     CULLEI PER MANDAY
GRMNCST   MED         3.074      SEST. PER MANDAY
WNGRCST   MED           .150     MODII PER MANDAY
WNWNCST   MED           .100     CULLEI PER MANDAY
WNMNCST   MED         3.074      SEST. PER MANDAY
GRAINCL                    0     TOTAL MEN PER YEAR
GRCULT                     0     TOTAL MANDAYS
GRWD                       0     TOTAL MANDAYS
GRRP                       0     TOTAL MANDAYS
GRFRT                      0     TOTAL MANDAYS
WINESL               16.000      TOTAL MEN PER YEAR
WNHARV              194.625      TOTAL MANDAYS
WNPRN               389.250      TOTAL MANDAYS
WNCULT              778.500      TOTAL MANDAYS
WNFRT                      0     TOTAL MANDAYS
WINEPR    HI        345.000      SEST. PER CULLEI
GRAINPR   MED         2.074      SEST. PER MODII
SHTSPR    MED      1036.966      SEST. PER JUGERA
WINEYD    LOW         2.500      CULLEI PER JUGERA
GRAINYD   MED        36.296      MODII PER JUGERA
SEED      MED           .110     PER CENT. OF YIELD
GRAINRT              50.000      MODII PER YEAR
WINERT                  .250     CULLEI PER YEAR
OWNER     MED         2.555      CULLEI PER YEAR
YREXP     MED      8000.000      SEST. PER YEAR
OLAND     MED           .149     PER CENT. OF TOTAL
OLIVEYD   HI        625.000      POUNDS PER JUGERA
OLIVEPR   MED           .500     SEST. PER POUND
OLPRSS               59.415      TOTAL MANDAYS
OLPICK              111.402      TOTAL MANDAYS
VLAND     MED           .057     PER CENT. OF TOTAL
VWORK                25.769      TOTAL MANDAYS
OLIVERT   MED       142.957      POUNDS PER YEAR
OLGRCST   MED           .150     MODII PER MANDAY
OLWNCST   MED           .100     CULLEI PER MANDAY
OLMNCST   MED         3.074      SEST. PER MANDAY
OLOLCST   MED           .509     POUNDS PER MANDAY
GROLCST   MED           .509     POUNDS PER MANDAY
WNOLCST   MED           .509     POUNDS PER MANDAY
OLIVECL                    0     TOTAL MEN PER YEAR
GARDCL                     0     TOTAL MEN PER YEAR


TOTAL COST IN GRAIN IS         808.672 MODII
TOTAL COST IN WINE IS           63.635 CULLEI
TOTAL COST IN OLIVES IS       2293.566 POUNDS
TOTAL COST IN MONEY IS       13451.324 SEST.
TOTAL GRAIN YIELD IS          2000.205 MODII
TOTAL WINE YIELD IS             68.706 CULLEI
TOTAL OLIVE YIELD IS          9283.529 POUNDS
TOTAL GRAIN SURPLUS IS        1191.623 MODII
TOTAL WINE SURPLUS IS            5.050 CULLEI
TOTAL OLIVE SURPLUS IS        7555.540 POUNDS
TOTAL COST FOR THE YEAR IS   37953.577 SEST.
TOTAL NET PROFIT FOR YEAR     4422.973 SEST.
PROFIT FOR THE YEAR IS         -11.654 PER CENT
```

Figure 11–8. Printout for Plantation with Low Wine Yield per Unit of Land

```
DO YOU WISH TO RUN AGAIN?
?YES
DO YOU WISH TO CHANGE ANY PARAMETERS?
TYPE UYES, NO OR LIST.
?YES
INPUT PARAMETER TO BE CHANGED (TYPE NO TO STOP)
?WINEYD
INPUT NEW RANGE OR NO
?HI
INPUT PARAMETER TO BE CHANGED (TYPE NO TO STOP)
?NO
DO YOU WISH TO LEASE OUT YOUR OLIVE LAND?
?NO
DO YOU WISH AN IMMEDIATE LISTING?
?YES
DO YOU WISH A LONG OR SHORT PRINTOUT?
?SHORT

TOTAL COST IN GRAIN IS       808.672 MODII
TOTAL COST IN WINE IS         63.655 CULLEI
TOTAL COST IN OLIVES IS     2293.566 POUNDS
TOTAL COST IN MONEY IS     13451.324 SEST.
TOTAL GRAIN YIELD IS        2000.295 MODII
TOTAL WINE YIELD IS           93.931 CULLEI
TOTAL OLIVE YIELD IS        9283.528 POUNDS
TOTAL GRAIN SURPLUS IS      1191.623 MODII
TOTAL WINE SURPLUS IS         30.276 CULLEI
TOTAL OLIVE SURPLUS IS      7555.540 POUNDS
TOTAL COST FOR YEAR IS     37953.577 SEST.

TOTAL NET PROFIT FOR THE YEAR IS    4279.911 SEST.
PROFIT FOR THE YEAR IS                 11.277 PER CENT.
```

Figure 11-9. Printout for Same Plantation Seen in Figure 11-8, except
Wine Yield Is High

but more conservative profit estimates ranged from 4 to 20 percent per year. Columella (III.3) used 6 percent per year as a reasonable return, and White [6, p. 244] estimated 13.3 percent as a likely profit on plantations with medium to high grape yields.

On an olive-producing farm (figure 11-11), the simulation shows an optimum of about 90 percent of the land might have been dedicated to olives, if the land between the trees were planted in grain, as is the case in many parts of the Mediterranean today. Olive yields are high only every other year, and the estimates in figure 11-11 reflect a high-yield year. On a good year, yields on a 100-jugera estate could be as high as 4,000 gallons (35 cullei) of olive oil. Boscoreale's olive storage could have held about 20 cullei [2, p. 181]. Profits were generally around 9 to 12 percent, but on a good year could be as high as 45 percent. A few low-yield years had negative profits. Information from runs of CATO indicates that the olive plantation would have needed to secure wine for rations and pay. To be profitable, olive farms must have had access to a cheap supply of wine. It is likely that an olive farm operator bought wine from neighbors or shipped it in from another of his farms.

Grain land also takes up half the area in the mixed farm (figure 11-12).

Figure 11-10. Some General
Conclusions about
Wine Plantations ▶

50% IN GRAIN
30% IN VINES
15% IN REEDS AND GARDEN
5% FOR BUILDINGS

YIELDS: 25 TO 95 CULLEI (WINE)
           (3000-12000 GALLONS)

PROFITS: 4% TO 20%

PROBLEM: GRAIN SUPPLY

90% IN OLIVE TREES (GRAIN INTERSPERSED)
5% IN GARDEN
5% FOR BUILDINGS

◀ **Figure 11-11.** Some General
Conclusions about
Olive Plantations

YIELDS: 15 TO 35 CULLEI (OIL)
           (1800 TO 4000 GALLONS)

PROFITS: 2% TO 14%

PROBLEM: WINE SUPPLY

Figure 11-12. Some General
Conclusions about
the Mixed Farm ▶

50% IN GRAIN
20% IN VINES
20% IN OLIVES
5% IN REEDS AND GARDEN
5% FOR BUILDINGS

YIELDS: 40 TO 85 CULLEI (WINE)
           (4800 TO 10000 GALLONS)

           4 TO 8 CULLEI (OIL)
           (500 TO 1000 GALLONS)

PROFITS: 6% TO 18%

PROBLEM: GRAIN SUPPLY

Several land combinations on mixed estates are stable and profitable. In this particular instance, 40 percent of the land is split between vines and olives. Wine yields on a mixed farm can be as high as 84 cullei, and olive yields of 15 cullei would be average for a good year. Profits go as high as 60 percent, but on the average are around 6 to 18 percent.

On a mixed farm like this, most of the profit per jugera is still derived from the wine yields even though olives are grown. Grain supplies still cause problems, and there is a risk of a deficit, unless land is not fallowed. Mixed farms benefit most from small olive orchards because the orchards reduce food expenses by providing oil and also allow more land to be planted in grain between trees. If a farmer had the capital needed for the additional investment, olives would be an excellent crop to add to an already profitable wine plantation.

Computer's Contribution

The computer allows for a fast computation of algorithms using over fifty variables and for the input of random variables, which makes the simulation more realistic. Using the computer gives the operator control over the variables so that the effect of each on the system as a whole can be tested. Although there are no comparative data, it is clear that the results given by the computer could never have been calculated with such accuracy in any reasonable time. The major cost of the project was in programming and debugging the program, which is estimated to have taken about 80 hours. Actual computer time and storage were provided by UCC. Complete records were not kept, but a typical run of CATO cost $.90.

Research Prospects

CATO provides the opportunity to learn much more about the internal factors which operated within the plantation system of ancient Roman Italy. Each variable can be tested and manipulated, as in the example of proportions of crop land given above. Once all the important internal variables are identified, they can be considered in their larger economic and social contexts (figure 11-1). For example, the cost-effectiveness of slave versus hired labor is a constant source of controversy in Roman history. Political and economic factors throughout Roman times altered the availability of slave and free labor. With CATO, it has been determined that the profitability of maintaining slaves varies according to the kinds of crops being grown and the size of the farms. This knowledge demonstrates the danger of making generalizations about which type of worker is less expensive.

Several additions could be made to CATO to make it even more useful. First, the program could be expanded to compute output and profitability over several years, instead of just one. This would increase the chances of attaining a "realistic" plantation. Second, another computer program could be written to compile and interpret the results of many runs of CATO. As it is, the user must still sort through an enormous amount of data by hand.

Finally, the modeling and simulation of a series of plantations could enable the study of the evolution of the plantation. Once the key characteristics of each plantation are understood, the changes taking place over time can be modeled and simulated. This process should stimulate the development of careful generalizations about plantations in all time periods as well as about the evolution of the plantation type of agriculture.

Simulation has unlimited potential for studying ancient social, cultural, and economic systems. This approach has already been used in various other fields, particularly business, control sciences, and social sciences, and will continue to be an essential tool for studying systems as a whole, as well as the relationships of the variables that make up those systems.

Acknowledgments

We would like to thank Dr. Peter C. Patton, director, and the University of Minnesota Computer Center (UCC) for support and computer time.

Notes

1. A system has been defined as "an intercommunicating network of attributes or entities forming a complex whole." D. Clarke, *Analytical Archaeology,* 2d ed. (London: Methuen, 1978).

2. A model is a representation of a system, object, or theory in some form other than the entity itself.

3. Simulation is the process of designing a model of a real system and conducting experiments with this model to test specific hypotheses concerning the system and to better understand the system and how it works. R.E. Shannon, *Systems Simulation: The Art, the Science* (Englewood Cliffs, N.J.: Prentice-Hall, 1975).

4. Interactive processing is a mode of running jobs in which the user may intervene after each step. Interactive processing allows the user to take appropriate action depending on the outcome of the previous command.

References
1. Carrington, R.C. "Studies in the Campanian 'Villae Rusticae'," *Journal of Roman Studies* 21(1931):110–130.

2. Day, J. "Agriculture in the Life of Pompeii," *Yale Classical Studies* New Haven: Yale University Press, 1932, pp. 166–208.
3. Frank, Tenney. *Economic Survey of Rome,* Vols. 1–5. Baltimore: Johns Hopkins University Press, 1933.
4. Rostovtzeff, M.I. *The Social and Economic History of the Roman Empire,* 2d edition, Oxford, England: Clarendon Press, 1963.
5. White, K. "The Productivity of Labour in Roman Agriculture," *Antiquity* 39(1965):102–107.
6. White, K. *Roman Farming,* Ithaca, New York: Cornell University Press, 1970.

Bibliography

Doran, J. and Hodsen, F., *Mathematics and Computers in Archaeology.* Cambridge, Mass.: Harvard University Press, 1975.
Doran, J., "Systems Theory, Computer Simulations and Archaeology," *World Archaeology* 1(1969):289–298.
Lehman, R.S., *Computer Simulations and Modeling.* Hillsdale, New Jersey: Lawrence Erlbaum Associates, 1977.

12 Caesar's Army in Gaul: A Computer-Aided Prosopography

Linda M. Ricketts

The value of prosopographical research to the study of ancient history has been demonstrated by the revolutionary work of R. Syme[1] and the various contributions of W. Peremans and E. van't Dack. Lists such as the *Prosopographia Attica* by J. Kirchner[2] and the *Prosopographia Ptolemaica* by Peremans and van't Dack[3] are indispensible for the study of Greek inscriptions and Greek papyri (the writing material of ancient Egypt), while T.R.S. Broughton's collection of Roman officeholders is a worthwhile preliminary for a cautious examination of Roman officials in the Republic (509 to 31 B.C.).[4] Prosopography, or more accurately, proposographical study, takes into focus the biographies of a select group of individuals to provide an analysis of historical events, political procedure, and social and economic structure through an examination of the careers, family, offices, and the like of these same individuals. A prosopography or prosopographical list is a collection of biographical sketches which form the basis of this analysis.

The Problem

Caesar's army in Gaul offers an appealing perimeter for a Roman prosopographical study. The participants in Caesar's Gallic campaign, which lasted from 58 to 50 B.C., include a representative cross section of members of traditionally influential and ascending Roman families, many of whom graduated from Caesar's staff to become significant powers in the tumultuous era of the civil wars (48 to 30 B.C.). In addition, the number of persons named as serving in the Gallic campaign is not so large as to be prohibitive for a limited study. In his commentary, *The Gallic War,* Caesar names fifty officers and soldiers serving with him in Gaul. Other classical sources for the period, including writings of Caesar's contemporary, Cicero, and the works of first-, second-, and third-century A.D. authors (such as Plutarch, Dio Cassius, and Suetonius) add five names to Caesar's staff as well as additional information about the officers mentioned in *The Gallic War.* The material is also open to original research. This point is best made by briefly reviewing the most noteworthy scholarship concerning the topic.

Such a discussion must begin with T. Rice Holmes's lengthy volume *Caesar's Conquest of Gaul.*[5] The book, published in 1911, is the standard exposition of the events in the Gallic War. In part 2 of the work, Holmes discusses various topics related to the Gallic campaign, among which is a section on the military. His emphasis throughout the chapter is on the nature of the army and the offices, not the individuals involved in the command. One exception is the subsection on Caesar's legates (lieutenant generals), in which Holmes lists the names of both the legates mentioned by Caesar and the officers whom Holmes considered to be of uncertain rank. A prosopography was not Holmes's intention, so there is no attempt at including complete textual references to the officers or descriptions of their functions, although he does provide a fair discussion of the identity of the officers of uncertain rank. Of those officers of uncertain rank, P. Crassus and D. Brutus are now generally considered to have been prefects in command of the cavalry and fleet, respectively, while comparative prosopo-graphical work based on *The Gallic War* and other primary sources brings new clues to the identity of other officers.

Holmes's discussion of the officers of uncertain rank draws largely on the conclusions reached by W. Drumann in his *Geschichte Roms* in 1906.[6] In addition to his summaries of the staff positions of these officers, Drumann offers an updated version of P. Willems's table of Caesar's legates.[7] Drumann's table lists Caesar's legates according to their years of service. This table is quite useful for any commentary on the legates, although it does not present a prosopography. This chapter offers a few additions to Drumann's table including M. Messius (54 B.C., Cicero, *Ad Atticum* 4.15) and perhaps Q. Numerius Rufus (c. 57 B.C.; *Corpus Inscriptionum Latinarum,* volume 2, number 759).

Two other works containing lists of officers active during the Gallic wars are T.R.S. Broughton's *The Magistrates of the Roman Republic* and J. Suolahti's *The Junior Officers of the Roman Army in the Republican Period.*[8] Broughton's *Magistrates* is a year-by-year list of Roman officeholders from 509 to 31 B.C. The account includes the names and textual references to the officers and junior officers of the legions (quaestors or quartermaster generals, legates, prefects, and military tribunes). Broghton's work is certainly open for revision, especially in the names of and textual references to the junior officers (prefects and tribunes). Suolahti's *Junior Officers* improves Broughton's lists with several additions to the list of prefect appointments. However, even Suolahti's roster can be increased. Moreover, the scope of my study of Caesar's Gallic staff is quite different from both Suolahti's and Broughton's efforts: It concentrates on Caesar's legions in Gaul alone and involves the lower grades of the army, the legates, and the junior officers, as well as increases the prosopography to include information such as the location of an individual's activities.

Other prosopographical studies of the late Republic (first century B.C.) are useful for a commentary on Caesar's staff, but they in no way limit the originality of this Caesar project or present a comparable prosopography of the staff. Major contributions, such as F. Munzer's pioneering *Romische Adelsparteien und Adelsfamilien*[9] and R. Syme's *The Roman Revolution* are valuable as references to family influence and participation. Likewise, biographies of important Roman officers and politicians of the period, such as E. Huzar's[10] and O. Bengtson's[11] books on Mark Antony and R. Syme's article on T. Labienus[12] have useful material on a few of the participants in the campaign. Thus, the focus of this Caesar prosopography is original, and where the project draws on material common to related studies, the Caesar prosopography substantially enlarges and revises the other works.

The Project

It now remains to discuss the aim and projected organization of the project. The purpose of this prosopographical study of Caesar's army in Gaul is twofold: first, to present a prosopographical list of Caesar's staff according to Caesar's narrative of the war and the supporting evidence from other classical and inscriptional sources; second, to provide a commentary on the prosopography which includes an analysis of the staff by rank, reevaluation of the officers of uncertain rank, an examination of Mark Antony's activities in Gaul, and a composite look at Gallic campaign officers who later deserted Caesar's standards or joined the conspiracy against his life. The prosopographical list has been generated by means of a data-base management system. System 2000 was chosen as the data-management system for this project because its hierarchical data-base capability is appropriate for prosopographical research. It also allows simple data entry as well as easy data updating and several options for retrieval. The REPORT WRITER feature enables retrieval of the information in a format organized according to the user's specifications.

Each entry in the data-base definition (figure 12–1) represents one text reference to a staff member in the Gallic campaign. The entry consists of his personal name (*praenomen*), clan name (*nomen*), additional name (*cognomen*), if any, his position on the staff (if this is stated in the reference), the date of the reference, the approximate location of his activities, the textual source for this information, and space for additional notes about that particular entry. There are several levels in the hierarchy of a data base in System 2000, at the top of which is level 0, containing the fundamental information for the entry. For the Caesar project, level 0 includes the name of the staff member, stored in three components (*nomen, praenomen,* and *cognomen*). There are three levels beyond the root (level 0). Since most of the data can be repeated within each entry (for example, there can be several

1. *Praenomen* (first name)

2. *Nomen* (second name)

3. *Cognomen* (third name)

4. Notes

   This repeating group allows the insertion of comments or explanations concerning the data entries in the remaining components.

   5. Note entry

6. Position information (military title)

   7. Position

   8. Date and location information

      Each entry—one text reference to a staff member—is dated and the activities of the participant located according to the textual reference.

      9. Date

      10. Geographical location

      11. Reference

          The text reference for the above information is given in this repeating group.

          12. Classical text or inscription

              The abbreviations CT or INS show that the following information refers to either a book and chapter of a classical text or the volume and inscription number of an inscription.

          13. Author

          14. Title

          15. Book or volume

          16. Chapter or inscription

Level 0 Level 1 Level 2 Level 3

Figure 12-1. Data-Base Definition for System 2000

note entries or more than one position reference in each text reference to an individual), the components beyond level 0 occur within what are termed *repeating groups.* The data base created for this project is described in figure 12-1. Components 1 through 3 contain the name at level 0. The hierarchical nature of the data described in this data-base definition is illustrated by successive indentation of the components. Thus, level 1 information, such as that contained in components 7 and 8, can occur more than once as data within the level 0 repeating group designated by component 6 (position information) for each entry. Similarly, there can be multiple occurrences of the level 3 components 12 through 16 for each occurrence of the level 2 repeating group 11 (reference), which is itself an element of the level 1 repeating group 8 (date and location information).

Results and Prospects

The REPORT WRITER feature of System 2000 enables the data in the data base to be printed according to a user-defined format. The material is organized alphabetically according to the *nomen* (clan name) and the *praenomen* (personal name), and the entries for each staff member are further placed in chronological order of service. Figure 12-2 is an example of the Caesar prosopography (preliminary list). Each text reference is

```
PROSOPOGRAPHY                                           PAGE   1


   1.  AEMILIUS         LUCIUS

           --58
             DECURIONIS EQUITUM GALLORUM
             HELVETII
             CAESAR              GALLIC WAR              1        23

   2.  ANTISTIUS        GAIUS        REGINUS

           --53
             LEGATUS
             GAUL
             CAESAR              GALLIC WAR              6        01

           --52
             LEGATUS
             ALESIA
             CAESAR              GALLIC WAR              7        83

           --52

             AMBIVARETI
             CAESAR              GALLIC WAR              7        90

   3.  ANTONIUS         MARCUS

           --52
             LEGATUS
             ALESIA
             CAESAR              GALLIC WAR              7        81

           --52
             AD QUAESTURAM PETENDAM
             GAUL
             CICERO              PHILIPPICS              2        49

           --51
             QUAESTOR
             GAUL
             CICERO              PHILIPPICS              2        50

           --51
             QUAESTOR
             GAUL
             CICERO              PHILIPPICS              2        71

           --51
             QUAESTOR AND SUIS PRAEFECIT HIBERNIS
             BIBRACTE
```

Figure 12-2. Sample Page from Prosopography

chronologically arranged under the heading of the name of the staff member. The names are in alphabetical order according to the *nomen* (for example, Antonius), and the *nomen* is followed by the *praenomen* (for example, Marcus) and *cognomen* (additional name, if any). The order of each entry after the name is date of the reference in years B.C. (for example, 52), position reference, if any (for example, *legatus*), location of activities (for example, Alesia). and the author, text, book, and chapter in which the information is found (for example, Caesar, *Gallic War,* book 7, chapter 81).

The prosopographical list has been evaluated in a commentary.[13] First, an examination by position progresses according to rank: quaestors, legates, military tribunes, prefects, centurions, decurions, standard bearers, interpreters, envoys, and scouts. Second, the commentary attempts to identify the positions of officers of uncertain rank by focusing on not only their commands in Gaul, but also the officers' subsequent careers. Third, the commentary discusses Mark Antony in Gaul. It is the intention here to isolate Antony's activities in Gaul in order to analyze his leadership as Caesar's quartermaster general and legate and to trace his developing favoritism with Caesar, who had already nominated him augur (a respected religious position in Rome) in 50 B.C. Fourth, and finally, the commentary includes a study of conspirators and deserters among Caesar's former Gallic staff. This offers a fresh approach to the turn of events in 44 B.C. It is curious that among the plotting senators who assassinated Caesar on the Ides of March, 44 B.C., there numbered several of Caesar's previously loyal legates in Gaul. The desertion of his principal subordinate, Labienus, to the Pompeian cause in 49 B.C. is likewise remarkable. Syme attempts a rationale for Labienus's desertion in "The Allegience of Labienus," and J. Collins likewise established a justification for Roman indignation toward Caesar in "Caesar and the Corruption of Power."[14] The group study of the conspirators from among Caesar's Gallic staff could suggest a further reason for their behavior.

The advantage of using a computer in this project is that it provides a much more efficient system for creating the prosopography, and the computer can handle a complex set of data entries. Furthermore, the fact that an entry requires only four levels in the hierarchical tree of System 2000 makes the program inexpensive to run. It is hoped that the Caesar data base will serve as a model for future prosopographical studies.

Acknowledgments

The research for this project has been supported by the University Computer Center, University of Minnesota. I am indebted to Debra Katz for her help in setting up the data-base definition and description and to Renee Holoien for her assistance with System 2000 and its REPORT WRITER feature. I also wish to thank Professors Tom B. Jones and Peter C. Patton for their guidance and encouragement.

Notes

1. Ronald Syme. *The Roman Revolution,* rev. ed. (London: Oxford University Press, 1952).

2. J. Kirchner, *Prosopographia Attica,* 2 vols. (Berlin: G. Reimer, 1903).

3. W. Peremans and E. van't Dack, *Prosopographia Ptolemaica,* 8 vols., Studia Hellenistica Universitatis (Louvain: E. Naewelaerts; Leiden: E.J. Brill, 1950–1975).

4. T.R.S. Broughton, *The Magistrates of the Roman Republic,* 2 vols., American Philological Association Monograph 15 (Cleveland, Ohio: Case Western Reserve University Press, 1952).

5. T. Rice Holmes, *Caesar's Conquest of Gaul,* 2d ed. (Oxford, Ohio: Clarendon Press, 1911).

6. W. Drumann, *Geschichte Roms in seinen Ubergange von der Republikanischen zur Monarchischen Verfassung oder Pompeius, Caesar, Cicero und ihre Zeitgenossen,* 2d ed., edited by P. Groebe, vol. 3 (Leipzig: Gebruder Borntraeger, 1906).

7. P. Willems, *Le Senat de La Republique Romain: Sa Composition et Ses Attributions,* vol. 2 (Louvain: Ch. Peeters, 1883).

8. Jaakko Suolahti, *The Junior Officers of the Roman Army in the Republican Period.* Suomalaisen Tiedeakatemian Toimituksia, Annales academiae scientiarum fennicae, ser. B, 97. Helsinki, 1955.

9. Friedrich Munzer, *Romische Adelsparteien und Adelsfamilien* (Stuttgart: J.B. Metzler, 1920).

10. Eleanor Goltz Huzar, *Mark Antony: A Biography* (Minneapolis: University of Minnesota Press, 1978).

11. Hermann Bengtson, *Marcus Antonius: Triumvir und Herrscher des Orients* (Munich: C.H. Beck, 1977).

12. Ronald Syme, "The Allegiance of Labienus," *Journal of Roman Studies* 28 (1938):113–125.

13. Linda M. Ricketts, *Caesar's Army in Gaul: A Prosopographical Study,* Technical Report 80001 (University Computer Center, University of Minnesota, 1980).

14. John H. Collins, "Caesar and the Corruption of Power," *Historia* 4(1955):445–465.

Bibliography

Primary Sources

Appian. *Civil Wars; Gallic History.*
Athenaeus. *Deipnosophistai.*
Aurunculeius Cotta, L. *Roman Constitution* (in Athenaeus).
Caesar. *Gallic War.*
Cicero. *Ad Atticum; Ad Familiares; Ad Quinum Fratrem; In Vatinium; Philippics; Corpus Inscriptionum Latinarum.*
Dio Cassius. *Roman History.*
Florus. *Epitome of Roman History.*
Hirtius. *Gallic War* (Book 8 of Caesar's *Gallic War*).
Livy. *Summaries.*
Lucan. *Pharsalia.*
Plutarch. *Caesar; Pompey.*
Strabo. *Geography.*
Suetonius. *The Deified Julius; Galba.*
Valerius Maximus. *Factorum Ad Dictorum Memorabilium Libri IX.*

Secondary Sources

Bailey, D.R. Shackelton. "The Roman Nobility in the Second Civil War." *Classical Quarterly* 10 (1960):253–267.
Bondurant, Bernard Camillus. *Decimus Junius Brutus Albinus: A Historical Study.* Chicago: University of Chicago Press, 1907.
Gelzer, Matthias. *Caesar: Politician and Statesman.* Translated by Peter Needham. 6th ed. Cambridge, Mass.: Harvard University Press, 1968.
————. *The Roman Nobility.* Translated by Robin Seager. Oxford, Ohio: Basil Blackwell, 1969.
Gruen, Erich S. *The Last Generation of the Roman Republic.* Berkeley: University of California Press, 1974.
Kraner, F., and Dittenberger, W. (commentary). *C. Iulii Caesaris Commentarii "De Bello Gallico."* 19th ed. by Heinrich Meusel. 3 vols. Berlin: Weidmann, 1960–1961.
Parker, H.M.D. *The Roman Legions.* 2d ed. New York: Barnes and Noble, Inc., 1958.
von Pauly, August Friedrich, and Wissowa, Georg, eds. *Paulys Realencyclopadie Der Classichen Altertumswissenschaft.* Stuttgart: J.B. Metzler, 1894–.
Walser, Gerold. *Caesar und Die Germanen: Studien zur Politischen Tendenz Romischer Feldsberichte.* Historia Einzelschriften 1. Wiesbaden: Franz Steiner, 1956.

13 Minnesota Archaeological-Survey Data Base

Ruth Tate

Since the time that archaeological expeditions have been conducted by students of human culture rather than by antiquarians gathering objects for their age or beauty, the quantity of data recorded by expeditions has become less and less manageable. Expeditions conducted during the nineteenth century were generally oriented toward plundering rather than learning, and much important information, particularly that relating to the location of individual finds, was lost. Modern archaeologists, in order to learn as much as possible about ancient peoples and their cultures, record precise details about each artifact they find. These details fall into two general categories: first, an artifact's provenance (location) is described in terms of a three-dimensional grid system which delineates the boundaries of the site; second, the attributes of an artifact, such as its design motif, shape, material type, and function, are recorded. Using these types of information, archaeologists seek to reconstruct possible social, cultural, and economic activities of the people who produced the artifacts. Before such hypotheses can be formulated, however, data about large numbers of artifacts must be collected and organized for comparison. The broader the time span or area to be studied, the more information is needed for a thorough archaeological study, and this quantity of information creates a vast data-management problem.

The Problem

An example of the type of investigation with which archaeologists are often concerned is the comparative study of the materials of a single excavation site. The archaeologist looks at the provenance information (recorded as the excavation proceeds) and the record of artifacts found and analyzed. The number and attributes of artifact type A are compared to those of artifact type B. Comparative studies of the artifacts of type A found in level X as compared to level Y and so on may also be undertaken in the preparation of a single site's excavation report. Excavation reports from many sites may be examined by archaeologists who are looking for possible behavior patterns as manifested in the archaeological remains. Studies of types of shelter used by prehistoric peoples, for example, require searching an area's site reports

205

for possible like behavior; for example, did early people use rock shelters only occasionally, or were they used in a regularly established pattern for shelter? Results of such research would be based on evidence of the numbers of rock shelters in an area, the density of artifact scatter in the shelter, and absolute or relative chronology.

The study of artifact-type chronologies is often considered to be an effective methodology for establishing cultural sequences within an area. Archaeologists compare artifacts of similar types from various sites (basing type on artifact attributes) in order to create hypotheses about coexisting groups of people or peoples with a direct-contact pattern (exchange of goods) or other types of contact which allowed the exchange of ideas. Curators of archaeological collections often have been concerned with cataloging and chronologically ordering the vast collections which became a part of a museum's holdings during an earlier era when archaeological expeditions collected artifacts on the criteria of beauty or uniqueness, with little regard for provenance. Large numbers of items stored in museums must therefore be correlated with the scant records of early excavations.

Archaeological excavation records serve an important role in the planning of future land-expansion projects. Federally funded projects require that the archaeological significance of proposed highway right-of-ways, national park improvement areas, and other sites be determined. Known archaeological sites must be carefully surveyed and tested in order to plan for development which will not disturb major archaeological sites. Lengthy literary and archaeological research is therefore a necessary preliminary step in federal project planning and development. The above examples of the widely diversified interests of archaeologists point to the need for an organized archaeological-data filing system.

The Project

The research project described here involves the development of an archaeological data base for the state of Minnesota. The data base was designed with the widely diversified needs of archaeological research in mind. Archaeological excavation and research information was categorized into three specific groups: general site information, provenance, and artifact data. The general site category (figure 13-1) includes information such as the site's state identification code (line 1) (state-county-site number), site type (line 3) (habitation, burial, artifact scatter, and so on), cultural associations (line 4) (Paleo-Archaic, Woodland, and so on), excavation participants (line 10), and laboratory analysis data (line 17). The locational information field (figure 13-2) contains specific site data which record individual excavation units. Horizontal and vertical provenance (lines 22 to 26) are also incorpo-

Site information is to be filled in once per excavation site.
Information in parentheses guides entry format to the computer.
A prepared form (listing possible choices from which the
analyst chooses answers) is used with the catalog.

1. Site Number (Refers to state assigned number) (letters & numbers x 7)
2. Registration (State or National) (letters x 5)
3. Site Type (numbers x 2)
        1. artifact scatter
        2. artifacts with features
        3. habitation-campsites
        4. habitation-village
        5. burial(s)/cemetery
        6. mound(s)
        7. cave/rockshelter
        8. quarry
        9. kill site
       10. pictograph/petroglyph
       11. finds spot
       12. other
4. Cultural Components (number x 2)
        1. Paleo-Indian
        2. Early Archaic
        3. Late Archaic
        4. Early Woodland
        5. Middle Woodland
        6. Late Woodland
        7. Mississippian
        8. Historical/Aboriginal
        9. Uncertain aceramic
       10. Uncertain ceramic
5. Upper Zone Limit (Depth of artifact zone when starting level)
        list in c.m. (numbers x 3)
6. Lower Zone Limit (Depth of artifact zone when sterile) (numbers x 3)
7. Site Condition (Before this excavation) (letters x 9)
            Existent - never really excavated
            Disturbed - some excavation
            Destroyed - under city buildings, etc.
            Unknown
8. Reports Published? (Yes/no)
9. (Not used)
10. Participants (This marks the beginning of a repeat group; a repeat
                 group allows for the entry of multiple sets of information.)
       11. Archaeologist (last name, first initial) (letters x 10)
       12. Institution sponsoring (letters x 10)
       13. Project Name (letters x 15)
       14. Excavation Date(s) (possibility of several years) (letters &
            numbers x 15)
15. Collection Data (This is another repeating group)
       16. Collection Repository (Where is the collection) (letters x 1)
17. Lab Analyst (Who was in charge) (last name, first initial)
       (letters x 10)
       18. Analysis Date(s) (letters & numbers x 10)
       19. Cataloguer (Who was in charge) (letters x 10)

Figure 13-1. Categories of Information about the Archaeological Site

rated. Post molds, as evidence for possible semipermanent structures, may
also be recorded. Individual artifact information (figure 13-3) includes data
which are valuable in preparing analytical reports on specific artifacts. This
information may also serve as a catalog so that archaeologists, museum
curators, and other researchers will be able to use the collected artifacts for
future comparative studies. Figure 13-3 shows categories of information

```
20. Location (repeating group)
      21. Feature (number) (numbers x 2)
      22. Level Number (numbers x 2)
      23. Upper Level Limit (numbers x 3)
      24. Lower Level Limit (numbers x 3)
      25. East/West coordinate (letters & numbers x 15)
      26. North/South coordinate (letters & numbers x 15)
      27. Postmold evidence (yes/no)
      28. Cultural Component (numbers x 2)
             1. Paleo-Indian
             2. Early Archaic
             3. Late Archaic
             4. Early Woodland
             5. Middle Woodland
             6. Late Woodland
             7. Mississippian
             8. Historical/Aboriginal
             9. Uncertain aceramic
            10. Uncertain ceramic

The above information is filled out for each excavation level, square,
or feature in the excavation site. Location information is not
included if it is not known. The analyst would then begin with the
artifact information. (See Figure 13-3)
```

Figure 13-2. Information Concerning the Location of an Artifact

which could be recorded for each ceramic artifact. The catalog number assigned to an artifact (line 31) is recorded. Ceramic attributes are recorded if relevant (lines 33 to 36), including temper, shape, design, surface treatment, and additional decorative treatment.

The Minnesota Archaeological-Survey data base was designed by first researching the types of information Minnesota archaeologists were interested in recording and the types of reports they generated from their data. The next step was to make a list of the categories of data to be included and to outline how they are related. This list was used to create a System 2000 data-base definition. These fields of information were divided into three groups, as described above: general site information, locational data, and specific artifact description. The general site group has eleven categories of data (figure 13-4, components 1 to 10, and 15), with some categories (components 10 and 15) having additional levels of detail (components 11 to 14, 16 to 19). The provenance group (component 20) contains the artifact descriptions under the catalog entry (component 30) in addition to locational data. Modifier lists of possible field values were then established for many of the data categories. Numeric codes were created for each modifier entry. For example, a cataloger enters the number 07 in category 33 (figure 13-3) when recording that the ceramic temper of a piece of pottery was shell.

This is an illustration of the types of information which can be
recorded about artifacts. The information recorded tells type of
artifact plus analytical information.

30. Catalog (repeating group of 20 but also the beginning of another
    repeating group)
    31. Artifact Number (letters & numbers x 8)
    32. Category of Artifact (numbers x 2)
        1. Botanical
        2. Ceramic
        3. Faunal (shell has separate category)
        4. Fire-Cracked Rjock
        5. Historical Contact Evidence
        6. Human Skeletal
        7. Lithics
        8. Metal
        9. Other Remains
        10. Shell
    33. Ceramic Temper (numbers x 2)
        1. Broken Pottery
        2. Fiber
        3. Gravel (large granules)
        4. Grit
        5. None
        6. Sand
        7. Shell
        8. Shell & Grit
        9. Shell & Sand
        10. Unknown
    34. Ceramic Shape/Design (numbers x 2)
        1. Base
        2. Bead
        3. Body Sherd Decorated
        4. Body Sherd Undecorated
        5. Complete Vessel
        6. Crumb
        7. Handle
        8. Incomplete Rim (lip present, incomplete decoration,
           lower edge is gone)
        9. Near Rim (lip present, lower edge of decoration not
           present)
        10. Neck (lip not present; lower edge of decoration is)
        11. Pipe
        12. Rim (lip to body; shows all decoration)
        13. Split sherd (entire sherd is not present; part has
            broken away)
        14. Shoulder
    35. Ceramic Surface Treatment (numbers x 2)
        1. Cord-Wrapped Paddle
        2. Cord-Wrapped Stick
        3. Net/Fabric Impressed
        4. Smooth/Brushed
    36. Ceramic Decorative Treatment (numbers x y to allow for
                                     multiple decoration)
        1. Cord Impressed
        2. Dentate
        3. Incized/Engraved
        4. Noded/Bossed
        5. Punctate
        6. Rocker Stamped
        7. Scalloped
        8. Trailed/Wide Incized

Figure 13-3. Characteristics of an Artifact

```
 1*  Site number (name x(7))
 2*  Registration (name x(5))
 3*  Site type (integer number 99)
 4*  Cultural components (name/ x15))
 5*  Upper Zone Limit (integer number 999)
 6*  Lower Zone Limit (integer number 999)
 7*  Site condition (name x(9))
 8*  Reports published (name xxx)
 9*  Dummya (name x (10))
10*  Participants (rg)
    11*   Archaeologist (name x(10) in 10)
    12*   Institution (name x(10) in 10)
    13*   Project name (name x(15) in 10)
    14*   Excavation date (name x(15) in 10)
15*  Collection date (rg)
    16*   collection repository (name x10) in 15)
    17*   Lab analyst (name x(10) in 15)
    18*   Analysis date (name x(10) in 15)
    19*   Cataloger (name x(10) in 15)
20*  Location (rg)
    21*   Feature (integer number 99 in 20)
    22*   Level number (integer number 999 in 20)
    23*   Upper level limit (integer number 999 in 20)
    24*   Lower level limit (integer number 999 in 20)
    25*   Eastern feature coordinate (name x(15) in 20)
    26*   Northern feature coordinate (name x(15) in 20)
    27*   Postmold evidence (name xxx in20)
    28*   Cultural component (integer number 99 in 20)
    30*   Catalog (rg in 20)
       31*   Artifact number (name x(8) in 30)
       32*   Category of artifact (integer number 99 in 30)
       33*   Ceramic temper (integer number 99 in 30)
       34*   Ceramic shape/design (integer number 99 in 30)
       35*   Ceramic surface treatment (integer number 99 in 30)
       36*   Ceramic decorative treatment (integer number 99 in 30)
       37*   Faunal material (integer number 99 in 30)
       38*   Mammal category (integer number 99 in 30)
       39*   Fish category (integer number 99 in 30)
       40*   Reptile category (integer number 99 in 30)
       41*   Amphibians category (integer number 99 in 30)
       42*   Bird category (integer number 99 in 30)
       43*   Specific bone info (integer number 99 in 30)
       44*   Bone shape/function/design (integer number 99 in 30)
       45*   Shell type (integer number 99 in 30)
       46*   Shell shape/function/design (integer number 99 in 30)
       47*   Metal type (integer number 99 in 30)
       48*   Metal shape/function/design (integer number 99 in 30)
       49*   Botanical remains (integer number 99 in 30)
       50*   Fire-cracked rock category (integer number 99 in 30)
       51*   Specific stone material (integer number 99 in 30)
       52*   Lithic color (integer number 99 in 30)
       53*   Geological characteristics (integer number 99 in 30)
       54*   Lithic shape/function/design (integer number 99 in 30)
       55*   Human skeletal material (integer number 99 in 30)
       56*   Burial type (integer number 99 in 30)
       57*   Age (integer number 99 in 30)
       58*   Sex (name x in 30)
       59*   Cause of death (integer number 99 in 30)
       60*   Other wounds (integer number 99 in 30)
       61*   Deficiency diseases (integer number 99 in 30)
       62*   Pathological lesions (integer number 99 in 30)
       63*   Grave goods (name xxx in 30)
       64*   Other remains (integer number 99 in 30)
       65*   Evidence of historical contact (name x(15) in 300)
       66*   Remarks (name x(240) in 30)
       67*   Remark included (name xxx in 30)
```

Figure 13-4. System 2000 Data-Base Definition

Results

Once the data were collected, they were keypunched and entered into System 2000 data-base files. An interactive terminal was used for entering the data, which the data-base management system could then access and list as requested. Some examples of data retrieval are shown in figure 13–5. An additional feature of the Minnesota Archaeological-Survey data base is its ability to list artifact information in a format which can serve as a museum catalog (figure 13–6). The data-base definition established in this project was used by Hamline University in the summer 1978 survey and field school. In addition, the definition has been expanded to include categories of information relevant to the archaeological analysis of historic sites. Experimentation has shown that the data base, which was designed for a large data set, is not cost-effective for small sets of data with less than 300 entries. It is the need for a method to add to and manipulate a large amount of data which has been addressed in the Minnesota Archaeological Survey data-base project.

Although archaeologists would be the most obvious users of this data base, the information which is recorded is also of interest to historians and

```
---
PR COUNT C32 WHERE C32 EQ 7:        Statistical count of lithics in test
CNT 32* 13                          sample
---
PR COUNT C54 WHERE C54 EQ 13:
CNT 54* 6                           Statistical count of lithics which
---                                 are in a chip shape
DITTO WHERE C54 EQ 37:
CNT 54* 6
---


TALLY C32:
************************
ELEMENT-      CATEGORY OF ARTIFACT
************************
FREQUENCY     VALUE
--------------------
        1        1
        1        2
        1        3               Statistical count of each artifact
        1        4               category in test sample
        2        5
        1        6
       13        7
        1        8
        1       10
--------------------
        9    UNIQUE VALUES
--------------------
       22    OCCURRENCES
--------------------
```

Figure 13–5. Examples of Data Retrieval

```
---
PR C1, OB C1 WH C4 EQ 5 AND
C32 EQ 7 AND C54 EQ 13:
1* 21AN141
1* 21GO03
---


---
PR CO,OB C1 WH C1 EXISTS:

1* 21AN141
3*    4
4*    5
5*   10
6*  130
7*    2

  11* CAINE
  12* HAMLINE
  13* RICECK
  14* 78

  16* HAMLINEU
  17* CAINE,C
  18* 78
  19* PANCHA,D

  22* 15
  25* W124-125
  26* N37-38

   31* YF714
   32*   7
   51*  21
   52*  22
   53*   5
   54*  13

   31* YF715
   32*   7
   51*  21
   52*  22
   53*   5
   54*  13

   31* YF716
   32*   7
   51*  21
   52*  22
   53*   5
   54*  13
```

List of site numbers exhibiting like cultural components which contained like artifacts.

A listing of the information recorded about the excavation site 21AN141 (individual artifact information is included.)

Figure 13-5 continued

art historians. Historians use information from prehistory to build theories about early contacts with the first explorers. In addition, tracing lines of development from prehistoric to historic groups permits the examination of culture traits, such as ceremonies which are difficult to reconstruct from the archaeological record. Art historians often investigate the development of design elements on ceramics and other artifacts. A data base which allows the organized cataloging of artifact designs in relationship to those from other sites and periods facilitates in-depth studies of design development. The art historian may also use the data base to trace the evolution of artistic techniques, delineate the selection of subject matter, or map geographic areas of influence. The widespread applicability of data-base systems to

Museum catalog record tells where the item was found, its
museum catalog number, type of object and description of
object (numeric code of description is based on categories
in catalog).

SITE NUMBER	ARTIFACT NUMBER	ARTIFACT CATEGORY	ARTIFACT DESCRIPTION
21AN141	YF714	7	21 22 5 13
21AN141	YF715	7	21 22 5 13
21AN141	YF716	7	21 22 5 13
21GD03	1084	7	21 22 5 13
21GD03	1085	7	21 22 5 37
21GD03	1086	7	21 22 5 37
21GD03	1087	7	21 22 5 37
21GD03	1088	7	21 22 5 13
21PN17	3157846	7	21 22 5 13
21PN17	3157847	7	21 22 5 37
21PN17	3157848	7	23 22 0 35
21PN17	3157849	5	21
21PN17	3157850	7	9 1 4 37
21PN17	3157851	7	6 6 0 37
21PN17	3157852	3	5 2
21PN17	3157853	8	1 7
21PN17	3157854	18	11 9
21PN17	3157855	1	7
21PN17	3157856	4	1 9 17
21PN17	3157857	2	7 7 9 8
21PN17	3157858	5	
21PN17	3157858H	6	7 1 5H 6 7 yes

Figure 13-6. List of Data in Museum Catalog Format

research questions which require the manipulation of large amounts of data
is apparent. A data-base system can serve various needs, such as accessing
data relevant to historically documented events and tracing the development
of industries, genealogies, and land-ownership relationships.

Archaeological excavations generate an extremely large amount of
data. The sheer volume of related paperwork can make site analysis and
related research very time-consuming. Hour upon hour is required to
manipulate the collected data to determine what artifact class(es) and which
type(s) were found in particular excavation units. The need for a computerized data filing system is obvious. Computer-assisted data management
allows systematic information recording and easy retrieval of site, feature,
or artifact counts, systematic grouping of site and related data, and so
forth. Although archaeologists in Minnesota have used computers for limited problem-related projects, there has not previously been a statewide data
survey system. In other parts of the United States, however, statewide site
and artifact data-base systems have been established. Among the research
projects which have been aided by a data-base management system is the
work in the Mississippi Valley, where a system has been developed to allow
detailed site and artifact information to be accessed not only for comparative studies, but also for detailed site analysis, cluster analysis, and predic-
tive probability studies [1]. The state of Arkansas [3] makes widespread use

of its survey data base for land-management purposes. Proposed land developments are scrutinized for possible disturbance of archaeological sites. The National Museums of Canada [2] have developed a data-base system which combines archaeological site information, excavation data, and information about museum collections into a large, computerized cataloging system.

Acknowledgments

I wish to acknowledge the assistance of University Computer Center staff, especially Debra Katz, for her guidance in System 2000. Also to be acknowledged are Professors Sheila J. McNally and Peter C. Patton for their guidance and encouragement. Thanks are also due to Christy Caine of Hamline University in St. Paul for the development of ceramic categories, to Orrin Shane of the Science Museum of Minnesota in St. Paul for faunal categories, and to the archaeology department staff of the Minnesota Historical Society.

References

1. Limp, W. Frederick. "Oracle System Survey Method." Report #3, Draft. Indiana University, Glenn A. Black Laboratory of Archaeology-Research.

2. Loy, T., and Powell, G.R. "Archaeological Data Recording Guide." *British Columbia Provincial Museum Heritage Records,* no. 3. Victoria: British Columbia Provincial Museum, 1977.

3. Scholtz, Sandra. "A Management Information System Design for a General Museum." *Museum Data Bank Research Report,* no. 12. Museum Data Bank Committee, Rochester, N.Y.: Margaret Woodbury Strong Museum, November 1976.

Bibliography

MRI, Inc. "System 2000 Reference Manual." MRI Systems Corporation, P.O. Box 9968, Austin, Texas 78766. November 1971, rev. August 1972, July 1973, August 1974.

14 Computer-Aided Instruction in Archaeology

Vicky A. Walsh

Archaeology is concerned with the retrieval and study of the remains of past cultures or peoples in order to attempt the reconstruction of their environment, their culture, and their daily lives. The primary means of retrieving these remains is the excavation of archaeological sites. Once a site is excavated, all that remains are the artifacts themselves and the data noted and collected by the excavators. It is therefore especially important to excavate and record everything precisely. Excavation techniques have improved greatly since the early days of archaeological exploration, but there is still a need for the careful training and education of student archaeologists. Nothing can replace actual excavation experience, but we can provide students with experience in research design, sampling strategy, data recording, artifact and site analysis, and report generation before they actually begin excavating.

The Problem

In the past, students have been taught archaeological technique almost exclusively through courses on method and theory and in summer field schools. Courses are a necessary and important source of background material, but they do not give students the necessary real experience in excavation and rarely give the student the opportunity to design and carry out a project of her own. Field schools are the best method of teaching excavation and recording skills. However, the actual site data are unknown before excavating, which makes it difficult to fairly assess the skills of the students. Since real sites are excavated, important information about the site may be missed or recorded incorrectly through the inexperience of the excavators. Also, the project design, sampling strategy, and so on, are already determined by the field school director(s) (especially in the case of a long-term excavation), and students have no means of trying out the theories they have learned in class. Recent attempts to avoid these difficulties include the creation and subsequent excavation of an artificial archaeological site.[1] This entails creating features and burying artifacts with careful recording of all data and then excavating the site at a later date or with a different group of students. Since the expected data are known, the results of the excavation

215

can be compared with the known data to assess the accuracy of the techniques and of the recording. Sandbox excavation has also been set up in a laboratory setting for the same purpose, although on a much smaller scale. [2]

Solution Approach

This project proposes yet another solution to the problem of providing adequate experience and competence in archaeological methods before the student actually goes to work on an excavation. This computer simulation is designed to be used as part of a regularly taught course in archaeology. The use of this module depends on the purposes of the course and the desires of the instructor. For example, it can be used either to illustrate sampling and analysis techniques in a methods and theory course or to provide data from an actual site for a survey or history course. It is projected that it will be used within courses in anthropology, classics, history, art history, and other areas dealing with the study of archaeological sites. The use of a simulation[3] of an archaeological excavation for teaching purposes is not new,[4] but the use of a computer to operate the teaching module is, and has several advantages over the manual method. Very little instruction is needed to operate the "excavation"; the computer program itself leads the student through a logical and straightforward set of decisions. Each student may design and execute a different excavation strategy based on varying problems or experience. Two of the key advantages to using a computer simulation are that each student may operate at his own speed with a minimum of teacher intervention and that the "results" of each grid excavated are returned to the student immediately and can thus be used in deciding future strategy if desired. The computer can also provide a variety of graphic displays and additional information about the archaeological site at the instructor's or student's direct request while the "excavation" is in progress (see below). Beyond the advantages for instructing student archaeologists, the simulation of an excavation, using data from an actual excavated site, can be used to test the validity of a series of sampling strategies by comparing each "excavation" with the actual excavation results, especially if the excavation was reasonably complete.

Methodology

In this case, the general approach to the problem of simulating a site excavation is to create a series of site data bases to be used with a single computer program. This program will retrieve the data from the data base on request and return the information to the student. Each data base contains the data describing a selected site from a particular geographical area and chronological period. A variety of sites is used in order to facilitate employing the simulation in courses on Old World as well as New World archaeology: prehistoric as well as historic. Using just one program for several courses makes updating the simulation procedures much easier and ensures some continuity from course to course. By utilizing certain selective features, the instructor can increase the complexity of the simulation exercise and thus successfully challenge students having varied experience and expertise with the same basic module.

Because of the desirability of independent and affordable computing for individual departments, microcomputers are being employed in a variety of computer-assisted instruction (CAI) projects supported by UCC (see chapters 17 and 18 on Greek and Latin courses). In particular, the Terak microcomputer is being used for this project because of its graphic capabilities. To minimize equipment costs, a single-disk, Pascal operating system, similar to the University of California at San Diego (UCSD) system,[5] is used. This system offers excellent file handling and editing capabilities for program creation and maintenance, and it runs the actual simulation as well. The simulation program (ARCHSIM) is written in the University of Minnesota version of UCSD Pascal, utilizing the facility for loading the program in small chunks or segments. This feature reduces the amount of memory needed to run the program, which is, of course, an important consideration in using microcomputers, since space is limited. ARCHSIM interfaces between the student and information contained in a series of subordinate files. These files contain the site-excavation data as well as archaeological-analysis information and program-operation data.

The kind and amount of background information about the site (figure 14-1) given the student are up to the discretion of the instructor. Armed with this information, the student must then design an excavation strategy based on the problem(s) she wishes to investigate. She then begins to "excavate" the site using ARCHSIM. ARCHSIM gives the student brief instructions (figure 14-2) on how to operate the simulation. It explains the grid system (figure 14-3) and the three sampling strategies (figure 14-4) which the program can implement, and it requests (figure 14-5) the student to select one of these. If the student has elected to personally choose each grid to be excavated (intuitive), she then requests the grid and depth to be dug (figure 14-6). For all strategies, the program will output the results of the "excavation" (figure 14-7). These results include the depth of each level (7.1), a physical description of the level (7.2), and artifact or feature (7.3) descriptions. When the excavation is completed, any of several analysis files (figure 14-8) may be listed. An additional feature of ARCHSIM is the recording of the cost of the excavation (figure 14-9). The student starts with a set budget; each grid excavated and each analysis chosen subtract from the total, and deficit spending is not allowed (figure 14–10)! This requires the student to be aware of the very real problem of finances in archaeological excavations. This, then, is the basic simulation or teaching module. The student can also request additional graphic output (figure 14–11) at various points in the excavation. This consists of a plot of the grid, by level, of the artifacts and features located in that grid.

```
                    PHYSICAL GEOGRAPHY AND CLIMATE

    SOME 32 SITES HAVE SO FAR BEEN LOCATED IN THE REGION OF BROKEN TERRAIN
IN WHICH OUR SITE IS FOUND.  PRINCIPAL REGIONAL COMPONENTS ARE LIMESTONES
AND FLYSCH, BUT EXTENSIVE AREAS OF SERPENTINE OCCUR IN THE NORTHERN AND
WESTERN SECTORS, WHILE OUTCROPS OF CHLORITE AND STEATITE ARE FOUND IN A
VALLEY TO THE NORTHEAST OF OUR SITE.  ALL OF THE SITES WHICH HAVE BEEN
LOCATED IN THE AREA HAVE BEEN SITUATED NEAR MODERATELY FERTILE SOIL --
EITHER IN BASINS OR AT THE MOUTHS OF VALLEYS CONTAINING ALLUVIAL DEPOSITS.
NUMEROUS GULLIES SEPARATE MARL RIDGES, SOME OF WHICH BEAR A THIN,
LIGHT-COLORED SOIL CONTAINING LARGE AMOUNTS OF CALCIUM CARBONATE.  ON
MANY SLOPES, MAN-MADE TERRACES FOLLOW NATURAL CONTOURS AND RETAIN A
DEPTH OF SIMILAR SOIL WHICH IS SUITABLE FOR CULTIVATION.

    OUR SETTLEMENT IS SITUATED ON THE HIGHEST OF FOUR HILLS (66.3 M ABOVE
SEA LEVEL) RISING ABOVE THE SOUTHERN END OF A RIDGE SOME 3.5 KM EAST OF
A MODERN VILLAGE.  THE SETTLEMENT HILL IS CAPPED ALL OVER WITH SLABS OF
BEACH ROCK (SAND GRAINS AND MOLLUSC SHELLS CEMENTED BY CALCITE).  SIMILAR
DEPOSITS ELSEWHERE IN THE AREA HAVE BEEN ASSIGNED, ON THE BASIS OF THEIR
MOLLUSCAN FAUNA, TO A PHASE OF THE PLEISTOCENE PERIOD.

    BETWEEN HILLS, THE RIDGE HAS AN ALMOST FLAT SURFACE CUT ACROSS
WHITE OR GREY MARL AT ABOUT 51 M ABOVE SEA LEVEL.  A DEEP GULLY SEPARATES THE
RIDGE FROM RISING GROUND TO THE NORTH, WHILE THE SOUTHERN SLOPES (IN WHICH
STRATA OF BEACHROCK ARE VISIBLE) FALL ALMOST DIRECTLY DOWN TO A NARROW
SAND BEACH.  WESTERN AND EASTERN SLOPES GRADE INTO SMALL, FLAT PLAINS
WHICH OPEN DIRECTLY ONTO THE SEA.  STREAM CHANNELS LEADING FROM THE INTERIOR
ARE ABOUT 2 M DEEP, AND MOST RADIATE FROM THE FLAT AREA BETWEEN TWO HILLS.
THIS SEEMS TO ACCOUNT FOR THE ALMOST TOTAL LACK OF SOIL COVER THERE,
THOUGH A THIN SOIL IS FOUND UNDER PINES ON THE HIGH NORTHWESTERN SLOPES
AND IN PATCHES BENEATH SCRUB.

    NO PERENNIAL WATER SUPPLY IS NOW AVAILABLE ON THE RIDGE; THE PRESENCE
OF MARL MAKES ITS AVAILABILITY IN THE PAST UNLIKELY TOO.  AT PRESENT, THE
NEAREST WATER SOURCES ARE WELLS IN THE PLAINS BELOW THE RIDGE; IN WINTER
THESE ARE SUPPLEMENTED BY SURFACE FLOW IN STREAMS.  EROSION OF THE RIDGE
HAS PROBABLY LOWERED THE LOCAL WATER TABLE, BUT IT IS UNLIKELY THAT THE
SETTLEMENT COULD HAVE DRAWN UPON ANY OTHER SOURCES IN THE PAST UNLESS THESE
WERE SPRINGS AT THE CONTACT POINT BETWEEN THE MARLS AND THE CONGLOMERATES.

    TEMPERATURE DATA SHOW THAT THE REGION IS WARM YEAR ROUND (ANNUAL
AVERAGE 20.1 DEGREES C.):  JANUARY AND FEBRUARY ARE THE COLDEST MONTHS
(12.9 AND 13.1 DEGREES C. RESPECTIVELY), AND JULY AND AUGUST THE HOTTEST
(28.4 AND 28.2 DEGREES C.).  ALTHOUGH THERE IS AN EXTREME RANGE OF AVERAGE
MONTHLY TEMPERATURES OF 15.5 DEGREES C., HIGH WINTER HUMIDITY REDUCES THE
DIFFERENCE BETWEEN THE TWO SEASONS.

    MOST PRECIPITATION IS RECEIVED IN THE COOLEST PART OF THE YEAR, BETWEEN
OCTOBER-NOVEMBER AND FEBRUARY-MARCH.  IT FALLS IN SUDDEN, HEAVY DOWNPOURS
ON AN AVERAGE OF 9.6 RAIN-DAYS PER MONTH, AND IS BROUGHT BY WARM, OFTEN
DUST-LADEN WINDS FROM THE SOUTH AND SOUTHWEST.  THE PERIOD FROM APRIL
TO OCTOBER IS MARKEDLY ARID, WITH THE ONLY RAINFALL BROUGHT BY AN
OCCASIONAL THUNDERSTORM IN LATE SUMMER.
```

Figure 14–1. Site Description

VEGETATION

MOST OF THE LAND IN THE AREA IS COVERED BY SCRUB OF VARIOUS KINDS.
NEAR THE SEA THIS SCRUB IS SCATTERED, AND THERE ARE LARGE AREAS WITHOUT
BUSHES. FURTHER INLAND, SCRUB BECOMES MORE CONTINUOUS AND PINE TREES
LINE THE HILL TOPS. IN THE NORTH OF THE REGION THE PINES ARE JOINED
BY OTHER TREES AND THERE ARE SCATTERED TRACTS OF MORE REGULAR WOODLAND.
THE SEAWARD PLAINS ARE HIGHLY CULTIVATED TODAY WITH EARLY TOMATOES, WHICH
GROW DURING THE WINTER RAINS, AND WITH BANANA, CITRUS FRUIT, AND OTHER
TREES WHICH ARE PARTLY IRRIGATED. OLIVE GROVES ARE EXTENSIVE IN PARTS
OF THE VALLEY AND PLAIN, AND ARE SCATTERED AMONG THE HILLS. THE
BOUNDARIES OF CULTIVATION ARE OFTEN INDEFINITE, AND RUINED TERRACES
AND DERELICT CAROB TREES SHOW WHERE FARMING HAS RECEDED.

THE SOFT LIMESTONE HILLS WHICH HAVE BEEN RECENTLY CULTIVATED ARE
COVERED MAINLY BY FOUR TYPES OF SCRUB:

TYPE 1   DOMINATED BY SOME COMBINATION OF CAROB, WILD
           OLIVE, PISTACHIO, AND A TALL SUMMER-DECIDUOUS
           SHRUB. CONFINED TO GULLIES, HOLLOWS, AND
           NORTH-FACING SLOPES.

TYPE 2   THE COMMONEST TYPE: DOMINATED BY PISTACHIO AND
           THE LESS FREQUENT JUNIPER.

TYPE 3   WIDELY-SPACED PISTACHIO BUSHES AND LARGE TUFTS
           OF COARSE GRASS. A GREEN, LEAFLESS SHRUB IS
           CHARACTERISTIC. THE TYPE OCCURS MAINLY IN
           SOMEWHAT DEEPER SOILS ON LEVEL GROUND NEAR THE SEA.

TYPE 4   DOMINATED BY COARSE GRASS AND A SILVERY SHRUB.
           NOT SEEN MORE THAN 400 M FROM THE SEA; PROBABLY
           FLOURISHES ONLY IN SALINE SOIL.

FRAGMENTS OF STREAM-SIDE COMMUNITIES, REQUIRING GROUND-WATER THROUGHOUT
THE YEAR, OCCUR IN THE PLAIN. TYPICAL WOODY PLANTS ARE THE PLANE, MYRTLE,
OLEANDER, AND CHASTE TREES. FURTHER INLAND ARE SCATTERED PATCHES OF
TALL EVERGREEN MAQUIS 3-5 M HIGH. THE DOMINANT SHRUB IS A SPECIES OF OAK.

THE ONLY WOODLAND TREE FOUND IN THE REGION IS PINE. CLOSED WOODLANDS
OCCUR MAINLY ON NORTH-FACING SLOPES AND ARE PATCHY EVEN THERE: THEY GRADE
INTO AREAS WITH SCATTERED PINES AMONG SCRUB. PINE WOODS ARE PROGRESSIVELY
MORE ABUNDANT FURTHER INLAND, WHERE THEY ARE SOMETIMES MIXED WITH OTHER
TREES SUCH AS THE DECIDUOUS WILD PEAR.

CEREALS (MAINLY BARLEY AND OATS) ARE NOW CONFINED TO PARTS OF THE PLAIN
AND TO GOOD LAND ELSEWHERE. DERELICT TERRACES ON THE SOFT LIMESTONE SLOPES
ARE SAID TO HAVE BEEN LAST PLOUGHED UP DURING THE "WET YEARS" OF WORLD
WAR II. RECENTLY ABANDONED ARABLE LAND PASSES THROUGH A STAGE WITH
NUMEROUS ANNUALS AND VARIOUS THISTLES: A LATER STAGE (LASTING FOR MANY
YEARS) IS DOMINATED BY THYME, WHICH OFTEN FORMS A DENSE STAND TO THE
EXCLUSION OF OTHER SHRUBS. THE NORMAL SCRUB SPECIES INVADE VERY SLOWLY,
USUALLY FROM TERRACE WALLS. ON THE EXCAVATION SITE ITSELF CERTAIN
SPECIES OF DWARF GREY SHRUBS SUGGEST LONGER ABANDONMENT THAN ELSEWHERE.

OLIVE AND CAROB GROVES (WITH ALMONDS AND FIGS ABOVE 600 M) FORM ANOTHER
TYPE OF SEMI-CULTIVATION. THE WILD OLIVE IS AN IMPORTANT SCRUB SPECIES,
BUT THE CAROB -- ALTHOUGH GENERALLY SUPPOSED NATURAL TO THE REGION -- IS
NEARLY ALWAYS PLANTED AROUND THE MODERN VILLAGE NEAR THE SITE. WHEN NOT
IN REGULAR GROVES, IT IS GENERALLY ASSOCIATED WITH CULTIVATION: THE TREES
ARE ALL OLD AND DO NOT REGENERATE, ALTHOUGH NUMEROUS UNSUCCESSFUL
SEEDLINGS ARE PRODUCED. FOLLOWING USUAL PRACTICE, THE GROUND UNDER OLIVES
AND CAROBS IS REGULARLY PLOUGHED. OLIVE AND (ESPECIALLY) CAROB GROWING
IS NOW IN DECLINE. MANY OF THE OUTLYING GROVES ARE NEGLECTED, THE GROUND
VEGETATION RESEMBLING THE DIFFERENT STAGES OF ABANDONED ARABLE LAND.

DENSE STANDS OF THE GIANT REED "ARUNDO DONAX" COVER MUCH OF THE PLAIN.
THESE REED-BEDS MAY BE PLANTED, AND CUT REEDS ARE AN IMPORTANT SUBSTITUTE
FOR TIMBER.

Figure 14–1 continued

COMPARATIVELY LITTLE GRAZING APPEARS TO GO ON IN THE REGION AT PRESENT.
IT IS POSSIBLE THAT IN WINTER ITINERANT FLOCKS MAY DO SOME DAMAGE, BUT
LITTLE EVIDENCE OF CROPPED BUSHES AND TREES COULD BE FOUND. ONLY IN THE
MOUNTAINS IS THERE MORE INTENSE GRAZING. ALTHOUGH THE WOODY VEGETATION
OF THE REGION MAY HAVE BEEN REDUCED TO ITS PRESENT STATE BY HUMAN
ACTIVITIES IN THE PAST, THE EVIDENCE SEEMS TO SUGGEST THAT SUCH ACTIVITIES
DO NOT NOW LIMIT ITS FUTURE DEVELOPMENT.

THE VEGETATION HISTORY OF THE REGION IS LITTLE KNOWN. WITH ITS BASIC
SOILS, OXIDIZING CLIMATE, AND LACK OF LAKES IT IS UNLIKELY THAT A POLLEN
DIAGRAM WILL BE PRODUCED. THE CLASSICAL AUTHORS (CHIEFLY STRABO AND
THEOPHRASTUS) GIVE LITTLE RELEVANT TOPOGRAPHICAL INFORMATION. THE
VEGETATION PATTERN OF THE AREA WAS PROBABLY ESTABLISHED IN PRE-CLASSICAL
TIMES, THOUGH AN INDICATION OF PREHISTORIC VEGETATIONAL CHANGES COMES
FROM THEOPHRASTUS' MENTION OF THE WOODLAND, WHICH MAY HAVE BEEN SECONDARY
FOLLOWING DRASTIC LOGGING OR THE RETREAT OF AGRICULTURE (CYPRESS READILY
INVADES EX-FARMLAND) AT SOME EARLIER PERIOD.

CONCLUSION:

THE REGION IN ANCIENT TIMES MAY BE PICTURED AS SURROUNDED BY LOW,
INTERRUPTED EVERGREEN WOODLANDS DOMINATED BY OAK. ON SOUTH-FACING SLOPES
THIS WOULD GIVE WAY TO A MORE SCRUBBY WOODLAND PROBABLY DOMINATED BY
WILD OLIVE OR JUNIPER. MUCH OF THE MORE EASILY CLEARED WOODLAND WOULD
HAVE BEEN TURNED INTO PASTURE, VINEYARDS, AND OLIVE GROVES -- THE LAST
PERHAPS GRAFTED ONTO NATIVE WILD OLIVES. ENOUGH OF THE OAKWOOD REMAINED
WITHIN REACH TO PROVIDE A PORTION OF THE TIMBER. PINE, NOT READILY
AVAILABLE, PERHAPS GREW ON THE HARD LIMESTONE. COASTAL PLAINS WOULD
HAVE HAD LAGOONS WITH REED-BEDS, WHILE THE REMAINDER OF THE PLAINS WOULD
HAVE BEEN LESS SUITABLE FOR AGRICULTURE SINCE THEIR MYRTLE AND PLANE
TREES WOULD HAVE BEEN DIFFICULT TO DESTROY. A FEW TREES OF THE NATIVE
DATE PALM, WHICH STILL GROWS IN A FEW SIMILAR COASTAL LOCALITIES,
MAY HAVE BEEN PRESENT; THOUGH ITS DATES ARE SAID TO BE INEDIBLE, THEY
MAY HAVE BEEN STOMACHED IN DROUGHT YEARS.

Figure 14-1 continued

ARCHSIM is a computer simulation of an archaeological excavation. The
student or USER is presented with information about the physical attributes
of the area and has in hand descriptions of the codes used in the output
from ARCHSIM. The user then selects a sampling strategy, based on prior
formulation of the problem to be investigated. The computer will provide
grid selections for random or systematic sampling, but the user can select
the grids she wishes to "excavate" based on her own intuition or professional
judgment. After the grids are selected, the computer will print the results
of the "excavation" including stratigraphy, artifacts found and features.
When all the grids have been processed, the user may choose any of several
analyses to be performed on the excavated data. The results of these
analyses will be printed by the computer.

The site consists of four large squares divided into 25 grids. To select
a grid for excavation, enter the square disignation (R,S,V or W) and
two coordinates (1 to 5) to indicated the grid to be processed.
Some examples of valid grids are: R13, S55, V52, W11.

The program will keep track of the costs of this excavation. Your excavation
season is budgeted for $2000. Each grid excavated costs $150 and each analysis
costs $100. The program will end if you go beyond this budget, so plan your
strategy accordingly.

Figure 14-2. Program Introduction

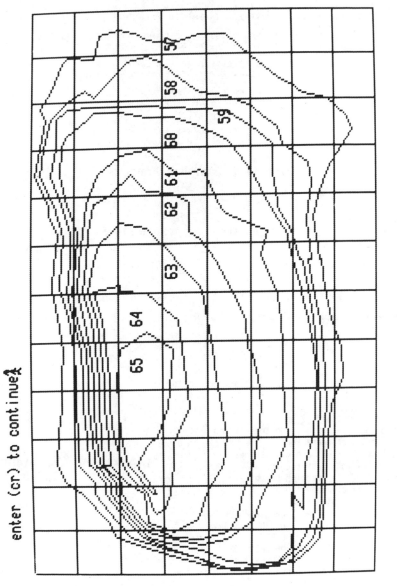

Figure 14–3. Site Grid System

SAMPLING

ARCHAEOLOGICAL SAMPLING PROCEDURES ARE DESIGNED TO RETRIEVE A REPRESEN-
TATIVE SELECTION OF ANY CULTURAL MATERIAL VISIBLE ON THE SURFACE OF A
SITE. THIS MATERIAL IS ANALYSED WITH A VIEW TO PLANNING STRATEGY TO BE
EMPLOYED IN THE ACTUAL EXCAVATION (WHERE TO DIG, WHAT TO EXPECT, ETC.).

YOU MAY SELECT FROM THE FOLLOWING THREE "SAMPLING" METHODS, EACH OF WHICH
PRESUPPOSES A GRID SYSTEM OVERLYING THE SITE:

SYSTEMATIC: ALL MATERIAL IS COLLECTED FROM SQUARES AT REGULAR INTERVALS
             OVER THE GRID (I.E. EVERY 4TH SQUARE, EVERY 5TH SQUARE).

RANDOM: THE GRID SQUARES FROM WHICH MATERIAL IS TO BE GATHERED ARE
             DETERMINED ON THE BASIS OF A RANDOMLY GENERATED SERIES OF
             NUMBERS.

INTUITIVE: THE EXCAVATOR SELECTS SQUARES WHICH HE HAS REASON TO BELIEVE
             WILL PROVIDE APPROPRIATE CULTURAL MATERIAL.

Figure 14–4. Sampling Strategies

what is your sampling strategy? intuitive   ◀ **Figure 14–5.** Request for
                                                              Sampling Strategy

enter grid designation...(cr) to stop: R13   ◀ **Figure 14–6.** Request for Grid
                                                              and Depth
enter depth (in cms) to excavate next grid: 50

enter depth (in cms) to excavate next grid: 50
grid R22

cm (from top)
7.1   0 to 5   Surface and topsoil 7.2
      0 artifacts were found
      5 to 15   lt brn with stones
      0 artifacts were found   ◀ **Figure 14–7.** "Excavation"
      15 to 20   reddish brown   ▼   Results
      5 artifacts were found
              STONE (00)   7.3
                    LENGTH 25.0-35.0
                    WIDTH 12.5-30.0
                    QUERN   7.4
                    MATERIAL 02   7.5
                    NUMBER 3
      enter (cr) to continue
              STONE (000)
                    DIAMETER 7.5 (FLAT FACE)
                    TOOL
                    MATERIAL 02
                    SPHERICAL; WITH ONE FACE FLATTENED BY GRINDING AND POUNDING.
      enter (cr) to continue⧗

```
THE FOLLOWING IS A LIST OF ANALYSES THAT CAN BE CARRIED OUT
ON THE DATA RECOVERED FROM YOUR EXCAVATION. KEEP YOUR OVERALL
RESEARCH STRATEGY IN MIND IN SELECTING ANALYSES.

THE POSSIBLE ANALYSES ARE:
CERAMICS
SHELLS
PLASTER
METAL
OBSIDIAN
BONES
```

Figure 14–8. Available Analysis Files

```
ENTER NAME OF ANALYSIS...ENTER (CR) TO END:
CONGRATULATIONS..YOUR EXCAVATION IS COMPLETED.
YOU HAVE EXPLORED 12 GRIDS AND FOUND
CULTURAL REMAINS IN 8 OF THEM.

YOUR COSTS FOR THIS SEASON ARE $1800
```

Figure 14–9. Cost of Current Excavation Run

```
enter grid designation...(cr) to stop: R11

enter depth (in cms) to excavate next grid: 10
grid R11

cm (from top)
0 to 25      Surface and topsoil
0 artifacts were found
enter grid designation...(cr) to stop: R11
SORRY...YOU HAVE OVERRUN YOUR BUDGET!
```

Figure 14–10. Result of Overspending the Budget

The amount of descriptive information given the student by the computer can be controlled by the instructor or programmer by changing the information in the program operating files. For example, only the text to the right of the category code (figure 14–12) will be printed (figure 14–7, at 7.4), and codes without corresponding text will be printed as is (figure 14–7, at 7.5). By altering these files, the information listed by the computer can be changed. In addition, handouts (figure 14–13) for the course may contain relevant information concerning artifact and feature description. A simulation based on the excavation of a prehistoric Greek site[6] is now available for use with two classics courses, "Introduction to Greek and Roman Archaeology" and "Introduction to Greek Prehistory." A second data base, the Agora in Athens,[7] is in use with the course "Greek Archaeology: Archaic, Classical and Hellenistic." Other data bases being developed include one on a pre-Columbian site in the Southwest United States.

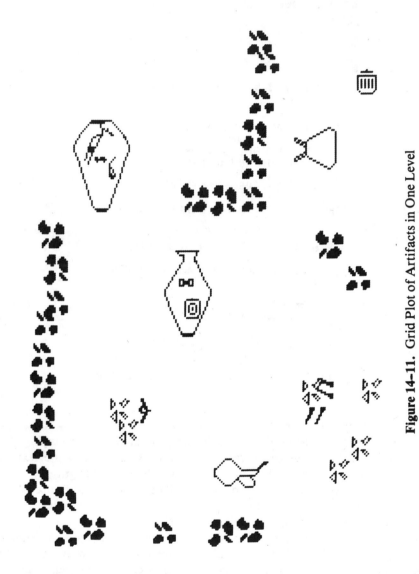

Figure 14-11. Grid Plot of Artifacts in One Level

STONE OBJECT SHAPES

01: TOOL

02: WEIGHT

03: DISK

04: QUERN

05: FIGURINE

06: WORKED RECTANGULAR BLOCK

07: SMOOTH PEBBLE

08: SPINDLEWHORL

09: LOOMWEIGHT

10: VASE

11: STAMP SEAL

12: SEE COMMENT

Figure 14-12. Category Code Descriptions for Stone Object Shapes ▶

FABRICS

01: PURE BUFF   PURE, WITH FEW OR NO GRITTY (TEMPERING) INCLUSIONS; USUALLY FAIRLY SOFT, SOMETIMES FIRM TO HARD; USUALLY BUFF-COLORED, SOMETIMES GREYISH-BUFF OR ORANGE-BUFF.

02: GRITTY   FIRM TO HARD BUFF COLORED WITH PURPLISH TO BLACK GRITS.

03: FINE BROWN   FINE, SANDY BROWN (SOMETIMES GREY-BROWN OR ORANGE) WITH TINY WHITE AND OFTEN GOLD (MICA) GRITS.

04: PITHOS FABRIC   COARSE WITH DISTINCT PURPLE, DARK, AND SOMETIMES WHITE GRITS; FIRM TO HARD; USUALLY BUFF, BUT VARIES FROM GREY CORE TC PINK AT SURFACE EDGES.

05: COARSE, FRIABLE, WITH DARK GRITS; BRICK RED TO DARK BROWN TO PURPLISH BROWN IN COLOR.

06: THIN ORANGE   VERY THIN-WALLED, FIRM TO HARD, WELL-FIRED; ORANGE (SOMETIMES BROWNISH) IN COLOR WITH TINY WHITE GRITS.

07: FINE GREY   PURE, LIGHT GREY FABRIC WITH NO GRITTY INCLUSIONS; SOFT AND THICK-WALLED

08: FIRM TO HARD, LIGHT BROWN OR ORANGE IN COLOR, WITH WHITE MARBLE GRITS.

Figure 14-13. Pottery and Stone Artifact Code Description

09: PALE BUFF   PURE, WITH NO GRITS; PALE, CREAMY BUFF IN COLOR; GIVEN
                   A PALE CREAMY OR IVORY SLIP WHICH IS BURNISHED.

10: OTHERS   A: SOFT, ORANGE TO GREENISH-GREY; VERY GRITTY. (3)
                   B: PALE PINK (1)
                   C: DEEP PINK (1)
                   D: PLAIN BUFF (1)
                   E: THIN REDDISH (1)
                   F: DARK GREY, POORLY FIRED (1)

SURFACE TREATMENTS

01: RED TO BROWN PAINT, UNBURNISHED, ALL OVER THE SURFACE

02: DARK, PURPLISH-BLACK OR BLACK PAINT, UNBURNISHED, ALL OVER THE
    SURFACE

03: RED, BROWN, YELLOW AND BLACK PAINT, MOTTLED, BURNISHED, APPLIED
    ONTO A BUFF SLIP ALL OVER THE EXTERNAL SURFACE EXCEPT THE BASE

04: BROWN-BLACK TRICKLE DECORATION PAINTED ONTO A BUFF SLIP

05: DARK PAINTED PATTERNS ON A BUFF SLIP

06: PURPLISH/REDDISH/BROWNISH PAINT APPLIED ALL OVER THE SURFACE OR
    ON THE INTERIOR SURFACE ONLY

07: RED-BROWN PAINT, BURNISHED, ALL OVER THE SURFACE

08: PALE GREY SLIP, ALL OVER, LIGHTLY BURNISHED; OCCASIONALLY INCISED

09: BROWN SURFACE, NO SLIP

10: PALE YELLOW OR IVORY SLIP, ALL OVER, BURNISHED

11: PSEUDO MOTTLED & BURNISHED -- RED, BROWN, BLACK AND YELLOW MOTTLED
    PAINT, ALL OVER, UNBURNISHED BUT LUSTROUS

12: OTHER   A: PLAIN BUFF SLIP   (4)
                   B: WHITISH SLIP   (1)
                   C: PURPLE-RED BURNISHED   (1)

                        STONE OBJECTS

MATERIALS CODE

01: LIMESTONE

02: SANDSTONE

03: MARBLE

04: BASIC IGNEOUS

05: STEATITE   *Figure 14-13 continued*

06: SERPENTINE

07: OTHER   A: CALCITE
               B: METAMORPHIC
               C: DOLOMITE

08: OBSIDIAN

FORMS CODE

01: TOOL   A: POUNDER
              B: GRINDER
              C: AXE
              D: BORER
              E: PESTLE
              F: RUBBER

02: WEIGHT

03: DISK

04: QUERN

05: FIGURINE

06: RECTANGULAR BLOCK

07: SMOOTH PEBBLE

08: SPINDLEWHORL   *Figure 14–13 continued*

09: LOOMWEIGHT

10: VASE

11: STAMP SEAL

12: SEE COMMENT

The simulation program ARCHSIM requires a single-disk Terak microcomputer with keyboard and CRT (video screen) and the University of Minnesota version of the UCSD Pascal microcomputer operating system [5]. The system, the program, and the secondary files are all stored on magnetic diskettes (floppy disks), which are inexpensive and easily transportable. The only disadvantage of these disks is that their small storage capacity necessitates frequent disk changes midprogram in order to access a large-site data base. The software-technology needs for this simulation are adequately satisfied by the UCC Pascal system. Future improvements in the speed and storage capabilities of the equipment will, however, increase the ease of use of ARCHSIM and allow for special enhancements to be made to the program.

Some of the advantages of using a computer to operate the simulation of an archaeological excavation as a teaching exercise are mentioned above. The Terak microcomputer offers the added benefit of presenting a graphic representation of the topography, the grid system and spatial relationships of artifacts and features during the excavation process. Also, the use of a CRT (video screen) instead of a hard-copy printer forces the student to develop good note-taking skills which are indispensable in a field situation. After the initial purchase or rental of the equipment, the cost of running the simulation program involves only equipment maintenance and the electricity to run the machine. Since these costs can be shared by offering several CAI courses simultaneously, the actual cost per teaching module can be minimized. The additional expense of providing enough copies of the simulation for student use is usually alleviated by charging a laboratory fee or having the students buy their own disks. Therefore, the main expense other than equipment is hiring personnel to maintain the programs and to monitor the computer laboratory where the students will run the simulation.

Computer simulation is a useful technique for teaching archaeological concepts and methods such as research design and strategy, sampling, stratigraphy, and artifact analysis. In general CAI will be used with greater frequency and with greater sophistication as technology improves and as archaeologists and others better appreciate its advantages. Simulation as a CAI technique can have even greater impact on education than conventional CAI methods because it goes beyond computer drills and exercises. Simulation provides the student with the challenge to design his own research strategy, analyze the results of the research, and synthesize the whole into a coherent report. Using data from actual excavations (or any real situation) both allows the instructor to evaluate the student's work in relation to what is known and presents the student with a real-life situation, not a hypothetical one.

Once the data are available in machine-readable form, other research projects can be undertaken using these data: The simulation can also be used to test hypotheses concerning the data themselves or the sampling of these data. If many data bases are available, comparisons of simulations of different sites but using similar strategies can be made; or the data bases can be merged to provide one data base for use in research that deals with chronological, cross-cultural, or areal questions. Statistical and other analyses can also be applied to the data contained in any of these data bases.

Acknowledgments

Without the hard work and persistence of Marta Nichols-Vellios and Sharon DeHoff, this project would not have survived. To them was allotted much of the drudgery, boredom, and frustration, and a grateful thank you is long overdue. A large portion of thanks is also due Professor Peter C. Patton and Professors A.T. Kraabel and Ellen Herscher (classics) for their help and encouragement.

Notes

1. J.H. Chilott and J.J. Deetz, "The Construction and Use of a Laboratory Archaeological Site," *American Antiquity* 29(1964):328–337.

2. Introductory archaeology course in the anthropology department at the University of Minnesota at Duluth.

3. See chapter 11, note 3.

4. J. Specter, *Prehistoric Midwestern Woodland Indians,* (unpublished teaching package) Minneapolis, Minnesota, 1973.

5. K.L. Bowles, *Microcomputer Problem Solving Using Pascal* (New York: Springer-Verlag, 1977).

6. Peter Warren, *Myrtos,* BSA Supplement 7, 1972.

7. *The Athenian Agora:* ASCSA, vol. 14 (1972); H. Thompson and R. Wycherley, vol. 12 (1970); B. Sparks and L. Talcott; and various other smaller references.

Part III
Computing in
Humanistic Education

Peter C. Patton

Research in computer-aided instruction and the psychology of learning has a long tradition at the University of Minnesota. Professor Russell W. Burris, of the consulting group on instructional design, was a pioneer in this technology, and his annual seminars for faculty interested in incorporating this technology into their own teaching encouraged applications in many different areas, from language instruction to calculus and physics, and, most recently, even to legal education.[1] Our interest in Part III is to report recent coursework developments at the University of Minnesota, with a special emphasis on the use of the microcomputer technology and the "off-loading" of large-computer computer-aided instruction (CAI) developments onto small computers.

Early research and development in CAI at Minnesota by Professor Burris and the late Professor Cecil Wood of the German Department resulted in a high-quality computer laboratory section in a German grammar course. The success of this course in teaching German led directly to its extension by Professor Ray Wakefield to teaching Dutch and indirectly to a PLATO course in classical Greek written by Michael Kunin under the direction of Professor Gerald Erickson. The PLATO system developed at the University of Illinois and sponsored commercially by the Control Data Corporation has represented for at least a decade the most advanced CAI technology available.[2] The first two chapters in Part III illustrate some of the capability of this system. The course teaching reading of Sumerian economic texts in cuneiform (chapter 15) had two goals. The first was to capture the inductive methodology employed in the Sumerian seminar for many years by Regents Professor Tom B. Jones. The second goal was to attempt something that would stress the PLATO technology in order to better understand the limits of its capability to deal with reading instruction in logographic agglutinative languages. As the reader will see, the PLATO system proved more than able to meet the challenge. The course has been successfully used by Professor Daniel Reisman as a supplement to his literary Sumerian course. It has been used for independent study by students wishing to gain a research capability with Sumerian source materials in ten weeks. During this period the student must master ninety documents dealing with a wide variety of economic transactions employing more than 350 logograms.

The Egyptian hieroglyphics course (chapter 16) was suggested by Kenneth Decker and his advisor, Professor M.A.R. Barker of the Department of South Asian Studies. Control Data Corporation (CDC) made the development of the course possible by a matching grant. Chapter 16 is a summary of the resulting technical report to CDC,[3] which was in turn an extension of Decker's master's thesis in ancient studies.[4] The goals for the development of this course were again double: to stress the technology to the breaking point and at the same time to integrate the course fully in the PLATO technology so that it would not be dependent on non-CAI materials. The course was simultaneously taught to a total of six graduate students on the Minneapolis and Duluth campuses (University of Minnesota). Recent attempts to reformat these courses for small computers have served not only to clarify the limit of PLATO technology, but also to better define the vague territory between large-computer and small-computer applications in CAI. As a result of these efforts, the authors of chapter 16 were led to specify, design, and implement a microcomputer able to perform most of the complex CAI functions that a large computer enables.[5]

Chapter 17 on Greek CAI describes the effort required to transform a large computer course into a microcomputer-based course. The Terak computer may lack by only a factor of 2 the ability to display and store Sumerian or Egyptian writing, but it is very well suited to instruction in Greek and Latin. Similarly, the Terak is well equipped to handle other languages with non-Latin alphabets such as Russian, Hebrew, and Sanskrit, but research at UCC in these areas is too premature to describe in this book. The Terak Greek course was derived from its PLATO predecessor, but the Latin course described in chapter 18 was designed and built from the ground up. Although the Latin course developers did not have to overcome the design problems of a new alphabet for the Terak, they did choose to attempt some challenging instructional capabilities. The Greek and Latin courses hold the promise of teaching classical scholars to be able to read these languages as rapidly as they do their native languages. We hope such techniques will overcome the objections of new students and allow them a whole new appreciation of Greek and Latin as fascinating literatures, not just ancient languages or philological and cultural resources.

The classics department at the University of Minnesota opened a small-computer laboratory at the start of the 1979/1980 academic year. It consists of seven Terak microcomputers plus a shared printer. The laboratory supports the instructional program of the department by means of the classical Greek, New Testament Greek, and Latin courses and a Greek prehistoric archaeology course described by Dr. Walsh in chapter 14. Under the enthusiastic leadership of the classics department, with some technical support from the University Computer Center, this laboratory is rapidly growing to become a computing services center for both instruction and research in the humanities.

The chapters on computer-assisted music instruction (19) and analysis (20) by Professor Dorothy Gross present quite a different range of computer application problems than do those on the language courses. Gross has done pioneering work in these areas, not only on large computers and using the PLATO system, but also experimentally on the very small-scale APPLE II personal computer. Originally it was intended to devote an entire part of this book to computer applications in music, but it was not feasible for lack of applications at the University of Minnesota. The work by Gross represents an important contribution to this fascinating area of computer application.

Notes

1. Burris, R.W. "Computer Network Experiments in Teaching Law" (Princeton, N.J.: EDUCOM, 1980).

2. Control Data Corporation, "PLATO User's Guide," Pub. No. 97405900 (Minneapolis, Minn.: Control Data Corporation, 1976).

3. K.W. Decker, O.J. Schaden, P.C. Patton, M.A.R. Barker, W.R. Brookman, and R.J. Kubat, "A PLATO Course for Egyptian Hieroglyphics," Technical Report 79003 (University of Minnesota, University Computer Center, September 1979).

4. K.W. Decker, "A Computer-Aided Course in Ancient Egyptian," master's thesis, University of Minnesota, March 1980.

5. W.R. Franta, "Joyce: A Next Generation Personal Computer," Proceedings of the Third Symposium on Small Systems, *Sigsmall Newsletter* 6, no. 2(September 1980):108–113.

15 Sumerian: An Experiment in CAI Language Learning

William R. Brookman,
Geri Hockfield, and
Peter C. Patton

Language learning through the use of computer-aided instruction (CAI) is by no means a novel idea. Many self-contained instructional programs exist which lead the eager student through the paradigms of a new language. Historically these computer-aided courses have focused on the rather traditional languages usually offered in college, so that German, French, Spanish, and Russian constitute the core of language lessons available on computer. Encouragingly, some attention has been directed to the realm of the classical languages, that is, Latin and Greek; even the biblical languages, Hebrew and Koine Greek, have been included into the growing list of languages readily available through CAI. However, the need is evident for CAI programs to provide for language-learning opportunities in nontraditional areas. Toward this end, a unique language course has been developed and employed at the University of Minnesota. The course is unprecedented in several respects. First, this CAI program teaches students the oldest language known, the Sumerian language. Second, Sumerian is a nonalphabetic language written in cuneiform logograms, thereby eliciting special interest because of many atypical problems involved in programing and in the presentation and development of basic skills required to use the language productively.

Regardless of the size of an educational institution, it is not feasible to have instructors always available for language courses of relatively low demand. Individuals who are not enrolled at one of the very few universities having a Sumerologist on the staff are simply out of luck if they wish to learn Sumerian. Existing books and teaching aids usually require a teacher or experienced guide to their contents. Few exercises are provided for reinforcement, and those exercises presented are not provided with answers. Still, the need to fulfill the desires of interested and highly motivated students who may wish to study such a language is paramount. One of the prime motivating factors in the development of the Sumerian CAI course was a desire to fill this gulf, a task to which the concept of CAI is ideally suited.

In 1977 we were fortunate to have participated in the last ancient history seminar taught by Regents Professor Tom B. Jones before his retirement from the history department at the University of Minnesota. The purpose of this seminar was to initiate history students into Jones's methodology for analyzing Sumerian economic documents of the Ur III period.[1] Most of the students had no previous experience reading such texts; in fact, many had no experience reading any Sumerian at all. Yet, by the end of the year, not only were the students able to read the texts, but also they could use them to describe and analyze problems in the economic and bureaucratic history of the third dynasty of Ur.[2] We became interested in preserving both the method and the content of Jones's seminar, based on the inductive approach which he employed to teach ancient languages. Thus, another goal in the development of this course was to impress in a computer program the essence of particular instructional design.

A further motive in the development of this course was to demonstrate that the most modern "writing" technology, that is, computer graphics, could be applied to the study of the world's most ancient written language. Previous to the work on this course, the University of Minnesota Computer Center was already involved in projects applying computer technology to language instruction. The university was using Control Data's PLATO instructional system for several traditional language courses. The excellent graphic capabilities of the PLATO system make it ideal for teaching languages written in scripts other than the alphabets of English or European languages. However, the very nature of the Sumerian language itself is so radically different from that of any alphabetic language that the capacity of the computer system for dealing with the graphics of nonalphabetic languages was rigorously tested.[3]

The Problem

The design of the Sumerian course fell into two problem areas, instructional design and the solving of difficulties related to computer programming, including especially those concerning graphic display. The scope of the project and the overall approach used in the development of the Sumerian course can, in a general way, be examined within these categories. The merit of CAI speaks for itself. Much has been written about the theoretical basis for CAI. Yet, it is the positive results of studies on computer-assisted language learning that have been most encouraging. The evidence of such studies shows that students learning a language via CAI comprehend more, faster, and achieve higher scores than students working on the same material with conventional instructional methods [1, 2, 3, 4, 5]. This is not, therefore, the appropriate place to defend the construction and implementation of a CAI language course. Still, simply incorporating the use of a terminal does not guarantee instruction of redeeming value. For this reason, an effective instructional design is a critical element of any CAI program.

Planning for instruction, especially computer-based instruction, is a complex process that requires balancing many separate elements and continually reevaluating the relationship of each part of the plan to the whole, because one element may affect the development of another. The need to anticipate unexpected student responses is paramount. Consequently, the important questions which had to be addressed initially were these: In terms of present abilities and knowledge, how do we define purposes, organize content, select learning methods, and utilize technological developments to meet the multiple needs of the student?

Fortunately the model provided by Jones's "sink or swim" teaching method eliminated a detailed analysis of several of these potentially vexing questions. The purpose and scope of the course have been already noted; the learning method was to be based on Jones's inductive model. The remaining pedagogical problem, that of content organization, was based primarily on the time element: while the original seminar lasted thirty weeks, it was thought a ten-week, single-quarter, condensed version was more appropriate for this experimental computer-aided course. Thus, there was a consolidation of the large amount of potential material. This included selecting texts of graded difficulty and varied subject matter to include in the course, while preserving the inductive approach which depends on cumulative language experience applied to new problems in translation. Finally, the problem of utilizing the computer technology to develop the graphics required for Sumerian orthography, and the physical construction of the program itself, had to be confronted. This area of implementation proved to be the most troublesome and time-consuming.

This combination of approaches resulted in a self-contained language course which introduces students to the Sumerian language as exhibited in a specific genre: economic documents. Such administrative texts constitute the largest corpus of Sumerian tablets, which are untranslated and thus largely unavailable to students of ancient economic and cultural history. The CAI course is designed to teach the historical scholar to read and deal with such primary-source material. The course was designed to enable a true beginner, without prior knowledge of cuneiform signs or Sumerian grammar, to work with actual ancient texts.

The Solution

The format of the Sumerian course is such that the student works through a series of short economic documents. Each document comprises one lesson; the sixty-two-lesson progression through the course is carefully graded from simple to difficult. The first lesson presents the simplest kind of material so that, after having read several texts, the student will develop an intuitive grasp of the structure or "formula" of a single type of document. Successive lessons continue to expand vocabulary and the general sense of economic activity, progressing through a broader scope of business and trade affairs. Before the student begins working with the actual texts, however, the PLATO computer terminal is introduced. Next an introductory lesson to the Sumerian course itself is available to the student. This section includes a specific statement of course goals, historical background of the Ur III period (figure 15-1), the Sumerian number system (figure 15-2), and conventions to be employed when transliterating and translating the texts (figure 15-3). In addition, exercises are included to enable the student to master this material before ever entering a text lesson (figure 15-4).

The introductory lesson concludes with an index from which a student can access literally any element of the course (figure 15-5). As has been suggested [2], this is helpful in avoiding predetermined 'branching' in the program. Therefore, while a sequenced program is available, an unsequenced presentation is possible. This allows student flexibility and eliminates the computer's exercising strict control over what the student sees.

The Ur III Period

Ur III economic texts were produced during a relatively short period of time; about 125 years. They are usually assigned a date of around 2000 B.C.$^{\pm}$ 100 years. The texts included in this course come from the time of four kings. Listed below are the kings and the length of their reigns.

Šulgi	48 years
Amar-Sin	9 years
Šu-Sin	9 years
Ibbi-Sin	24 years

However, most tablets come from the middle period (the last 10 years of Šulgi to the first few of Ibbi-Sin). So the study of economic organization is generally limited to only about 30 years.

The texts were dated by means of month and year formulae. There are certain problems with the sequence, for example, whether Šulgi actually reigned 48 or 49 years is still unclear. But, for the purposes of this course, these problems are not very significant. For more background, see S.N. Kramer, The Sumerians, pp.68-70.

Figure 15-1. Historical Background of the Ur III Period

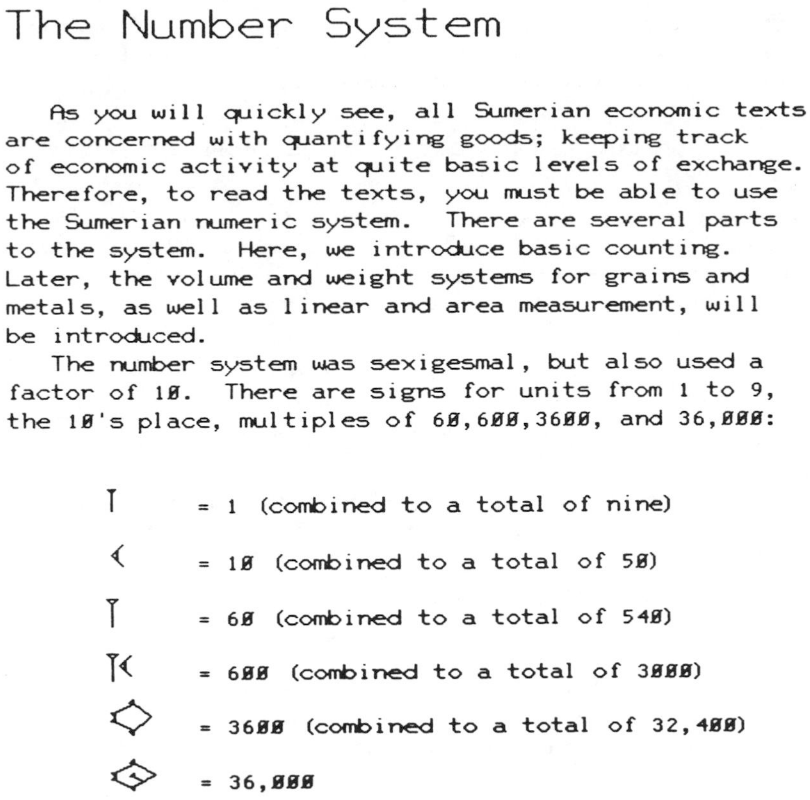

The Number System

As you will quickly see, all Sumerian economic texts
are concerned with quantifying goods; keeping track
of economic activity at quite basic levels of exchange.
Therefore, to read the texts, you must be able to use
the Sumerian numeric system. There are several parts
to the system. Here, we introduce basic counting.
Later, the volume and weight systems for grains and
metals, as well as linear and area measurement, will
be introduced.

The number system was sexigesmal, but also used a
factor of 1Ø. There are signs for units from 1 to 9,
the 1Ø's place, multiples of 6Ø,6ØØ,36ØØ, and 36,ØØØ:

T   = 1 (combined to a total of nine)

<   = 1Ø (combined to a total of 5Ø)

T   = 6Ø (combined to a total of 54Ø)

T<   = 6ØØ (combined to a total of 3ØØØ)

◇   = 36ØØ (combined to a total of 32,4ØØ)

◇   = 36,ØØØ

Figure 15-2. Sumerian Numeration

Beyond the introductory material, there are essentially four main elements of the course: texts, a sign list, a dictionary, and HELP lessons. As
noted, the point is for the student to work inductively through the texts.
Upon entering lesson 1, the student is presented with a graphic representation of an ancient Sumerian document (figure 15-6). The student must then
transliterate the document by typing into the terminal the phonetic value of
each sign. In tablet 1 (figure 15-6) there are seven lines to be transliterated,
each of which is "judged" by PLATO.[4] If the line is judged to have been
correctly transliterated, the student proceeds to the next line; but if the
transliteration is incorrect, PLATO gives the student a "no" response. The
student is then given three chances per line to enter the correct transliteration. After the third incorrect response, the correct answer is provided for
the student, who must then type in the correct transliteration.

The use of hyphens in names has already been mentioned.
As in literary Sumerian, hyphens separate syllables
which form a single word. For example:

$$Du_{11}\text{-ga } i_3\text{-tum}_2 \quad \text{"Du-ga received"}$$

The first word has hyphens in both transliteration and
translation because it is a personal name. The second
has a hyphen to show the connection of the verbal prefix
and the verb stem. By contrast, the phrase

$$1 \text{ gu}_4 \text{ še} \qquad 1 \text{ barley fed ox}$$

has no hyphens since all signs represent separate
words.

Certain groups of signs have two transliterations,
grammatical and phonetic. The most frequent ones are:

    ZU.AB   abzu
    EN.ZU   Sin

The first is written in capital letters with a <u>period</u>
separating syllables. The second has no hyphens.
Either transliteration is correct and will be judged
correct by Plato. In translating, only the second example
(<u>abzu</u>, <u>Sin</u>) is correct. When such alternatives exist,
they will be listed in the dictionary.

Figure 15-3. Conventions Used in Transliterating the Sumerian Language

<u>Translate</u> this Sumerian phrase in the form which you
will use when doing a tablet.

$$\gamma \quad \text{ⅲ} \quad \diamondsuit$$

$$\gg u_4 \; 3 \text{ kam}$$

Figure 15-4. Sample Student Exercise

```
Below are all the tablets.   Indicate which one you
wish to work on by typing  in the appropriate number.
```

Lesson I (Animal texts)		Lesson III (ba-zi,zi-ga texts)	
Number	Name of Text	Number	Name of Text
1	AO7 28	16	B3 183
2	AO7 23	16a	B3 183a
3	AO7 26	17	B3 178
4	AO7 29	17a	B3 178a
5	AO7 30	18	TRU 319
6	AO7 33	18a	TRU 319a
7	AO7 34	19	B5 47
8	KI 13	20	B5 73
8a	KI 13a	20a	B5 73a
Lesson II (Animal texts)		21	B3 15
Number	Name of Text	21a	B3 15a
9	TRU 91	22	KI 138
10	B3 181	22a	KI 138a
11	B3 184		
12	B3 186		
13	KI 23		
14	TRU 107		
14a	TRU 107a		
15	AO7 13		
15a	AO7 13a		

```
Type the number of the tablet you wish to see
(or "quit" to stop or NEXT for more lessons)>
```

Figure 15-5. Partial Index of Lessons

After the entire document has been correctly transliterated, the display screen would appear as figure 15-7. Notice in line 5 of figure 15-7 the transliteration bi_2, bil. This illustrates a PLATO judging feature that enables the course designed to specify a number of acceptable answers, all to be judged correct. In this case a response of either bi_2 or bil is accepted as correct.

The student now turns to a translation of the text; as with the transliteration, it is done line by line. Here the designer encounters a problem with PLATO judging since it is difficult for PLATO to judge long strings of words. It may be impossible to anticipate all the correct variations of syntax that may occur in a phrase of more than a few words. Thus, a situation may arise where, for all practical purposes, the student has translated a sentence correctly, yet that answer may not have been anticipated by the designer and a "no" response is given by PLATO. Fortunately, the formulaic nature of the economic documents eliminated most of this problem. In the introductory material, the student is taught how to translate certain formulaic phrases that occur over and over in the texts.

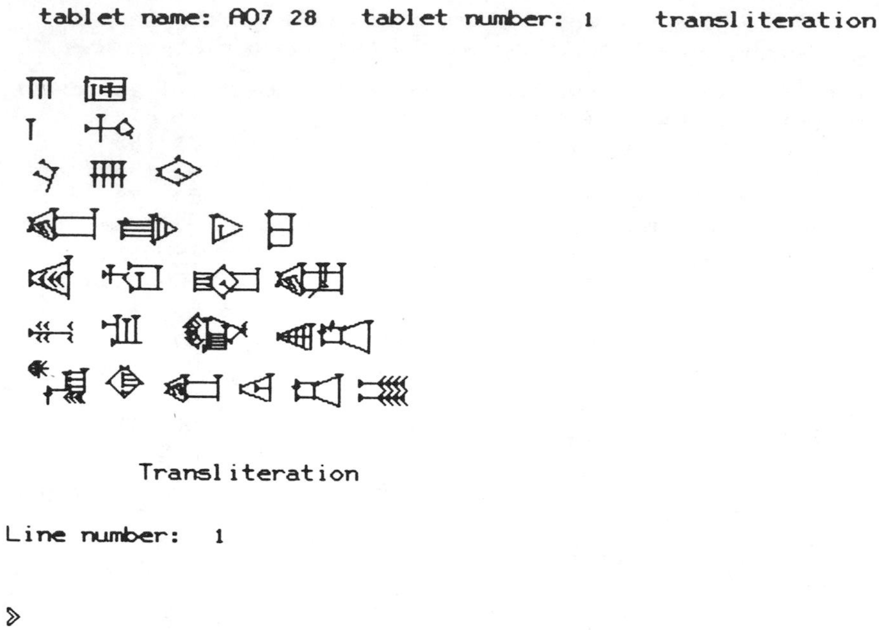

tablet name: A07 28   tablet number: 1   transliteration

Transliteration

Line number: 1

Figure 15-6. Computer Graphic of an Ancient Sumerian Tablet

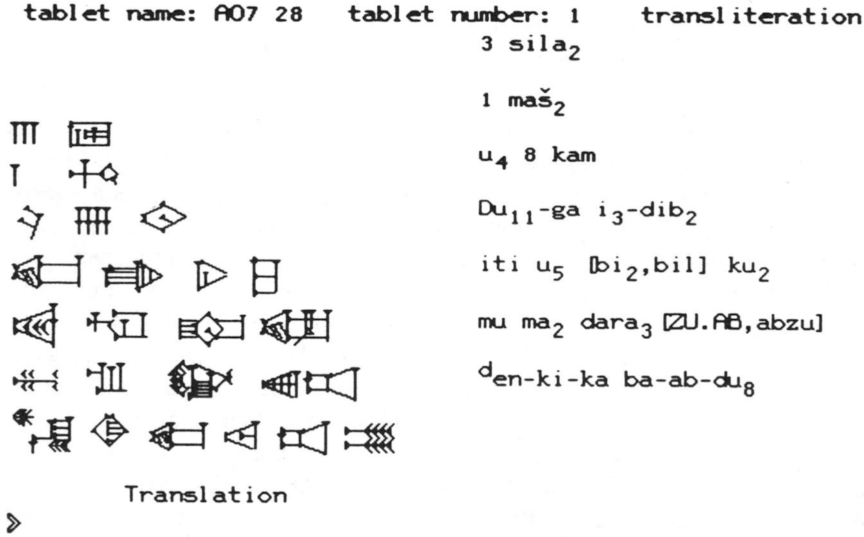

tablet name: A07 28   tablet number: 1   transliteration

3 sila$_2$

1 maš$_2$

u$_4$ 8 kam

Du$_{11}$-ga i$_3$-dib$_2$

iti u$_5$ [bi$_2$,bil] ku$_2$

mu ma$_2$ dara$_3$ [ZU.AB,abzu]

^{d}en-ki-ka ba-ab-du$_8$

Translation

Figure 15-7. Sumerian Tablet Transliterated

Syntactically the most complex elements of these documents are the
year and month formulas which occur in nearly every text. These are not
presented to the student as translation problems. However, a system of
abbreviations was devised for the student to use in lieu of translation. In
figure 15-8, the final two lines of translation are "D 3" and "ŠS 2." The
abbreviation D3 represents the translation of the Sumerian phrase *iti u₅-bi₂*
ku₂. Literally, the phrase means "the month of the eating of the *ubi* bird."
Each Sumerian city-state had its own calendar. This particular text is from
the city of Drehem, and D3 is the third month in the Drehem calendar. The
final translated line of text 1 is ŠS 2. The Sumerian phrase *mu ma₂ dara₃*
abzu en-ki ba-ab-du₈ might well be translated as "the year Enki's boat,
Antelope of the Deep, was finished." There are several slightly variant ways

tablet name: A07 28   tablet number: 1   transliteration 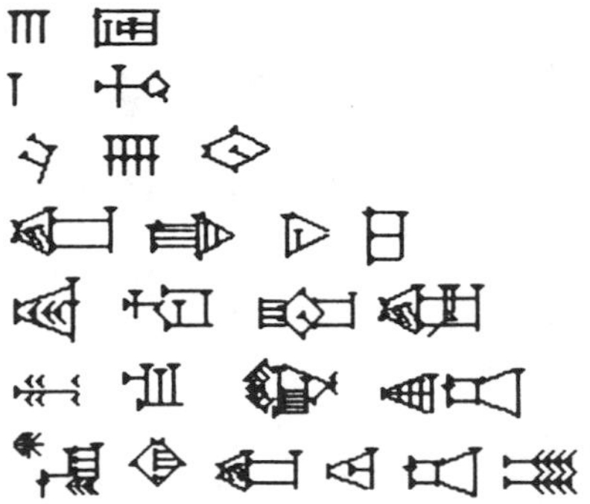
                                    3 sila₂

                                    1 maš₂

                                    u₄ 8 kam

                                    Du₁₁-ga i₃-dib₂

                                    iti u₅ [bi₂,bil] ku₂

                                    mu ma₂ dara₃ [ZU.AB,abzu]

                                    ᵈen-ki-ka ba-ab-du₈

          Translation
3 lambs
1 goat
on the 8th day
Du-ga received
D 3

ŠS 2

Type the number of the tablet you wish to see, "quit" to stop,
NEXT for next tablet in sequence, or BACK for the index⟩

Figure 15-8. Sumerian Tablet Transliterated and Translated

of translating this phrase correctly. Since this is the second year of the reign of Shu-Sin, the king of Sumer, the appropriate designation is ŠS 2. There is a HELP lesson which provides the student with abbreviations used in the course (figure 15-9). In this manner, the student works through the sixty-two tablets which comprise the course.

The second major element of the course is a sign list. This is simply a nine-page display of all the cuneiform signs used in the course. The sign list is really an index to the third element of the course, the dictionary. Each cuneiform sign is assigned a reference number according to the standard reference work, Labat's *Manuel d'epigraphie akkadienne* [5] (see figure 15-10 for the sign list). Using this reference number, the student may then access any dictionary entry. The student may gain access to the sign list and dictionary in several ways, depending on what the student is investigating.

```
mu a-ra2-3-kam-aš Si-mu-ru-um-ki ba-ḫul              Š 33

mu Amar-dSin lugal                                    AS 1

mu dAmar-dSin lugal-e giš-gu-za dEn-lil2-la2
   in-dim2                                            AS 3

mu dAmar-dSin lugal-e Ša-aš-ru-ki mu-ḫul             AS 6

mu dAmar-dSin lugal-e Ur-bi2-lum-ki mu-ḫul           AS 2

mu An-ša-an-ki ba-ḫul                                 Š 35

mu bi2-tum-ra-bi2-um-ki ba-ḫul                       AS 7

mu bad3 ma-da ba-du3                                  Š 38

mu dGu-za dEn-lil2-la2 ba-dim2                        AS 3

mu dNanna kar-zi-da ba-ḫun                           AS 9

mu dŠu-dSin lugal                                    ŠS 1

mu dŠu-dSin lugal-e bad3 mar-tu mu-du3               ŠS 4

mu dŠu-dSin lugal-e na-maḫ mu-du3                    ŠS 6
```

NEXT to continue, BACK to return to tablet

Figure 15-9. Sumerian Year Formulas

Figure 15-11 describes the options available with the sign list and the dictionary.

The dictionary consists of approximately 400 entries. Each entry display gives the student the cuneiform sign, all the possible transliterations, and all the possible meanings (figure 15-12). The student may go to any dictionary entry from any location in the course. From the dictionary, the student is then returned to that point in the course from which he or she exited.

The final major element of the course is a series of small HELP lessons to aid the student in specific problems. They may also be accessed from any point in the course. Seven HELP units are available: personal names, place names, gods' names, month formulas, year formulas, a map, and a biblio-

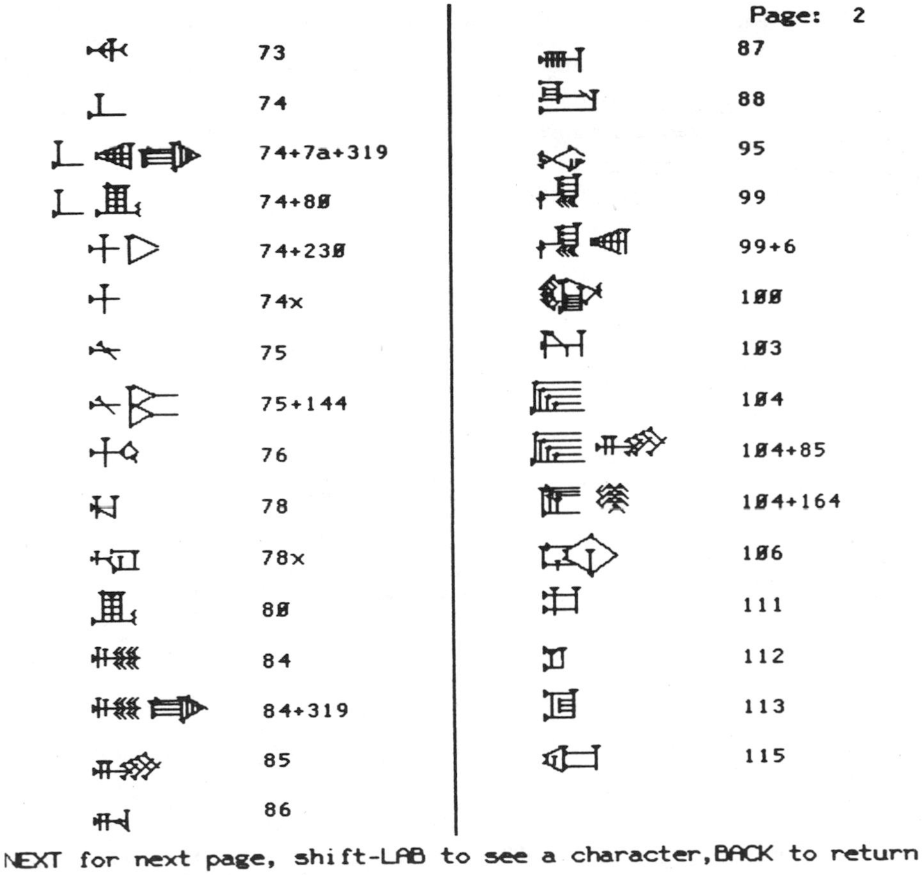

Page: 2

Sign	Number	Sign	Number
⟨cuneiform⟩	73	⟨cuneiform⟩	87
⟨cuneiform⟩	74	⟨cuneiform⟩	88
⟨cuneiform⟩	74+7a+319	⟨cuneiform⟩	95
⟨cuneiform⟩	74+8Ø	⟨cuneiform⟩	99
⟨cuneiform⟩	74+23Ø	⟨cuneiform⟩	99+6
⟨cuneiform⟩	74x	⟨cuneiform⟩	1ØØ
⟨cuneiform⟩	75	⟨cuneiform⟩	1Ø3
⟨cuneiform⟩	75+144	⟨cuneiform⟩	1Ø4
⟨cuneiform⟩	76	⟨cuneiform⟩	1Ø4+85
⟨cuneiform⟩	78	⟨cuneiform⟩	1Ø4+164
⟨cuneiform⟩	78x	⟨cuneiform⟩	1Ø6
⟨cuneiform⟩	8Ø	⟨cuneiform⟩	111
⟨cuneiform⟩	84	⟨cuneiform⟩	112
⟨cuneiform⟩	84+319	⟨cuneiform⟩	113
⟨cuneiform⟩	85	⟨cuneiform⟩	115
⟨cuneiform⟩	86		

NEXT for next page, shift-LAB to see a character, BACK to return

Figure 15-10. Sign List of Cuneiform Characters

a.   Search sign list for specific sign from the
     text. (You will have to designate the
     search sign.)

a1. Same as above except that you may choose a
     different starting page for the sign list.

b.   Search sign list but not for any specific sign
     (You will go directly to the sign list.)

b1. Same as above but you get to choose an alternate
     page to start the sign list from.

c.   Go directly to the dictionary. (You must
     designate a sign by Labat number.)

c1. Same as above, but no specification of a
     search sign.

     Choose an option⟩

Figure 15-11. Student Options for Searching

name= tum_2 number= 286
tur_x to deliver
tum_2 to deliver
tu_3 to deliver
du   part of name
du   to go
ra_2 part of name
gub   part of name
gub   stationed
gin   to go
gin   ordinary

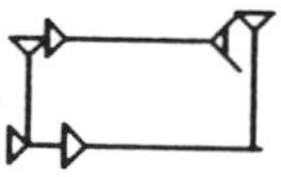

BACK to return, LAB for table, shift-LAB for another character

Figure 15-12. Sample Lexical Entry

graphy of the course. An example display from the personal-names HELP lesson is shown as figure 15–13. Note that the transliteration, translation, meaning of the name, and the number of the text in which the name originally occurs are provided. So although the novice may be unsure whether a particular Sumerian phrase is a proper name, one need only access this HELP unit to verify it. The other HELP lessons are similarly designed. The map HELP lesson details the geographical area of southern Mesopotamia, noting the cities from which the Ur III tablets originated.

Thus far, only the instructional design of the Sumerian course has been discussed. The second major division of this project was the actual design and solving of graphic-display problems. It is perhaps ironic that this course implements the most modern writing technology to reproduce the most ancient, perhaps original, writing technology. The scribes of old molded clay into a small, workable tablet. Then, with wooden stylus in hand, they

Personal Names

transliteration	translation	Meaning	Text
ab-ba-ša$_6$-ga	Ab-ba-ša-ga	father is favorable	2
a-ḫu-ni	A-ḫu-ni		22a
a-ḫu-ni-šu	A-ḫu-ni-šu		3
al-la-mu	Al-la-mu	my Al-la	6
^{d}amar-^{d}EN.ZU	Amar-Sin		8a
a-pil-i$_3$-a	A-pil-i-a		20a
a-tu	A-tu		17
ba-ba-ti	Ba-ba-ti	Ba-ba is life	33a
ba-la-a	Ba-la-a	Ba is abundant	28
ba-ša$_6$	Ba-ša	Ba is good	25
da-da	Da-da	force	13
da-da-ga	Da-da-ga		44a
DINGIR-ba-ni	DINGIR-ba-ni		50
du$_{11}$-ga	Du-ga	his word	1
du$_{11}$-ga-li	Du-ga-li	having pure speech	33
^{d}en-lil$_2$-la	En-lil-la	he is Enlil's	11
^{d}en-lil$_2$-zi-ša$_6$-gal$_2$	En-lil-zi-ša-gal	Enlil is an encouragement	16
en-dingir-mu	En-dingir-mu	the prince is my god	21a
ḫu-wa-wa	Ḫu-wa-wa		45a
ib-la$_2$	Ib-la		43
in-ta-e$_3$-a	In-ta-e-a	who has left from...	7
ir$_3$-mu	Ir-mu		22a
la-ni-mu	La-ni-mu	my La-ni	38
lu$_5$-a-mu	Lu-a-mu		5

Figure 15–13. Display of Sumerian Personal Names

impressed the cuneiform signs into the moist clay. Attempting to duplicate the ancient cuneiform writing provided an opportunity to test the limits of this modern technology for graphics of nonalphabetic languages. After several months of experimenting and attempting to find the best method of duplicating cuneiform tablets on a terminal display, a program was devised which allowed the programmers to "write" Sumerian characters on the computer screen.

All the signs were constructed by using two simple components, much as the ancient scribes did: a wedge (▷—) and a crescent (◁). Each of the approximately 400 signs employed in the course was constructed piece by piece by using these two basic picture elements. Each character created was given a name (usually the most common phonetic value of that sign) and a number (Labat number). First the sign was placed on the display grid, and the relative size of the element was determined. The program also allowed any angle of rotation to be set for any element of the sign. The programmer decided if a crescent or a wedge was desired, indicating the length where a wedge was specified. From this point, more elements (wedges or crescents) could be placed in positions relative to the first element to build a cuneiform sign. In this way, all the signs included in the course were built. Some of the signs contained as many as twenty-five to thirty picture elements.

Acknowledgments

We wish to acknowledge the assistance of Eric Inman and Joel Halpern, who experimented with cuneiform graphics, and the programming support of Richard Kubat. We especially acknowledge Professor Tom B. Jones, who taught us all Sumerian and to whom the course is dedicated. Professor Daniel D. Reisman was willing to first employ the PLATO course as a language laboratory in his literary Sumerian course. We thank him for his interest, encouragement, and many helpful suggestions.

Notes

1. The Ur III period generally is dated circa 2000 B.C. plus or minus 75 years. During this time span, several city-states flourished in the area of southern Mesopotamia. From these urban centers, hundreds of thousands of economic documents have been recovered.

2. For a methodological model for studying the Ur III texts, see Jones's *Sumerian Economic Texts from the Third Ur Dynasty* (in Bibliography).

3. For a brief discussion of the Sumerian language, see chapter 3.

4. When a student types in a response, the PLATO system makes two copies. One copy is stored for later reference while the other copy, called the judging copy, is used for determining how well the response fits the answer(s) specified by the author. It is extremely important to remember that this form of answer judging is not the same as determining if the student's response is correct. If the student responds with a word of phrase that, while correct, was unanticipated by the author, the response is still judged incorrect.

References

1. Abboud, Victorine, and Bunderson, C.V. *A Computer-Assisted Instruction Program in the Arabic Writing System.* Technical Report no. 4. The University of Texas at Austin Computer Assisted Instruction Laboratory, 1971.

2. Allen, John R. "Current Trends in Computer-Assisted Instruction." *Computers in the Humanities* 7 (September 1972):47-55.

3. Dick, W., and Lalta, R. "Comparative Effects of Ability and Presentation Mode in Computer-Assisted Instruction and Programmed Instruction." *A V Communication Review,* no. 18 (1970):33-37.

4. Holtzman, Wayne H., ed. *Computer-Assisted Instruction, Testing, and Guidance.* New York: Harper & Row, 1970.

5. Labat, Rene. *Manual D'Epigraphie Akkadienne.* Paris: Librairei Orientaliste Paul Geuthner, S.A., 1976.

6. Morrison, H.W., and Adams, E.N. "Pilot Study of a CAI Laboratory in German." *The Modern Language Journal* 52, no. 5 (May 1969): 279-287.

Bibliography

Adams, E.N. *The Use of CAI in Foreign Language Instruction.* IBM Research Report RC 2377. Yorktown Heights, New York, 30 October 1968.

Adams, E.N.; Morrison, H.W.; and Reddy, J.M. "Conversation with a Computer as a Technique of Language Instruction." *The Modern Language Journal* 52, no. 1 (January 1968):3-16.

Alford, M.H.T. *Computer Assistance in Learning to Read Foreign Languages.* Cambridge, England: Literary and Linguistic Computer Centre, 1971.

Allen, John R. "ELSE at Dartmouth: An Experiment in Computer-Aided Instruction in French." *The French Review* 44, no. 5 (April 1971):902–912.

————. "Individualizing Foreign Language Instruction with Computers at Dartmouth." *Foreign Language Annals* 5, no. 3 (March 1972):348–349.

————. "The Use of a Computer in Drilling." *Die Unterrichts-Praxis,* Spring 1972.

Alpert, D., and Bitzer, D.L. "Advances in Computer-Based Education." *Science* 167, no. 3925 (March 1970):1582–1590.

Anastasio, Ernest J. "The Study of Factors Inhibiting the Use of Computers in Instruction." *EDUCOM* 7, no. 1 (Spring 1972):2–10.

Anisfeld, Moshe. "Psycholinguistic Perspectives on Language Learning." In *Trends in Language Teaching,* edited by A. Valdman. New York: McGraw-Hill, 1966.

Atkinson, Richard C., and Wilson, H.A. *Computer-Assisted Instruction: A Book of Readings.* New York: Academic Press, 1969.

Avner, R.A. "How to Produce Ineffective CAI Material." *Educational Technology* 14, no. 8 (1974):26–27.

Banathy, Bela. *Instructional Systems.* Belmont, Calif.: Fearon Publishers, 1968.

Bloomfield, Leonard. *Outline Guide for the Practical Study of Foreign Languages.* Baltimore, Maryland: Linguistic Society of America, 1942.

Brookman, William R.; Hockfield, G.; and Patton, P.C. "Computer Aided Instruction in Reading Sumerian Cuneiform Economic Texts." Report 79004. University of Minnesota Computing Center, November 1979.

Bushnell, Don D., and Allen, Dwight W., eds. *The Computer in American Education.* New York: Wiley, 1967.

Byerly, Gayle A. "CAI in College English." *Computers in the Humanities* 12(1978):281–285.

Chastain, Kenneth. "Behavioristic and Cognitive Approaches in Programmed Instruction." *Language Learning* 20, no. 2 (1970):223–235.

Crothers, E., and Suppes, P. *Experiments in Second Language Learning.* New York: Academic Press, 1967.

Eraut, Michael R. "An Instructional Systems Approach to Course Development." *AV Communication Review,* Spring 1966, pp. 90–101.

Gage, William. "Uncommonly Taught Languages." Special Report No. 4 in *ERIC Bulletin,* no. 17 (1970).

Gagne, Robert M. *The Conditions of Learning.* New York: Holt, Rinehart and Winston, 1965.

Heinich, Robert. *Technology and the Management of Instruction.* Department of Audiovisual Instruction, Washington, 1970.

Jones, T.B. "Sumerian Administrative Documents: An Essay." *Sumerological Studies in Honor of Thorkild Jacobson.* Assyriological Studies, no. 20. Chicago: University of Chicago Press, 1976.

Jones, T.B., and Snyder, J.W. *Sumerican Economic Texts from the Third Ur Dynasty.* Westport, Conn.: Greenwood Press, 1974.

Kemp, Jerrold E. *Instructional Design.* Belmont, Calif.: Fearon Publishers, 1971.

Kramer, Samuel Noah. *The Sumerians.* Chicago: University of Chicago Press, 1963.

Lane, Harlan. "Models of Learning and Methods of Teaching." In *Language Learning: The Individual and the Process,* edited by E. Najam. Supplement to *International Journal of American Linguistics,* 1966.

Levien, R.E., ed. *Computers in Instruction.* Santa Monica, Calif.: The Rand Corporation, 1971.

————. *The Emerging Technology: Instructional Uses of the Computer in Higher Education.* New York: McGraw-Hill, 1972.

McPherson-Turner, Cherry. "CAI Readiness Checklist: Formative Author Evaluation of CAI Lessons." *Journal of Computer-Based Instruction* 6(November 1979):47–49.

Pribram, Karl H. "The Neuro-physiology of Remembering." *Scientific American,* January 1969, pp. 73–86.

Reigeluth, Charles M. "TICCIT to the Future: Advances in Instructional Theory for CAI." *Journal of Computer-Based Instruction* 6(November 1979):40–46.

Rosenbaum, P.S. *The Computer as a Learning Environment for Foreign Language Instruction.* IBM Research Report RC-2352, Yorktown Heights, New York, 1968.

Selzer, R.A. "Computer-Assisted Instruction: What It Can and Cannot Do." *American Psychologist* 26, no. 4 (1971):373–377.

Stevick, Earl W. *A Workbook in Language Teaching.* Nashville, Tenn.: Abingdon Press, 1963.

Stolurow, Lawrence M. "The Harvard CAI Laboratory." *Educational Technology,* September 30, 1968, pp. 11–12.

Valdman, Albert. "Programmed Instruction and Foreign Language Teaching." In *Trends in Language Teaching,* edited by A. Valdman. New York: McGraw-Hill, 1966.

Waite, Stephen V.F. "Computer-Supplemental Latin Instruction at Dartmouth College." *CHum* 4, no. 5 (May 1970):313–314.

Wardhaugh, Ronald. "Some Current Problems in Second-Language Teaching." *Language Learning* 17, nos. 1, 2 (1967):21–26.

16 A Computer-Based Course in Ancient Egyptian Hieroglyphics

*Kenneth W. Decker,
O.J. Schaden, Peter C. Patton,
and Kellen C. Thornton*

Ancient Egyptian, although it survives in only its written hieroglyphic form, can nonetheless be taught as a participatory activity when gleaned from dusty tomes and recreated on a computer terminal screen. An introductory course of this nature, taught by an unaided computer, was conceived in June 1978 at the University of Minnesota. Two general concerns prompted cooperation between the disciplines of ancient studies and computer science. First, the quality and availability of instruction in ancient languages, particularly those written in logographic (word-picture) characters, and specifically Ancient Egyptian, desperately wanted improvement. Second, the developers of a special computer-based education system known as PLATO sought means for testing the pictorial capabilities of their equipment. The product is an effective tool for individual, independent study of Egyptian hieroglyphics when a trained Egyptologist is not available as a teacher.

Language teaching, particularly the teaching of ancient languages, has not changed very much since the turn of the century and may not have changed much since the Middle Ages.[1] Until the audiolingual method was introduced in the 1940s, students were expected to speak the language in class, to learn dialogues, memorize passages from literature, memorize grammatical patterns, and read large quantities of text. This is the way Ancient Egyptian is taught today. On the other hand, the audiolingual approach revolutionized the teaching of modern languages by giving priority to the task of listening and speaking a new language, while treating reading and writing as secondary skills. With the audiolingual approach, the student alters and builds phrases with the rules of the grammar being learned, according to transformational and generative theory. So far only one manual, John Callendar's *Middle Egyptian*,[2] teaches Ancient Egyptian from the Middle Kingdom with this approach.

The primary reference for Ancient Egyptian is still Sir Alan Gardiner's *Egyptian Grammar*.[3] Enormously detailed, the work delineates thoroughly the complex structure of Middle Egyptian. Virtually everyone who has seriously studied Egyptian since 1927 has employed this grammar, yet its literary style is archaic, and lables used to describe parts of speech and sentence

253

structure are incomprehensible to the beginner. Furthermore, the exercises which conclude each chapter contain vocabulary items and grammatical issues not discussed until many pages later and include no answers. An experienced teacher is essential for most students. Consequently, a machine teaching system suggests a most attractive solution for the beginner attending a university that does not employ an Egyptologist.

The Problem

Interest in doing a computer-based Egyptian course arose from a previous project for a PLATO Sumerian course also reported in this book (chapter 15). Control Data Corporation acquired PLATO from its creators at the University of Illinois in 1967. PLATO (Program Logic for Automatic Teaching Operations) is a sophisticated teaching tool delivering information contained in a large-scale computer to the user via special terminals possessing a touch-sensitive screen and a keyboard. The system is one whereby the student and the terminal interact; instantaneous query and response give the illusion that one monopolizes the computer's time when its size and speed actually make it capable of sustaining numerous other interactive terminals simultaneously. PLATO is employed internationally by business and educational institutions as a training device with which an individual is taught standardized courses. Control Data's interest in this project lay in ascertaining the useful limits of PLATO screen resolution, graphic-design capabilities, and data-structuring capability.

Programs on PLATO requiring characters other than the Latin alphabet are rare. The most difficult combination of teaching and graphics until Egyptian was a course in Sumerian (reported in chapter 15), the world's first written language. Sumerian was written by pressing cuneiform (wedge-shaped) characters into damp clay tablets with a reed stylus. As reproduced on the PLATO screen, the cuneiform signs consist of short straight lines linked to form wedges and longer straight lines. Once formatted and scaled to the desired size, these wedges can be placed together to form any cuneiform sign. Egyptian signs, however, are much more complex since they are pictorial, consisting of many tiny line segments strung together to form curves and straight lines, making them much more difficult to reproduce. For this reason the generation of hieroglyphics stresses most thoroughly PLATO's graphic abilities.

The audiovisual method used in this course has never been used previously to teach Egyptian. Using an oral approach in a language whose vowels are long lost may seem odd, but the method is based on the assumptions that language learning is a process of habit formation and that students learn more efficiently by speaking than by reading. The approach used here concentrates on the former. This course is designed to provide grammatical information about Egyptian and to have the student practice using this new knowledge many times. Instant evaluation is provided by PLATO. Three kinds of exercises are used in the course:

1. Common phrases or sentences are transliterated (converted to another script with appropriate symbols) to Latin script and translated (converted to another language) into English.
2. Finger pressure on the touch panel of the screen indicates responses to multiple-choice questions.
3. Students build phrases by adding to or replacing words or phrases in preceding phrases. Known as the *microwave format* because it consists of nearly identical phrases patterned after the first in the series, the technique was perfected during the 1960s when hundreds of Peace Corps volunteers had to learn exotic languages. Entire courses consisted of nothing but microwave dialogues, which prove most effective when combined with other formats and methods.[4] PLATO is well suited to the microwave format because short sentences whose short answers minimize stylistic variance allow PLATO to judge the student's answer quickly. Further, fewer possible answers require fewer answers PLATO must be programmed to accept.

The Solution

Two other courses in ancient languages developed for PLATO at the University of Minnesota predate Egyptian: Classical Greek and the aforementioned Sumerian. Classical Greek is a free-standing (requires no classroom training) reading course that starts with the Greek alphabet and eventually incorporates most classical Greek grammar. A series of brief, animated grammatical discussions is followed by pertinent reinforcing questions. The Egyptian and Greek courses differ only in that Greek has no reading exercises and Egyptian grammatical presentations tend to be longer and more formal and employ more examples. The Sumerian course differs greatly from the other two for it requires a certain amount of classroom preparation. Furthermore, the orientation is textual rather than grammatical. A long series of transcriptions of Sumerian tablets is printed on the screen, and the student translates and transliterates them line by line with the aid of a dictionary and sign list. Finally, since the Sumerian course is the prototype, its programming is more primitive; consequently, printing is slower than for the other courses.

Developing of individual hieroglyphs on PLATO took approximately three months, although the time to create a single sign diminished significantly with practice. Before signs were made, however, a decision had to be made as to which signs of the more than 500 used by the Egyptians should be included. A preliminary vocabulary was derived by choosing the most common signs from the Gardiner reference. A second harvest incorporated hieroglyphs not considered particularly common, but used in common words. Hieroglyphs were added throughout course development as required by grammatical constructions. The sign style used by Gardiner was copied because it is simple, aesthetically pleasing, and available. To reproduce the signs on the PLATO screen, pages of Gardiner's sign list were copied, specific signs circled, and copied again onto transparent plastic sheets. An overhead projector enlarged the images to a maximum of 3 inches and displayed them on white paper taped to a wall for tracing. Transparencies made of the hand copies were then cut out and taped to the PLATO screen.

Using the PLATO system, the author of instructional material is not required to function as a programmer. Instead, a special author language called TUTOR, described in a PLATO reference manual, is used to issue standardized instructions for constructing lessons. The PLATO system converts TUTOR to instructions which can be executed by the computer. Commands are categorized by the type of manipulation to be performed. To create a picture, authors used a package or set of instructions called insert display (ID) mode. ID mode allows a person to locate and manipulate a cursor around the screen with arrow keys. Pushing appropriate keys generates, in any size, text, lines, circles, and arcs; moves text and pictures; and permits virtually any sort of screen design. Thus each hieroglyph was taped to the screen and traced by the cursor. A succession of many short lines approximated the irregular curves of figures such as birds, insects, and humans.

A second package of instructions to the machine allows one to reexamine work and edit it. Show display (SD) mode uses the same system commands as ID mode, but requires a preexisting code to display. SD mode reduces the size of the hieroglyphs: If the symbols are left 3 inches high, only one word or a short phrase can be displayed on the 8½ × 8½ inch screen. The screen display emanates from 26,121 dots of neon light arranged in a 511 × 511 grid, making some limit on reduction possibilities inevitable. Experimenting with different sizes proved even the most complicated signs could be shrunk to a 1-inch maximum (30 dots) without losing legibility; hence, no sign is allowed to extend beyond 1 inch in any direction. Gardiner's text demonstrates the proper proportions for the smaller signs. The hierarchy of size in his sign list shows the following relations: full, ¾, ½, and ¼ wide; and full, ¾, ½, ¼ high. For example, tall, thin signs tended to be full-size high and ¼ size wide. Incorporating his systems means full sized is 30 dots, ¾ is 20, ½ is 15, and ¼ is 7 or 8 dots.

Next, all characters were shrunk by approximately the same amount. At this point exceptions to the PLATO screen's ability to produce legible characters appeared. It does not represent round or curved objects very well, especially if smaller than a certain size. Round signs tend to become octagonal when their radii are eight dots, and oblong if the radii are less; therefore, nine dots seems the smallest diameter possible for circles. The irregular signs respond uniquely to shrinking and have to be handled individually. Consequently, not all signs could be reduced to the prescribed size, and the solution was to recreate the signs by hand. Fortunately, none of the really complex signs required this treatment, since most were signs with small arcs or embedded circles. This procedure, while tiresome, evinces excellent results.

Transliterating Egyptian phonemes requires a special character set because Egyptologists use special symbols to show singularly Egyptian sounds: ', 3, ḫ, ḥ, h, š, ḳ, ṭ, ḏ. In order to keep clear the distinction between transliterated and translated answers in PLATO's judging program, a whole new character set was created for the transliterations. It is a modified form of an italic type already available on PLATO. The first two special symbols, ' and 3, are created outright, while all other symbols, special and otherwise, are made by typing the italic base character and adding diacritics with special arithmetic keys. Symbols and text are arranged for presentation as if they reside on a page. A programmer engaged through the University Computer Center (UCC), University of Minnesota, wrote a program which made the arranging process simpler, faster, and cheaper than the existing procedure. Because the new program allowed two persons at a time to create pages, the approximately three-year production time was reduced to six months. The figure from the computer terminal screen (figure 16–1) illustrates an exercise taken from unit four.

The course is designed to be a free-standing introduction to Egyptian hieroglyphs and the basics of Egyptian grammar, and it should require no additional instruction or textual material. Besides a limited vocabulary, only the most common grammatical forms are introduced. On completing the course, students should be able to read simple sentences, identify the various parts of speech, and read such simple pieces of Egyptian literature as royal annals, *The Story of Sinuhe,* and funerary inscriptions.

To make it easier for students to both learn Egyptian and use PLATO, the first lesson introduces the "alphabet" and nouns. This gives students practice recognizing hieroglyphs without having to worry about phrase or sentence structure. This basic beginning also allows students to become familiar with the PLATO system and the terminal with its special keys. Essential, as well, is a clear introduction to the different uses of individual hieroglyphs. A sign can be an ideogram having the meaning of the object it resembles, a phonetic symbol, or a determinative which has no phonetic value, but serves as an aid to understanding the rest of a word. Without understanding these distinctions, reading Egyptian is impossible.

The next lesson introduces short phrases, first by using suffix pronouns

4.060

Exercise 1

mni·n·ʃ wi m s3t·ʃ wrt
He married me to his eldest daughter.
(it is interesting to note that mni literally
means to <u>moor</u> a boat, but the Egyptians
used the concept to describe marriage.
The image the Egyptians wanted to project
was probably one of constancy, security
and of coming home after a long journey alone.)

2.    ḥˤm·i sn
                              I approach them.

3.   ˤḥ3·ṯw
                              Beware!

                              niwt·i st
4.   It is my town.

                              mk wi im·s
                              See, I am in it.
5.

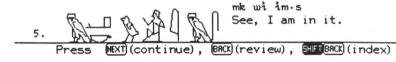

Press [NEXT](continue), [BACK](review), [SHIFT][BACK](index)

Figure 16–1. Sample Student Exercise

and demonstratives (words such as *that* which point out) and then by introducing the word *iw* to illustrate the word order of nonverbal sentences, for
example, sentences with adjectival predicates. Throughout the initial chapters, examples introduce new signs and new vocabulary. Biliteral and tri-
literal signs are introduced with new vocabulary using those signs. At this
point, students have mastered simple phrase rules and are ready for sentences with more interesting content and problems, as well as for the presentation of verb forms.

Students of Egyptian will appreciate the problem of choosing a verb
form to introduce first. The selected verb form (sdm.f) is simple, but its
range of meanings can be staggeringly complex, depending on whether

Gardiner's or Callendar's interpretation is accepted. Gardiner's system has prevailed here because it is less complex and less confusing to beginners. The authors, however, changed some of Gardiner's ponderous nomenclature to more easily understood terms.

In later chapters, the course begins to stress some aspects of hieroglyphic texts which incorporate idioms peculiar to Ancient Egyptian. The authors believe that the students should learn how to interpret titles, how to recognize common abbreviations, and how to detect honorific transpositions. These skills make it possible to read the funerary and dedicatory inscriptions that are introduced. Without an introduction to these idiomatic uses, many texts can be incomprehensible. Because the course is designed to be used without textual materials, we included HELP units to which the student could refer at any point in the lesson. These include a sign list, dictionary, index, and map of the Nile Valley.

The Results

During spring quarter 1979, six University of Minnesota students at the Duluth and Minneapolis campuses used the course as sole material for an introductory class in Middle Egyptian. At the beginning of the quarter, they received instruction on the PLATO system and a short pamphlet explaining keyboard use and the mechanics of the course. They were polled twice regarding their experiences with and feelings about the course. Both polls indicated that the Duluth students were suffering from the lack of local PLATO instructors to answer their questions about the setup. A note file for student questions helped resolve the absent-teacher problem. As the quarter progressed, students became much more adept with the equipment because questions about the keyboard dwindled, and reports of errors then increased. Each error was corrected as soon after it was reported as possible, although some errors in sign placement or judging routines were not easy to fix. There were no programming errors. At quarter's end, all the students reported that learning about Egyptian on PLATO had generally been a positive experience. They observed that one of the main benefits of computer-aided instruction is that one may proceed at one's own pace. This means that students can work when they want to or when it fits into their schedule, and they can review parts of the course repeatedly at their leisure. Students are thus freed from the tyranny of the classroom schedule. The human administrator of the course monitored student progress by referring to a special file kept by PLATO. The file holds a record of each access to the course; it holds the student's name, date, lesson number, number of questions asked, number answered correctly on the first try, number of times wrong answers were given, and time elapsed since the student signed on. These data reflect the confusion of the students on initial unaided encounters with PLATO.

The final examination consisted of nineteen questions. In the first section, the students transliterated and translated thirteen words. In the second section, they translated six short phrases or sentences. PLATO did not judge the results; it only recorded the students' answers. The purpose of the test was to demonstrate that students had committed the commonest signs to memory, knew the phonetic values of those hieroglyphs, had absorbed the simpler word-order rules of Middle Egyptian, and could remember a simple set of vocabulary items. In grading, course administrators considered the difficulty in taking an experimental course, the number of errors found by each student, the number of astute suggestions for change, as well as final-examination scores. Out of a possible 57 points, final-examination scores ranged from 39 to 57, and all were judged to be above average.

Research Prospects

The PLATO Egyptian course in its present form is designed to introduce the hieroglyphic writing system and the grammar of Middle Egyptian. Theoretically, the course could be expanded into a full two- or three-year course including the whole Middle Egyptian grammar, a discussion of linguistic problems, and several hundred reading exercises taken from the Middle Egyptian literary corpus. Included as well could be a complete treatment of Old Egyptian and Late Egyptian grammar with associated reading exercises numbering in the thousands. Finally, PLATO could be very useful in teaching students to read hieratic, the cursive form of Egyptian writing. More realistically, however, we think this course could become a complete course in Middle Egyptian grammar with many interesting reading exercises. The time required to do so would be eighteen to twenty-four months, depending on the number of persons assigned to put in material. One Egyptologist and two full-time typists could incorporate all the material in Gardiner's grammar in that time, although the typists should know something about hieroglyphics or be artistically inclined. Similar introductions to Old and Late Egyptian, each requiring a full-time typing staff of two and one Egyptologist, could be completed in eighteen months. An introductory course in reading hieratic would take somewhat longer because character-placement problems would be more complex and a whole new corpus of signs would have to be created, a task requiring six person-months of constant work. Sign placement is a problem in hieratic because, as in most cursive systems, the signs are sometimes run together or connected by curved lines. One revolutionary implementation would run the introductory course in two modes, presenting a page in both hieroglyphic and hieratic characters changeable at the touch of a key.

The present course is still incomplete as an introduction to the language. The addition of a few reading exercises would be an improvement. Elements of great importance which are lacking at present are pseudo-participial forms, participles, negatives, imperatives, number system, calendar, royal titularies, and funerary formulas.

Additions to the existing sign list and vocabularies, inclusion of the materials listed above, certain additions to existing chapters, and corrections would give the course all the elements of Middle Egyptian grammar. After completing the course, the student would be able to glean a certain amount of information from many of the monument inscriptions and have the basic elements needed to identify royal names and the like.

With the ever-increasing costs of higher education and the general inaccessibility of instruction in Egyptian, the course fills a special need. Although it is only an introduction, it offers certain advantages. First, the course is available wherever a PLATO terminal exists. Second, since the course consists of exercises and quizzes for the student, it does more than merely list rules of grammar and vocabularies. Third, the interaction of student and machine recreates in some measure that which exists between student and teacher, since PLATO's responses are related directly to the student's answers.

The PLATO course is by no means a substitute for the slow, methodical, and detailed study necessary for the specialist. Should the course inspire anyone to go on to further study in the more traditional manner, however, it will have provided a thorough introduction to the language of Ancient Egypt.

Acknowledgments

We wish to acknowledge the technical assistance of W.R. Brookman, who developed PLATO Sumerian; of Richard Kubat, who did much of the TUTOR programming; and the support and encouragement of Professor M.A.R. Barker. We also acknowledge the financial support of the Control Data Corporation, which awarded a matching grant, and the University Computer Center for encouragement and assistance.

Notes

1. E.W. Sterick, *Adapting and Writing Language Lessons* (Washington: Foreign Service Institute, 1971), p. 1.

2. J.B. Callendar, *Middle Egyptian,* Afro-Asiatic Dialects, vol. 2 (Malibu: Undena Press, 1975).

3. A. Gardiner, *Egyptian Grammar,* 3d ed. rev. (Oxford: Griffith Institute, 1957).

4. Sterick, *Adapting and Writing Language Lessons,* p. 314.

Bibliography

Control Data Corporation. "PLATO Subsystem." Pub. No. 97405200, Minneapolis, Minn.: CDC, 1974.

———. "PLATO Users Guide." Pub. No. 97405900. Minneapolis, Minn.: CDC, 1976.

———. "PLATO Author Language Reference Manual." Pub. No. 97405100. Minneapolis, Minn.: CDC, 1977.

Decker, K.W. "A Computer-Aided Course in Ancient Egyptian." Master's thesis, Center for Ancient Studies, University of Minnesota, March 1980.

Patton, P.C.; Brookman, W.R.; and Hockfield, G. "Computer-Aided Instruction in Reading Sumerian Cuneiform Economic Texts." UCC Report 79004. Univerity of Minnesota, November 1979.

Sherwood, B.A. *The Tutor Language.* Urbana: University of Illinois, 1974.

17 A Small-Computer CAI Course in Classical Greek

Dale V. Gear

The development of a system on a small computer for computer-assisted instruction in languages with a non-Latin alphabet was begun in June 1978 by George Gonzalez, Meg Tarbet, Paul Sonkowsky, and Dale Gear, members of the computer-assisted instruction (CAI) systems group of the University Computer Center (UCC) at the University of Minnesota. There were several motivations for this project. The first was economic. Prior to the development of this system, anyone who wanted to use a computer to teach a language with a non-Latin alphabet, such as Greek, was forced to rely on the Control Data Corporation PLATO system, which has the capability of presenting text on a cathode-ray tube (CRT), using any character set the user designs. However, it is very expensive to use the PLATO system; further, the user must endure such problems inherent in a time-sharing system as system down time and lack of available ports. If an adequate system could be written for a microcomputer, many of these problems could be alleviated. A microcomputer might require an initial investment equivalent to the annual cost of a PLATO port, but this would be a one-time-only expense. Maintenance contracts for a microcomputer are much cheaper than the fee for a PLATO terminal. Since microcomputers are self-contained units, the loss of one does not affect any others. If five microcomputers are available for use in a facility, then all five can be used at once, regardless of the number of users in other facilities. It was clear, therefore, that a good delivery system on a microcomputer would be more economical and efficient than the computerized instructional system available at that time.

The second motive was closely related to the first. Granted that an inexpensive, yet fully capable, delivery system was needed and that the microcomputer was the obvious choice for such a system, it was not at all certain that the realization of a system with the necessary sophistication was possible. A very small computer would be required to perform basically the same functions as the PLATO system without the benefit of the latter's faster and more extensive hardware. This project would push the microcomputer to the limit of its abilities and give an accurate picture of the current state of microcomputer technology and its capabilities. If the delivery system were successfully implemented, a new tool would be available for teaching via computer.

Complementing these two purposes was the desire to make the system as portable as possible. This required that the system not be written in code executable by only one machine. In order to accomplish this goal, we had to write the program in a high-level computer language. What was needed was a general-purpose language which had flexible data structures, modular programming capabilities, and wide availability. The one language which fulfilled these requirements was Pascal. By June 1978, the University of Minnesota possessed several Terak microcomputers equipped with the Pascal language. In addition, the powerful LSI-11 processor, coupled with graphics features, made the Terak the computer of choice for this project.

We decided that the best test of the completed system would be the conversion of a program already running on PLATO. The PLATO course "Classical Greek," written by Professor Gerald Erickson and Michael Kunin, was ideal because it was designed to teach a language which does not use the Latin alphabet. It is a freestanding course that starts with the Greek alphabet and goes on to deal with nearly all Classical Greek grammar, but does not include any reading exercises. It is presented in a workbook format, that is, as a series of grammatical discussions (using some animation) followed by reinforcing questions about the material just presented. This course uses the most important abilities of the PLATO system (text presentation, drills, and branches to review units), and the conversion project would be deemed successful if the new system could duplicate these abilities within the limitations imposed by the Terak's hardware.

The Problem

Before we could begin writing the new CAI system, its purpose had to be defined completely, including what features were necessary and what were optional. This was accomplished by first studying PLATO courses (especially the Greek course) carefully to determine which features of the PLATO system were used most often and with the best effect and then discussing the merits of various aspects of these examples. At the same time, we always had to keep in mind the limitations imposed by the size and power of the Terak microcomputer.

Eventually it was determined that the following capabilities were necessary to an adequate CAI system:

1. To format and display text from a text file in two character sets with the ability to switch character sets in midline
2. To erase the screen and position text on the screen under program control
3. To branch to different areas of the program depending on criteria determined at time of execution

4. To drill randomly and sequentially with fully programmable help, hints, and answers
5. To evaluate expressions and have the features of a simple computer language

The features which were desired but not absolutely necessary to the system were graphics capabilities (line drawing, picture displaying) and error processing, to aid those who are unfamiliar with the system in designing working programs. Because of the limited amount of storage capacity (56K bytes) available on the Terak, we decided very early that only the most rudimentary graphics features of line drawing and automated box drawing could be made available to the user. The amount of error processing possible was also dependent on the amount of storage available after the necessary features were installed. The exact configuration of this processing was left indeterminate until the main system was completed. All the above features are available in some form on PLATO, and the performance of the new system was to be judged by comparison with PLATO.

In addition to all these features, we wanted a system which was easy for a person unfamiliar with computers to learn and use, and which allowed changes to be made in courses very quickly and with a minimum of effort. Further, the system had to be able to handle large amounts of text in a single course, with no delay between the change of text for the course and execution of the course. This feature was needed in order to minimize testing time for the course writer.

Approach

In determining the form of the new system, the CAI systems group had not only the PLATO system at hand, but also the Minnesota Instructional Language (MIL) and the Computer-Assisted Language Learning System (CALLS) to use for developmental ideas. These three systems use different methods for programming computer-assisted instruction.

After considering these three systems, we decided that the best method of implementing the features outlined above and achieving the overall purpose of the project was to use the CALLS model of a text-file-driven interpreter with text and commands incorporated into the same file. This new system, originally designated SUPERCALLS, but later renamed Course Programming Language (CPL), would be much more flexible and powerful than CALLS because of the capability of using more than one character set and the ability to do more than just text presentation and drilling. It would have some graphics capabilities and a variety of drilling and input judging methods which would rival PLATO's. At the same time, a good course could be written without knowledge of the intricacies of computer programming, although much more could be accomplished with effort on the part of the course author.

The format of these text files was the next item which required a decision. The files would be indexed for random accessing and would contain the text to be displayed, questions to be given to the students (along with the answers against which the students' responses would be checked), and commands to be executed by CPL. We decided that the indexing should be handled as in MIL and CALLS with labels in the text file at each point where access was desired. This would allow the course to branch to areas in the text file which had been previously designated by the course programmer.

In order to allow CPL and the label processor to make decisions about text in a file, it was decided that column 1 of each line would be the determining factor. If this column contained a percent sign, the line would be considered a text label. If it held a dollar sign, then a command to CPL followed. Lines beginning with a plus or minus were to be part of the student-response processing sections. Lines with a slash or space in the first column were to be printed on the screen.

After these decisions were made, there remained only the slight matter of designing, writing, and testing the system.

The Solution

Designing the System

Since the project was specifically concerned with languages which use non-Latin characters, the group had to deal with the design and display of a character set which, because of aesthetic considerations, could not be shown on the Terak screen using its normal character-display mode. Each character, then, had to be drawn on the screen by using the Terak's intrinsic graphics capabilities. A couple of very basic points were established at the outset. Because this project was experimental and was using Greek as its first test, efforts were directed toward only those features which are required by languages whose writing systems are alphabetic (as opposed to syllabic or ideogrammatic) and proceed from left to right. This is not to say that the idea of a more general program was permanently discarded, merely that the first effort was to be limited to meeting these requirements. When we had determined the results of our first efforts, possible extensions could be considered.

A program was written to automate the process of designing the new character sets. This character-set editor allows the user to specify the matrix size and create characters of variable width on the Terak graphics screen, defined as a matrix 320 dots wide by 240 dots high. Experimentation showed that the most acceptable character size was 10 dots wide by 16 dots high. One of the side effects of drawing the characters on the screen was that letters could be of variable width. That is, a letter "i" could be drawn in less space than a letter "w," and so on. The actual drawing of the characters on the screen turned out to be the easiest part to do. By using the Terak's DrawBlock intrinsic, it is easy to move a two-dimensional array (matrix) onto the Terak screen. By indexing an array of the matrices with the char data structure of Pascal, it proved relatively simple to associate a character from the text file or keyboard with a particular matrix in the character set. From there it was moved to the screen where the letter appeared miraculously. Figure 17-1 illustrates the character set. Controlling the

LETTER	NAME		SOUND AS IN
α	ἄλφα	(alpha)	father
β	βῆτα	(beta)	beg
γ	γάμμα	(gamma)	go
δ	δέλτα	(delta)	dig
ε	ἒ ψιλόν	(epsilon)	met
ζ	ζέτα	(zeta)	glazed
η	ῆτα	(eta)	fate
θ	θῆτα	(theta)	hothouse
ι	ἰῶτα	(iota)	meteor/police
κ	κάππα	(kappa)	kin
λ	λάμβδα	(lambda)	let
μ	μῦ	(mu)	met

LETTER	NAME		SOUND AS IN
ν	νῦ	(nu)	net
ξ	ξῖ	(xi)	sex
ο	ὄ μικρὸν	(omicron)	obey
π	πῖ	(pi)	pet
ρ	ῥῶ	(rho)	run
ς,σ	σίγμα	(sigma)	such
τ	ταῦ	(tau)	tar
υ	ῦ ψιλόν	(upsilon)	beep
φ	φῖ	(phi)	slophouse
χ	χῖ	(chi)	key
ψ	ψῖ	(psi)	gypsy
ω	ὦ μέγα	(omega)	note

Figure 17-1. Character Set

placement of characters so that text was not written beyond the edges of the screen was accomplished by keeping track of where the last character was drawn and the amount of room left on the screen. For output from a text file, a formatting routine automatically started a new line if there was not room for displaying the next complete word on the screen. Another program module scrolled the screen and prevented writing beyond the bottom of the screen.

The question of switching character sets and other proposed special features of the output modules had to be considered. In order to make editing as easy as possible, all text in text files would be entered by using the standard Terak character set. The program, therefore, required some method of determining which character set it must use for display purposes as it printed out the current line of text. The easiest way to do this was to have a special character in the text file itself which caused CPL to switch from the current character set to the other one (only two 128-member sets can be resident at any one time). There was also the question of indicating to CPL that the next character was to be displayed above the line or below the line. Moreover, if diacritical marks had to appear directly over or under characters, then there also had to be a way to indicate this to CPL. Each of these separate cases required a special character to indicate the necessary formatting. However, if characters were reserved exclusively for these uses, the number of displayable characters would be correspondingly reduced. Circumstances could be envisioned in which all or nearly all possible printing characters would be needed to represent adequately the writing system of a language which was being taught by using CPL.

The most economical solution appeared to be the reservation of a single character which would indicate to CPL that the following character should be interpreted as a control or force character, causing one of the actions described above to be initiated. The character chosen for this job was the back slash (\), since it is seldom used in English text and could, it was hoped, be avoided in other languages. Up to this point, the reserved use of this character has not presented any problems.

The force characters and their effects are:

\f   Toggle between character sets. Returns to character stored in slots 0 to 127 (the "default" set) at the end of each line in the text file.

\b   Place the following character centered in the previous character's screen position.

\d   Print the following character two dots lower than normal on screen; then revert to normal level.

\ D   Print all characters two dots lower than normal until another
"\D" is encountered.

\ u   Print the following character two dots higher than normal on
screen; then revert to normal level.

\ U   Print all characters two dots higher than normal until another
"\U" is encountered.

\ _   Underline all characters following until another "_" is
encountered.

Provision was made so that these force characters could be used in combination, in order to allow diacritical marks to be placed above or below the previously printed character.

Testing a student requires that there be some way to ask questions and obtain answers from those taking the computerized course. Before the student can respond, there must be something to which a response is required, that is, a question of some sort. The CPL designers had to come up with a workable method for presenting these questions to the student in various formats. First, CPL should be able to ask a single question at a time, judge the answer, and continue with the course. It should also be able to ask a series of questions, as in a drill, and pass the student on to the next section according to the number of questions answered correctly. The actual proportion of correct answers required should be controlled by the course programmer. Also, it should be possible to send the student to remedial sections of the course if too many questions were missed. The number of attempts a student makes for a question before she is counted incorrect should also be under the control of the course writer, as well as the number of attempts made before passing along to the next question, whether or not the current one is answered correctly. Answers should be available to the student if she is unable to answer the question herself or requests that kind of help by pressing a special key. The presence or absence of this aid should be also under the control of the programmer. The order of the presentation of the questions should be either random or sequential, and questions missed once should be noted and reasked if the student has not yet reached the passing level.

The judging should also have various features to allow as much latitude as possible in the programming of the course. The answers against which the response is to be compared must be present in the text file in a format that is easy for the programmer to master and decipherable by CPL. Allowances should be made for irregular answers by a student. Every student will not present an answer in the same way. The judging routines should be general enough to allow the programmer easily to program alternate or optional parts of answers without being forced to rewrite those parts of the answer which do not change. It should be possible to look for more than one answer or set of answers. CPL should also check for specific, programmed wrong answers and be able to respond to the student's answer with corrective information, if the course writer so desires. These were some of the ideas that went into the creation of the CPL judging routines.

In writing the judging module, a couple of assumptions were necessary. First, it was assumed that the student's answer would be passed to the procedure in a string. (A string is an array or sequence of characters. This sentence is an example of a string.) This string would contain the force character mentioned previously, which tells what character set is in use, and all character strings would be recorded in their fully expanded form, so that although the student, under specific circumstances, may press only two keys to display up to ten characters, all the characters actually displayed in that situation are recorded. Second, it was assumed that the answer in the text file would be passed to or obtained by the judging procedure from the text file in another string, which would then be compared in some as yet undefined way with the student's response.

In order to be able to take into account certain allowable irregularities such as extra spaces or different punctuation, it was decided that the best way to do the judging was to split the string into separate sections on word boundaries. These word boundaries were defined as spaces and punctuation characters between alphanumeric substrings, that is, between parts of the string containing letters and numbers.

Judging takes place in the following manner. The student's answer is divided into substrings according to the placement of blanks and punctuation marks which are not considered in the judging. The same action is taken with an answer found in the text file, and then the substrings are compared. If they are all exactly alike, then a good match has been made between the student's response and the expected answer. This is the process for those questions which require that the student make an exact match, and it is the default method of judging.

If this method were the only one available to the programmer, however, entering answers into the text file could be tedious, especially if there are several answers which differ only slightly. For example, a question might require the answer *a temple*, but the programmer may wish to allow both *the temple* and *one temple*. If only the exact-matching method were available, then the text file would have to contain the full form of all three answers to ensure that all were accepted. In this case, the work of entering three separate lines of answers is trivial; but if the answers contained several words which had reasonable alternatives, one could end up with ten or more long lines of text for one answer to a question. From these considerations and from observation of the programming techniques used by PLATO authors, we determined that there were two necessary extensions to the default-judging routine: alternate parts of answers within a single answer and optional parts within a single answer. *Optional parts* were defined as words which can, but are not required to, appear in a student's response, and *alternate answers* as those from a group of which one must appear in the student's response.

It was decided to enclose optional answers in broken brackets (< >) and alternate answers in parentheses and to separate the alternates by using the Terak's broken-vertical-line character (¦), while the optional answers were to be separated by spaces or the broken vertical line or, in fact, any punctuation character. So, if the example above were listed in the alternate-answer format, it would appear as

$$(a \mid the \mid one) \; temple$$

indicating that *a* or *the* or *one* must appear in the answer in order to be counted correct. If the programmer decided that *a, the,* or *one* could appear but was not necessary, then the answer in the text file could appear as

$$<a \mid the \mid one> \; temple$$

In the former case, *a temple, the temple,* or *one temple* would be correct, while just plain *temple* would be incorrect. In the latter case, all four variants would be counted correct. CPL also allows for alternate answers within alternate answers. For example, in the symbolic group

$$A \; (B \; (C \mid D) \mid E)$$

the student response would require the presence of word *A* and either word *E* or word *B* plus *C* or *D*. In other words, the acceptable answers are

$$A \; E$$
$$A \; B \; C$$
$$A \; B \; D$$

In addition to the normal, or default, type of judging, which requires the student to enter an answer that can be matched exactly (within the tolerances allowed by alternate and optional answers) to the answer stored in the appropriate place in the text file, CPL can be programmed to accept an answer without regard for word order. This is extremely important in some drills when the language being taught is not word-order-dependent.

There are also some cases in which the exact form of the student's response is more or less insignificant, the important factor being the presence of one or more key words. In these cases it is useful to allow the student to enter as many words as desired and yet have CPL look for only certain words, counting the response correct regardless of the environment of those words. The ability to program this method of judging is another feature of CPL.

There are two basic formats in which questions can be presented to the student: singly or in groups. The one most used is the group method, that is, drills or tests. The questions can be presented randomly or sequentially, and questions missed by the student are re-presented until some criterion for termination, predetermined by the programmer, is attained. The number of tries allowed for each question, as well as the number of tries within which a question will be considered correct, is under the control of the programmer, as is the availability of help, hints, and correct answers. The character set in which the student's responses will appear is also controlled by the programmer.

Transferring the Course from PLATO to Terak

As was stated above, CPL was created with the intention of using it to implement on the Terak the Classical Greek course already present on CDC's PLATO system. The most important task, namely, writing CPL, was completed in about three months. Transferring and editing the Greek course were to take another three to five months.

In order to make the conversion from PLATO to the Terak, a tape of the whole course had to be obtained from Control Data Corporation and placed on the University of Minnesota's computer system. From there, after some preliminary editing, it would be transferred to the Terak for the final editing phase. After some difficulty, this transfer was accomplished.

The transfer of information from the UCC computer to Terak was carried out by using a program which allowed communication between the two computers, so that much of the transfer was done automatically, with little human intervention. All the actual manipulation of the text was done on the Terak after transfer, since the University of California at San Diego (UCSD) Pascal operating system for Terak has a very good screen-oriented editor, which is easier to use than the line-oriented editor residing on the UCC system. The CAI group wrote several programs to remove and reformat parts of the PLATO program, so that CPL could recognize appropriate sections and present them to students correctly.

Even with these programs to speed the transfer process, however, editing the text files was still a time-consuming task. Many things required repeated testing and correction before they could be considered ready for students. The smaller Terak screen made it necessary to write text on the screen in smaller installments. This change required visual inspection in order to ensure consistency and coherence. All the charts, diagrams, and paradigms in the Greek course had to be reformatted to fit on the screen of the Terak. Again, this was a job requiring constant human intervention.

One of the most arduous tasks was adjusting the test questions so that the student's answers were short enough to fit on a single line of the screen. The course as it is presented on PLATO also has this restriction; however, its screen is eighty characters wide, while the program allowed an average of only thirty-five to forty characters per line. Having a line so short meant rethinking the questions and answers in the drills. In many cases this made the questions and answers more concise and meaningful, although in other instances it merely cut down on the student's range of possible responses. For the most part, the shortened responses save the student from much frustration resulting from typing errors which are bound to occur in long responses.

After the conversion of each PLATO program file to a CPL text file, there was testing to do. This consisted of running each section of the course and checking it from both the student's and the instructor's point of view. Also, it was sometimes necessary to modify the presentation of text in order to ensure that each full-screen display was relevant to the subject at hand and divided in reasonable places.

The Classical Greek course was completed in January 1979. At this time, the transfer of the New Testament (Koine) Greek course, also resident on the PLATO system, began. The same process as before was repeated, with the experience gained from the Classical Greek course greatly speeding the work.

During the summer of 1979, the CAI systems group hired two graduate students from the classics department to go through both courses in an effort to remove as many mistakes as possible before students actually started using the programs in the fall. After a short period of training in the use of the Terak editor and the syntax of CPL, these students were able to find and correct many problem areas, as well as indicate areas where they thought there might be pedagogical problems. If it was possible to fix these without substantially altering the nature of the course, it was done; but many of these problem areas still await correction or modification.

By the end of the summer, the courses were as near to correct as possible. It was recognized that many errors and problems must still exist in both CPL and the Greek courses themselves, but these were well enough hidden that they could not be found except under actual student use. The first students who used the programs would probably discover the problems which remained, and it was hoped that they could be easily and quickly fixed so as to reduce any inconvenience as much as possible.

Results

Even before this project began, the classics department was interested in using the computer as an instructional medium. The Greek courses which were transferred from PLATO to the Terak had been developed by members of the University of Minnesota classics department. Unfortunately, since the University of Minnesota's involvement with PLATO was deemphasized, the Greek courses became harder and harder to access. In addition, the terminals available were nowhere near the department itself, nor even to one another. This caused some difficulty for both students and instructors. It was best for the instructors to be near to students who were working on the course in order to help them over the rough spots, which were bound to occur since these courses were really the first of their kind. These courses were also incomplete, with minor gaps in the grammatical sections, where the student would require the help of an instructor.

Microcomputers have many advantages, not the least of which is the fact that they are independent computers. They do not need access to a telephone or to a larger computer in order to work. They can be placed wherever they are most necessary or convenient. To the classics department, this meant that it was possible to create a computer laboratory near the offices of the faculty and teaching associates who would be directing the courses. Students would not feel so alone when working with the computer. Since the computers would be grouped in a single area, it would be possible to staff the laboratory using only one person at a time, instead of one per terminal area. So both the hardware and the workforce would be less costly by using microcomputers.

Even with this lower cost, the expenses involved in a relatively large laboratory such as the one desired by the classics department are substantial. The department felt that a minimum of six computers should be available in the laboratory for students. At that time this represented a cost of about $32,000. This cost and the staffing expenses are a little more than a small department can bear alone. Even leasing the computers instead of buying them would cause a strain on a department with such limited resources. Fortunately the University Computer Center was able to come to the aid of the classics department. Since this was all part of a research project for the UCC, the laboratory could be funded in part by the UCC, at least for the first year. After that, it was hoped that more of the language departments in the same building as the classics department would use the laboratory and help with expenses as more material was made available on the Terak.

Now two computerized Greek courses were available, Classical Greek and New Testament (Koine) Greek. Both of the computer courses were intended as beginning courses, assuming no knowledge of Greek on the part of the student. This meant that there were opportunities to use computer-aided instruction in two different ways. The first was as an alternative to a course already taught in the traditional fashion. This would allow those who thought the traditional method too fast or too slow to take Classical Greek at a pace of their own choosing. It would also give those who would not normally be able to take the course because of a scheduling conflict, for instance, a chance to learn Greek.

The second way to use the computer was as a supplement to the normal schedule of courses. The New Testament Greek program would allow the insertion of a new course into the curriculum. Students whose primary interest was New Testament Greek would no longer have to go through an entire year of Classical Greek in order to get to it. Many students who avoid Greek because they must take the Classical Greek section first might enroll in a course in which New Testament Greek is the only subject.

When the courses were first written for the PLATO system, the Classical Greek program was used at the University of Minnesota for a short time. As PLATO became harder and harder to use at the University of Minnesota, the Greek course was used less and less. By the time CPL was ready for use on the Terak, very few people were left in the classics department who had any experience using the computer as a teaching medium. This meant, of course, that those who were going to teach Greek via the computer had to gain some experience with it, even if it was only enough to stay ahead of the students and to answer most of the questions posed. The department was fortunate in being able to find two graduate students who were able, in spite of initial skepticism and fear, to acclimate themselves in time to begin teaching the courses. They tackled a difficult and unfamiliar subject (computers, not Greek) and acquitted themselves well. If these courses have been successful, much of the credit must go to them. Without their patience and understanding, both with the students and with the sometimes unruly computers, this important attempt to join modern technology and a very traditional subject might never have passed its initial stages.

So that students who took these computer-aided courses would be as free as possible to choose times which were most convenient to them to use the computers, the department decided to keep the laboratory open at least forty hours a week for the first quarter (fall of 1979). Most of the open hours coincided with normal university business hours, with two days a week having later evening hours. By using information on laboratory use obtained during the first quarter, open hours for succeeding quarters were determined later. The laboratory was staffed whenever it was open, both for the students' aid and for the protection of the easily transportable microcomputers, by graduate students from the classics department. Little training was required for those who staffed the laboratory. Their chief duty was to record any problems which occurred while they were present. All were given training in running the courses, so they could offer some help to students.

As with any new method of doing things, there are expectations, hopes, and desires, on one side, and, on the other, there is the real world. This is especially true with computers. Their reputation for speed and accuracy sometimes misleads people into forgetting that humans have the sole responsibility for what computers accomplish, whether as programmers or as users. Computers are only tools. How they are used determines their utility and success. Just as with other tools, computers can do some jobs well, other jobs passably, and yet other jobs not at all.

Computer-assisted instruction depends on people, perhaps more than any other computerized task. Not only must the programmers create a system which works well with people, but also those who create the courses must work with the computer system and with the subject matter of the course, in order to obtain a program that puts both system and course together in a package that yet another human, the student, can use easily and effectively. Ideally the student should note only the advantages of using the computer as a teacher. The student should be aware of the accurate, timely, and exact responses; the flexibility; the patience of the computer. Its impersonal nature should be disguised as much as possible (at least until students become accustomed to the idea of computers in the classroom).

Instructors who use the computer must also be considered by those who create systems and courseware. They must not feel threatened or frustrated by the computer. They must feel that they are using another teaching tool, not retreating before the encroachment of the computer, nor acceding to their eventual replacement in the classroom. Nor must they assume that modern technology will be able to work miracles, that it will be able to take the entire load from their shoulders. There will always be a need for qualified instructors. Computer-assisted instruction will, it is hoped, be able to take over some of the less pleasant, repetitive tasks which teachers currently face, leaving them more time to pursue with students deeper and more intense studies than are currently feasible.

Adding to the problems faced by the creators of a CAI system or a CAI course is the fact that in spite of several years of existence, there is still no research which either proves or disproves that a particular technique works any better than another. The best that system creators can do is discuss with users, those who write CAI courses, what they think they might need now or in the future; but the users themselves are merely making educated guesses based on past experience with or present theories of teaching. Until such research is done, CAI will be a matter of trial and error, and the big losers in that situation are the students.

The above discussion concerns all CAI, not just CPL and the Greek courses. However, much of it can be applied to the experiences with the

Greek courses over the 1979–1980 school year. It was hoped that the computer-assisted Greek courses would allow instructors to spend less total time with their classes than the traditional teaching methods. In fact, some feared that jobs would be wiped out because of the advent of these courses. However, it was found that the amount of time required of an instructor teaching these courses was approximately the same on a per student basis. The difference was in the quality of time spent with the students. Part of the time was made necessary by deficiencies in the courses. These deficiencies forced the instructors to cover some topics in a classroom situation. There are other deficiencies such as unclear instructions, unresponsive responses, and so on, which caused problems for many students. Errors in the text and drill answers also created problems, but these were removed as soon as they were reported.

After all these problems are taken into consideration, there remains the majority of the time spent with students participating in these courses. It is here that the strong point of the courses becomes evident. Instead of spending classroom time trying to get students to learn their grammatical forms and drilling them on these forms, a task done by the computer, most of the classroom time was spent reading Greek texts. Students who made it through the course were found to have better knowledge of grammar and more reading experience than those who participated in the traditional courses.

Thus, even though the results were different from the expectations, even though the time required of an instructor was not substantially different from that required by the traditional method, the program was successful. It may not have required less time, but it certainly produced better-educated students. With different and improved courses, both these goals might be met.

Current and Future Developments

Since CPL was developed primarily for second-language teaching and since its first use was for teaching Greek, it seems reasonable that the first entirely original program development in CPL should be a Latin course. This development began in June 1979, and the results are reported in chapter 18 of this book. The University Computer Center has recently received word that instructors at the State University of New York at Albany have also been developing courseware using CPL.

Professor Cesar Farah has been developing an Arabic course on PLATO at the University of Minnesota, and future plans for CPL include transferring this course to the Terak. At present this is not possible. Because of the nature of Arabic script and the necessity for right-to-left writing,

CPL will require some modifications before the transfer is possible. Although these modifications are relatively minor, the Terak does not have enough memory to handle them. Therefore, Arabic will have to wait until a computer comparable to the Terak but with more memory becomes available.

18 A Latin Course on a Small Computer

George Vellios,
Gerald M. Erickson, and
Rosanne Gulino

The University of Minnesota's computer-assisted Latin course is an attempt to improve on previously established methods of teaching Latin, a language which, at best, is a difficult subject for speakers of English. We are all experienced teachers of Latin who have utilized many different texts and methods of instruction through the years; it is our goal to create a complete Latin course which will allow the student to proceed at his or her own pace, will ensure mastery of grammar, and will, at the same time, cultivate the ability to read fluently. Previous methods of teaching Latin have tended to overemphasize one or the other of these skills, with the predictable result that students of Latin may have conspicuous weaknesses in vocabulary, grammar, or reading skills after a three- or four-year course in high school or a one-year course in college using the traditional methods. Patience may overcome such difficulties, but in an age when the teacher's endurance is frequently overtaxed, his or her patience may be strained. Students, moreover, often wish to pursue a foreign language no further than the minimum number of language credits required for a diploma. The problem, then, is to create for students of Latin who have only a year in which to absorb the necessary vocabulary, grammar, and reading skill, an experience through which they can learn, or even utilize, Latin in their day-to-day pursuit of aesthetic enjoyment.

Previous methods of teaching Latin have fallen into two general categories. The first method confronts a student immediately with a set of grammatical forms which are to be memorized, usually with almost total lack of understanding on the part of the student as to the material's use. The dissimilarity of English noun forms (which generally make no distinction between subject and direct-object forms) and the Latin noun system with its complicated set of endings, each of which signals at least one syntactic function, makes Latin very difficult for a student with little or no acquaintance with foreign languages, if the analytic approach to learning is used. The second method for teaching Latin, a method used in the *Cambridge Latin Course* and in *Lingua Latina Secundum Naturae Rationem Explicata,* stresses the importance of reading at the outset of a student's exposure to the language and introduces vocabulary and grammatical forms in the context of their use in stories of increasing complexity. This method's lack of emphasis on grammatical analysis, however, frequently leaves the student at sea when confronted by a complicated original text by a classical author.

The Problem

Admittedly, many people have managed to learn Latin quite well, using texts which espouse one or the other method described above. This happy occurrence, however, has often been due to the efforts of the teacher to establish a balance by supplementing texts of the first sort with easy readings and texts of the second sort with grammatical analysis and drills. Our goal has been to achieve this balance in a carefully designed text with copious attention to all the important skills needed by the student of Latin.

In designing a computer-assisted Latin course, we kept in mind three important considerations:

1. Syntactic and morphological function must be presented, as much as possible, in the order of importance and frequency in the language.
2. Drills must be coordinated with the text, must be thorough, and must allow for individual differences of ability to grasp material by providing remedial aids.
3. Reading practice must be included, must be interesting, and must stress comprehension of content.

In conjunction with these desiderata, we determined that this course should consist of a written text, in which the student can find grammatical material and morphology introduced and explained, and of computer drills, in which the student may practice each lesson. The twofold nature of the course allows the student to study at home (where there may not be access to a computer) and to engage in intense drilling at her or his own pace with a computer using a program designed to cover material introduced in the text, with remedial aids to clear up difficulties in comprehension.

The first task was to decide on a general outline for the written text, in which Latin syntax and morphology are broken into essential elements, beginning with areas which have traditionally given beginning students the greatest difficulty. It was decided to first consider the noun system in Latin, which is an inflected language (that is, syntactical relationships are signified by means of word endings, known as cases), because of its radical dissimilarity to the noun system in English. Rather than introduce the entire noun system at once, as beginning texts traditionally do, the authors started with the relatively straightforward subject-object relationship signified by the nominative and accusative cases, respectively. Each chapter subsequently introduces a new syntactical relationship until the case system is completed; it is a step-by-step building process whereby the student acquires a firm comprehension of Latin sentence structure. To avoid muddying the student's grasp of nouns, verb forms are kept simple (third person, present, active, indicative) until the noun system is completely covered. When the noun system is finished, the step-by-step building process is applied to the Latin verb, whereby the student's knowledge of tenses, voices, and moods is expanded chapter by chapter, parcel by parcel, rather than by means of unwieldy paradigms which must be diligently memorized.

The text, of course, is the skeleton of the language course, and it directs the student to coordinated, computerized drills after each concept is introduced in the text. We desired a computer program which would display a problem or question to the student, wait for a response, provide a hint if needed, judge the student's responses, tally the responses, determine whether remedial aid is necessary, and provide such aid if necessary.

Methodology

Because the classics department has access to Terak microcomputers, which employ floppy disks, typewriter keyboards, and cathode-ray tube (CRT) screens, it was necessary to devise a program using a computer language compatible with the Terak system. A further consideration was that the authors are classicists who are inexperienced programmers, who have little time or inclination to study the standard computing language of Pascal (which is compatible with the Terak). It was decided, therefore, to employ a program known as CPL which had been developed by the computer-assisted instruction (CAI) group at the University of Minnesota Computer Center for the instruction of Classical and biblical Greek. This program requires that the learning material be entered into the computer in a structured format (see next section) with relatively few computer-related commands.

The computer in the Latin course must first display instructions to the student. Using CPL, the programmer may enter the student's instructions into the computer, specifying the desired location on the screen by naming cartesian coordinates (the screen is 240 by 320 "dots" of light), using, for example, the command

$$\$AT\ 10,12$$

(This tells the computer to display the instructions beginning ten dots down from the top of the screen and twelve dots from the left of the screen.) The instructions are then typed on the succeeding line, being set off by a backward slash which tells the computer that what follows is a message to be displayed on the screen, for example,

/Answer the following in Latin.

The programmer may then specify for how long the message is to be displayed before it is erased by typing the PAUSE command followed by a number indicating for how many seconds the message is to remain on the screen, such as

$PAUSE 2

(The message is to be displayed for 2 seconds.) If the programmer wishes, a command which tells the computer to wait for the student to press the return key before erasing the instructions may be used:

$RETURN

Each question is entered into the computer with the following format:

1. A unique label
2. A command telling the computer a question is to be asked
3. A question to be displayed to the student
4. The answer which the computer must regard as correct
5. A command telling the computer to display an acceptable answer if the student fails to answer correctly and any extra comment is deemed desirable by the programmer
6. A command telling the computer to erase the screen when the student has either answered correctly or been shown the correct answer

In CPL, these lines would resemble the following:

1. %D1AQ1
2. $ASK
3. /What does "cognoscenti" mean to you?
4. + those who know
5. $ENDASK "those who know" (from "cognoscere," to learn or find out)
6. $RETURN

The programmer has the option, using CPL, of providing a hint if the student desires it. The hint option, utilized by the command

$HINT : = TRUE

tells the computer to display the answer (line 5 above) if the student presses a designated key. Other options allow the programmer to give the student access to paradigms, explicatory material, and so on, if certain keys are pressed by the student.

CPL keeps a tally of the correct responses made by the student during a given drill. This feature enables the programmer to utilize a command which sends the computer to drills and/or instructions under various labels provided a criterion score is not made on the initial drill. As a rule of thumb, the criterion score in the Latin program is 90 percent, so for a drill of ten questions, the command

$$\text{\$IF WRONG} > \; = 1 \; \text{THEN \#\$GOTO}$$

followed by the label of the desired remedial drill, tells the computer to set the condition necessary for proceeding to the remedial drill at one error out of ten, or 10 percent. The computer, if the condition is fulfilled by the student, proceeds immediately to the remedial drill. This process may be repeated several times, resulting in "layers" or "branches" of drills, and the programmer may add extra explanation as the branches increase in number. The beauty of this branching technique is that it allows the student who can quickly grasp new syntactic and morphological material to proceed through the computer drills very rapidly, since her or his high scores will not send the computer into the remedial branches. The student who requires extra aid, however, may find plenty of help in the remedial branches. Since the "hint" key, for example, may or may not be utilized by the programmer in each drill, the programmer may design the initial drill without a hint key available, add the "hint" option in the first remedial branch, and add the "hint" and paradigm keys in the second remedial branch. The programmer may, of course, simply choose to alter the difficulty of the questions in the various branches. This branching technique is very effective in making the computer more sensitive to the needs and abilities of the individual student.

Another feature used to great advantage in the Latin program is the above-mentioned PAUSE command to control the amount of time in which a message is displayed. We believe that timed reading followed by questions concerning the student's comprehension of what has been read is a valuable technique for forcing the student to actually read Latin rather than decipher it. To create a timed reading, the programmer merely enters, for example,

$$\text{\$PAUSE 60}$$

(that is, 60 seconds), followed by a text which the student should be able to read in the amount of time specified. The Latin course then displays questions concerning the content of the passage. If the criterion score is not met, a remedial branch is provided in which the text is fragmented, displayed with appropriate questions, and programmed not to erase until the student makes a response. If the student fails to meet the criterion score for this branch, another remedial branch is provided in which one sentence of text at a time is given with the applicable question. If the student's score meets the criterion of 90 percent, the initial timed reading is repeated in its entirety. If, however, the student fails to meet the criterion in the second remedial branch, a third branch is offered which displays a message with tips on how to improve reading, vocabulary, and so forth.

Results

Using the design features for the text and computerized drills described above, we have created a format for each unit or chapter in the course which is designed to maximize the skills mentioned in the above section. This format, divided between text and computer, is as follows for a typical unit:

1. Introduction of syntactic function X (text)
   a. Form of X
   b. Use of X
2. Drills for practice in syntactic function X (computer)
   a. Form of X
   b. Use of X
3. New Latin vocabulary and English derivatives (text)
4. Vocabulary drills (computer)
   a. Latin vocabulary
   b. English derivatives
5. Latin reading for comprehension
   a. Reading selection (text)
   b. Questions on reading (computer)
   c. Continuation of reading in timed reading (computer)
   d. Questions on timed reading (computer)

In order to avoid monotony for the student, the computer drills vary considerably in type, falling under the following categories:

1. Question and answer, for example,
   Question: What is the case of *insula*?
   Answer: Nominative
2. Multiple-choice questions, for example,
   Question: What is the case of *nautae*?
   a. Nominative   *b.* Dative
   c. Ablative   *d.* Genitive
   Answer: *b, c,* or *d*

3. "Clozes," for example,

Question: Because he was too young to walk about, the baby's parents pushed him in a per_____or.

Answer: Perambulator

These types of questions allow the programmer to limit the computer's expectations to very specific forms, saving considerable time and space in the computer memory.

The choice of content for each section of a unit is carefully interlocked with each other section in the Latin course. Although learning a particular grammatical form may be the purpose of a lesson and may be illustrated copiously in drills and the reading selection, the subject of the reading selection determines in large part the vocabulary of the chapter, and vice versa. Moreover, as new forms are explained, examples are taken from the reading material, so that the student finds no grammatical or lexical surprises when the Latin reading is done. We chose for the first half of the course the fourth Roman emperor, Claudius, and his Julio-Claudian relatives, since their saga, as preserved by Tacitus and Suetonius and popularized by Robert Graves, covers virtually the full spectrum of Roman culture, from military triumph, to construction, to love, to scholarly brilliance, and to depravity. To further the student's grasp of the cultural context of the readings, illustrations of each story are included in the text. The second half of the course uses selections (with slight adaptation) from Roman authors such as Cicero, Catullus, and Ovid, and medieval authors such as Isidore of Seville, Abelard, and Scaliser. Our aim is to expose the student to a variety of styles, as the long history of Latin literature so amply allows.

In no way can CAI replace a teacher. Rather, a skillful teacher and a well-designed educational program will employ CAI to accomplish those tasks for which it is well suited, and no more. The net results of the extensive employment of this medium in our department have been to increase the number of students who have contact with the classics department and to enable teachers to teach more advanced, specialized courses, thereby allowing them to use their skills and knowledge more fully.

The Latin program makes use of very simple computing techniques, all of which could be employed for didactic purposes in a number of fields in which drilling is desirable.

The text for The University of Minnesota's computer-assisted Latin course will be typed and photocopied in limited editions in order to keep costs minimal. Floppy disks for the computer drills will be copied as needed.

Other CAI programs developed and used by the classics department are

Basic Vocabulary Development (prerequisite for the following three)

Technical Terms for the Medical and Biological Sciences

Advanced Etymology (selected Indo-European roots with Greek and Latin derivatives)

Topics and Figures of Speech for Latin Poetry

Advanced Medical Terminology (taught through Indo-European roots)

Technical Terms for Nursing and the Paramedical Professions (this program has no prerequisite and has a more practical focus)

(All the above were developed with the assistance of a grant from the National Endowment for the Humanities.)

In addition, the classics department has developed the following courses or auxiliary programs:

Classical Greek—a sequence in which the student can progress at her/his pace

Biblical Greek—a self-paced course leading to a classroom course in Koine Greek

Simulated Field Exercises in Archaeology

A program for teaching the meters of Latin poetry and a program for beginning Latin are currently being developed; programs for teaching the technical terms of agriculture and for developing speed and retention in reading Latin and Greek texts are projected for the future.

Acknowledgments

We are grateful to the programmers of the CAI group of the University of Minnesota for their development of CPL, the program whereby the computer drills are made possible. We also thank Linda Mitchell, a graduate student in classics, for her skillful and creative illustrations for the student text which accompanies the Terak course.

19 A Computer-Assisted Music Course and Its Implementation

Dorothy Gross

While instruction in music fundamentals has never ranked among the most essential items of a secondary or postsecondary education, students intending to pursue a career in music need such instruction. Paradoxically, the same "back to basics" trend that has cut back or even eliminated music classes has also fostered a desire among music educators for providing a solid foundation in the basics of music. Historically, education in music fundamentals outside a classroom has taken place in instrument lessons, as an independent study, or with a programmed text. Computer-assisted instruction (CAI) in music offers a new way of approaching individualized music education, but the technology involved must be adapted to a musician's needs. This chapter first examines potential benefits and drawbacks of the use of computers to teach basic musical concepts. Described are the development and results of two related projects in computer-assisted instruction in music fundamentals.

The Problem

The specific area involved in this project—music fundamentals—includes music notation, scales, intervals, chords, and common musical terms. Computer-assisted instruction in this area would meet the needs of schools that do not offer music theory, as well as providing remedial assistance. Then, too, a complete computer-assisted course can be the basis of individualized study or a correspondence course.

While a computer-assisted course in music fundamentals has been created at Bloomsburg State College [13] and is being developed at the University of Delaware [1], most CAI in music fundamentals has been in the form of lessons on individual aspects of the subject matter. There are, for example, lessons teaching note reading [8], rhythm [12], and key signatures [11]. Some games are available as well [7, 11].

In providing music instruction, one technical problem is the adaptation of the numbers and letters available on most computer terminals to the non-verbal and nonnumerical elements of music. Specifically, the biggest problems lie with sound production and music notation. While technical solutions exist, some are so expensive that many schools will not be able to afford them [2].

The first requirement for music instruction, with or without a computer, is that students have the opportunity to listen to music. In the conventional teaching situation, students may hear live music, usually performed by the instructor, or else listen to recorded music. While the latter probably will be performed better, and hence be more appealing and informative to students, the former provides flexibility needed for instructional goals. For example, if there is a problem understanding a musical idea, the instructor may play small examples on an instrument to elucidate that point. Generally, both live and recorded sound are used in order to elicit greater student interest and achievement.

With the use of computers, there are several options for providing recorded sound. The easiest method is to have students listen to music on their own, between sessions at the computer. For a quicker interchange between computer use and music listening, the student may be asked to operate a cassette recorder at certain points in a lesson. On some computers, there are mechanisms that will permit computer control of recorded music [3], but not all computer networks have them. For live sound several computer devices exist that generate musical tones [3, 8] or play an electronic organ [9, 10]. Unfortunately, such devices are not normally standard equipment, and their acquisition therefore adds to the cost of the instruction. One further problem is that the sound produced by computer synthesis more closely resembles a synthesizer tone than one produced on a traditional instrument.

A second requirement for most music instruction is the presentation of written music. Since the symbols used for notation do not look at all like the letters, numbers, and punctuation marks on the computer terminal keyboard, getting a student to read and write music is no trivial matter in music CAI. Financially, the simplest solution is to create some kind of code [9] using common typewriter symbols. While this approach will work with highly motivated or intelligent users, music students should not have to master a special code prior to taking a computer-aided music course. Particularly in the case of music fundamentals students, many of whom do not come into the course reading music, there is a danger of becoming more familiar with a substitute than with real, printed music.

Several techniques have been used to display written music on output devices for students. One approach is to create a large five-line staff made of hyphens, with musical characters approximated by typewriter characters [14]. While more similar to printed music than an alphanumeric code, this method is still too abstract for beginning music students. Most promising are computer terminals capable of displaying accurate music notation. Of these the most sophisticated is the PLATO terminal [11], whose screen not only displays music but also is sensitive to user touch. For instance, the PLATO terminal can show a piano keyboard which can be "played," that is, touched, by the student [8].

Unfortunately, such equipment often has been too costly to be widely available.

Assuming that such technical problems are overcome, a complete computer-assisted fundamentals course is desirable because a comprehensive course can offer guidance and organization as well as information. Also, by studying student progress through a sequence of lessons, educators may learn more about music-learning processes. While such a study might be undertaken by using separate lessons, a uniform, coordinated set of programs lends itself better to tabulation and further statistical processing of student results.

In general, CAI in music benefits two groups: music students and researchers in music education. Regarding the former, students would learn the rudiments in preparation for more advanced music instruction. Since music involves reading and counting, increased music reading ability can generalize to basic reading and arithmetic skills. In the area of music pedagogy, the path that students follow from less to more musical knowledge may help reveal how people acquire skills in music-reading and analysis and may even generalize to other skills, both nonverbal and verbal.

The role of the computer itself in computer-assisted music instruction is essentially to provide information and drills, but the machine can handle other tasks as well. The computer may be programmed to recommend which lesson a student ought to take next, based on that student's previous drill results. For example, given that the criterion for moving from one level of difficulty to the next is answering four out of five questions correctly, the computer can keep track of the student's score on the last five questions and determine whether the student is capable of handling the next lesson. This flexibility permits students to learn at their own pace.

Regarding research in music education, a computer-assisted instruction program can be modified to keep a record of student responses. Such research will be used to study music learning, but can also be valuable in studying music perception. For example, if students have great difficulty distinguishing between two musical sounds, then we know that those sounds are perceived as being similar. Data from music CAI can be studied intuitively or statistically for significant tendencies. Not only the results obtained by using the computer, but also the methodology developed to treat the material may be of help in further research in music or other fields.

Solution

As noted above, CAI sophistication varies from equipment that displays only alphanumerics to systems that can produce sound and show accurate music notation. Financial considerations aside, the superior technology of Control Data Corporation's PLATO system, a national computer network designed specifically for instructional use, provides computer-generated sound, accurate music notation, a large amount of memory, and a touch-sensitive screen. For schools unable to afford PLATO, however, a less expensive medium for music CAI should be available. This chapter concerns the implementation of the same subject matter on both PLATO and an ordinary large-computer time-sharing network, Control Data Corporation's Cyber 73.

On both systems, the specific methodology employed was to provide an existing textbook-workbook [6] with computer-delivered drills. In this way, it was possible to build on previous pedagogical tradition, as well as give students instruction and musical examples. Each question in the computer drills was phrased in either a short-answer or multiple-choice format. Unless an answer was very short and simple, the latter was preferred, since otherwise a student might misinterpret computer instructions or make a spelling mistake. Such errors would register as wrong responses even if the student knew the correct answer.

The version of the course programmed for use on the Cyber 73 was designed for the time-sharing network of the Minnesota Educational Computer Consortium (MECC). Included in this course are thirty-five written drills, seven aural drills, two practice tests, and a program for the recording of student scores on drills and tests. Subjects covered are music notation, scales, intervals, chords, and terminology. On PLATO the course consists of twenty written drills and two practice drills, and it covers the same subject matter as the course on MECC. Because of the high-quality ear-training lessons already available on PLATO [6] there did not seem to be a need to provide other aural drills on that network.

On the MECC network, technical requirements are an ASCII time-sharing terminal, the textbook-workbook, and a cassette recorder. Another necessity is a table or surface large enough to hold the textbook on one side of the terminal and the recorder on the other. The only human resource needed is someone available to answer questions regarding computer use or the subject matter. For PLATO the required materials are a terminal and the above-mentioned textbook. As with the MECC network, some available consultation must be provided. An important resource requirement, for both networks, is money to pay for operation of the terminals. Not only is funding for music CAI problematic, but also there may not even be an appropriate bureaucratic channel for a student willing to pay for CAI. Economics based on the classroom may not adapt well to more individualized modes of instruction.

The role of the computer in the complete music-fundamentals project varied somewhat between the two networks. Since the MECC network provides only the ASCII character set, other audiovisual aids are necessary in addition to the computer drills. For music notation, students look at music printed in their textbook, and for aural musical examples, they hear recordings of music performed on conventional instruments. The computer is used to ask questions about the book or tapes, evaluate the answers, and give students their scores at the end of each drill. If the instructor wants records kept, the program stores each student's scores and competencies.

On the PLATO network, the computer has all the technology necessary for producing music notation and sound. Even so, for straightforward presentation of information, a book serves the same purpose at a far more reasonable cost. Moreover, students prefer to have material to take home between sessions at the terminal; PLATO does not print on paper—it only displays on a screen. Therefore, the textbook is retained, not because it is indispensable, but because it presents information more cheaply and conveniently than does PLATO. For drilling and testing, however, music notation appears on the PLATO screen itself. This is advantageous because computer examples need not be limited to those in the textbook. For aural drills, the existing courses on PLATO provide sound produced by the computer, so tapes are not necessary.

Results

The two courses have both been used by nonmusic majors, on MECC with students at the University of Minnesota, and on the PLATO network with students at the University of Nebraska at Omaha [4]. At this writing, the Minnesota programs are being reviewed by MECC for publication. The other course, called MUSFUND, is available on PLATO. To determine how successfully the lessons were instructing the students, students not only were asked for their opinions, but also were observed while using the lessons.

While no students had trouble working the ASCII terminals, there were not enough terminals available for full student use. On PLATO, there were problems at first, because of the lack of experience of the author and the staff at the University of Nebraska at Omaha with the PLATO system. After these problems were eliminated, the only problem was the frequency of times when, for any number of reasons, the computer was not working.

Regarding actual student achievement at either school, a study of the pilot project at the University of Minnesota showed that students who used the computer drills improved more than those who did not. As shown in figure 19-1, students who used the drills improved 65 points (out of 100) from pretest to posttest, while students not using the computer improved 56 points. Since the group using the computer averaged lower on the pretest than the other students, it seems that students with weak musical backgrounds can use the programs for remedial work.

test	computer users	non-computer users
pre-test	25%	36%
post-test	90%	92%
improvement	65%	56%

Figure 19-1. Test Results of University of Minnesota Students in Music-Fundamentals Pilot Project

To illustrate the two courses, consider the following examples, which are coordinated with a note-reading exercise in the textbook. Figure 19-2 shows part of a lesson from a note-identification drill from the MECC course. First, the student is referred to a note printed in the textbook. Then the student types in the letter name of that note, that is, a letter from A through G. In this example, the correct answer is C, but the student has answered D, so the computer prints a message to that effect. Later in the lesson, this question is asked again since the student answered incorrectly the first time. At the end of a lesson, as shown in figure 19-3, the student receives a score (0 to 100 percent). If this score is above a cutoff point, usually 85 percent, the terminal displays a congratulatory message. Otherwise, the computer advises students to "hit the books."

Figure 19-4 is a copy of a PLATO lesson covering the same topic. Now the exercise is displayed completely on the screen, with an arrow pointing to the note to be identified. As in the MECC lesson, students type in a letter from A through G and receive an immediate evaluation of their answer. Notes not identified correctly on the first try are presented again. At the end of each lesson, students receive a numerical score and appropriate message, in the same way as in the MECC version.

Concerning cost-effectiveness, the MECC network is rather inexpensive, with necessary equipment quite available throughout the state of Minnesota. More problematic, though, is getting access to the equipment, for many terminals are situated in mathematics rooms or engineering buildings, without provisions for use by students in the arts and humanities. PLATO is more expensive and not as available, but access, for people who can afford it, is possible through learning centers.

Research Prospects

Future prospects in CAI of music fundamentals include revision of the PLATO lessons to include more of PLATO's advanced graphics technology

```
1 THE THIRD NOTE IN EXERCISE #6 IS

  ANSWER ? E
  GREAT

2 THE FIRST NOTE IN EXERCISE #1 IS

  ANSWER ? D
  SORRY ABOUT THAT, BUT THE CORRECT ANSWER WAS : C
```

Figure 19-2. Note-Identification Drill on MECC

```
     RECYCLE THROUGH INCORRECT ANSWERS

  1 THE FIRST NOTE IN EXERCISE  #1 IS

    ANSWER ? C
    GREAT


  WELL, DOROTHY, YOU ANSWERED  23
  QUESTIONS CORRECTLY ON THE FIRST TRY.
  SCORE : 96 PERCENT CORRECT.
  CONGRATULATIONS, YOU HAVE SUCCESSFULLY
  COMPLETED DRILL : WS2
```

Figure 19-3. End of an MECC Lesson

Type the name of the note beneath the small arrow, then press NEXT.

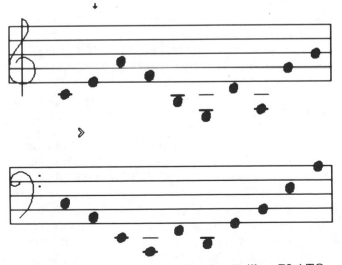

Figure 19-4. Note-Identification Drill on PLATO

and to refer students to other lessons available on that network. Another feature yet to be implemented on the PLATO course is recordkeeping of student scores. Beyond this project, many other areas of music instruction, such as ear training, music history, and more advanced theory, can benefit from CAI.

Currently, many musicians, including myself, have been developing lessons on microcomputers. This new development lowers the cost of instructional computing to where computers are available not only in schools, but also in homes. The current technology permits music notation to be displayed on a screen, even on a home television screen; sound production of up to six simultaneous notes is also possible. If the trend toward lower cost and increased capability continues, computer-assisted instruction will have more of an impact on students in the arts and humanities.

Eventually programs such as those discussed above can be adapted to keep detailed records for use in pedagogical studies. Results from these will add specific verification (or possibly contradiction) of generalizations drawn intuitively from traditional music instruction. Empirical research can also help in settling disputed issues. CAI in musical skills can be used as one part of a cross-disciplinary study of general educational theories and strategies.

The course developed on the MECC network has been reported at the 1978 convention of the Association for the Development of Computer-Based Instructional Systems, the 1978 convention of the Music Educators National Conference, the 1978 fall conference of the Minnesota Music Theory Consortium, and the 1979 midwinter clinic of the Minnesota Music Educators Association.

The PLATO course has been reported by myself at the 1979 convention of the Association for the Development of Computer-Based Instructional Systems and by Roger Foltz, of the University of Nebraska at Omaha, at the 1979 convention of the Midwest Theory Society.

Acknowledgments

Financial support for the MECC programs was provided by grants from the University of Minnesota Center for Educational Development and the University of Minnesota Council on Liberal Education, Small Grants Program. Funding for the PLATO course comes from the University of Nebraska Computer Center. While many people made some contribution to the projects, I would like to acknowledge my reviewers, Andrew Ahlgren, Linda Borry and Roger Foltz; project assistants, Scott Kallen, Myrna Johnson, and Thomas Moher; and all the students involved in the pilot projects.

References

1. Arenson, M. The Development of a Competency-Based Education Program in Music Theory. *Proceedings of the 1979 Conference of the Association for the Development of Computer-Based Instructional Systems,* San Diego, Calif.: 1979, 289.

2. ———. "An Examination of Computer-Based Educational Hardware at Twenty-eight MCCBMI Member Schools. *Journal of Computer-Based Instruction* 5(1978):38–40.

3. Eddins, J. "Random Access Audio in Computer-Assisted Instruction." *Journal of Computer-Based Instruction* 5(1978):22–29.

4. Foltz, R. "Integration of PLATO into a Music Curriculum" (Paper presented at the 1979 convention of the Midwest Theory Society, Madison, Wis.).

5. Gooch, S. "PLATO Music System." *Proceedings of the 1978 Conference of the Association for the Development of Computer-Based Instructional Systems.* Dallas, Tex.: March 1978, 314–324.

6. Hill, F.W., and Searight, R. *Study Outline and Work-book in the Elements of Music.* Dubuque: Wm. C. Brown Company, 1976.

7. Hofstetter, F.T. Interactive Simulation/Games as an Aid to Musical Learning. *Proceedings of the 1977 Conference of the Association for the Development of Computer-Based Instructional Systems,* Bloomington, Del.: 1977, 104–117.

8. ———. "GUIDO: An Interactive Computer-Based System for Improvement of Instruction and Research in Ear-Training." *Journal of Computer-Based Instruction* 1, no. 4 (1975):100–106.

9. Killam, R.N., and Lorton, P. "Computer-Assisted Instruction in Music: Ear-Training Drill and Practice." *Proceedings of the Fifth Conference on Computers in the Undergraduate Curricula.* Pullman, Wash.: Washington State University, 1974.

10. Lamb, M.R. and Bates, R.H.T. "Computerized Aural Training: An Interactive System Designed to Help Both Teachers and Students." *Journal of Computer-Based Instruction* 5(1978):30–37.

11. Peters, G.D. "The Complete Computer-Based Music System: A Teaching System—a Musician's Tool." *Proceedings of the 1977 Winter Conference of the Association for the Development of Computer-based Instructional Systems,* Wilmington, Del.: February 1977, 93–100.

12. Placek, R.W. "Design and Trial of a Computer-Assisted Lesson in Rhythm." *Journal of Research in Music Education* 22(1974):13–23.

13. Stanislaw, R.J. "Computer-Assisted Instruction for Beginning Music Theory" (Paper presented at the 1978 meeting of the Society for Music Theory, Minneapolis, Minn.).

14. Thostenson, M.S. "Two Important Principles for Constructing Computer-Based Music Instruction Programs—the Circle of Fifths, and Key Transposition." *Proceedings of the 1977 Conference of the Association for the Development of Computer-Based Instruction Systems,* Bloomington, Del.: 1977, 80–92.

Bibliography

Articles and Monographs

Allvin, R.L. "Computer-Assisted Music Instruction: A Look at the Potential." *Journal of Research in Music Education* 19(1971):131–143.

Arenson, M. "Guidelines for the Development of Computer-Assisted Instruction Materials in Music Theory. *Proceedings of the 1977 Winter Conference of the Association for the Development of Computer-Based Instructional Systems,* Wilmington, Del. February 1977, 101–103.

Deihl, N.C. "Computer-Assisted Instruction and Instrumental Music: Implications for Teaching and Research." *Journal of Research in Music Education* 35(1973):299–306.

Gross, D. "Computer-Assisted Music Fundamentals in Minnesota Public Schools" (Paper presented at the 1979 mid-winter clinic of the Minnesota Music Educators Association, Minneapolis, Minn.).

———. "Starting up in Computer-Based Music Instruction" (Paper presented at the 1979 convention of the Association for the Development of Computer-Based Instructional Systems, San Diego, Calif.).

———. "What to do Until the Hardware Comes" (Paper presented at the 1978 convention of the Association for the Development of Computer-Based Instructional Systems, Dallas, Tex.).

———. "A Computer-Assisted Music Fundamentals Course" (Paper presented at the 1978 Fall conference of the Minnesota Music Theory Consortium, St. Peters, Minn.).

Hullfish, W.H. "A Comparison of Two Computer-Assisted Instructional Programs in Music Theory." *Journal of Research in Music Education* 20(1972):354–361.

Killam, R.; Lorton, P.; and Schubert, E. "Interval Recognition: A Study of Student Accuracy of Identification of Harmonic and Melodic Intervals." *Journal of Music Theory* 19, no. 2 (1975):212–234.

Kuhn, W.E. "Computer-Assisted Instruction in Music: Drill and Practice in Ear-Training." *College Music Symposium* 14(1974):89–101.

Peters, G.D. and Eddins, J.W. "Applications of Computers to Music Pedagogy, Analysis, and Research: A Selected Bibliography." *Journal of Computer-Based Instruction* 5(1978)41–44.

Taylor, J.A. and Parrish, J.W. "A National Survey on the Uses of, and Attitudes Toward Programmed Instruction and Computers in Public School and College Music Education." *Journal of Computer-Based Instruction* 5(1978):11–21.

Conference Proceedings

Alonso, S.; Appleton, J.H.; and Jones, C.A. "A Special Purpose Digital System for the Instruction, Composition, and Performance of Music." *Proceedings of the 1975 Conference on Computers in the Undergraduate Curricula*. Fort Worth, Tex. June 1975.

Hultberg, M.L.; Hultberg, W.E.; and Tenny, T. "Project Clef: CAI in Music Theory—Update 1979." *Proceedings of the 1979 Conference of the Association for the Development of Computer-Based Instructional Systems*. San Diego, Calif.: March 1979, 928–934.

Lorton, P., and Killam, R.N. "Data Analysis and Retention: Experience and Recommendations." *Proceedings of the 1977 Winter Conference of the Association for the Development of Computer-Based Instructional Systems,* Wilmington, Del. February 1977, 298–307.

Wittlich, G. "Computers and Music Instruction at Indiana University (Bloomington)." *Proceedings of the First Annual Meeting of the National Consortium for Computer-Based Music Instruction*. Newark, Del.: 1973.

20 A Computer Project in Music Analysis

Dorothy Gross

Music analysis is a systematic investigation into the structure and function of music. The first step in any analysis is the isolation of basic musical elements, such as rhythm, notes, chords, instrumentation and dynamics. The frequency, succession, and changes of those elements are then studied, statistically or intuitively, in order to determine the salient and characteristic features of the music.

The Problem

As with other arts and humanities, both emotional and intellectual factors enter into a musical work. This dichotomy has produced many types of analysis, as well as much debate on how music should be analyzed. With the more intuitive analytical techniques, analysts draw conclusions based on their impressions from hearing a piece and studying the score, without rigorous, logical proof. For example, in defining *accent* in music, two theorists maintain that accent "is understandable as an experience but undefined in terms of causes" [5, p. 7]. Since such processes are subjective, it is entirely possible for two respected theorists to apply the same techniques, yet arrive at different results.

Intellectual processes, on the other hand, entail a step-by-step procedure that leads inevitably to a single solution. Usually such techniques concentrate on details relatively untouched by the complex interaction of the many variables which contribute to our understanding of music. One such device is the measuring of the difference in pitch between two notes. By counting the number of piano keys between two notes, a theorist has an accurate measurement of their distance, or interval. Results of such analysis may be used to compare composers or to study the connection between quantitative results and intuitive impressions on the listener.

Since analysis of intervals forms a significant part of the programs described in this chapter, an example of interval calculation done without a computer is helpful. As mentioned earlier, intervals are defined as the distance in pitch between two notes. For each piano key passed between them, we count one semitone. For example, from E up to F-sharp (or G-flat) is two semitones. Figure 20–1 shows the first line of *Twinkle, Twinkle, Little Star,* indicating the interval between each note and its successor.

Figure 20–1. *Twinkle, Twinkle, Little Star*

While understanding the artistic, creative nature of music often requires an intuitive approach, sometimes intuition is used in lieu of a valid but impractical, intellectual procedure. In the analysis of long compositions, for instance, traditionally the intuitive has prevailed over the intellectual approach. This is because even where an intellectual process might be fruitful, the analysis would take too long. For instance, in just figure 20–1 there are thirteen intervals. Considering that music generally is considerably longer than that and contains other notes in addition to the melody, a detailed study of interval use in the piece would be very time-consuming and tedious. For this reason, musicians have preferred the quicker, albeit less precise, route of subjective investigation.

In view of the need for a means of performing routine operations, such as the one described above, quickly, accurately, and without boredom, computers seem to offer an ideal solution. However, the reality of computer use has demonstrated that music notation cannot be read accurately by computer without considerable intermediate human effort. Usually this effort consists of representing music in a code using only characters available on a computer keypunch, specifically letters, numbers, and punctuation marks. After encoding, someone must enter the data into a computer before computer-assisted analysis can begin.

The process of representing music in a code necessitates putting in much of the time-consuming work that computer intervention was supposed to eliminate. Furthermore, errors in coding and typing may require considerable editing before a musical composition is ready for analysis. To add to these difficulties, many different codes have been invented, with the unfortunate result that one analysis program may not accept a code that worked for another program. To avoid having to represent a piece in several different codes in order to run the same composition through different analytical routines, a single, coordinated set of programs, all using the same code, is desirable.

The focus of this chapter, therefore, is to provide a comprehensive group of computer programs to aid in the application of some of the more objective, intellectual techniques of music analysis. Specific areas covered include finding and counting melodic, rhythmic, and chord patterns and applying some procedures from mathematical set theory to music analysis. An explanation of set-theoretical applications to music is beyond the scope of this chapter. Readers wishing more information should consult Allen Forte's *The Structure of Atonal Music* [7]. Additionally, some attention is paid to the composer's instructions about how to play the notes—how loud, how smoothly, at what speed.

Many researchers have designed programs to meet specific needs, such as harmony [1] and melodic problems [10] and set theory applications [6]. Prior to this project, however, no one had developed a comprehensive set of programs, all using the same data base. Since the beginning of this project, a similar set of programs has been developed at Ohio State University [12]. A different solution effort is a programming language designed specifically for use in music analysis [9], an approach which can help the analyst but requires the learning of a computer language.

The immediate value of this project is the development and use of a tool for music analysis. The ultimate merit will be the value of results of the programs as contributions to musical knowledge and theory. Since areas within music tend to overlap, significant analytical discoveries can contribute to music history, composition, performance, and pedagogy. For example, in one study [2], a computer was used to determine the composer of a piece of disputed authorship.

Besides the direct benefits of results from running the programs, the methodology itself will lead to more rigorous definitions of many musical terms. Particularly, the problem of grouping notes into meaningful units within a composition is troublesome with a computer, since this has only been done intuitively in the past. While much theory exists to categorize and describe a group once it has been isolated, the actual separation of notes into groups is not a clear process.

In general, both the results and methodology will illuminate the value of using computers and doing empirical research in music. Moreover, since the value of quantification in an aesthetic field is subject to debate at this time in other areas of the arts and humanities, as well as in music, these findings can have an impact ranging from specific techniques to general philosophies. Certainly, progress in one nonscientific field lends support to people involved with computers in similar fields.

The Solution

The overall approach to the problem of computer-assisted music analysis has been to offer the user both convenience and flexibility. Since a given musician may not necessarily be involved with computer science, one criterion in development was that no programming knowledge be required in order to run the programs. Yet, since some control by the user is desirable, a method of allowing users to select from options contained within the programs was needed. These structural goals, as well as the substantive goals described earlier, form the basis of the specific methodology.

There were three distinct stages of the project: encoding the music, translation from the encoding language to a largely numeric data base, and the musical analysis itself. The first stage, encoding, involved conversion of music from the printed score to an alphanumeric code. After several codes were researched, the MUSTRAN encoding language, designed by Jerome Wenker [3], was selected because it included representations of all the dynamic and articulation markings and descriptive words, as well as pitch and rhythm. Also, the code was reasonably easy to learn and use. Encoding was done without the aid of a computer, although some computer assistance was used in checking data for errors.

The second stage, translation, involved the conversion of music from MUSTRAN to a data base more suitable for electronic data processing. Translation was entirely computerized, consisting of a sequence of three programs connected automatically to one another, so that one set of instructions from the user directed the computer to run all three programs in the correct order. As it became evident that faulty data would be a problem with even the most careful users, error-checking routines were included in the translation programs. Finally, when corrected to the user's satisfaction, the translation was stored on a magnetic disk or tape for future use.

The last and most important stage was analysis itself. At this point, five programs were developed, which could be used sequentially or individually as the analyst desired.

1. The LINEAR program was created to find and count patterns of events occurring in succession. Depending on user-controlled parameters, these events could be pitches, intervals, rhythms, chords, dynamics, or articulations. Since the music-analytic procedures used usually were not concerned with patterns of more than twelve events in a row, this pattern length was the maximum for which the programs were designed. Analysts had available several options in this program, such as disregarding rests and repeated notes, or setting a minimum number of occurrences in order for a pattern to be listed.

2. The VERTICL program was developed to find and to count patterns of the same elements studied in LINEAR, only instead of tracing events occurring in succession, this program followed events occurring within the same time span. Once again, the user could choose from different options regarding the exact analytical techniques. For example, the time span could be varied from simultaneities to all events occurring within a piece. With time spans greater than simultaneity, each pattern could also be listed in either ascending or chronological order. Another control permitted the user to include or disregard the octave in which a note occurred.

3. The THEMES program searched translated data for themes submitted and labeled by the user. According to user-selected choices, slight pitch variations and rhythmic changes might or might not be considered significant. THEMES produced a schematic diagram tracing the themes through the piece, including any transpositions (moving a theme up or down) and incomplete occurrences. While the latter were limited by default to fragments beginning with the first note of a theme, it was possible to search for fragments beginning with succeeding notes as well. After diagraming the piece, THEMES counted occurrences of each theme, breaking them down according to transposition and fragment length.

4. The HARMSET program read in the results of VERTICL and labeled them with chord symbols. Depending on the nature of the sounds and the wishes of the user, the vertical groups could be labeled in two ways. For combinations of notes resembling traditional chords, the computer applied chord labels from traditional music theory. For example, a G major chord appeared as "G M." With this program, an analyst could identify traditional chords with traditional names. More modern sounds required a method of labeling that is not tied down to the harmonic vocabulary of chords. For such sounds, set-theoretical methods [7] measuring sounds in terms of semitones were applied.

With either chords or sets, HARMSET results could be sent automatically to LINEAR. Doing so provided a count of chords or sets, as well as successions of up to six chords or sets. According to user preference, the rhythm of each group could be included in the tabulation.

5. The COUNT program kept a running count of results from music written by the same composer. For COUNT, the data consisted of cards punched by either LINEAR or VERTICL. For this program, there were no user-controlled options.

Required for this project were a computer with 100,000 words of memory (on a Control Data Corporation machine), a keypunch, a printer, and disk space. Another requirement was computer time, roughly 15 seconds per program per page of music, and enough human time to encode and correct data and to run programs. While the original programs were written in CAL SNOBOL on a Control Data Corporation computer, they were later adapted to SPITBOL for use on an IBM 370/168. On both versions, the computer was employed for translation of data, and for the analytical processes described above. Interpretation of computer results was left to the user.

Results

The principal result of this project is that a tool has been developed for performing a considerable amount of analysis with a minimum amount of user computer work. Since the programs can use the same routines to analyze different compositions, they lend themselves very well to objective comparisons of music from different styles and cultures.

With the programs and their many options, as described above, a variety of analyses too numerous to discuss here is available to the user. As an example, Luigi Dallapiccola's *Quaderno Musicale* No. 11 has been run through each of the five different analytical routines. Figure 20–2 exhibits the first two lines of that piece.

Figure 20–3 shows results of the LINEAR program's search for rhythmic values. (For the sake of clarity, one column of the actual printout has been omitted.) The first column represents each tone's duration as a fraction of a whole beat, according to the chart in the upper left area of the printout. For instance, in this example 1.0 is a quarter note and 2.0 is a half note. Subsequent columns list the number of occurrences of each rhythm in the highest melody ("soprano"), other voices, and total.

This example tells us much about Dallapiccola's use of rhythm. First, a wide variety of values is used, including the division of the beat into two, three, and six parts. Second, a traditional texture of faster notes (one beat or less) in the melody over a slower accompaniment has been retained, despite the variety of rhythmic values. Finally, since rhythms appear in this list in order of appearance, a steady increase in rhythmic complexity is apparent, giving the piece a sense of rhythmic growth.

Figure 20–4 shows another application of LINEAR, to count the dynamics occurring during the piece, by sorting them into five general classes, ranging from very soft ("PP") to very loud ("FF"), with additional words for changes in loudness. The results show that only the quieter ranges of sound (P, PP) are used, as well as many gradual changes in loudness (CRESC, DIM).

Figure 20–5 is a page from the output of VERTICL, showing a count of groups of simultaneously occurring notes. Pluses after letters indicate sharps, for example, "F +" means F-sharp; and minuses stand for flats. Following each letter is a number indicating how high or low the note is, with C1 being the lowest C on the piano. (The few notes below that C are shown by the number 0.) The first column following each group shows the total number of occurrences of each group. Following that, the total is broken down according to the duration of the occurrence. In this example, there are four classes of durations, ranging from long sounds (three beats or longer) to very short sounds (less than half a beat). Finally, the total duration of each group is listed.

From these results, it is apparent that a wide variety of sounds occurs, with few patterns recurring. Further, an examination of the score shows that recurring groups do not have very large total durations, in spite of their recurrence. One interesting observation about Dallapiccola's use of notes is

Source: Reprinted with permission from Dallapiccola, *Quaderno Musicale Di Annalibera.*

Figure 20–2. First Two Lines of the Dallapiccola Piece

LINEAR GROUPING PROGRAM

TITLE   QUADERNO MUSICALE NO. 11
COMPOSER   DALLAPICCOLA
SCANNING OF DURATION PATTERNS
BEGINNING AT ATTACK TIME 0.0:
   '0.500' = EIGHTH NOTE
   '1.0'   = QUARTER NOTE
   '2.0'   = HALF NOTE

1-NOTE PATTERNS

TOTALS

PATTERN		FREQUENCY	
	SOPRANO	OTHER VOICES	TOTAL
1.0	12	1	13
1.500	7	3	10
4.500		2	2
3.0		33	33
0.500	19	3	22
6.0		4	4
4.0	1	1	2
2.0		4	4
0.166	6	0	6
0.416	2	0	2
0.250	2	0	2
0.750	2	0	2
1.250	1	0	1
5.500		1	1
0.833	2	0	2
1.333	1	0	1
0.666	1	0	1
3.500	1	0	1

ALL PATTERNS HAVE BEEN PRINTED.

Figure 20–3. Sample Result of LINEAR: Rhythm

that in any group, if a pitch is used in one octave, it does not appear simultaneously in another octave. This results in a very economical use of sound, with no duplication.

After pitches have been grouped by VERTICL, they may then be analyzed according to set-theoretical methods in HARMSET. Then, these results can be run through LINEAR in order to count pitch sets or set successions. Figure 20–6 shows a count of two-set successions in the Dallapiccola piece.

In each set, numbers refer to intervals above a theoretical zero point. The actual music contains varying octave arrangements of those intervals. For example, "0" could be a unison, an octave, or several octaves. One striking feature of these results is that many sets contain only even numbers,

```
                        LINEAR GROUPING PROGRAM

TITLE          QUADERNO MUSICALE NO. 11

COMPOSER       DALLAPICCOLA

SCANNING OF DYNAMIC PATTERNS

                        1-DYNAMICS PATTERNS

                    TOTALS

                    PATTERN                         FREQUENCY

                                            OTHER
                                  SOPRANO    VOICES     TOTAL

              P                      1          0          1
              CRESC                  8          1          9
              PP                     1          3          4
              DIM                   13          3         16


ALL PATTERNS HAVE BEEN PRINTED.
```

Figure 20-4. Sample Result of LINEAR: Dynamics

meaning that they have only even intervals (known to musicians as the whole-tone scale). The remaining sets turn out to be segments of a major scale. As a result, the music provides the listener with many familiar sounds. Note also the tendency of sounds to be followed by similar sounds, for example, "0 2 6 8" succeeded by "0 2 4 8". This aids the listener in recognizing familiar sounds by providing areas dominated by a particular sonority, rather than an even distribution of sounds. Regarding the bottom line of the example, the user has selected an option to set a minimum number of occurrences, in this case two, in order for a pattern to be printed.

Figure 20-7 is part of a map of occurrences of themes called P, I, R, and RI, as shown in figure 20-8. Numbers along the tip of figure 20-8 are beat numbers, counting from the beginning of the piece. Since there may be more than one note at a time on a staff, each staff has been subdivided by the computer into "voices" consisting of one note at a time. Rows in the chart represent each voice.

The result of THEMES is a schematic diagram, showing occurrences of each theme, fragment size (if incomplete), and transposition, regardless of octave. Fragment size is shown by "FR" followed by the number of notes in the incomplete theme. This indication is omitted if the theme is complete. Transposition is "T" followed by the theme's transposition, ranging from 0 (not transposed) to 11 (transposed eleven semitones higher). For example, "P T0" means theme P transposed zero semitones, but the same label would apply to the theme transposed up or down any number of octaves.

TOTALS

NUMBERS AFTER LETTER NAMES INDICATE REGISTER (E.G. A440 = A4).
ALL SETS HAVE BEEN PRINTED.

SOUND	SET	FREQ	3.0+ BEATS	DURATION 1.0+ TO 3.0	0.500+ TO 1.0	0 TO 0.500	TOTAL DURATION
B-3		1			1		1.0
A 4		1			1		1.0
D+3	B-3 C 4 C 4 A 4	1				1	0.500
D+3	B-3 C 4 G 4 F 5	1				1	0.500
B-3	E 4 E 4 G+4 D 5	1				1	0.500
B-3	E 4 E 4 G+4 C 5	2			1	1	1.500
B-3	F 4 F+4 G+4	1				1	0.500
B 3	F 4 G 4 A 4	2		1		1	2.0
B 3	F 4 A 4 D+5	1				1	0.500
B 3	F 4 A 4 C+5	1			1		1.0
F+3	D 4 F 4 G+4 C+5	1		1			1.500
F+3	B 3 D 4 F 4 C+5	1				1	0.500
E 2	F+3 D 4 A 3	1		1			1.500
E 2	C 3 C 3 A 3 A 3	2				2	1.0
E 2	C 3 C 3 G 3 A 3	1				1	0.500
E 2	C 3 C 3 G 3 A 3 F+6	1				1	0.500
E 2	C 3 D+3 A 3 B 5	1			1		1.0
E 2	C 3 D+3 D 4 B 5	1				1	0.500
G+3	C 3 D+3 B 4 B 5	1		1			1.500
G+3	D 4 D+3 B 5	1			1		1.0
G+3	B-3 E 5 B 5	1				1	0.500
F 3	B-3 D 4	1				1	0.500
F 3	B-3	3				3	1.500
F 3	B-3	2				2	0.750
A 2	D 3 C+4 F+4	1			1		1.0
A 2	D 3 C+4 F+4 C 5	2				2	0.750
A 2	D 3 F 3 B-3 C 5	1				1	0.500
C+3	F 3 F 3 B-3 G 4	1				1	0.500
C+3	G 3 F 3 B-3 E 4	1			1		1.0
C+3	G 3 E 4 A 4	1				1	0.500
C+3	G 3 B 4 D+4	1				1	0.250
C+3	G 3 C 4 D+4	3				3	0.750
F+3	G 3 D 4 E 4	1				1	0.500
F+3	C 4 E 4 G+4	1				1	0.250
F+3	E 4 E 4 G+4	1			1		1.0
F+3	B-3 B 3 E 4	1				1	0.500
D+3	G+3 B 3 C+4	1		1			1.500

Figure 20-5. Sample Result of VERTICL

2-SONORITY PATTERNS

TOTALS

PATTERN		FREQUENCY
0 2 6 8 0 2 4 8		2
0 2 4 6 0 2 4 6		3
0 2 6 8 0 2 6 8		4
0 2 6 0 2 6		4
0 1 5 8 0 1 3 7 8		2
0 1 3 5 8 0 1 3 5 8		3
0 1 3 5 8 0 1 5 8		2

ONLY PATTERNS OCCURRING 2 TIMES OR MORE HAVE BEEN PRINTED.

Figure 20-6. Sample Result of HARMSET

Figure 20-7. Themes in the Dallapiccola Piece

Results from this program show that fragments of the themes are used to accompany the complete occurrences in the highest voice, particularly at the beginning of the piece. What makes this especially noteworthy is that in the actual technique used by the composer to write this piece, the accompaniment was created by using thematic fragments as chords. The existence of similar harmonic and melodic patterns in this piece is definitely a unifying feature.

THE FOLLOWING BEGINS IN MEASURE 1 .

BEAT:	2.500	4.500	6.0	15.0	19.0	21.500	25.0	25.500	36.0
STAFF 1 VOICE 1	P T0					RIFR6 T8		R T2	
STAFF 1 VOICE 2									
STAFF 2 VOICE 1			IFR3 T10		RIFR3 T8				
STAFF 2 VOICE 2		RFR3 T1							
STAFF 3 VOICE 1				IFR3 T1					
STAFF 3 VOICE 2							PFR3 T8		PFR3 T7
STAFF 3 VOICE 3									
STAFF 3 VOICE 4									

THE FOLLOWING BEGINS IN MEASURE 14 .

BEAT:	39.500
STAFF 1 VOICE 1	I T2
STAFF 1 VOICE 2	
STAFF 2 VOICE 1	
STAFF 2 VOICE 2	
STAFF 3 VOICE 1	
STAFF 3 VOICE 2	
STAFF 3 VOICE 3	
STAFF 3 VOICE 4	

Figure 20–8. Sample Result of THEMES

Since the original version of the programs was completed in 1975, it has contributed to ongoing efforts in music analysis around the country. At Northwestern University, students and faculty have used these programs for research purposes, including dissertation research. During this time, several revisions have occurred, including the development of an IBM version for Lehman College (CUNY).

While interpretation of the significance of the results obtained from running programs in the package is left up to the user, there is no question that the availability of information previously difficult (if not impossible) to collect will place music analysis in a new light. So far, applications of these programs range from studies of Bach to twentieth-century music, both classical and popular. Two typical uses are the analysis of a single composition [8] and the comparison of two pieces or composers [11].

Since the aim of the programming was to achieve accurate results, cost was not the first consideration in development, although a less expensive version is possible in the future. Compared with traditional methods, the package will be cheaper, even if not so revised, when a data base of musical scores in MUSTRAN is available.

In general, future prospects for the use of the programs in music analysis are to study more compositions and to test the validity and significance of empirical techniques in music research. The latter use relates to all the arts and humanities, since the use of computers in these fields is not totally accepted. Unlike more scientific fields, where empirical data are welcome, the arts contain many excellent scholars who believe that hard, cold facts supplied by a computer cannot contribute positively to an understanding of the spontaneous, inspired process involved in creating a work of art. Future research will reveal the extent to which empirical data can aid in analysis of the fruits of largely intuitive thought processes.

Research Prospects

Desirable extensions of this project are (1) the creation of a library of music in computer-readable form, to avoid the inconvenient process of getting music into a machine; (2) economization, so that more programs may be run; and (3) analyzing results with programs that perform statistical analysis, so that statistical significance and correlations may be established in a methodical fashion.

My work has been published as a Ph.D. dissertation [8] and in the proceedings of the 1975 Indiana University Computer Network Conference. The programs are reviewed favorably in the Spring 1977 *Computer Music Journal,* in an article about the Indiana University Computer Music System [4]. I have read papers at the 1975 CUNY Forum on Computers in Music and at the 1978 Central Midwest Theory Society meeting. Furthermore, Rosalie Sward, a user from Northwestern University, presented papers about her use of the programs at the 1978 International Computer Music Conference and at the 1979 International Conference on Computers and the Humanities.

Acknowledgments

Development of the programs was aided by Dr. Gary Wittlich, Rosalie Sward, and computer center personnel and grants at the University of Minnesota, Indiana University, Lehman College, and Northwestern University.

References

1. Bernstein, L.F., and Olive, J.P. "Computers and the 16th-Century Chanson: A Pilot Project at the University of Chicago." *Computers and the Humanities* 3(1969):153–160.

2. Brantley, D.L. "Disputed Authorship of Musical Works: A Quantitative Approach to the Attribution of the Quartets Published as Haydn's Opus 3." Ph.D. dissertation, University of Iowa, 1977.

3. Brook, B.S., editor. *Musicology and the Computer.* New York: The City University of New York Press, 1970.

4. Byrd, D. "The Indiana University Computer Music System." *Computer Music Journal* (Spring 1977).

5. Cooper, G., and Meyer, L. *The Rhythmic Structure of Music.* Chicago: The University of Chicago Press, 1960.

6. Forte, A. "A Program for the Analytic Reading of Scores." *Journal of Music Theory* 10, no. 2 (1966):330–364.

7. Forte, D. *The Structure of Atonal Music.* New Haven: Yale University Press, 1973.

8. Gross, D. "A Set of Computer Programs to Aid in Music Analysis." Ph.D. dissertation, Indiana University, 1975.

9. Mendel, A. "Some Preliminary Attempts at Computer-Assisted Style Analysis in Music." *Computers and the Humanities* 4(1969):41–52.

10. Suchoff, B. "Computerized Folk Song Research and the Problem of Variants." *Computers and the Humanities* 2(1968):155–159.

11. Sward, R. "The Computer Assists in Attempting to Solve a Problem of Twentieth Century Music (Paper delivered at the 1978 International Computer Music Conference, Evanston, Ill., 1978).

12. Whitney, T.G. "Music Analysis: SLAM Simplified or How the Computer Compares 16th Century Bourgeois with Eighteenth Century Bach." *Creative Computing* 3, no. 2 (1977):88–89.

Bibliography

Articles and Monographs

Brender, M.P. and Brender, R.F. "Computer Transcription and Analysis of Mid-Thirteenth Century Musical Notation." *Journal of Music Theory* 10, no. 2 (1966):198–221.

Patrick, P.H. "A Computer Study of a Suspension-Formation in the Masses of Josquin des Prez." *Computers and the Humanities* 8(1974): 321–331.

Roller, G. "Development of a Method for Analysis of Musical Compositions Using an Electronic Digital Computer." *Journal of Research in Music Education* 13(1965):249–252.

Suchoff, B. "The Computer and Bartok Research in America." *Journal of Research in Music Education* 19(1971):3–16.

Books

Dallapiccola, L. *Quaderno Musicale di Annalibera*. Milan: Edizioni Suvini Zerboni, 1953.

Kostka, S. *A Bibliography of Computer Applications in Music*. Hackensack, N.J.: J. Boonin, 1974.

Lincoln, H.B., editor. *The Computer and Music,* Ithaca: Cornell University Press, 1970.

Part IV
Computer Applications in the Fine Arts

Kevin McMahon

Throughout history, art and technology have reflected the human condition and the collective human experience. The collective experience is the total of all the thought, feelings, and individual living experiences that have occurred until the instant in which they are perceived. The artist, ever searching for a medium which best expresses his or her inspiration, employs familiar, available materials, thus relying on the latest technological developments. Each new medium used for artistic expression is added to the pool of art media from which future artists will draw. In order to move forward, technology cannot escape its symbiotic relationship with art, as expressed through the artistic process. The technologist relies upon the artistic process to nurture the mind's creative abilities. Albert Einstein emphasized this creative process in a paper entitled "Principles of Research,"[1] in which he wrote that the physicist's supreme task is to arrive at universal elementary laws, which can be used to build up the cosmos by pure deduction, and that not logic, but intuition, resting on sympathetic understanding of experience, can reach those laws. Part IV focuses on the pride of technology, the computer, and explores how the potential of this tool may be more closely realized by exploring it within a context involving a broad range of people with widely differing interests and experiences. Because the computer's design requires a strictly logical and structured thinking process, until recently it has been used primarily by technically trained professionals. This specialized thought process is typically mastered by the scientist, the mathematician, the logician, and the technologist. Contrarily, one sees relatively few artists, linguists, or humanists using this tool, since their training and experience do not typically prepare them for such processes. Because of this highly specialized prerequisite, computer use has evolved along a rather narrow path, lacking the wider perspective which encompasses all facets of the collective experience.

As each field of study becomes more complex and requires more preparatory training, tangential fields that are not directly relevant to one's chosen field of interest are often necessarily neglected. In this age of specialization, the scientist is no longer trained in philosophy, history, nature, and art, nor the humanist in anatomy, physiology, natural science, and logic. This specialization severely limits exploration of the collective experience

315

and promotes a shift toward a more distilled and undernourished value system.

Part IV poses the computer as an art medium, removes the technical prerequisites for the person who uses it, and reviews the use of computers in the setting of the fine arts. A brief historical perspective precedes an overview of computer fundamentals. These topics are followed by a somewhat detailed description of a flexible, image-making computer program named ARTPRIN. A variety of art programs currently available at the University of Minnesota is then briefly described, in addition to the several computer display devices available on which visual imagery can be explored. Following this, several chapters detail the works and personalities of those involved in creating fine art with the aid of a computer. This context illuminates the issue of creativity and its effect on the collective experience, and will be of interest to the artist, the technologist, and the educator. The educator will readily recognize how this approach can be useful for introducing to a general audience the issues, possibilities, and idiosyncracies of this twentieth-century phenomenon. Chapter 21 draws some conclusions about the state of the art and discusses possible directions for the future.

A historical analysis tracing the development of the computer would undoubtedly include reference to counting pebbles and beads, the abacus, the Incan quipu (knotted-string records), and the numerous astral monuments on which the ancients could "read" the astronomical rhythms. Mention of logic, the theories of numbers, and the philosophical development of time as measurable and evenly parceled would be unavoidable. Discussions of levers, gears, theories of mechanical contraptions, engines, and automation would also be present—and it would be a monumental undertaking.

Another development which spans the entire human time line and which, in my view, is intimately intertwined with the above-mentioned one, is the expression of the human need to create, often referred to as the artistic process. Traveling along this path through time, one sees pictures made with plant dyes on cave walls and on tree bark. Egg and wax mixtures then carried the extracted pigments and were used to make pictures on cloth. There are charcoal pictures on paper and oil paintings on canvas, as well as acrylic paints and phosphorescent pigments on practically any substance. One encounters solid forms hewn from stone or fired in clay and marvels at objects carved from wood and those cast in metal. The fire of a torch has welded steel, aluminum, and now plastics into new shapes. One can even find that "solid" shapes are not solid, as the hand passes through focused holographic laser beams. One hears rhythms and harmonies coming from clicked stones and sticks; from sticks tapping skin-covered hollows, metal tubes, and sheets; from air rushing past holes drilled into bamboo shoots and long twisted metal tubes; from taut strings plucked, stroked, vibrated, and hammered; and from squeaking, groaning electronic devices. Words, spoken or sung, add new dimensions to the sounds.

The more recent history of the creation of pictures with the aid of a computer can be traced to the late 1930s, when the first computers were being built. At that time cathode-ray oscilloscopes were used for aesthetic experiments well before the concept of computer art had developed. One of the earliest computer artists, Maughan Mason, was inspired for his graphic experiments by pendulum motions. R.K. Mitchell of the Batelle Memorial Institute in Columbus, Ohio, and Ivan Finkle of the Rand Corporation in Santa Monica, California, made Lissajous figures by means of digital computers. The use of these Lissajous figures for design purposes as, for instance, on wallpaper was first proposed as early as 1937 by C. Burnett. In 1958, A. Rich of Johns Hopkins University wrote a program for the design of wave patterns for textiles, and by 1963 systems for such designs had been developed at the Massachusetts Institute of Technology.[2]

In addition to the incredible growth in computer technology during the 1960s and the increased availability of computers, several important events occurred. In 1963, the periodical *Computers and Automation* (currently *Computers and People*) sponsored a contest in which computer-graphics works were judged on the basis of aesthetic criteria.[3] This contest, now an annual event for the monthly magazine, continues to attract a variety of creative imagery from a diverse range of participants. Unfortunately, as with any black-and-white reproduction technique, the absence of scale, texture, and color severely inhibit the full impact of the works displayed. In 1968, the first major exhibition of actual works, entitled "Cybernetic Serendipity," was held by London's Institute of Contemporary Arts. This event, resulting from the efforts of Jasia Reichardt and Max Bense, focused worldwide attention on the phenomenon of computer graphics as it related to the fine arts. This international exhibition, with its varied program of lectures, music, and film, helped to bring artists and technologists together in a spirit of collaboration. A subsequent exhibition was arranged by Käthe Schröder in Hamburg, Germany, in 1969 and traveled to Munich, Hamburg, Oslo, Brussels, Rome, and Tokyo, contributing toward the popularization of this art form in Europe.[4] The Computer Arts Society was formed by Alan Sutcliffe as a part of the British Computer Society in 1968.[5] This organization provides a support community and an information exchange for its members with its semiannual publication "Page." The formation of a special interest group (SIGGRAPH) of the Association for Computing Machinery (ACM) for the area of graphics has accelerated the growth of computer graphics.[6] The annual gathering of this group has helped to develop very sophisticated programming techniques for representing and displaying three-dimensional effects.[7]

Finally, the technological development of computers and computer display equipment during the 1970s has opened up an entirely new field for computer graphics. Increased quality of the display, less technical environments, and increased availability of equipment present today's artist with new media for expression. The artist who decides to use a computer, even as a toy, is using a communication medium whose short and rich history lies within a complicated social context which necessarily affects the artist's work.

Human need and the capacity to create link the development of art with that of technology. In exploring art, one focuses on creativity as embodied in beauty and harmony, without being distracted by the utilitarian aspects of technology typically accompanying the often overlooked creative process of technology. This creative process, which draws from the collective experience and returns a unique expression of the moment back into the collective experience, is essentially the same for both art and technology.

Following chapter 21, Part IV presents a gallery of computer artists. Selected works of these artists are presented here as examples of the use of computer technology in aid of artistic expression. It was not possible to present figures 22-1, 22-2, 23-1, 23-2, 24-1, 24-2, 24-3, 25-1 to 25-3, 26-2, and 26-3 in color in this book, but the interested reader is invited to write to the University of Minnesota Computer Center to obtain color plates of these figures at no cost beyond the price of the book. Write to Professor P.C. Patton, Director, University Computer Center, University of Minnesota, 208 Union Street S.E., 227 Experimental Engineering Bldg., Minneapolis, Minnesota 55455.

Notes

1. Albert Einstein, *The World as I See It,* translated by Alan Harris (London: John Lane, 1941).

2. Herbert Franke, *Computer Graphics, Computer Art* (London: Phaidon Press, 1971), p. 60.

3. See the September issues of *Computers and People* for the annual computer-art contests.

4. See Franke, *Computer Graphics, Computer Art,* p. 70.

5. Computer Arts Society: Chairman, Alan Sutcliffe, 4 Binfield Road, Workingham, Berkshire, England; U.S. branch: Coordinator, Kurt Lauckner, Mathematics Department, Eastern Michigan University, Ypsilanti, Michigan 48197 USA.

6. Association for Computing Machinery, 1133 Avenue of the Americas, New York, N.Y. 10036.

7. Jonathan Benthall, *Science and Technology in Art Today* (New York: Praeger Publishers, 1972), p. 50.

21 Computer Fundamentals for the Artist

Kevin McMahon

The computer will now be set up as an artist's sketch tablet to explore the variety of marks and shapes that can result from its use. Any general-purpose digital computer can be described as having four basic activities: input, processing, storage, and output.[1] Figure 21-1 shows these activities in a block diagram and indicates the paths over which information travels while in the computer system. A typical computer task involves all four activities. For example, a human sends some information into the computer by using some input device, and the computer stores this information as coded numbers in its storage unit, processes this information according to the human's instructions, and finally prints out the results on some output device in a form that the human can interpret.

Typically, a computer is described with reference to its hardware and software. *Hardware* refers to the overall computer system and each of the individual electrical and mechanical components that are electrically interconnected. *Software* refers to the "programs" or sequences of instructions

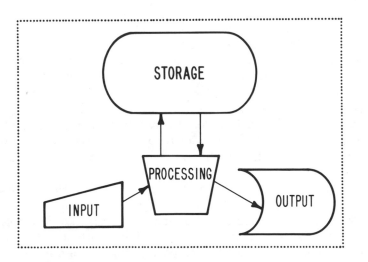

Figure 21-1. Block Diagram of a Computer

319

for the various computer tasks. These tasks are temporarily stored in the computer's storage unit or memory only while being performed, and they can be cleared out of the machine or stored on some machine-readable medium for future use.

The computer must be told what to do at every step. Setting up a procedure for the computer is called programming the computer. Each computer has a set of very basic operations that it can perform. A program consists of a sequence of these operations and is stored as machine instructions in the computer's storage unit or memory. Each memory location has a unique number or address associated with it, so that the computer's processor can conveniently read its contents or store a new number there. When the human causes the machine to run the program, the computer gets the first instruction from memory, performs that operation, then retrieves the next instruction, performs that one, and so on, until the last instruction has been completed, at which time the computer awaits another task.

In this fashion, the computer is a "sequential instruction performer." When the run button is pushed, the procedure and results are entirely defined, thus making the computer useful in performing a task over and over. Many different tasks can be defined and run on the same computer, which gives rise to the "general purpose" attribute mentioned earlier. The phenomenal speed and inherent accuracy of performing the instructions are determined by the current technology and the manufacturer's machine design. Typically, a few million sequential operations can be performed in one second.

Tasks for the computer can be made even more flexible than implied above, primarily because of two instructions found in all digital computers: the "jump" and "condition action" instructions. The sequential processing of the instructions can be altered if one of the instructions is the jump instruction, which causes the computer to start its sequential processing at a new location in the task. This nonsequential aspect is carried even further by the conditional-action instruction. This instruction allows portions of a task to be done only if certain conditions are met; otherwise, these portions are skipped. By means of these two instructions, the single task can be run over and over with results each time depending on the conditions set up in the task.

The instruction set for a typical computer is very cumbersome for humans to use. It involves a series of 1s and 0s which are grouped in a way defined by each of the multitude of manufacturers. For example, the machine instruction to add whichever number is currently stored in memory location 3 to the number in a temporary location in the processor might look like this:

0 101 000 000 000 011

For this fictitious computer, the instruction is decoded by taking the first four digits, or bits, which are this machine's "add" instruction, and performing this operation on the contents of the memory location indicated by the remaining digits. This instruction causes the machine to retrieve the number stored in that location and to add it to the value in a temporary storage location in the processor.

Because of this painstaking process, a series of "higher level" languages was developed for programming. Pascal, BASIC, FORTRAN, and COBOL are a few of the more common programming languages in use today. These languages are standardized so that humans can learn a language and program for any computer that has the appropriate conversion program. A single instruction in a higher-level language is converted to several machine instructions by the conversion program, thus greatly simplifying the process for the human.

Figure 21-2 shows a simple Pascal program. These instructions would be decoded by the Pascal conversion program, and a series of machine instructions would be placed in the storage unit. At this point, each time the computer was caused to run PROGRAM SAMPLE, the machine would locate Program Sample's first instruction and begin to process each subsequent instruction, eventually printing the message "THIS IS A SIMPLE SAMPLE" on its printing device. In this case, the actual printing process is the result of many separate machine instructions, as indicated in figure 21-3.

```
PROGRAM SAMPLE(OUTPUT);

(* THIS PROGRAM PRINTS OUT A SIMPLE MESSAGE *)

BEGIN
    WRITELN('THIS IS A SIMPLE SAMPLE')
END.
```

Figure 21-2. A Pascal Program

```
STEPS 1-5   --PREVIOUS INSTRUCTIONS--
STEP    6   GET THE NEXT LETTER FROM STORAGE.
STEP    7   SEND IT TO THE OUTPUT DEVICE.
STEP    8   IF THERE ARE MORE LETTERS
                GO TO STEP 6.
                OTHERWISE, PERFORM THE NEXT INSTRUCTION.
STEP    9   STOP. (TASK HAS BEEN COMPLETED).
```

Figure 21-3. Program Steps at Machine Language Level

In carrying this development one giant step further, applications programs are written in these high-level languages and create yet *higher*-level "application" languages for describing the desired task. These programs, while being performed by the computer, wait for and interpret these special commands. The program designer anticipates a variety of related tasks and incorporates them all into one program. The user of that program learns what the flexibilities of the program are and how to select the various features in order to create the desired effects. How general these programs can be made will depend on the point at which the complexity of the selection process for the variety of features available in the programs surpasses the complexity of the programming itself—a point which appears to be a long way off. With this approach, a person does not have to learn computer programming in order to use this tool, providing that the selected task is suited for a computer, an appropriate program is available, and, more importantly, such a program is flexible enough to include all the facets of the new task. This last point causes much frustration. Most often, compromises are made in redefining the new task to coordinate it as much as possible with existing programs.

Computer Software

This section reviews several of the applications programs that relate to the creation of visual imagery and fine art. A detailed description of one program, ARTPRIN, will help to clarify one method that the artist can use for designing and producing images with a computer. This is followed by a general description of several other art programs. These programs are currently being used at the University of Minnesota; in general, they contain their own task language, which pertains to the range of imagery determined by the program's design. The primary emphasis is on describing the range of images possible.

In general, the artists who use the computer as their art medium perform some degree of "postprocessing" of the raw images that result from their use of the computer programs. Postprocessing in this context means altering the resulting image in a way that is not possible by the computer alone. In the simplest sense, this merely means cropping, matting, and framing the image, but it also includes carrying the idea further by mixing the image with other art media. Photography, lithography, drawing, painting, etching, film and video, collage and sculpture, and weaving and sewing name several of the traditional media that have been used as means of postprocessing raw computer images. This chapter focuses on only the creation of raw computer images, since a detailed description of these traditional art media used in postprocessing is beyond the scope of this work.

ARTPRIN

A program has been set up to print various geometric shapes on some output device. For this example, a printer is the output device. This program interprets an "art" language with which the human can select and place the shapes on the printer page. The program designer has decided that a sheet of paper 11 inches wide and 8 inches high is to be the usual format for the pictures. On this sheet there are spaces for 110 letters side by side across the page and 50 letters down the page. A sample from program ARTPRIN, a program that uses such an art language, is shown in figure 21-4. This pro-

FIGURE NAME	SPECIAL FIELD	LEVEL	SYMBOL	START ROW	START COLUMN	ROW LENGTH	COLUMN LENGTH
END							
FRAME		1.	.	1.	1.	20.	50.
BOX		1.	I	11.	44.	5.	6.
BOX		1.	/	14.	10.	2.	25.
BOX		1.	M	16.	16.	4.	32.
OVAL		1.		13.	50.	20.	20.
OVAL		1.	H	13.	50.	20.	32.
OVAL		1.		6.	15.	8.	24.
OVAL		1.	V	8.	17.	14.	32.
BEGIN							

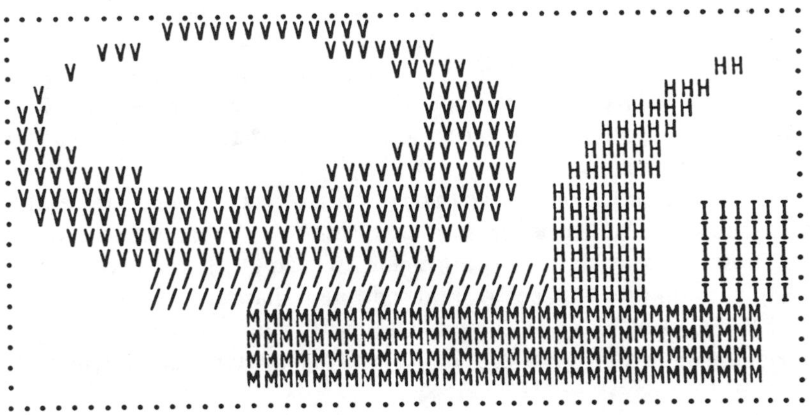

Figure 21-4. ARTPRIN Art Language and Resulting Picture

gram stems from the work pioneered by Katherine Nash and Robert Williams in 1968.[2] It is one of the art programs currently in use at the University of Minnesota in a studio arts course entitled "Art and Computers,"[3] which provides a nontechnical introduction to basic art concepts and the use of computers as an art medium.

Each shape in program ARTPRIN has a starting row and a starting column. For the oval shape, this starting location is its center. The frame shape starts at its upper left-hand corner. Figure 21–4 shows only the first twenty rows and the first fifty columns of the "usual" page for clarity. The location "row 1, column 1" is in the upper left-hand corner of the picture. A second example of program ARTPRIN is shown in figure 21–5. This picture has been made from oval and box shapes only. There are four separate levels on which the forms may be arranged. The final picture is a superposition of these four levels. Any shape that is placed on a given level "erases" any portion of the previous shapes on the same level that are "underneath" the latest shape.

To clarify this aspect, figure 21–6 shows three pairs of overlapping ovals. The ovals in the first pair are on different levels, so where they overlap, two symbols are printed. The right-hand pair of ovals is on the same level, so that the first oval printed is partially replaced by the second oval's symbols. The crescent was produced in the same manner as the right-hand pair, only the second oval was made out of the "blank" symbol.

Figure 21–7 shows the effects that can be achieved by sending an arrangement of shapes similar to those shown in figure 21–5 to a different output device, the dot plotter. If so instructed, program ARTPRIN exchanges a square-dot pattern for each of the letters used in the picture. The square used for the symbol is 10 dots high and 10 dots wide. The letters of the alphabet are replaced by a tone ranging in twenty-six steps from light to dark. The symbol "A" is a light tone with no dots present, "M" is a medium tone with about half of the dots present in the square, and "Z" is the black tone with all the dots in the square present. A selection of letters and their associated dot patterns is shown in figure 21–8. Figures 21–9 to 21–11 show a selection of images that have been made by using ARTPRIN and the dot plotter.[4]

In this manner, a program can be written which could be run repeatedly by anyone who had learned its nontechnical "art" language, with different visual results for each new arrangement of shapes. The person using this program could move shapes around, add new shapes, and alter the size of existing shapes as ideas developed. The most important considerations for developing such a program are that (1) the art language is straightforward,

Figure 21-5. ARTPRIN: Ovals and Boxes

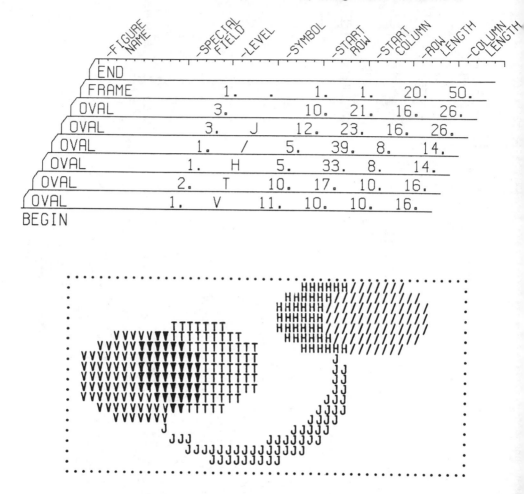

FIGURE NAME	SPECIAL FIELD	LEVEL	SYMBOL	START ROW	START COLUMN	ROW LENGTH	COLUMN LENGTH
END							
FRAME		1.	.	1.	1.	20.	50.
OVAL		3.		10.	21.	16.	26.
OVAL		3.	J	12.	23.	16.	26.
OVAL		1.	/	5.	39.	8.	14.
OVAL		1.	H	5.	33.	8.	14.
OVAL		2.	T	10.	17.	10.	16.
OVAL		1.	V	11.	10.	10.	16.

BEGIN

Figure 21-6. Effects of ARTPRIN's Levels

(2) the shapes are basic, (3) the instruction booklet is clear and easy to follow, and (4) the program is flexible. If these considerations are met, a wide variety of interesting and appealing pictures is possible; furthermore, the program may be enjoyed by a broad range of people. These types of "picture" programs can be useful in teaching basic art concepts and developing a sensitivity toward aesthetics. With this approach, a person with a non-technical background can use the computer in a visually creative way without being hindered by the technical details of computer programming.

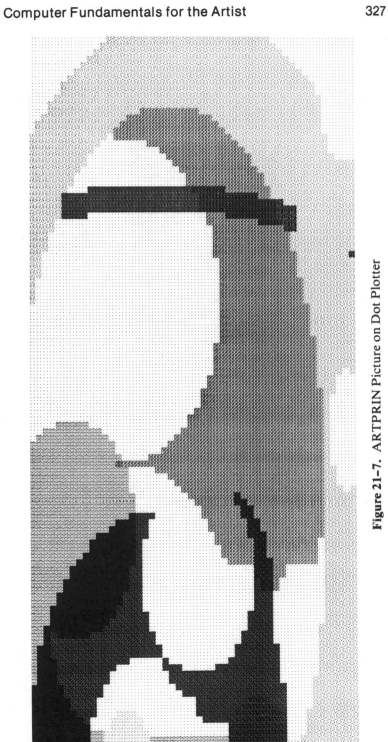

Figure 21-7. ARTPRIN Picture on Dot Plotter

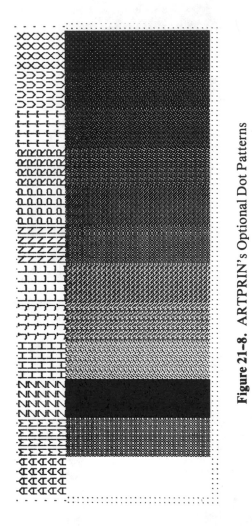

Figure 21–8. ARTPRIN's Optional Dot Patterns

Figure 21-9. ARTPRIN Picture by Caprice Glaser

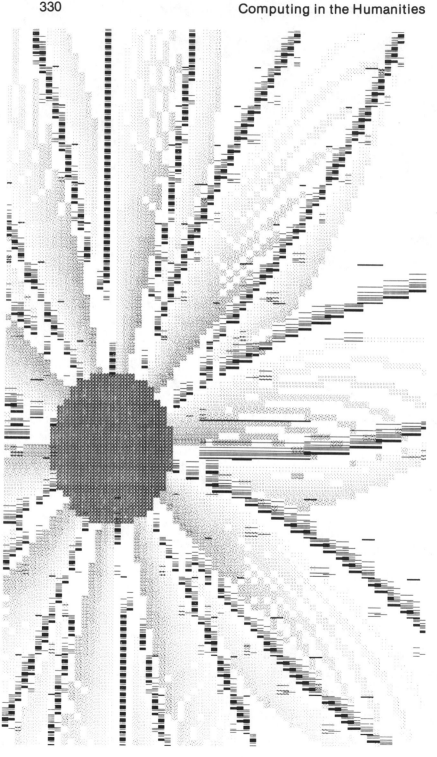

Figure 21–10. ARTPRIN Picture by Romulo Faria

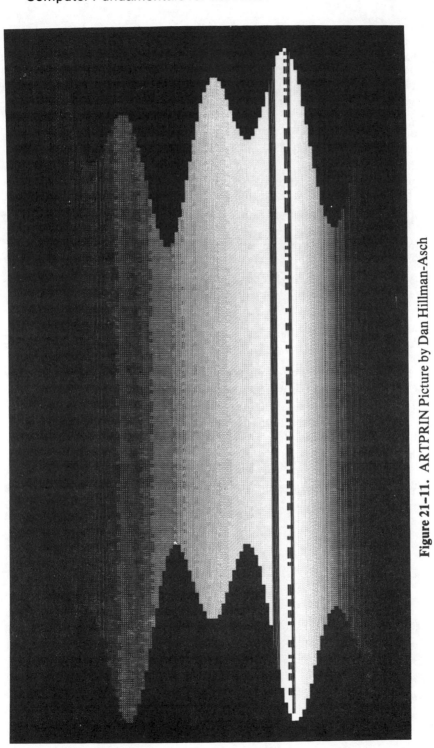

Figure 21–11. ARTPRIN Picture by Dan Hillman-Asch

ARTPLOT

Program ARTPLOT is conceptually very similar to ARTPRIN.[5] The main difference between the programs is that ARTPLOT uses a mechanical drawing device called a line plotter for its output device. ARTPLOT uses simple geometric shapes which can be placed anywhere on the drawing page and rotated or changed by a small amount, thus allowing for graceful curvatures not possible on ARTPRIN's output device, the printer. The variable format of ARTPLOT's drawing page is typically 10 inches wide by 12 inches high with its reference origin at the lower left-hand corner of the page. To specify a location on the page, one gives the number of inches horizontally from the left-hand edge and the number of inches vertically from the bottom of the sheet. Similarly, the sizes of the shapes are specified as their width and height in inches. Typically, each shape requires a new command as input to the program, although there is a "repeat" command, also found in program ARTPRIN, which generates any number of evenly varying shapes with a single command. Figures 21-12 to 21-14 show pictures that have been made by using program ARTPLOT.[6]

ARTSURF

With this program, one sets up any number of flat surfaces and specifies the position from which the surfaces will be viewed. The locations for peaks and valleys are then selected by telling ARTSURF their positions with respect to the left and bottom edges of the surface and by specifying their distance above or below the surface itself. These peaks and valleys are added to the surface and can be cone-shaped, spire-shaped, or wave-shaped (as if created by a pebble thrown into water). The program displays the resulting surfaces on a flat paper, using the line plotting output device in the fashion shown in figures 21-15 and 21-16.

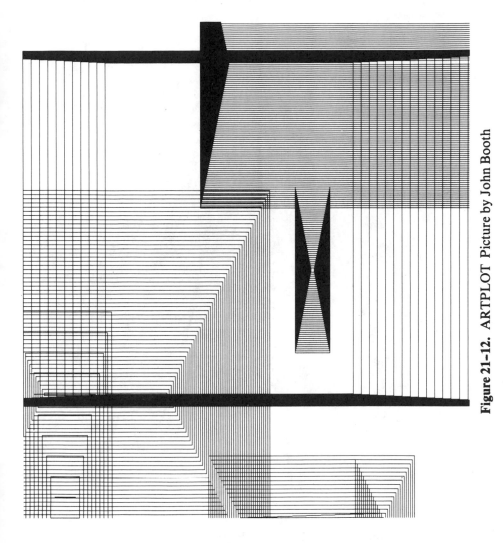

Figure 21-12. ARTPLOT Picture by John Booth

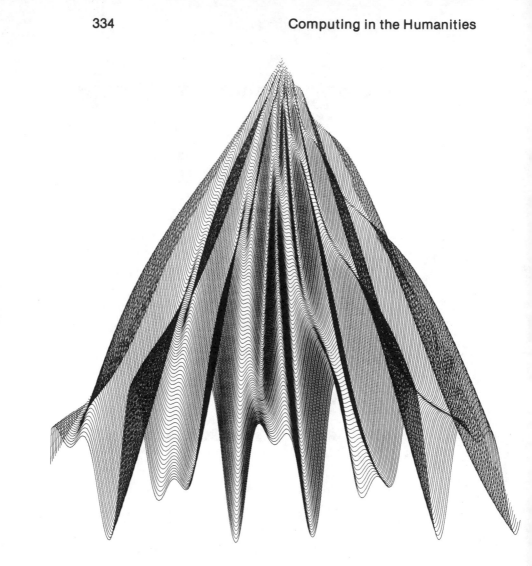

Figure 21-13. ARTPLOT Picture by Jerry Brandt

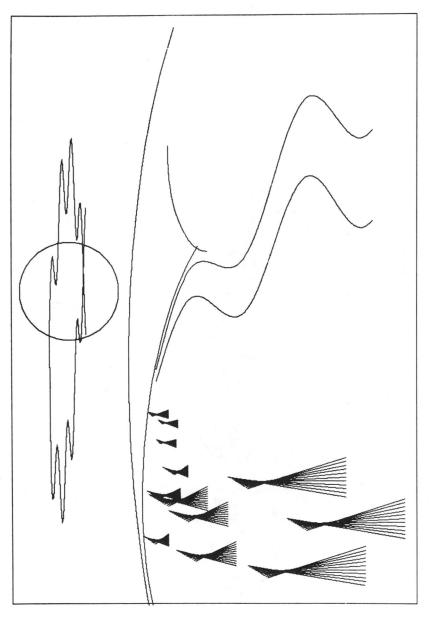

Figure 21–14. "Harvest Moon" by Kevin McMahon

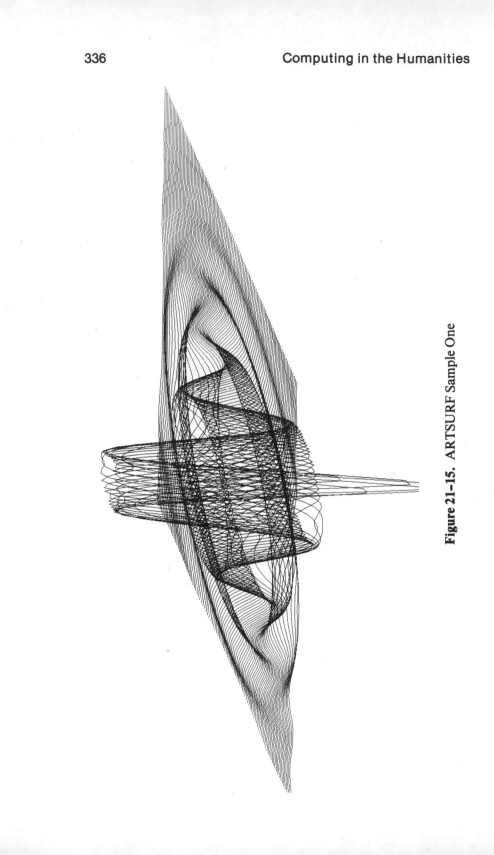

Figure 21–15. ARTSURF Sample One

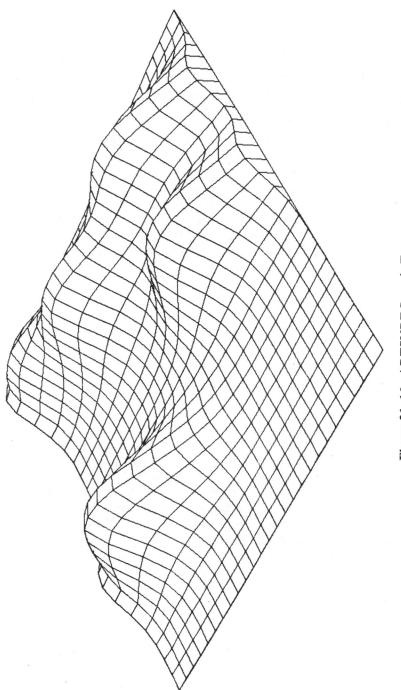

Figure 21-16. ARTSURF Sample Two

WEAVE

This program was designed for use by weavers and pattern designers. The program utilizes a series of pattern-manipulating routines called MEXPLOR which were written by Ken Knowlton at Bell Laboratories of New Jersey.[7] With this program, the weaver describes the way in which the harnesses and peddles of a loom are to be set, as well as the tone of the warp and weft materials. Four tones are allowed in this program: white, light gray, dark gray, and black. The peddle sequence is then given, and the resulting pattern is displayed. As a second method of using WEAVE, a pattern designer can describe a pattern unit and instruct the computer program to place that pattern at various locations on its display area of 140 rows by 140 columns. These units can be rotated or enlarged and mixed with other pattern units as the work develops. The finished pattern is then printed on either a dot plotter or a printer. Figures 21–17 to 21–19 were produced by using program WEAVE, by Debra Millard, whose artwork is reviewed in chapter 25 of this book.

ARTPICT

This program employs "picture processing" techniques similar to those used in reconstructing the picture signals sent to earth from spacecraft near the moon, Mars, and now Jupiter. The interested user begins with a 35-mm slide and has its image digitized by a special device in a fashion similar to that used for Wirephotos. During the digitizing process, a fine grid is superimposed on the slide, and the light transmitted through each small box or picture element (pixel) is recorded as a number between 0 (no light makes it through the slide) and 63 (all the light makes it through) onto magnetic tape similar to that used in a tape recorder. ARTPICT "reads" this tape of picture information along with the commands selecting the reconstruction method to be used, cropping and expansion values, and a selection of other features. The reconstructed image is displayed on a dot plotter by means of dot patterns from an evenly divided gray scale. A single photographic image can be reconstructed any number of times in different ways by which the user of the program can explore a broad range of visual effects. See figures 21–20 and 21–21.

Figure 21–17. "Interweave" by Debra Millard ▶

Figure 21–18. "A Measure of Light" by Debra Millard

Figure 21–19. "Fretwork" by Debra Millard

Figure 21-20. ARTPICT Image, Coarse Resolution

Figure 21-21. ARTPICT Image, Fine Resolution

ARTSINE

The basic visual element of program ARTSINE is a curved line. A sequence of these curves is positioned on a page 10 inches wide by 12 inches high. The height, length, and starting position of each curve are specified as input to the program. As each curve is drawn, it is divided into many parts and is optionally connected to the corresponding part on the last curve drawn. The curves can range from a dot to a fairly complicated curve. The final image is displayed on a line-plotting device. See figures 21-22 and 21-23.

ARTDOTS

Program ARTDOTS sets up a grid of small boxes. The size of these boxes is set by the user of the program. The boxes can be separated by a space, or touching, and are filled with dot patterns from sixty-four degrees of gray shades. The final image is displayed on a dot plotter. See figures 21-24 and 21-25.

MEXPLOR

The MEXPLOR package is a variation of the EXPLOR routines written by Ken Knowlton at Bell Laboratories of New Jersey.[8] This package consists of several FORTRAN routines that can be used to manipulate the tones stored in a grid of 140 by 140 cells. Each cell can be one of four tones: white, light gray, dark gray, or black. By writing a FORTRAN program, this display grid can be filled up with a phenomenal variety of different patterns and allows the user to explore various effects. This set of routines is extremely flexible and can be used in a wide range of applications. The final image can be displayed on either the dot plotter or a printer. See figure 21-26.

Today many programs exist all over the world which can be used by the artist to create visual imagery. These programs depend on the type of computer used, the type of input and output devices available, and the vision and proficiency of the designer. Many of the references at the end of this chapter include examples from a variety of these programs, most notably those books by H. Franke, J. Reichardt, F. Malina, R. Leavitt, and J. Benthall.[9]

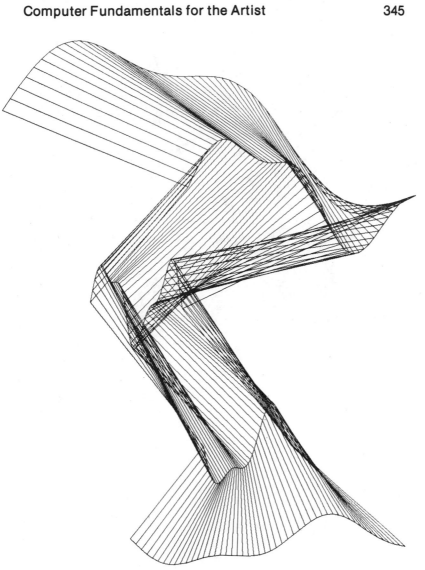

Figure 21–22. ARTSINE Sample One

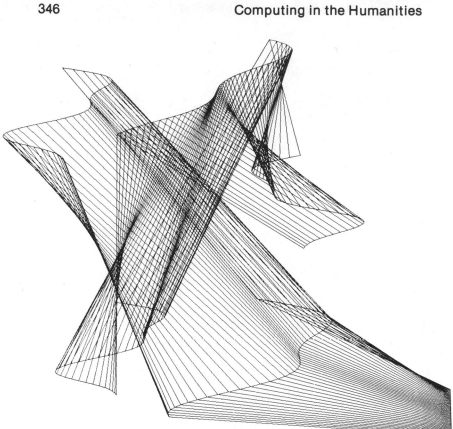

Figure 21–23. ARTSINE Sample Two

Figure 21–24. ''Perception'' by Kevin McMahon

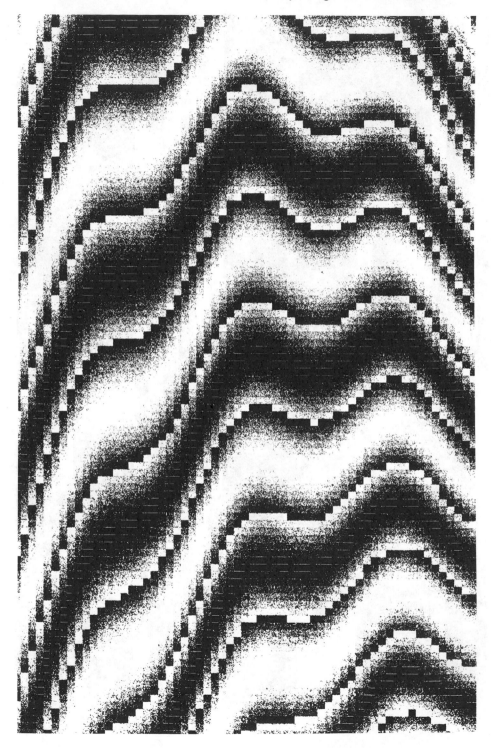

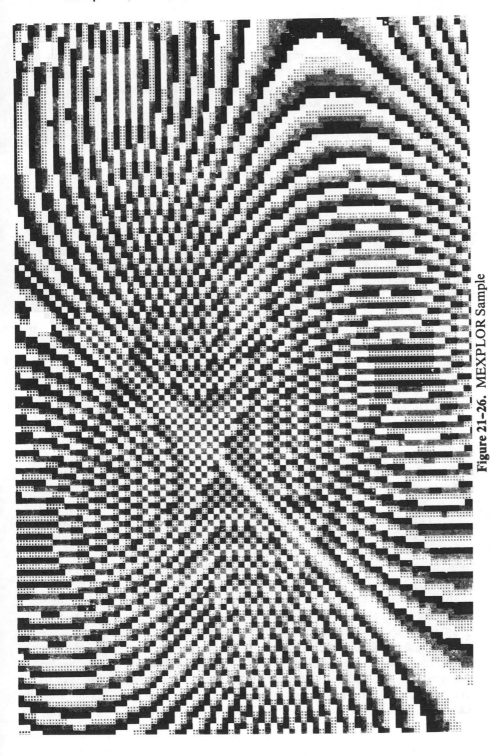

Figure 21-26. MEXPLOR Sample

Computer Hardware

To the artist, the most important aspects of computer hardware are those that relate to the creation and manipulation of the image. What are the methods that are used to "input" or send information into a computer, and on what type of "output" devices does the final image, be it a sketch or a completed work, appear? How is the idea transformed into a tangible visual image? This section reviews the multitude of input and output devices that can be used in the creation of visual imagery.

Input Devices

The characteristic process of an input device is that some human physiological action, usually a hand or an arm movement, is transformed into an electric signal that can be detected by a computer. Each input device has a finite set of unique options from which the human makes choices. This set can be likened to the English alphabet of twenty-six letters. To make a word, one chooses from one to several letters and arranges them sequentially. Only some of the arrangements of letters represent meaningful English words. In like manner, the designer of a computer program determines when and how the program will interpret a particular input sequence.

An example of a common input device is a modified typewriter. As a key is pressed, its characteristic, unique numeric code is sent to the computer. The computer can be programmed to detect any signals coming from this device and to store them in memory. From these stored codes, the identity and order of the keys that were pressed can be determined. By comparing the resulting sequence of numbers with a table of "meaningful" or anticipated codes, as determined by the program designer, various specific actions or effects, such as adding a shape to the picture, can be initiated.

A card reader is an input device that detects the unique code for each symbol or character punched in a standard computer card and then transmits this code to the computer. The letters, numbers, punctuation marks, and special symbols are printed across the top of the card, and their respective codes are punched into the columns below each symbol by means of a special typewriterlike device called a "keypunch machine." The particular computer program that reads the card information prescribes the arrangement and interpretation of that information. The person who uses the program learns this card format and selects the program features by typing the appropriate symbols in the card columns. The program instruction booklet describes these formats and interpretations in detail. Use of the card reader requires that this entire set of instructions for the program, in addition to accounting and program-access information, be included in one deck of cards. This deck of commands is read into the computer and treated as one complete task. For instance, if the program displays a picture, this image is determined completely by the information in the deck of cards. To vary the picture, new instructions could be added or removed from the deck, depending on the particular program design.

Another input device, the keyboard, is usually associated with an output device such as a printer or a screen (cathode-ray tube). As keys are pressed, a code is sent to the computer, and the symbol is displayed on the screen. After a row of symbols is typed and detected, the computer program determines the requested action and performs this action if the command is in its repertoire. In contrast to the card reader, each line of information is processed immediately, and depending on the associated display device and program, the action is performed or an error message such as "unrecognized command" is issued. This method of using a computer is called "interactive" computing. If the picture-making program is cleverly written and the display device is suitable for displaying the picture or a facsimile of it, the changes that are being made may be viewed immediately. (See chapter 23 for a description of one such interactive program.)

Magnetic tape or disk machines are often used as input devices for programs. The information on them is usually prepared by means of a computer program. A simple case would be a program that transfers information from a deck of cards onto a disk. This program would read the information from the input device, a card reader, and write the same information on its output device, the disk drive. A different program could then read the information from the disk drive, now an input device, and process it accordingly. The advantages of these flexible media are speed, compact size, and versatility (in that the same piece of magnetic material can be used over and over for coding new information). In contrast, the above-mentioned punched cards cannot be erased, so that only one set of information can be encoded on a given card. Disks are the most convenient storage medium, second only to the computer memory itself, which is used for only very short-term storage. Disks are often used for storage of programs and input data.

The graphics tablet is an input device that has a closely spaced grid similar to a piece of graph paper. As a penlike drawing instrument is moved around on the tablet, its position is sent to the computer. A program can be written that will read the current pen position hundreds of times each second and display a series of lines representing the path over which the pen has moved on an associated output display device. Further programming can allow portions of the stored path to be replaced with newly drawn paths or mixed with several earlier paths. Other variations such as enlargement, reduction, and distortion are possible. This device is typically used for tracing the outline of a map or other complex shape and storing it for future use.

The light-pen and its special screen are quite analogous to the graphics tablet. The screen has a grid that can detect where the light from a small flashlightlike pen strikes. A program can be written that records the path of this light-pen in the computer memory. Once the path is stored, it can be modified in the ways mentioned in the graphics-tablet description. As an example, a program could first record any path drawn on the screen and then detect ten additional screen positions. The initial path could then be repeated ten times, so that each copy started at one of the ten input positions. The final picture would then have eleven repeated curves.

A variation of the light-pen and screen is a special screen which has two thumb-wheel knobs and cross hairs. Each knob controls a line, one horizontal and one vertical, that is displayed on the screen. The horizontal line can be positioned across the screen at any position between the bottom and the top by rotating the appropriate knob. In like manner, the vertical line can be positioned anywhere between the left and right edges of the screen. The intersection of these two lines defines one screen position that can be read by a program. This technique for determining screen positions is similar to and slower than the graphics tablet.

A joy-stick input device also resembles the graphics tablet. In addition to the pen's horizontal and vertical locations being sent to the computer, the third dimension, the distance that the pen is above or below the tablet itself, is also sent. In this fashion the hand control can be moved through space, and the three-dimensional path of the drawing tool can be stored in the computer. With appropriate display techniques, a three-dimensional object can be represented on the output device. An alternative method of recording three-dimensional paths has been developed, employing the graphics tablet. In this case, several cross sections, or outlines, are drawn and interpreted by the program as the various levels in the third dimension.

Another input device is the tracking ball. This device is similar to the thumb-wheel knobs and cross hairs, and it combines the motion of the two knobs into a single rotational motion of a ball. As the ball is moved, two internal knobs are repositioned according to the horizontal and vertical elements of the rotation. This information is sent to the computer as finely spaced horizontal and vertical locations. One application of this device allows for the selection of a color from a range of graduated shades of primary hues. As the tracking-ball position is changed, a position marker on a color TV monitor is moved to the corresponding color patch of the color chart and indicates the current color. This color is then applied to the selected region of the picture, which is also being displayed.

The last input device to be described is the photographic slide digitizer. This device relies on a technique similar to that of the Wirephoto. A finely spaced grid is superimposed on the slide image, and the image is scanned with a beam of light. A sensor detects the amount of light that makes it through the slide at each grid position and records its numeric value on magnetic tape. For black-and-white information, the slide is scanned once through a neutral gray filter, and the light codes are scaled from 0 (no light comes through the slide) to 63 (all the light makes it through the slide). The same approach is used to digitize a colored slide, but the slide is scanned three times, each time through a red, green, or blue filter, in a fashion similar to the color-separation printing technique. Once the slide has been digitized and stored on magnetic tape, a program can read this picture information, process or alter the information, and display the new image on an output device.

Output Devices

Most computer output devices fall into one of three categories: printers, cathode-ray tubes (CRTs), or plotters. Within each of these categories there are three subcategories that describe the basic visual element: the character, the dot, and the line. Because of the rapid growth of technology during the last decade, these categories refer to the functional descriptions of the devices, rather than to the actual physical machines. Today, it is not uncommon for a single, versatile machine to fall into two or three of these categories. The characteristic process for an output device is that some code is received from a computer and, according to the design of the device, transformed to some electromechanical action which results in a mark being made on some medium, typically paper, film, plastic, or a phosphorescent screen. These marks are usually made with inks or light beams.

The printing device has a set of characters or symbols that can be printed. A computer sends a numeric code to the printing device, which in turn selects the associated character, prints it into the current column position on the paper, and moves the position marker to the next column on the row in a fashion similar to that of a typewriter. Printers are the earliest and the most commonly used of the output devices. These machines can print up to 1,200 lines of type in one minute, and usually they have fixed character spacing, such that an "m" receives the same space as an "i," for instance. Computer programs such as ARTPRIN can use this output device to display regions of texture rather than rows of English text and tables.

Cathode-ray tubes use a process that is quite similar to that of a television screen, in that the display is produced by means of a phosphor-coated screen. There is usually no "hard copy," or piece of paper, associated with the screen image, so that as a new image is created, it replaces the previous screen image. Most CRTs display characters on the screen in a fashion similar to the printers; namely, a code is sent from the computer, causing the associated character to be displayed at the current screen position and the screen position marker to be moved to the next screen position.

Line-plotting devices are mechanical drawing machines that typically move a pen on a piece of paper. The pen can travel a specified number of steps in either the horizontal direction or the vertical direction. There are up to 200 steps in 1 inch. The computer first sends a command to lift the pen off the paper or to place it down against the paper. It then sends a pen-movement command which specifies the direction and the number of steps of the movement. A higher-level language might request that a circle be plotted in the middle of the drawing page. The computer program that interprets this language would then check to see if the plotter is on, lift the pen off the paper, move it to the beginning of the circle, and move the pen in tiny steps along the various directions that approximate the circle. This type of plotting device can also plot letters or characters by making them out of small lines.

Dot-plotting devices utilize a different display technique. The computer sends a series of 1s and 0s to the device, causing it to display a row of dots. For the simplest case, the 1 corresponds to a white dot (or no dot). A picture is made by sending many rows of dots with the appropriate 1s and 0s. This type of plotting device can display lines by placing the dots close together. Typically, up to 200 dots can be placed in 1 inch.

This completes the basic functional descriptions of the typical output devices. As mentioned above, these techniques are combined in the more versatile, current output devices. Many printing devices can also plot by means of closely spaced dots, in the fashion of the dot-plotting devices. Many CRT screens are now color displays and can use the colored dot-plotting techniques as well. Many plotting devices now display colored dots or lines on film or paper. This wide range of innovative output display devices promises a future of more exciting possibilities for the artists of tomorrow.

Notes

1. For a perceptive, readable, and enjoyable overview, see Joseph Weisenbaum, *Computer Power and Human Reason* (San Francisco: W.H. Freeman and Co., 1976).

2. Katherine Nash and Robert Williams, "Computer Program for Artists: ART 1," *Leonardo* 3(1970):439–442; Robert Williams, "Statistical Shading Using Digital Computer Program ART2," *Leonardo* 4(1971): 365–367.

3. Tom Buck and Kevin McMahon, "Program ARTPRIN," University Computer Center documentation, University of Minnesota, 1980; Kevin McMahon, "Program ARTPLOT," University Computer Center documentation, University of Minnesota (1977).

4. Figure 21-9, courtesy of Caprice Glaser; figure 21-10, courtesy of Romulo Faria; figure 21-11, courtesy of Dan Hillman-Asch.

5. Kevin McMahon, "Program ARTPLOT," University Computer Center documentation, University of Minnesota (1977).

6. Figure 21-12, courtesy of John Booth; figure 21-13, courtesy of Jerry Brandt.

7. Ken Knowlton, "EXPLOR—A Generator of Images from Explicit Patterns, Local Operations, and Randomness," *Proceedings of the Ninth Annual UAIDE Meeting,* Miami Beach, Fla., 1970, pp. 543-583; "A Report on the Use of Fortran-Coded EXPLOR for the Teaching of Computer Graphics and Computer Art," *Proceedings of ACM SIGPLAN Symposium on 2-D Man-Machine Communication,* Los Alamos, New Mexico, October 1972.

8. Ken Knowlton, "EXPLOR—A Generator of Images from Explicit Patterns, Local Operations, and Randomness," *Proceedings of the Ninth Annual UAIDE Meeting,* Miami Beach, Fla., 1970, pp. 543-583; "A Report on the Use of Fortran-Coded EXPLOR for the Teaching of Computer Graphics and Computer Art," *Proceedings of ACM SIGPLAN Symposium on 2-D Man-Machine Communication,* Los Alamos, New Mexico, October 1972; "Collaborations with Artists—A Programmer's Reflections," in *Graphic Languages,* edited by F. Nake and A. Rosenfeld (Amsterdam: North-Holland Publishing Co., 1972), pp. 399-418.

9. Herbert Franke, *Computer Graphics, Computer Art* (London: Phaidon Press, 1971), p. 60; Jasia Reichardt, *The Computer in Art,* London: Studio Vista (1971); Jasia Reichardt, *Cybernetic Serendipity* (New York: Praeger Publishers, 1969); *Visual Art, Mathematics and Computers,* selections from the Journal *Leonardo,* edited by Frank Malina (United Kingdom: Pergamon Press, 1979); Ruth Leavitt, ed., *Artist and Computer,* (New York: Harmony Books, 1976); Jonathan Benthall, *Science and Technology in Art Today* (New York: Praeger Publishers, 1972).

References

Journal *Leonardo,* various issues, 1967-1980.

Computer Graphics and Art, various issues, 1976-1980.

Douglas Davis, *Art in the Future, A History-Prophecy of the Collaboration between Science, Technology and Art* (New York: Praeger Publishers, 1973).

Jeffrey Lomax, ed., *Computers in the Creative Arts,* (London: National Computing Centre, Limited, 1973).

Pierre Couland, ed., "IBM Informatique No. 13", (Paris: IBM France, 1975).

22

A Gallery of Artists: Katherine Nash

Kevin McMahon and
Renee A. Holoien

Katherine Nash is a pioneer in the field of computer art. A sculptor and art teacher by profession, she has readily seen ways in which computers could be used in teaching basic art concepts while simultaneously providing the student with a better understanding of this ubiquitous force. In general, art students are not exposed to the more technical courses in science; likewise, students in the sciences are not versed in art.

In 1968, Nash worked with Richard Williams, a professor in engineering at the University of New Mexico, on an art program called "ART 1."[1] This program was later brought to the University of Minnesota and implemented on the computer system there. This program set the stage for the program style and spirit of the development that was to follow. ART 1 and its successors form a series of art programs notable for their simplicity and the ease with which artists with no technological background can use them. Experience and innovation have altered the art languages drastically, yet the spirit of a nontechnical approach to computer imagery has remained steadfast. These art programs have been used by Nash in various computer art courses at the University of Minnesota. Because of the minimal computer training required to use them, they have been particularly effective as vehicles to introduce students to the computer. In addition, Nash believes that the educational value of personal contact with the machine should be stressed, for such contact serves as a strong motivational force and aids in alleviating some of the alienation an artist might feel toward a machine. She feels that twenty years of a computerized society make it apparent that in twenty years no artist will be able to ignore the computer and will have to adjust to it, cope with it, or use it. He or she will not be able to reject it, for it will influence the artist's creative thinking, as all aspects of society have always influenced the artist. The computer will be another tool for creativity.

Students have enthusiastically experimented with a variety of methods to enhance output from the art programs. These include multicolor overlays obtained from colored gels, lithographs and silkscreen facilitated by means of microfilm output and photographic techniques, sandwiches of glass and gels to give the illusion of depth, computer films, and special papers. Nash has lacked the preconceived notions that most computer programmers grow up with as to what computers can and cannot do, thus encouraging her stu-

357

dents to use their imaginations. Many effects were achieved after the usual immediate responses of "That's impossible!" or "That's too hard!" Her constant requests to the computer center to put fresh ribbons and unruled paper into the printers and not to fold the output continue to raise the eyebrows of the computer operators.

As a sculptor of international repute, Nash finds it interesting that several computer artists are sculptors and suggests that it is because they have minds that can deal with technological and mechanical problems, that their minds are more geared to contemplating a new kind of machine.[2] Nash's computer work involves bold geometric shapes, suggesting an influence of her sensibilities as a sculptor. Just as she has insisted on being active in every phase of production of even the large cast-bronze sculptures, Nash is reluctant to use computer programs that generate random forms automatically, preferring to remain directly involved with every aspect of the design process. To her, the artist necessarily creates the order and the form. She has no pretensions about why she works with a computer and regards the machine simply as a useful tool for the contemporary artist.

Through her untiring efforts at making the computer a tool accessible to her students in studio art, Nash has done great service to this developing field in the fine arts. Now Professor Emeritus at the University of Minnesota, she continues to coinstruct the "Art and Computers" course for the studio arts department and to share her philosophy of computer art. See figures 22–1 and 22–2.

Notes

1. Katherine Nash and Richard Williams, "Computer Program for Artists: ART 1," *Leonardo* 3(1970):439–442.
2. Bill Johnson, "Retractable Art," *Minnesota Technolog,* January 1973.

Figure 22–1. *Firefly*

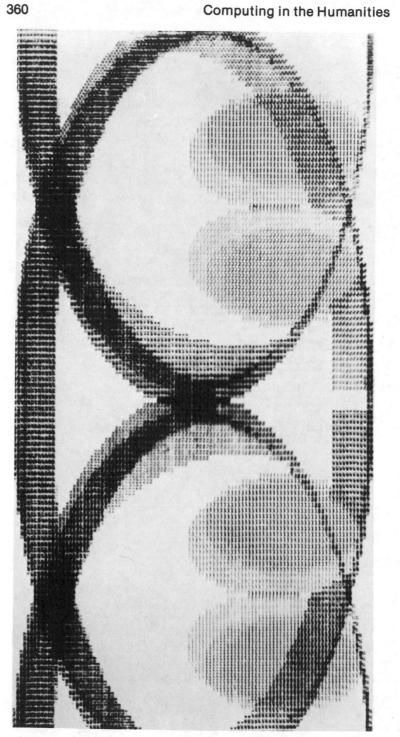

Figure 22–2. *Lobes in Space*

23

A Gallery of Artists: Ruth Leavitt

Renee A. Holoien

Ruth Leavitt produced her first professional one-woman show of computer-aided graphics at the Martin Gallery in Minneapolis, Minnesota, in 1972. The work exhibited was created with the aid of a program that allowed drawing with a light-pen and a cathode-ray tube housed at the University of Minnesota Space Science Center. This program, created by Jay Leavitt, detected the light-pen's movements across the screen and displayed a line indicating the path of the light-pen. An area of the screen could be optionally filled in with patterns and textures. Leavitt experimented with not only the imagery itself, but also enhancement of the output as well. The printer, for example, was made to print in color onto quality printmaker's paper. She transferred imagery from both the printer and the line plotter onto light-sensitive colored plastics, which were layered to create finished artworks, and individually phototransferred the images to produce editions of colored prints.

During 1973 and 1974, Leavitt's graphics were shown at many places across the United States, as well as in such countries as Japan, France, England, and Canada. She lectured to various groups and published papers on her work. In spite of the success that this work enjoyed, however, she felt limited by the computer program she had been using, for no matter how freely she drew with the light-pen, the designs created were ultimately resolved into a grid. Furthermore, she felt frustration as a painter unable to render as paintings the complicated images produced with the computer. This dissatisfaction, coupled with an increased knowledge of computers, led to the idea for Leavitt's "stretching" program. As a child, she had had a rubber dollar bill whose image could be distorted by stretching it in different ways. The stretching program would use the computer to simulate a rubber sheet so that the artist could stretch any pattern she chose to draw on it. The patterns would begin in a hard-edge, constructivist style, but distortion would impart the lyrical quality of abstract expressionism [1]. Many questions had to be answered before the program could be written. How would the surface move? How would the pattern deform? How would the artist communicate with the computer? After much discussion between the artist and the programmer, Jay Leavitt, the program was written.

The concern now became how things change. The Leavitts have been interested in the kind of shapes that appear in nonfigurative pictures, sometimes called "geometric abstract" and "concrete" art, and some of the ways that the shapes can be altered by a chosen procedure of deformation. In an example discussed in the Leavitts' 1976 article [2], the initial design consists of a pattern of repeated straight-line geometric shapes or design units, with a blank area in the middle of the composition. If forces are then applied at selected points in the design and essentially within the plane of the sheet, the design will be deformed. An initial design can be deformed into countless variations by varying the magnitude, direction, and location of the forces.

When the artist is about to begin a computer drawing, she makes a series of sketches showing the overall compositions of the pictures that she wishes to obtain. These sketches, which are simply gestures of movement, are drawn on graph paper, each within a 1.00×1.00 unit grid defined by an x axis and a y axis. The sketches are then used to decide where and how deforming forces are to be applied to the initial design. In the computer program, straight-line vectors are the means for representing applied deforming forces. The coordinates of the vector's tail indicate where a deforming force is first applied; those of its head define where it is terminated. A force need not be applied directly to any point in the design. Neither the head nor the tail may lie on or be outside an outer edge of the design. A list of the coordinate points of the heads and tails is compiled for instructing the computer.

The computer program is written in FORTRAN for an interactive system, which has the advantage that a display of the picture occurs immediately after the forces and patterns are specified and that changes can be effected within minutes. The program is stored on a disk. When the program is initiated, it requests: under what name the resulting picture representation should be stored for possible future processing and the number of times a pattern should be repeated along each side in making the initial design. The program permits the user to request from two to nine repetitions of the pattern unit. The program first scales the display to yield an initial design of the desired size. It then generates the full set of points needed to represent the entire initial design. The program poses three questions that are repeated for consideration while the picture is being made: (1) Is a display of its current picture with all its points desired? (2) Should the deformation procedure be terminated and the final picture be drawn on microfilm? (3) What are the coordinates of the tail and of the head of the next force vector to change the current picture? As soon as the coordinates of the head and tail are given, the computer adjusts every point in the design to reflect the new distortion. When work with the computer program is terminated, the final coordinates of the points for each of the selected pictures are stored on a disk for the next stage, for example, that of drawing the image onto microfilm. The primary advantage of microfilm is that reproductions in other print media and in other sizes can be made from it readily.

It is easier to store and significantly more economical than other media. To produce paintings with oils, Leavitt projects microfilm negatives onto the canvas. She also uses microfilm negatives to produce high-contrast separations for phototransfer graphic processes such as those used in serigraphy and lithography.

Leavitt has explored several patterns with this program: a linear one, one dealing with mass, a three-dimensional projected object, and so on. Each series is unique, comprises a new style, and even requires its own method of stretching. She has used this stretching program to create graphics and paintings and has begun to use a variation of the program which incorporates transformations for making animated films. She and the programmer collaborated to make the program allow expansion, contraction, and rotation of the surface, as well as provide the capability for transforming designs.

Previous to 1978, output from the computer had been in the form of lines drawn on black and white, 35-mm film. The artist projected the image onto the canvas to transfer the design and then painted in a traditional manner. In 1978, however, the program was extended to define within the machine each point on the surface of the image, adding the capability for design in three dimensions. This information allows the artist either to work in color, for the creation of color film animations, or to produce sculpture with a computer-driven milling machine. What Leavitt finds very exciting about this approach is that the computer allows her to consistently examine an idea while expressing it in different media.

Through this work, several different avenues of investigation have been presented. One idea is to "deform" color, that is, to use gradations to indicate stretching or contraction. Alternate procedures for deforming an initial unit are being considered. These include (1) deformations related to the phenomena of magnetic attraction and repulsion, (2) the simultaneous depiction of stages in the deformation of an initial design, and (3) the use of compound nonlinear vectors (spirals, for example). Leavitt considers that the use of a vector-oriented computer display would be an improvement in the method because the user could see the computer drawing while it is being made.

To Leavitt, the computer acts as a multifaceted tool which she controls. Although not actually writing the programs herself, by gradually becoming more familiar with the machine's operations, she knows better what can be expected of the computer and how to convey those expectations to the programmer. Just as Jackson Pollock would control the amount and direction of paint poured on a canvas, so, too, an artist using this method controls the amount and direction of deformation of a pattern. Like an abstract expressionist painter, a computer artist also finds that "nice accidents" occur. Each of the works begins its life in a static order and becomes "humanized" when an artist imparts a feeling of energy to the design. The orderliness of the "concrete" school of painting is not lost in the process of deforming the design. On the contrary, the artist feels that the "expression-ist" style intermingles with the "concrete" style to form a harmonious final picture [2]. In her book *Artist and Computer,* Ruth Leavitt writes that she will continue to use the computer as long as she has access to it, since it allows her to create artworks that would probably be impossible to produce in any other reasonable way. She finds that she can now explore areas about which artists in the past could only dream [1]. See figures 23-1 and 23-2.

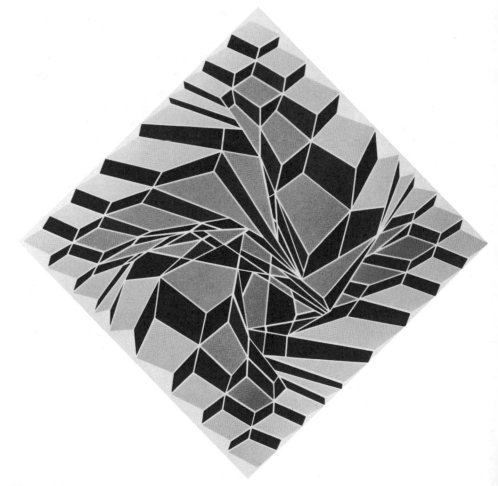

Figure 23-1. *Diamond, Variation I*

Figure 23-2. *Diamond, Variation II*

References

1. Leavitt, Ruth, ed. *Artist and Computer*. New York: Harmony Books, 1976, pp. 97–98.
2. Leavitt, Ruth, and Leavitt, Jay. "Pictures Based on Computer Drawings Made by Deforming an Initial Design." *Leonardo* 9(1976):99–103.

24
A Gallery of Artists:
Jean Davies Nordlund

Renee A. Holoien and
Kevin McMahon

Jean Nordlund is an artist and a weaver who has had an extensive background in design theory and application. While finishing her work at the University of Minnesota in 1977, she sat in on a lecture entitled ''The Computer as an Art Medium.'' Over the next few months, in collaboration with Kevin McMahon, the arts and humanities consultant for the University Computer Center, she helped design the WEAVE program. Nordlund had been weaving for several years and thus could provide technical knowledge in that area, in addition to working with the program and suggesting changes that would make it easier for a weaver to use for modeling particular loom weaving methods. The problems with which she was concerned involved placement of color by value (lightness or darkness) within a weaving pattern and development and variation of designs.

All this artist's work is double-woven, a process in which two layers of fabric are woven simultaneously, one above the other, intersecting each other at various intervals. The inherent nature of this weave creates startling juxtapositions of color fields, because one color can disappear below the surface into the lower level of cloth while the hidden color from the cloth below comes to the surface. The program WEAVE, discussed in some detail with regard to the work of Debra Millard in chapter 25 of this book, was written to accommodate specifications for the techniques of double-weaving. Using WEAVE, the artist determines a loom threading, a treadling tie-up, and a treadling sequence with a four-tone interpretation of the design. The finished computer sketch appears on either the printer or the dot plotter. The artist then interprets the plots with colors and, when a satisfying solution is achieved, sets her loom accordingly and weaves the design.

Use of the computer facilitates resolution of both design and color problems for the artist. There is the obvious advantage of speed which the computer offers, which allows the artist to test several designs in a short time. In addition, by systematically altering the pattern definition, a progression of subtle changes in the geometric design can be easily explored. This new perspective on the process of altering patterns and creating designs continues to serve as an essential tool in her weaving, even when she must work without computer assistance. Many design problems concerning the placement of color by value were resolved with the help of the positive-negative feature of WEAVE. By studying the often surprising changes resulting from this process, the artist became aware of the importance of visual contrast to the overall pattern and how this relates to the excess or lack of contrast in the design elements. A further dividend from using the computer was that unexpected "accidents" would occur and suggest pattern variations quite different from the current design. These variations would occasionally suggest a completely new direction in designing the pattern.

A random pattern-generating feature, on which Nordlund began to work with Kevin McMahon, but which was never operational while she was at the University of Minnesota, would be a valuable feature in the program, since it would allow for a more flexible design-creation process than presently available in WEAVE.

Jean Nordlund continues to show her weavings regularly in exhibitions across the country and still experiments with computer-assisted design when her travels bring her to the University of Minnesota. See figures 24-1 to 24-3.

Figure 24–1. *Relay*

Figure 24–2. Detail of *Relay*

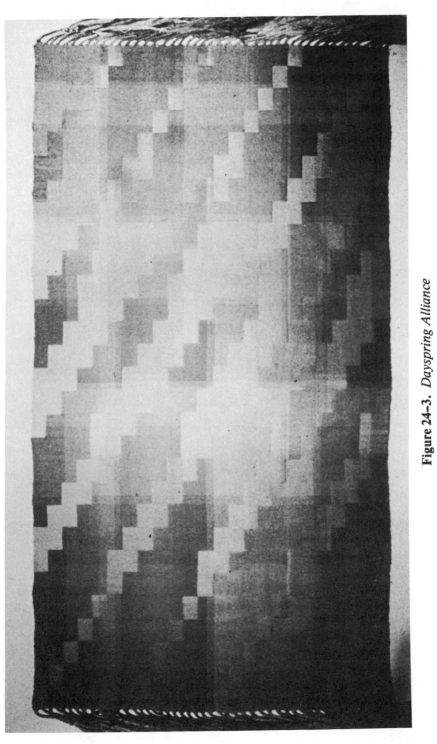

Figure 24–3. *Dayspring Alliance*

25 A Gallery of Artists: Debra Millard

Debra Millard

Debra Millard's master's-degree exhibition, *Exploration of Pattern: Computer Prints and Quilts,* shown in April 1979, was the culmination of a year's work developing patterns on a computerized design program and translating four of those patterns into quilts. The quilts were created with traditional construction techniques, using nontraditional color and pattern. Within each of three areas—pattern, color, and construction—limitations were established through preliminary studies so that alternative design solutions could be explored. The definition of the design problem for the quilts consisted of three basic limitations: the use of patterns created on a computerized design program, the use of subtle color gradations created by hand-dyeing fabrics, and the use of traditional quilt construction techniques.

Pattern

The essence of pattern is repetition, so that a unit of design, the module, is repeated to create the pattern. While repetition makes a pattern, variation makes it interesting. Variation, in this case, was created through the use of four values from black to white to create the module and through the rotation and placement of the module. The additional component of color was also involved in the design and construction of the quilts.

In this project, the module was a quilt block—a unit that can be stitched from small pieces of fabric. Squares were chosen as components of the modules for two reasons. First, woven fabric has horizontal and vertical structural lines and is therefore most easily handled when cut and sewn into squares or rectangles along these lines. Second, the computer is limited to working on a square grid. Features considered for future addition to the program might include the capability to incorporate such shapes as triangles or circles into a pattern.

The computer print patterns achieve variation and complexity through value changes in four steps from black to white. The values and their placement determine the character of the patterns. For example, when a square is adjoined by two other squares of the same value, one above or below it and the other on one side, the module and thus the pattern form right-angle shapes, creating a sense of solidness and weight (see figure 21-17). In contrast, when squares of the same value touch only at their corners, diagonal paths are formed (see figure 21-18). The diagonals create a sense of more movement and less weight. Further diversity can be achieved through the placement of values in relation to each other. For instance, the effect when black is placed next to white is quite different from the effect when black is placed next to dark gray. Black and white form the strongest of all contrasts, and the line created by their meeting is very definite. There is less contrast between black and dark gray, so the line created when they meet is less definite—almost out of focus, as illustrated by figure 21-19.

The Computer as a Tool for the Designer

Computers have long been used in the textile industry to design and mass-produce woven fabrics. However, they have been used very little by individual artists. The numeric and geometric structure of computer display machinery makes it particularly well suited to the needs of the quilt designer is producing strong, geometric patchwork designs. The computer manipulates design modules according to directions from the artist, and the result is an overall design or pattern. The machine does not take over the creative process, since the computer can do only what the designer tells it to do. The computer may actually enhance the creative process. Its main advantage is speed, by which it reduces the hours required to draw a complex pattern by hand to minutes. Since time then becomes a minor consideration, the artist can explore many designs. This may also encourage the artist to make changes, improving an already good design. As a tool for exploring many design alternatives quickly, the computer is invaluable.[1]

Computer programs written for the designer and the artist are generally written so that the user does not have to know computer programming. One program, WEAVE, is particularly suited for use by the contemporary patchwork-quilt designer. WEAVE was developed by Kevin McMahon, computer consultant for the arts at the University of Minnesota Computer Center. It allows quick exploration of design modules and the ways in which they work together to form patterns. Through various manipulations and repetitions of the module, the artist can create a series of related pattern designs.

The design module is defined in four values, black to white, and the modules are repeated across the page at locations specified by the designer. The work area is 140 rows by 140 columns. Design information is provided to the computer by punched cards. Key words—PATTERN, LOCATION, PRINT, PLOT, LIMIT, CLEAR, and NEGATIVE—and numeric directions for size and placement appear on these cards. The PATTERN card specifies the height and width of the module. The actual pattern-unit cards follow the PATTERN card. One pattern unit (module) row appears on each card with values defined as 0, 1, 2, and 3 (white to black). The LOCATION card indicates rows at which the previously specified pattern unit is to be "woven." PRINT and PLOT indicate the type of printing device to be used. The LIMIT card allows the designer to specify a beginning column and a number of times to repeat the design across the row. If this card is not used, the pattern design starts at column 1 and the module is repeated to fill up the workspace of 140 columns. The CLEAR card causes the design information to be erased with the computer. The NEGATIVE card produces a reversal of white to black values.

To make WEAVE more versatile, EXPAND and ROTATE functions were added to the program, at the suggestion of Millard. The EXPAND function increases the size of a small portion of the pattern. With the ROTATE function, the designer can include the number of degrees to rotate the module across the row and the position of the starting module. The rotation must take place in increments of 90 degrees. The module used must be a square and must have an odd number of rows and columns, so that the computer can identify a definite center for the module.

In the development of designs for these patterns, the speed at which the computer worked allowed over 100 patterns and their variations to be explored. The computer was able to produce a picture of a pattern in a matter of seconds, whereas a similar pattern hand-drawn on graph paper would have taken many hours. Thus, time that would have been needed for a tedious hand-rendered drawing could be devoted to the time-consuming task of creating the quilts.

Color

Since the patterns used for the quilts were visually complex in themselves, colors that were adjacent to each other in a color gradation and had common elements were chosen. A color gradation is a series of colors exhibiting a regular change. Two kinds of color gradations were used in this project: a hue circle and a value scale. A *hue circle* is a series of equally spaced hues such as red, orange, yellow, green, blue, purple, and magenta. A *value scale* is a series of evenly spaced steps from light to dark. A value scale can be either achromatic or chromatic. A chromatic scale would involve a single hue such as a scale from dark red to light red.

In this project, the two kinds of color gradations, hue and value, were explored through a series of fabric-dyeing experiments. The complexity of the patterns was balanced by selecting colors that would enhance rather than compete with the pattern. In *Language of Vision,* Gyorgy Kepes states that the eye's movement along a direction of hue or value gradation is similar to its movement along a line.[2] Thus, the value and hue gradations used in the quilts help to lead the viewer's eye into the pattern.

Fabric Dyeing

To obtain subtle gradations of hue and value, it was necessary to hand-dye the fabrics used in the quilts. One hundred percent cotton, unbleached muslin, and procion fiber-reactive dyes were chosen. The cotton muslin was selected for its ease of manipulation in hand-quilting and because it was relatively inexpensive, allowing the artist to experiment freely with the dyeing process. The procion dyes were chosen for their lightfastness and washability when used on natural fibers, as well as for their color intensity. They have the additional advantage of being cold-water dyes, so a heat source is not needed. The dye makes a permanent chemical bond with the fabric fibers during the dyeing process. The color samples resulting from systematic experimentation with the dyeing process for a twenty-eight-step circle of hues plus value gradations provided an excellent visual basis for color selection for the exhibited quilts.

Construction of the Quilts

The quilts were constructed by traditional sewing and quilting techniques. Before the large quilts were made, a series of 14 × 14 inch samples and small wall hangings were constructed to explore methods of piecing, quilting and binding, and the use of various types of battings and fabrics.

The pattern area for each quilt was selected by moving a window matte (a rectangular opening cut into a piece of paper) around the computer print to find the "best" area. Each of the quilts was based on an area of a computer print representing a single module, which was rotated so that it appeared in four orientations. The module was rotated down the first column and repeated in the same orientation across each row. The pattern area for each quilt was also chosen so that there was a central axis which gave a first impression of right-left symmetry. After the pattern area was selected from a computer print, experiments with colored pencils on the print helped to determine the placement of colors on the quilts. Fabric colors were chosen from the sample gradations created during the color studies.

Visual unity was achieved in each of the quilts in the series through a combination of hue and value gradations and through repetition of a single module to create the pattern. It was discovered that the pattern complexity needed to be balanced by a suppression of color contrast through use of color gradation. Interruptions of the color sequences were achieved through

subtle breaks in the color gradations and the use of a pure color for emphasis. Interruptions in the pattern were provided through rotations of the
module to create an asymmetrical balance. These same elements provide
visual unity in all the quilts, thus forming a related series of work. See figures 25-1 to 25-3.

Figure 25-1. *Maze*

Figure 25-2. Detail of *Maze*

Figure 25-3.
Counterpoint

Notes

1. Debra Millard, "Computer Quilts," *Craft Connection* (publication of the Minnesota Crafts Council) (Spring, 1979), p. 1.

2. Gyorgy Kepes, *Language of Vision* (Chicago: Theobald and Company, 1967), p. 49.

26 A Gallery of Artists: Kevin McMahon

Kevin McMahon and
Renee A. Holoien

Kevin McMahon was introduced to computer graphics as a student at the University of Minnesota when he saw a computer-generated film that described visually a physical principle about which he was learning. His instructor, Russell Hobbie, had produced the film and, when questioned about the film after class, agreed to demonstrate how it was made. As an apprentice to Dr. Hobbie, McMahon proceeded to learn the FORTRAN programming language and techniques for producing computer graphics. He subsequently published two films which are used as visual aids in describing two topics in physics that are difficult to demonstrate on a blackboard: the multiple-slit interference of light and the generation of Lissajous figures.

While learning these computer-graphics techniques, McMahon created a variety of geometric forms and designs and was captivated by the speed, precision, and delicacy of the images that he was able to create. After hearing of her directed-study class, in which artists worked with a computer in the creation of their images, McMahon met and began study under Katherine Nash, a sculpture professor in the studio arts department at the University of Minnesota. The open format and diverse range of discussion topics in this study group encouraged a sharing of ideas and backgrounds and contributed to his developing artistic awareness. This group taught him the necessity of speaking to others about this type of art and helped him to formulate a more coherent interpretation of it. When Nash retired, the teaching of this course was taken over by Kevin McMahon, who continues to teach it today.

In this class, entitled "Art and Computers," the computer is used as the primary art medium, with emphasis on using existing art programs as the vehicle for making pictures. After learning the process of using the programs, students create and print pictures which are critiqued and reworked weekly. Traditional media are freely mixed with the computer-generated sketches as the work develops. This "postprocessing" has included photography, film, lithography, silk screen, sculpture, drawing, painting, and collage. Although there is a continuing development of new and expensive computer display equipment, the approach of this class is to rely on existing computer facilities and to look at the variation in aesthetic quality of the products of each display device. Part of the purpose of "Art and Computers" is to enable the student both to mix the fields of art and computers without having to undertake several rather specialized courses in these separate fields and to apply formal attention to the combination of the two areas of study. McMahon finds that an inherent advantage of working in art education with a new, experimental medium is that there are no established techniques and methods textbooks to limit the inquisitiveness of the student in exploring what can be done.

McMahon is currently employed as the arts and humanities computer-applications consultant at the University of Minnesota Computer Center. Current projects that relate to use of the computer as an art medium can be grouped into three categories: art education, general lectures, and research. Art education refers to the above-mentioned "Art and Computers" course taught through the studio arts department. The general lectures and accompanying slide show describe this type of art, present an overview of the processes involved, and illustrate examples of the kind of work being done at this university. This approach has been well received by the audiences which have ranged from professionals in art and engineering to the more general, nontechnical groups, and it has been useful in defining many prevalent misconceptions concerning computers and computer art. The research in which McMahon is involved falls into three primary areas: quality and performance of each computer display device, effective programming techniques for software that is used by groups from nontechnical backgrounds, and consistent picture representation and treatment to facilitate transferring images to any of the available display devices.

In the creation of his own artwork, McMahon is attracted to the delicate marks and textures that can be made with a computer. He interprets an idea on different output devices, searching for the most suitable representation. He has recently begun to experiment with lithography in conjunction with computer-generated imagery, to move beyond the limits in tactile qualities presented by computer paper and film, and to work with colors and the richly textured stone surface. He also continues to take drawing and printmaking courses at the University of Minnesota.

McMahon is concerned with helping artists and those not trained in technical fields to use and influence the computer as a tool for producing art, as well as with showing scientists the importance of the emotional and subjective concept "aesthetic awareness," as it relates to the development of the highly specialized scientific fields. He believes that if we are to have reasonable applications of computer technology, we must involve a broader range of people and perspectives in the development. A necessary perspective in this process, he feels, is that of art and aesthetic awareness, which is an essential aspect of society. He emphasizes that the need is not for the computer to make the art of tomorrow, but for the artist to influence the development of the computer of tomorrow. See figures 26-1 to 26-3.

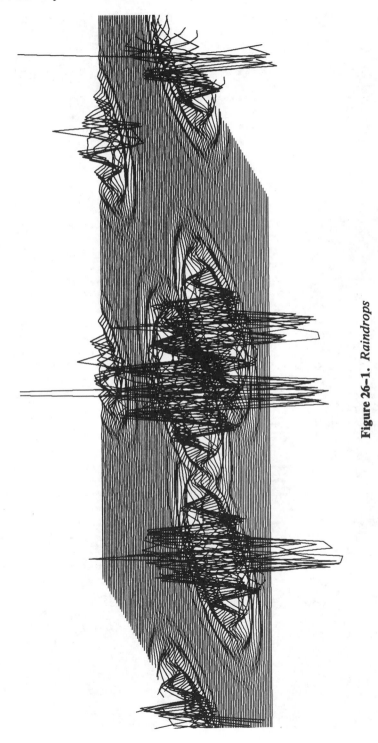

Figure 26-1. Raindrops

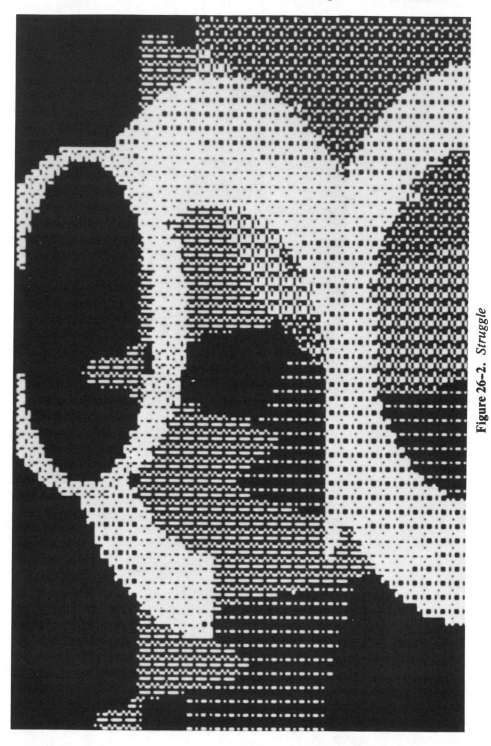

Figure 26–2. *Struggle*

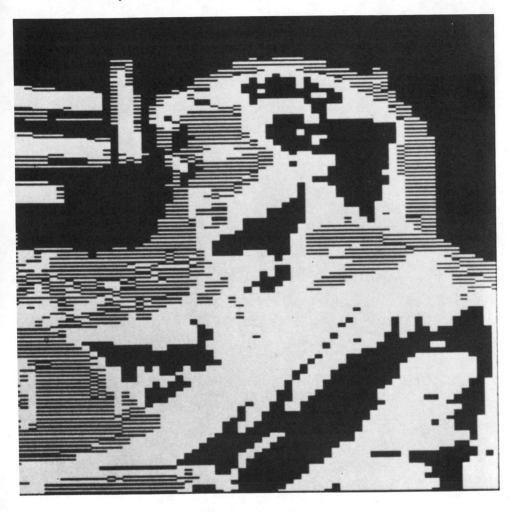

Figure 26–3. *Diffusion*

Index

Abacus, use of, 316
Abingdon Chronicles, 106
Abstract expressionism, 361
Accounting procedures, tax, 4
Aesthetic criteria: basis of, 317; enjoyment
    of, 279; quality concept, 381–382;
    sensitivity toward, 326
Afro-Asiatic: family groups, 137;
    languages, 140–142; text material, 139
Agencies, government, 122
Agriculture, factor of, 54
Ahlgren, Andrew, 294
Aircraft industry, 1
Akehurst, F.R.P., 12, 155–158
Akhmin, excavations at, 160
Akkadian: cognates, 10; grammar, 54; key
    words, 65–68; syllabary, 56; text
    material, 163–164
Alfred, King, 105, 111
Algonquian Indian tribe, 143
Algorithms and algorithmic format, 5, 86
Alphabet: Cyrillic, 137; English, 136, 350;
    graphic, 254; Greek, 255, 264; Latin,
    137, 254, 264; non-Latin, 12, 232, 263;
    symbols, 25; transliteration, 61, 64–65
Alphanumeric: code, 288; substrings, 270
American Indian languages, 143
American Oriental Society, 177
American Philogogical Association, 29
Analysis: artifact, 228; automatic, 177;
    cluster, 213; data, 176; discourse, 15–19,
    24–25, 145; grammatical 23–25, 30–31,
    35; graphemic, 135–137; historical, 316;
    language, 25, 86; linguistic, 72, 116–117,
    143, 164; manual, 145; semantic, 145;
    site, 213; sociometric, 177; statistical,
    159–160, 170, 174; syntax, 145; textual,
    145–146, 153; word, 22–23
Analytical Greek (New Testament)
    Concordance, 43–44
Anatolia, 136, 142
Ancient: Babylonia, 3, 174; collective
    literature, 115; cuneiform documents,
    159; Egypt, 253, 259, 261; Greece, 143;
    Iraq, 163; Italy, 190; languages, 3, 53,
    236, 256; Near East, 54; Sumer, 58
Anglo-Saxon Chronicle, 105–109
Anthropology and anthropologists, 58, 216
Antiquarians, profession of, 205
Antony, Mark, 199, 202
Apocrypha, 115
APPLE II personal computer, 4, 233
Application(s): hobby, 4; literacy, 2;

nonhobby, 4; nonmilitary, 1; pioneering,
    2
Applied mathematics, 1
Arabia, 137, 139; language of, 54; script of,
    277–278
Archeological Institute of America, 144
Archaeology and archaeologists: concepts,
    2–3, 58, 205–206, 228, 286; excavations
    and evidences, 181–182, 218; surveys,
    208, 211
ARCHSIM simulation program, 217, 227
Architecture and architects, 54
Archives, cuneiform, 3
Arithmetic. See Mathematics
Arkansas, 213
Art and artists: basic, 326, 357; concepts,
    299, 311, 317–318, 324, 350; and
    education, 326, 357, 382; fine, 3, 316;
    history, 212, 216; language, 323–324,
    359; programs, 322, 381
ART 1, 357
ARTDOTS program, 344
Artifacts: attributes and description,
    205–209; chronologies, 206, 228
Artificial language, 6, 8
Artist and Computer (Leavitt), 364
ART PICT Images, 338, 342–343
ARTPLOT program, 332–334
ARTPRIN program, 316, 322–331, 353
ARTSING program, 344–346
ARTSURF program, 336–337
ASCII character set, 290–291
Association for Computing Machinery
    (ACM), 317
Association for the Development of
    Computer Based Instructional Systems,
    294
Association for Literary and Linguistic
    Computing Bulletin, The, 2
Assyria, research in, 163–164
Astral monuments, 316
Astronomy and astronomists, 1
Atomic physics, 1, 9
Audiolingual methodology, 253–254
Authors and authorship studies, 8, 19, 42,
    86, 256, 270–271
Automation and automatic systems, 1, 31,
    34, 86–87, 90, 93, 177, 317
Automotive industry, social impact of the,
    3–5

Babylonia: Ancient, 3, 174; cuneiform texts
    of, 163; economic history and records

387

Index

Index

About the Contributors

F.R.P. Akehurst is an associate professor of French at the University of Minnesota. Dr. Akehurst received the Bachelor's and Master's degrees in French language and literature from Brasenose College, Oxford, England, in 1958 and 1962. He received the Ph.D. in French language and literature from the University of Colorado in 1967. He has taught in universities in France and the United States since 1960, and has been the recipient of a number of research and travel grants to further his study in French language and literature. Dr. Akehurst's special research interests focus on the medieval period of French literature and he has published extensively on Old French and Old Provençal poetry as represented by the troubadours. In recent years his research has led him to the study of the language and poetry of the troubadours, using quantitative methods and computer analysis.

William R. Brookman is a lecturer in ancient history and Old Testament studies at North Central Bible College in Minneapolis, Minnesota. He received the Bachelor's and Master's degrees in history at the University of Minnesota in 1975 and 1977, and is currently a Ph.D. candidate in ancient studies at the University of Minnesota. His research interests focus on Sumerian society, and he has developed expertise in Sumerian economic history. Mr. Brookman's current research involves building a computer data base of the entire cuneiform literature describing the Sumerian milling industry.

Roger Brooks received the Bachelor's degree at the University of Minnesota in 1979 and is currently a graduate student in the Department of Religious Studies at Brown University.

Kenneth W. Decker received the Bachelor's degree in ancient history and anthropology at the University of Minnesota in 1978. He received the Master's degree in ancient studies at the University of Minnesota in 1979, and currently is a graduate student in anthropology at Washington State University. Mr. Decker's research interests include the study of historic as well as prehistoric Egypt. He specializes in the study of Egyptian language and literature written in Egyptian hieroglyphics.

Gerald M. Erickson received the Bachelor's, Master's, and Ph.D. degrees at the University of Minnesota, and is an associate professor of classics at the University of Minnesota. His research interests include the use of computer-based methods for the teaching of classical languages and technical terminology.

Barbara Friberg received the Bachelor's degree in mathematics at John Brown University in 1967, the Master's degree in linguistics at the University of Saigon in 1973, and the Master's degree in computer science at the University of Minnesota in 1978. Ms. Friberg did field work in linguistics, literacy, and Bible translation in Vietnam and Cambodia from 1970 through 1975. She and Timothy Friberg have developed an extensive linguistic data base from the Greek New Testament text.

Timothy Friberg received the Bachelor's degree in Greek at Wheaton College in 1968, the Master's degree in linguistics at the University of Minnesota in 1978, and is currently completing work for the Ph.D. in linguistics at the University of Minnesota. Mr. Friberg did field work in linguistics, literacy, and Bible translation in Vietnam and Cambodia from 1969 through 1975. He and Barbara Friberg have developed an extensive analytical computer data base from the Greek New Testament text and have prepared a series of analytical aids for Bible scholars and Bible translators, to be published in 1981.

Dale V. Gear received the Bachelor's and Master's degrees in classics at the University of Kansas in 1973 and 1975. Mr. Gear is a Ph.D. candidate in classics and an analyst/programmer for the University of Minnesota Computer Center.

Dorothy Gross received the Bachelor's degree from Brown University in 1967, the Master's degree in music from the Manhattan School of Music in 1969, and the Ph.D. in music from Indiana University in 1975. She is an assistant professor of music at the University of Minnesota. Dr. Gross's research interests include computer-assisted music instruction and the use of computer methods in music analysis, and she has published a number of articles in these areas.

Rosanne Gulino received the Bachelor's degree at St. Louis University in 1970, the Master's degree in Spanish at New York University in 1974, and the Master's degree in classics and archaeology at the University of Minnesota in 1977. She is currently a Ph.D. candidate in classics at the University of Minnesota.

Nicki D.C. Harper received the Bachelor's degree in chemistry and the Master's degree in history at the University of Minnesota, and is currently completing work for a Ph.D. in history at the University of Minnesota where she is also a teaching associate in linguistics. Ms. Harper has published a number of articles on linguistic analysis and ancient Near Eastern history and archaeology, and has been active in an extensive computer-assisted study in graphemic analysis in her efforts to discover the underlying language behind the Minoan Linear A writing system.

Geri Hockfield received the Bachelor's degree from Carleton College, Northfield, Minnesota, in 1973, the Master's degree in ancient studies from the University of Minnesota in 1976, and is currently a Ph.D. candidate in ancient studies at the University of Minnesota.

Eric E. Inman received the Bachelor's degree in computer science at the University of Minnesota in 1980. As an undergraduate research assistant he developed software for computer-aided textual analysis. Mr. Inman is currently a member of the technical staff at the Space Technology Division of Inco, Inc., Boulder, Colorado.

Ruth Leavitt received the Bachelor's degree at the University of Minnesota. She is an artist, lecturer, and author and an authority on the use of computer technology in art. Her computer artwork has won numerous awards and is found in private and public collections in the United States and abroad. She is editor of *Artist and Computer* (1976).

Kevin McMahon received the Bachelor's degree in physics at the University of Minnesota in 1974. He has taught classes in computer art since 1975 and is currently an instructor in the studio-arts department of the Extension Division of the University of Minnesota, as well as arts and humanities consultant at the University of Minnesota Computer Center.

Debra Millard received the Bachelor's degree in music composition from Kenyon College in 1973 and the Master's degree in design from the University of Minnesota in 1980. She is a freelance designer and teacher, as well as a lecturer in the Extension Division at the University of Minnesota. She has participated in several exhibitions and has earned awards for her expertise in quilting and pattern design. Ms. Millard has done extensive research in the use of computers in the design of textiles and quilts.

J.L. Mitchell received the Bachelor's degree from King's College, University of London, in 1962, the Master's degree in linguistics at the University of Iowa in 1968, and the Ph.D. in English linguistics at the University of Iowa in 1970. He is an associate professor of English at the University of Minnesota and has been chairman of the English department since 1977. He is a pioneer in the use of computer technology in the study of Old English manuscripts, and has published extensively in this area.

Holly J. Morris received the Bachelor's degree at Kent State University in 1974 and the Master's degree in classics at the University of Minnesota in 1977. Ms. Morris is currently a Ph.D. candidate in the Center for Ancient Studies at the University of Minnesota. The focus of her research is economics and computer applications to the analysis of ancient economic systems.

John F. Mulhern was an undergraduate research assistant in the University of Minnesota Computer Center and received the Bachelor's degree in mathematics at the University of Minnesota in 1980. Mr. Mulhern has developed a number of sophisticated computer programs to aid researchers in language and literature, and made a major contribution to a research project to develop computer aids for Sumerian lexicography.

Katherine Nash received the Bachelor's degree at the University of Minnesota, advanced training at the Minnesota School of Art and the University of Minnesota, and a Doctor of Fine Arts degree at the University of Nebraska. She taught art at the Universities of Nebraska, Anaheim, and San Jose, and is currently Professor Emeritus of fine arts at the University of Minnesota. Professor Nash was a leader in the application of computing to the fine arts.

Jean Davies Nordlund received the Bachelor's and Master's degrees at the University of Minnesota in 1970 and 1977. She is a self-employed textile designer and weaver and is active in the application of computers to the design of textiles. Her weavings and designs have been included in several exhibitions throughout the country, and she has received various honors and awards for her work.

Linda M. Ricketts received the Bachelor's and the Master's degrees in history at Iowa State University in 1972 and 1975, and the Ph.D. in history at the University of Minnesota in 1980. She is currently on the faculty of Macalester College, St. Paul, Minnesota.

Tom Rindflesch received the Bachelor's degree in linguistics from the University of Minnesota where he is a Ph.D. candidate in linguistics and a graduate project assistant at the University of Minnesota Computer Center. His research interests include the application of computer technology to linguistics, and computer-aided graphemic analysis for the genetic classification of languages.

William C. Roos received the Bachelor's degree in mathematics from Waynesburg College, Pennsylvania, and is currently a principal research engineer at Sperry Univac Corporation. Mr. Roos's research interests include the development and implementation of artificial languages on computers and the impact of computer technology on society.

Donald Ross, Jr., received the Bachelor's and Master's degrees at Lehigh University in 1963 and 1964, and the Ph.D. at the University of Michigan in 1967. He is associate professor of English at the University of Minnesota and a pioneer in the use of computer techniques in the study of English literature. He is the author of a software package called EYEBALL and has used this package extensively in his study of literary style.

O.J. Schaden received the Bachelor's and Master's degrees in Oriental language and literature from the University of Chicago's Oriental Institute, where he specialized in Egyptian language and epigraphy. He received the Ph.D. in ancient history from the University of Minnesota. Dr. Schaden has done extensive research in Egypt and served as consultant in Egyptian language on the research project to develop a computer-based course in ancient Egyptian hieroglyphics.

Steven R. Sparley received the Bachelor's degree in classical Greek at the University of Minnesota, did graduate work in ancient studies there, and is currently completing requirements for the Master's degree in divinity at Bethany Theological Seminary, Mankato, Minnesota.

Ruth Tate received the Bachelor's degree in anthropology at the University of Minnesota and is currently completing requirements for the Master's degree in ancient studies at the University of Minnesota. Her research interests are in the development of computer data bases for archaeological applications.

Kellen C. Thornton received the Bachelor's degree in biology and telecommunications at Texas Technological University in 1973, and the Master's degree in science journalism at the University of Minnesota in 1977. Ms. Thornton is currently working as a freelance writer and editor of scientific articles.

George Vellios received the Bachelor's degree in philosophy in 1974, and the Master's degree in classics in 1976, both at Washington University in St. Louis, Missouri. Mr. Vellios has been a high-school Latin teacher and is interested in developing creative language-teaching methods.

Vicky A. Walsh received the Bachelor's degree in mathematics and philosophy at Iowa State University in 1970, the Master's degree in classics at the University of Minnesota in 1976, and the Ph.D. in Greek prehistoric archaeology at the University of Minnesota in 1980. She is currently humanities computing supervisor at the University of Minnesota Computer Center. Dr. Walsh's research interests include the application of statistics, data-base technology, and computer simulation methods to preclassical archaeology.

Richard D. Ward received the Ph.D. in ancient history from the University of Minnesota in 1973 and has studied at the Oriental Institute at the University of Chicago and the Lincoln Institute of Land Policy in Cambridge, Massachusetts. He is a former college and seminary teacher and has research experience as an archaeologist and epigrapher in the Near East. Dr. Ward has published in the area of ancient Sumerian and Babylonian real-estate and legal documents and is also the author of comparative studies of ancient and modern real-estate documentation methods. He is a management analyst at Ramsey County, Department of Property Taxation, St. Paul, Minnesota.

Tzvee Zahavy received the Bachelor's degree in mathematics at Yeshiva College in 1970, was ordained a rabbi in 1973, received the Master's degree in Jewish history in 1973 at Yeshiva University, and received the Ph.D. at Brown University in 1976, specializing in Judaism. He is currently associate professor in Ancient Near Eastern and Jewish studies at the University of Minnesota. Professor Zahavy's research interests include the application of computer technology to a general understanding of the structure of the rabbinical literature.

About the Editors

Peter C. Patton received the Bachelor's degree in engineering and applied physics from Harvard University in 1957, the Master's degree in mathematics from the University of Kansas in 1959, and the Ph.D. in aerospace engineering from the Technical University of Stuttgart in 1966. He is an associate professor at the University of Minnesota and a member of the graduate faculties in computer science, aerospace engineering, mechanics, and ancient studies, as well as a member of the faculty of the classical-civilizations program. He is director of the Center for Ancient Studies and director of the University of Minnesota Computer Center. In this combined responsibility Dr. Patton has had the unique opportunity to encourage research and instructional projects in the applications of computers to studies in the humanities at the University of Minnesota.

Renee A. Holoien received the Bachelor's degree in ancient music from the University of Minnesota in 1975, the Master's degree in ancient studies from the University of Minnesota in 1978, and is currently a Ph.D. candidate in South Asian languages and literature at the University of Minnesota, and an applications programmer in the University of Minnesota Computer Center. She has supervised many of the graduate research projects conducted jointly by the Center for Ancient Studies and the University of Minnesota Computer Center, and has assisted both students and faculty in developing and documenting computer data bases for their research.